CHARLES DICKENS' FAVORITE DAUGHTER

CHARLES DICKENS'
FAVORITE DAUGHTER

The Life, Loves, and Art of Katey Dickens Perugini

LUCINDA HAWKSLEY

LYONS PRESS
Guilford, Connecticut
An imprint of Globe Pequot Press

Lyons Press is an imprint of Globe Pequot Press.

Project editors: Ellen Urban and Lauren Brancato
Layout: Maggie Peterson

Library of Congress Cataloging-in-Publication Data is available on file.

ISBN 978-0-7627-8521-6

Printed in the United States of America

10 9 8 7 6 5 4 3 2 1

This book is dedicated to the memory of Andrew Xavier (1968–2011), a true friend without whom the world is a less happy and less witty place.

CONTENTS

LIST OF ILLUSTRATIONS AND PLATES

Photos and illustrations reproduced on the following pages are courtesy of:

Charles Dickens Museum, London: 17, 18, 41, 97, 109, 141, 145 (top), 203, 233, 266, 372
University of Hull Art Collection: 220
Royal Academy of Arts, London: 293, 294
The Bridgeman Art Library: xii, 70, 132, 140, 145 (bottom), 202, 254, 255, 300
Roger-Viollet/Rex Features: 4
Chris Forrest: 297
Topham Picturepoint: 2, 24, 44, 53, 57, 71, 95, 123, 172

All other images are supplied courtesy of the author.

FAMILY TREE

JOHN DICKENS (1785–1851) *m.* ELIZABETH BARROW (1789–1863)

Frances ("Fanny") Elizabeth Dickens (1810–1848) *m.* Henry Burnett (1811–1893)

Charles John Huffam Dickens (1812–1870) *m.* Catherine ("Kate") Thomson Hogarth (1815–1879)

Alfred Allen Dickens (1814–1814)

Letitia Mary Dickens (1816–1893) *m.* Henry Austin (1813–1861)

Harriet Ellen Dickens (1819–1824)

Frederick William Dickens (1820–1868) *m.* Anna Delancey Weller (1831–1868)

Alfred Lamert Dickens (1822–1860) *m.* Helen Dobson (1823–1915)

Augustus Newnham ("Boz") Dickens (1827–1866) *m.* Harriet Lovel (*b.*1829–*d.*?) ran away to America with Bertha Phillips in 1858

Children of Charles John Huffam Dickens and Catherine:

Charles Culliford Boz Dickens (1837–1896) *m.* Elizabeth ("Bessie") Matilda Moule Evans (*c.*1838–1907)

Mary ("Mamie") Dickens (1838–1896)

Katherine ("Katey") Elizabeth Macready Dickens (1839–1929) *m.* Charles Allston Collins (1828–1873) then *m.* Carlo Eduardo ("Charles Edward") Perugini (1839–1918)

Leonard Ralph Dickens Perugini (1875–1876)

Walter Savage Landor Dickens (1841–1863)

Francis ("Frank") Jeffrey Dickens (1844–1886)

Alfred D'Orsay Tennyson Dickens (1845–1912) *m.* Augusta Jessie Devlin (1849–1878) then *m.* Emile Rebecca Riley (1864–1913)

Sydney Smith Haldimand Dickens (1847–1872)

Sir Henry Fielding Charles Dickens (1849–1933) *m.* Marie Therese Louise Roche (1852–1940)

Dora Annie Dickens (1850–1851)

Edward ("Plorn") Bulwer Lytton Dickens (1852–1902) *m.* Constance Desailly (*d.*1914)

Children of Sir Henry Fielding Charles Dickens and Marie Therese:

Enid Henrietta Dickens (1877–1950) *m.* Ernest Bourchier Hawksley (1876–1931)

Henry ("Hal") Dickens (1878–1966) *m.* Fanny Runge (1876–1966)

Admiral Sir Gerald Charles Dickens (1879–1962) *m.* Anne Kathleen Pearl Birch (1889–1970)

Olive Nina Dickens (1881–1978) *m.* Robert Shirley Shuckburgh (1882–1954)

Elaine ("Bobbie") Dickens (1883–1978) *m.* Alexander Waley (1875–1934)

Philip ("Pip") Charles Dickens (1887–1964) *m.* Sybil Cunliffe Owen (1889–1934)

Cedric Charles Dickens (1889–1916)

A NOTE ON NAMES

Charles Dickens' wife, Catherine, is often referred to in his letters as Kate; however, in order that readers should not confuse her with her daughter, I have referred to her as Catherine throughout.

Kate Perugini was christened Catherine Elizabeth Macready Dickens, known throughout her childhood as Katey or Katie, and changed her name in adult life to Kate. Her siblings and many of her friends also knew her as Kitty or Kittie. I have referred to her as a child as Katey, which appears to have been Dickens' preferred spelling of her name. As an adult I have referred to her as Kate, as she preferred.

Confusingly, Katey's father, her eldest brother, and both her husbands were called Charles. To minimize the confusion, I have used the name "Charley" for her brother, as he was known by his family. Her first husband, Charles Allston Collins, was often called "Charlie" by his friends, so I have used this. The name of Katey's second husband is often anglicized to Charles Edward Perugini; I have, however, referred to him by his Italian name of Carlo, which is the name Kate called him.

Katey's sister Mary was almost always known as "Mamey" or "Mamie." The former spelling is the one her father favored when she was a child, but the latter is how the family and her friends referred to her as an adult and the name written on her grave, so I have gone with that spelling. In occasional, formal, circumstances she is referred to by Dickens as Mary.

William Thackeray's daughters were known as Anny, also spelled "Any" and "Annie," and Minny, also spelled "Minnie" (although her real name was Harriet). I have referred to them as Anny and Minny, which seem to be the preferred spellings.

FOREWORD

One of my most vivid memories from childhood is of a painting my parents owned. I loved it and would stare at it wondering who the beautiful woman was, dressed all in black standing with her back to the viewer, her head turned just enough to enable you to see her face, but not quite enough to prevent her from being mysterious. Two aspects particularly fascinated me: the bustle of her dress with its thick satin bow perched on the top and the way her hair was arranged, which I would try to emulate (without success).

I remember asking my father who the person in the painting was. He told me she was Kate, Charles Dickens' daughter, and my great-great-great aunt. The painter, he said, was John Millais, a very famous artist. At the age of eight, I was not particularly interested in Millais, but the desire to find out more about Kate, or Katey as I came to know her, intensified. Later, while I was studying for a post-graduate degree in the history of art, her name—in its several incarnations—kept appearing: Katey Dickens, Kate Collins, Kate Perugini. Usually mentioned as an adjunct of her famous father, she was however also given separate status as an artist, as a model, as one of Lord Leighton's circle, and as the wife of two artists.

I became obsessed with finding out more about this talented relative and about her long and interesting life. The more I researched, the more fascinating she became. Here was a woman who achieved considerable fame in her lifetime: an intimate friend of such people as Lord Leighton, William Thackeray, and George Bernard Shaw; a prolific artist who exhibited regularly at the Royal Academy and at the Society of Lady Artists and whose works sold consistently well—and yet no one, save the most ardent art lovers or Dickensians, recognizes her name.

In 1939 a writer named Gladys Storey published a book entitled *Dickens and Daughter*. It was based on the friendship Gladys and her mother had built up with Katey in the last decade of her life. It is not so much a biography as a collection of anecdotes around a loose biographical structure. It is a fascinating historic document, but often inaccurate

Portrait of Mrs. Perugini (1880) by Sir John Everett Millais

and—necessarily—biased by Gladys' and Katey's close relationship. *Charles Dickens' Favorite Daughter* aims to redress the balance and to bring Katey into what should be her recognized place in the history of British art.

Sadly, *Portrait of Mrs. Perugini* (1880) no longer belongs to the family. It is, however, in the possession of a private collector.

PROLOGUE

In the early nineteenth century, the most prestigious art school in Britain was London's Royal Academy and its preparatory school, known as Sass's. In 1838, Sass's accepted its youngest-ever artist, a nine-year-old boy from Jersey who was already being hailed as a genius. While still in his twenties this artist would find his works derided by the novelist Charles Dickens and by the country's most influential art critic, John Ruskin (whose ex-wife the young artist had recently married). Yet he would rise above the controversy to become the highest-paid artist in Britain, be created a baronet by Queen Victoria, and become President of the Royal Academy. His name was John Everett Millais.

Millais first grew to prominence over a scandal—a scandal associated with the artistic movement of which he was a founding member: Pre-Raphaelitism. He was one of seven young artists, all of whom were Royal Academy trained, who formed a group called the Pre-Raphaelite Brotherhood (known as the PRB). They disagreed with many of the principles of art as defined by the rigid government of the Royal Academy and wanted to paint in the style that had been popular in Italy before the advent of Raphael. When the authorities and the public discovered—by an unfortunate chance—what the letters PRB stood for, they were furious at the group's perceived arrogance and actively turned against them, their followers, and anyone who assumed a Pre-Raphaelite style of painting. It was several years before artists who painted in this style were accepted back into mainstream galleries. Millais was one of the fortunate few who was not ruined by the furor, largely because he was kept financially secure by family money.

By the 1870s Millais had overcome quite overwhelming criticism of two of his works, *Christ in the Carpenter's Shop* (1850) and *Sir Isumbras at the Ford* (1857); he was now adored by the masses and the establishment, and it seemed that nothing he painted could ever disappoint the art collectors. Yet despite his large and steady income, Millais' expenses were sometimes prohibitive, with an ever-growing family, studio costs, and an expensive lifestyle to be supported. Until this time, he had concentrated on crowd-pleasing genre paintings and, during the 1860s in particular, book illustrations, but as the 1870s progressed, Millais decided it was time for a change. Now in his forties, he began a new phase in his career, as a portrait painter—a profession that could prove highly lucrative.

The precocious nine-year-old genius—who had once so maddened his older, fellow Royal Academy pupils that they had dangled him out of a window by his feet until he passed out with fear—and a one-time Pre-Raphaelite rebel was now at the height of his fame. He could choose precisely whom to paint and what price to charge. His portraits, which would later include the society beauty Lily Langtry (1878) and the portrait painter Louise Jopling (1879), excited the rich and famous to clamour for his attention.

During the first half of 1874, Millais began a portrait that he intended to give as a wedding present; he found the subject so difficult to capture on canvas that this painting would not be finished for six years. The woman whose features he found so hard to re-create to his satisfaction had earlier been the model for one of his most popular paintings, *The Black Brunswicke*r (1860). Since then, she had become one of his closest friends. Her name was Kate Collins and she was the pretty young widow of the Pre-Raphaelite artist Charles Allston Collins, whom Millais had known since adolescence.

At the time of sitting—or, rather, standing—for her portrait, Kate was thirty-four and about to be married for the second time. A respected portrait painter herself, Katey (as she was then known) had first met Millais while she was a teenager, living at her father's house, which happened to be one of the most celebrated homes in London. She was the daughter of Charles Dickens, a man who had become a loyal friend to Millais—despite having almost wrecked the young man's career with his blistering review in 1850. With this former unfortunate incident forgotten, by the mid-1850s Millais was a regular visitor to the Dickens household. Katey's looks and her own budding artistic ability enchanted him, and in around 1859 Millais begged permission to paint the novelist's youngest daughter. With the clarity of purpose for which he was famed, Millais had decided she would be perfect for what was to become one of his most famous paintings.

Fourteen years later, after the deaths of both Kate's father and her first husband, Millais had asked her if he could paint her again. The result is a stunning, unusual portrait that captures the artist's feelings toward a mature, intelligent, fellow artist. It is a world away from his earlier depiction of Kate as a virginal young fiancée who knows with frightening prescience that her brave soldier lover is about to face death at the Battle of Waterloo.

According to the portrait's provenance, Kate entered Millais' studio wearing a fashionably styled all-black dress, positioned herself with her back toward him, turned her head so she was looking at him over her left shoulder and told him that this was how she wished to be painted. The result is a sexually provocative painting, indicative of Kate's forceful personality. It can be seen as a precursor of John Singer Sargent's risqué *Portrait of Madame X*, the painting of Madame Virginia Gautreau that was to cause a celebrated scandal two decades later. Although Kate's dress is not revealing, unlike the dress of Madame X, her stance, the prominent bustle positioned near the center of the portrait, and the way in which Millais captures the sitter's haughty self-possession are provocative in more ways than one, drawing the eye and creating questions in the viewer's mind.

The black dress is exquisitely rendered, with its enticing sheer sleeves providing a welcome relief from the more funereal tones of the bodice and the rich satin of the bustle's bow gleaming in contrast with the more sombre material of the skirt. Millais manages to make the several subtle shades of black appear as varied as a patterned silk, emphasizing the femaleness of the sitter by deliberately highlighting the movement of the fabric around her corseted curves. In contrast with her dress, Kate's pale, slightly strained-looking face and auburn hair seem to glow with light.

Kate's decision to wear black was, ostensibly, because she was still in mourning for her first husband and had no other fashionable dress in her wardrobe—but it is also known, from one of Kate's letters, that black was her favorite "color." She felt that she looked at her best when wearing it, so one can assume (when knowing more about Kate's personality) that the choice of dress had less to do with mourning convention and rather more to do with very understandable vanity.

In spite of his eagerness to paint Kate again, Millais found this portrait surprisingly difficult to complete. The wedding took place on June 4, 1874, but *Portrait of Mrs. Perugini* was not declared finished until 1880—and, even then, Millais admitted he was not happy with it. He felt it did not do justice to her looks or personality. The painting had pride of place in the Peruginis' London home, to which Millais was a regular visitor, but Kate was to recall how Millais would stare sadly at it and tell her "It is not you, my dear." It is certainly not the image of the extremely pretty Kate Perugini of contemporary description, but it is a triumphant image of a woman who has been recently bereaved, yet has managed to find new excitement in life. Overall, *Portrait of Mrs. Perugini* is a painting made of a friend at a deeply felt moment in her life as well as being a true depiction of an artist at an exciting time in her own career. The face that glances almost slightingly at the viewer from over her left shoulder hints teasingly at a lively personality and rich experience from behind those knowing eyes.

1

THE EARLY YEARS

The first years of Queen Victoria's reign were marked by exciting advancements. To the most fortunate of her subjects—those not suffering from poverty or any of the many prevalent social injustices—it must have seemed like a wonderful era. There appeared to be great changes and exciting discoveries taking place all over the world, with new opportunities opening up throughout the vast British Empire. The young Victoria, aged eighteen on her accession to the throne, had been proclaimed Queen in 1837 after the death of her uncle King William IV. Just a year later, the very first telegraph message was sent, British-owned slaves in the Bahamas were finally granted emancipation,[1] the National Gallery was opened in London, and Queen Victoria was crowned in Westminster Abbey. In 1839 the scientific world was amazed by Louis Daguerre's first photographic image of the moon, Fox Talbot brought photography to Britain, and the British public were thrilled to hear that their young queen had become engaged to a German prince. In addition, several great British traditions were begun: The first shipment of Indian tea arrived, the first Grand National horse race was run, and Henley staged its inaugural Royal Regatta. It was a time of challenges and impossibilities becoming reality, an era in which ambitious men could really believe their dreams might come true.

At the start of Victoria's reign, the young Charles Dickens was enjoying the early stages of fame. His first books, two series of *Sketches by Boz* (published in 1836), had led to widespread interest in this new writer whose real identity was unknown, but who wrote so humorously

---

1 Slavery had actually been abolished in the British Empire in 1833, but many slave owners were reluctant to adhere to the new law.

Catherine Dickens by Samuel Lawrence in 1838, a year before her daughter Katey was born. It was made as a companion piece to Lawrence's portrait of Charles.

and observantly about London life. It was his very next book, *Pickwick Papers*, that was to reveal the identity of "Boz" and make Charles Dickens a household name. The ludicrously funny tales of Mr. Samuel Pickwick and his companions were printed in twenty monthly installments. The stories were highly addictive and immediately had literate London laughing over the characters' antics and extolling the phenomenon of this new author. At the time the public was enjoying the first chapter of *Pickwick*, its author was just twenty-four years old.

In the year of the young queen's coronation, Charles Dickens' *Oliver Twist*, having been serialized in the periodical *Bentley's Miscellany*, was published to great acclaim and the first chapters of *Nicholas Nickleby* were printed in monthly installments. Both novels highlighted terrible social problems in modern Britain and started Victoria's subjects talking in earnest about what could be done to help the poor and the disenfranchised. *Oliver Twist* brought the shameful truth about workhouses and baby farms to the masses and *Nicholas Nickleby* caused investigative journalists to converge on Yorkshire to find out if what Mr. Dickens had written about the "Yorkshire Schools" was true. They discovered that these horrifying schools, to which unwanted children were sent, were a terrible reality. Dickens had brought the plight of these children, and the appalling way in which they had been treated by their parents, guardians, and "educators," into the public domain. The effect was tremendous. Within a few years of the publication of *Nicholas Nickleby* almost every one of the Yorkshire Schools had been closed down.

For centuries, writers had been revered in Britain, albeit often—as in the case of the Scottish poet Robbie Burns—most lauded after their death. At the time Charles Dickens was beginning his career, poetry and literature in general were enjoying a period of great creativity. The works of Sir Walter Scott, who had died in 1832, were much loved and widely read, as were those of Jane Austen (who had died in 1817). Among popular living authors were Thomas Carlyle, author of *The French Revolution* (1837), and Edward Bulwer Lytton, who wrote *The Last Days of Pompeii* (1834). There were also renowned poets, such as Robert Browning and Alfred Tennyson, whose work was widely read by all social classes. When the gently irreverent and clever works of Boz made their entrance

Charles Dickens by Samuel Lawrence, dated 1837. This was the year in which the first chapters of *Oliver Twist* were published (in monthly installments).

into this erudite world, they were considered a welcome addition to the ranks of popular fiction. In those days before radio, television, and cinema, writers provided one of the most popular forms of public entertainment. Theaters were hugely popular, but books were even more accessible to the masses. Even though a large percentage of the British population could not read, it was common for those members of a community who could do so to read to the illiterate. Publication of novels in monthly installments meant that crowds would gather to hear the latest chapter of a new book being read aloud. At the time Dickens began publishing his works, the word "celebrity" had not yet entered the *Oxford English Dictionary*. It was first recognized in the dictionary in 1849, by which time Dickens was indisputably one of the most famous celebrities in the British Empire. He was the first "modern" author: He went on book tours at home and abroad and worked hard on creating a prominent and recognizable public image. He managed not only to conquer his own country but almost the entire literate world.

In 1839, an indication of just how much the British public had taken this extraordinary new writer to its heart was demonstrated by a new ship launched in Chester: Its name was the *Pickwick*. This was a wonderfully exciting year for Charles Dickens. He was enjoying the fruits of a sudden and almost overwhelming success, his family life was happy, and fame had not yet become a problem. It was also the year in which his daughter Katey was born.

Three years earlier, Charles had married well—and socially somewhat above his own class. His wife, Catherine, was the daughter of George Hogarth, one of Charles' senior colleagues at the newspaper the *Evening Chronicle*. Charles had been writing for both the *Morning Chronicle* and the *Evening Chronicle,* and it was George Hogarth who had originally commissioned from Charles a series to be called *Sketches of London*, the precursor to *Sketches by Boz*. At the time of the marriage, Catherine Thomson Hogarth (often referred to as "Kate" in Dickens' letters) was twenty years old. She was an attractive, lively young woman at the head of a clique of pretty sisters, almost all of whom would fall under the spell of Catherine's husband as they grew to adulthood. The wedding had taken place on April 2, 1836, at St. Luke's Church, Chelsea. With a fecundity that was to take a considerable toll on her happiness and their marriage, Catherine became pregnant almost immediately. Katey's eldest sibling, Charles Culliford Boz Dickens—known to his family as "Charley"—came into the world on Twelfth Night, January 6, 1837. Fourteen months later, on March 6, 1838, the Dickenses' eldest daughter, Mary—nicknamed "Mamey" or "Mamie"—was born. Mary was named after her much mourned Aunt Mary Hogarth, who had died ten months previously. Dickens was enchanted by his babies. He was to prove a loving and indulgent father, far less strict than the typical image of a Victorian paterfamilias. He was also exacting, expecting the same high standards of his children as he presented in his works; an expectation that was to see him sorely disappointed as the Dickens children developed into adulthood.

On October 28, 1839, five days after the publication of the complete *Nicholas Nickleby*, and when his wife was nine months pregnant, Charles Dickens wrote to a friend that he was suffering "such a violent and annoying cold" that he was compelled to stay at home and nurse it. There is no mention in his letter of Catherine; Charles is entirely preoccupied by his own "sneezing, winking, weeping, watery state." One imagines that Catherine, aware she would shortly give birth, was not entirely sympathetic to her husband's "annoying" cold. After an uncomfortable night, she went into a "violent" labor on the morning of Tuesday the 29th. Thirteen hours later, in the master bedroom of 48 Doughty Street in central London, baby Catherine Elizabeth Macready Dickens made her entrance into the world. Her father, banned of course from the birthing room, spent his day pacing anxiously, waiting for his wife's attendant, Pickthorn, to come out with news. Childbirth was not always a joyous occasion in Victorian England: It could often prove fatal, both to the baby and mother. At nine o'clock that evening, Dickens wrote a relieved letter to his friend John Forster: "Thank God it is just now all safely over, and that Kate and the child—another little girl—as well as possible."

The prospect of Katey's arrival had thrown her father into a frenzy. Their home at the time was a comfortable Georgian townhouse, in London's Bloomsbury. The tall, slender, five-story house—now the Charles Dickens Museum—was, however, too small for an ever-growing family and their several servants. As the baby's due date approached, Charles had already spent several weeks seeking a new home. The census return for 1841 would show that, in addition to the family members, the Dickens household held four maidservants and a manservant. Now, on occasions when the museum is filled with guests, all wearing slender modern-day dress, one wonders how on earth the servants and female members of the Dickens household managed to move around their home's narrow hallways wearing such voluminous skirts.

For Charles the process of house-hunting proved frustrating, but eventually the perfect house was discovered and, when Katey was just over a month old, they moved into One Devonshire Terrace. Charles felt a tremendous sense of achievement as he signed the lease for this large, elegant home, across the road from fashionable Regent's Park.[2] Sadly, the house and its gardens were destroyed in the 1950s. Of all the homes in London that Charles Dickens lived in, the only one remaining today is 48 Doughty Street, the place of Katey's birth.

The new house was the end one of three Georgian terraced houses, built in 1776. There was a large garden, as well as stables and a coach house, with rooms above to accommodate stable staff. The house had a prepossessingly grand entrance: Its door and railings were painted vivid green, and above the door was a typical eighteenth-century fanlight window, which, made of stained glass, filled the hallway with color on sunny days. Charles Dickens, who could not abide poor hygiene, would no doubt have been pleased that there was an indoor bathroom (as well as two lavatories in the garden for the lesser mortals). The house was built over five floors, including a basement and two attic floors. The family lived in the two main stories, while the basement and part of the attics were the domain of the servants. The remaining attic rooms were the nursery and, later, Katey and Mamie's bedroom. The rooms on the main two floors were very spacious with extremely high ceilings and plenty of tall

2 The park and its local area had undergone extensive landscaping during the early decades of the 1800s, in accordance with the wishes of the now-deceased Prince Regent (George IV) and to the designs of the architect John Nash. In 1841, shortly after the Dickens family moved into the area, the greater part of the park was opened to the public.

windows to allow daylight to stream through; even the attics were well supplied with windows. Charles turned the ground-floor library into his study—and apparently erected a gate between the first and ground floors, so that the children could be kept at bay while he was working. There were steps leading from his study straight into the garden and the door that led into the hallway was covered with green baize in an effort to minimize any household noise that might disturb his writing. Also on the ground floor was a spacious dining room, big enough for Charles and Catherine to be able to entertain enthusiastically; they were excellent hosts.

Shortly after the move to Devonshire Terrace, as a reward for the rigors of yet another birth, and perhaps to help her overcome the inexplicable depression childbirth seemed to plunge her into, Charles bought his wife a carriage of her own (to put inside their grand new coach house). Catherine always experienced great difficulty in giving birth; she seems to have suffered agonizingly on each occasion and taken several months to recover, both physically and emotionally. Catherine's experience of post-natal depression was recorded in a letter by her young sister Mary in 1837, after Catherine had given birth for the first time. Mary wrote to a cousin:

> *my dearest Kate . . . has not gone on so well as her first week made us hope she would. After we thought she was getting quite well and strong it was discovered she was not able to nurse her Baby so she was obliged with great reluctance as you may suppose to give him up to a stranger. Poor Kate! it has been a dreadful trial for her. . . . Every time she sees her Baby she has a fit of crying and keeps constantly saying she is sure he will not care for her now she is not able to nurse him. I think time will be the only effectual cure for her—could she but forget this she has everything in the world to make her comfortable and happy.*

This unhappy pattern of Catherine's depression was to be repeated many times.

For the people of England, the few months following Katey Dickens' birth were a time of great excitement. The young Queen Victoria married Prince Albert of Saxe-Coburg in February 1840; in the same year, Nelson's Column was erected in Trafalgar Square, a proud symbol of Britain's control over the seas; the Penny Post was introduced; and the very first bicycle was made. Katey was born at an exhilarating, somewhat confused time and she was to live an equally exciting—and frenetic—life. Ironically, Britain was also suffering from its worst ever economic depression.[3]

When Katey was a baby and a child, both her parents suffered from regular bouts of depression and erratic mood swings. The depressive tendency was a condition that would pass from parent to newborn daughter. Considering how exposed Katey was to the condition throughout her formative years, it is unsurprising she should have inherited the tendency to depression.

In view of several circumstances of Charles Dickens' own childhood, it is also no surprise that the novelist himself suffered from depression. His early childhood had been nothing out of the ordinary, but his life changed dramatically when he was twelve. At the time of Charles' birth in 1812, his father, John, was a clerk in the Navy's pay department at Portsmouth Docks. When Charles was two, his father's job was transferred to London, but in 1817 the family moved to Chatham in Kent. Charles was very happy in Kent and, at the age of nine, started going to a school run by a popular master named William Giles. He greatly enjoyed school and, in 1821, wrote his first work, a "tragedy" entitled *Misnar, the Sultan of India*. As a boy, Charles must have entertained vivid dreams of all the things he would do when his education was complete; perhaps he hoped to attend a university, he may already have envisaged himself as a great writer, but it was more likely that he saw himself as a playwright rather than a novelist, as from a young age Charles longed to be an actor, touring the country and performing comic monologues like his hero Charles Mathews. Whatever his other dreams were at this time, he felt sure of one thing—that he was going to be a gentleman. Unfortunately, in 1822, just a year after Charles had started his schooling, John Dickens found himself in deep financial trouble. At the same time his job required relocation back to London and

---

3 In *The Victorians* A.N. Wilson writes that it is estimated "more than a million paupers starved from simple lack of employment" in Britain between 1837 and 1844.

his financial situation worsened considerably. Initially, Charles remained in Kent, living at school. At the end of the year, he was put on a coach to London to join his family, who were now living in reduced circumstances in Camden Town, north London.[4]

Charles was the second oldest child in a large family. His one elder sibling was his sister Fanny, already a promising musician and singer whose education was deemed of paramount importance to the family's future earning potential. In 1823, the family moved to the slightly more reputable area of Bloomsbury, where his mother, Elizabeth, attempted to salvage the family's worsening finances by opening a school "for young ladies." Sadly her efforts didn't attract a single pupil and the situation grew increasingly desperate. In February 1824, John Dickens was arrested for debt and imprisoned in the Marshalsea, a debtors' prison in the borough of Southwark, south London. At first, Elizabeth and their younger children remained at home, attempting to make the school viable. Eventually they gave up the venture and moved into John's prison cell. In the 1850s, the adult Charles Dickens would re-create his memories of the prison in *David Copperfield* and, most notably, *Little Dorrit*.

At the time of their father's arrest, Fanny was a scholarship boarder at the Royal Academy of Music and her parents chose not to remove her from school; Charles alone was left to fend for himself. He remained understandably bitter about this in later years (though the bitterness was aimed at his parents, not his sister). When his father was in prison, Charles had to live on his own in a lodging house, buy his own food, and work to support his imprisoned family. All this for a boy who had only just passed his twelfth birthday. A young cousin of Elizabeth's had found Charles a job at Warren's, a "blacking factory," where shoe polish and lead blacking were made. It was located at Hungerford Steps, near the Strand, in a crook of a dirty, smelly section of the River Thames (then a busy working river used heavily for industry). Charles' job was to paste the labels onto bottles of "blacking," a ubiquitous liquid used widely in Victorian homes for blacking shoes and boots, front steps, kitchen ranges, carriage hoods, and anything else that needed to be gleamingly black. A

---

4   His teacher, William Giles, did not forget the young Charles Dickens. When the author first found fame with *The Pickwick Papers,* William Giles sent him a letter of congratulations and an engraved silver snuff box.

sad vision of Charles' life at the time his father was first imprisoned is given in a book written many years later by his eldest daughter:

His mother and the rest of the family, with the exception of his sister Fanny . . . lived in a poor part of London, too far away from the black-ing warehouse for him to go and have his dinner with them; so he had to carry his food with him, or buy it at some cheap eating house, as he wandered about the streets, during the dinner hour. . . . When Charles had enough money he would buy some coffee and a slice of bread and butter. When the poor little pocket was empty, he wandered about the streets again, gazing into shop windows . . .

Although only a few months passed before the family was released from prison, some longer time went by before Charles was released from working life; the experience was never to leave him, nor the bitterness he felt about it. In *David Copperfield*, Charles writes of his eponymous hero being forced by his bullying stepfather to work at Murdstone and Grin-by's warehouse. As an adult, Charles almost never referred to this humili-ating episode in his childhood; it seems the only people he ever confided the truth about his history to were Catherine and John Forster. After Charles' death, when John Forster published his *Life of Charles Dickens* and the novelist's children learned the truth of their father's childhood, Charles' son Henry recalled an incident that had remained in his memory, although he had not known why. A few months before his father's death, at Christmas time, the family was playing a word-association game. One of the phrases Charles threw in was "Warren's Blacking, 30, Strand." Henry recalled, "He gave this with an odd twinkle in his eye and a strange inflection in his voice which at once forcibly arrested my attention and left a vivid impression on my mind for some time afterwards. Why, I could not, for the life of me, understand."

After leaving Warren's, Charles was able to return to school and he spent a year at Wellington House Academy in London. A willing pupil, liked by his peers and eager to learn, he must also have been terrified of his fellow pupils or teachers discovering his shameful secret. Although he was pleased to be back in education, Wellington House, and in par-ticular its sadistic headmaster, William Jones, was not a pleasant place to be. In 1827, at the age of fifteen, his parents' poor financial management led once again to Charles leaving school and, this time, to Fanny leaving the Royal Academy of Music. Fifteen was not considered young to leave school and Charles now began his career in earnest. His first job was as a solicitor's clerk with Ellis & Blackmore in Lincoln's Inn; it was this experience that was to give him such superb material when writing about the legal profession, especially notable in *Bleak House*.

Even with his childhood many years behind him, Charles was never to get over the terrible impressions the events of 1824 had left upon him. With every step he took toward success, each of which would inevitably move him farther and farther away from the specter of the Marshalsea, he was dogged by his childhood memories, which never stopped haunting him. As such, the exhilarating ability to provide his family with a home such as One Devonshire Terrace was all the more keenly enjoyed. His experiences may also suggest a reason behind the irritation he exhibited about the large number of children he and Catherine were to have: his own parents had kept having children, despite not being able to afford them. His youngest brother, Augustus, had been born in 1827—the same year in which Charles was forced to end his education and find a permanent job because John and Elizabeth had been evicted from their home.

Throughout the early years of fatherhood, Charles' behavior was unpredictable. On occasion he would suddenly appear from his study and call his children into the garden for raucous games, yet everyone—friends and family alike—learned never to approach him when he was attempting to work out a problem or was engrossed in thought. Eleanor Christian, who became friends with Charles and Catherine in 1840, recalled how his moods could swing from being excited and jovial to sulky and miserable— how one evening he could be adoring, slightly flirtatious, and chivalrous and yet the next morning would barely give her and her friend a second glance. She wrote:

> There were times when we gave Mr. Dickens "a wide berth," and Milly and I have often run round corners to get out of his way, when we thought he was in one of these moods, which we could tell by one glance at his face. His eyes were always like "danger-lamps," and

warned people to clear the line for fear of collision. We felt we had to do with a genius, and in the throes and agonies of bringing forth his conceptions, we did not expect him to submit to be interrupted by triflers like ourselves: at these times I confess I was horribly afraid of him. I told him so, to his great amusement . . .

This erratic behavior is key to understanding Katey's father's personality and the highly charged atmosphere within which she grew up. Of all his children, Katey was the most like Charles in temperament (as well as appearance) and she would live her life in a similarly impetuous manner. As she grew from a squalling, needy infant into a pleasingly chubby and delectable baby, so Charles' attachment to her grew. He became besotted with her and was deeply distressed when, at ten months old, she was extremely unwell while he and Catherine were away, visiting his parents in Devon. It was normal at that time for parents to leave young babies with the servants, and Katey had been left with the ever-reliable Pickthorn. On their return home, the anxious parents were informed of Katey's condition and assured that the family physician, Dr. Davis, had been called. After scaring them all, the infant Katey rallied, although her father noted anxiously that she had become terribly thin and was much paler than she should be. Sudden and alarming illnesses were to become a regular feature of Katey's life.

It was perhaps this early debilitating illness (undiagnosed in her father's letters) that prompted her parents to organize a christening as hastily as possible. Why she had not been christened already, as would have been more usual, is unknown, but on August 17, 1840, Dickens wrote to a friend, "A babby is to be christened and a fatted calf killed on these premises on Tuesday the 25th. Instant. It (the calf; not the babby) is to be taken off the spit at 6. *Can* you come?"

Katey was duly christened in the presence of three godparents and an "impatient . . . parson" who was furious at the non-appearance of another baby due to be christened at the same time. Her godfather was the actor William Charles Macready, after whom she had already been named. He gave a "watch and chain" as a christening present, which he was "pleased to see very much admired." Macready's diary for this date records how, after the christening ceremony and lunch were over, he and Charles left the ladies to coo over the baby and paid a visit to Coldbath Fields Prison, where they were shown around by the governor. It seems an amusingly anomalous appointment for Charles to have made for the date of his daughter's christening. That evening, Macready "went to dine with Dickens. Met some relations of his. . . . Rather noisy and uproarious—not so much *comme il faut* as I could have wished."

One of Katey's godmothers was also her aunt, Fanny. It seems that the other was a family friend, Miss Ayrton. By now, Fanny had married a fellow musician, Henry Burnett, and their eldest son, Henry Augustus, was born in the same year as Katey. He suffered from an unspecified disability, described only as being "weak" and "crippled"; he was Charles' inspiration for both Tiny Tim in *A Christmas Carol* and Paul Dombey in *Dombey and Son*. In 1841, Fanny and Henry would have a second son, named, in honor of his much-loved uncle, Charles Dickens Burnett. At this time, the Burnett family was living in London and socialized regularly with the Dickenses; Charles was extremely proud and fond of his talented sister.

A few days after Katey's christening, Charles took his young family on a holiday to Broadstairs, in Kent, a place he had grown to love and would often escape to. This holiday was the start of what would become a family tradition; Katey and her siblings were to spend long periods of their childhood playing on the sands and hiding behind the rocks of the coastal resort. The popular holiday spot was not far from Chatham. It seems Charles wanted his own children to experience the area where he had been so content; perhaps he himself wanted to remember life as it had been before the move to London, the shame of the debtors' prison, and his rudely interrupted education.

Despite Charles' frustration at the ease with which Catherine became pregnant, he did nothing to prevent conception.[5] Six months after Katey's christening, on February 8, 1841, she was usurped from her position as baby of the family by the arrival of Edgar. His was considered a "good honest Saxon name" by Charles—before he changed his mind and renamed the baby Walter Landor Dickens (after his friend the poet Walter Landor). A couple of weeks after the birth, Charles described his new

---

5 Several effective methods of contraception were available at the time, including condoms.

son as "very fat, when being washed looks like a plump turkey." Walter's birth was, however, about to be outshone in Charles' mind by the illness of his pet raven Grip. The bird had been a part of family life for many years and Charles had grown deeply attached to him, though Charley, Mamie, and Katey had little fondness for Grip as he was aggressive in play and made frequent attempts to bite their ankles. Despite the ministrations of a vet, Grip died on March 12. Charles noted wryly that his children were "rather glad" about it. In a somewhat macabre move, he had Grip stuffed and mounted in a glass case, from where the raven could look down upon him at work.[6] A second raven was soon bought and also named Grip, in honor of the deceased.[7]

Charles was congenitally restless and, having fathered four children in less than five years, he craved excitement. The realities of marriage, family life, and London were beginning to grow irksome and he had ambitions to conquer the new world. The United States of America was an important—and well-populated—market; if he wanted to make serious money he would need to become known on the other side of the Atlantic. Although his books were now bringing in a regular and enjoyable income, he would never feel secure in the knowledge that he was earning enough. Terrified of ending up like his father—who still found himself constantly in debt—Charles had a need to maximize his earning to its full capacity. This fear of becoming like John Dickens was no doubt one of the factors that led to Charles becoming what, today, is described as a workaholic. Charles' childhood forever drove him to earn greater and greater amounts of money to ensure his family's financial security.

Already there was a growing American market for his books and Charles' publishers had come up with an idea to increase his celebrity status through a lecture tour. The trip would involve a long journey by ship and several months of touring North America. It was a huge undertaking and one that was further complicated by the presence of four young

---

6   After Dickens' death the stuffed raven was sold for the very high price of £126. The person who bought Grip was an American, who bought the bird in memory of Edgar Allan Poe, who was said to have been inspired by Grip (in *Barnaby Rudge*) when he wrote "The Raven." Grip now resides in the rare books department of the Philadelphia Free Library.

7   Henry Fielding Dickens remembered a third raven also called Grip, who used to terrorize their large mastiff, Turk; he would steal the choicest bits of food from Turk's dish while the terrified dog waited submissively for the raven to finish.

children. During a summer season in Broadstairs, Charles worked on the feasibility of the plan, which included having to persuade Catherine of the importance of their going away. Initially, Charles insisted his entire family should make the trip, but as the plans progressed he could see how impracticable such an entourage would prove. By mid-September, Catherine was dissolving into dismal tears every time her husband mentioned America; she knew she must accompany him, but the prospect of leaving her children for several months was tearing her apart. Her baby was barely seven months old and her eldest child was not yet five. In addition, Catherine found herself having to deal with the sudden death of her brother, George Thomson Hogarth, in October 1841.

Although initially sympathetic to his wife in her distress and similarly reluctant to leave his children, Charles became increasingly enthusiastic about the proposed trip. Ignoring Catherine's unhappiness, he made concrete plans, such as insuring his life in case he should die abroad. Perhaps his erratic personality was being whispered about: The Eagle insurance company would not agree to cover him before investigating a bizarre rumor that he was suffering from dementia. Having satisfied themselves of Charles' sanity, his life was insured for £5,000.

Catherine's doubts were continually swamped by her husband's enthusiasm, and she was won over by an offer from Katey's godfather. Catherine had long been in awe of Macready, so, at Charles' request, the actor wrote to Catherine begging her not to take the children on such an arduous journey. He and his wife would, he offered, be happy to take care of Charley, Mamie, Katey, and Walter, acting *in loco parentis*. In addition, Charles' younger brother Fred would live in the house, so there would always be someone with the children. Unable to offer any further objections, Catherine finally agreed to the journey. Charles assured her they would be gone for only three months; however, in a letter to Fred, he admitted they would be away for "five or six months (but I don't tell her how long)."

Before they left London, Catherine was presented with a beautiful, circular sketch of their four children—and the infamous raven—by their friend Daniel Maclise. Catherine was to keep it with her all around America and Canada. The picture now hangs in the Charles Dickens Museum in London and is a wonderful insight into Victorian family life. The children, all so young but so perfectly dressed like mini-adults, sit in contented harmony, as though rowdy playing would not occur to them. They are seated upon tasseled cushions with an enormous book in between them. Four-year-old Charley is distinguishable purely by dint of being the oldest of the four, as he is dressed in a fetching off-the-shoulder number that makes him look extremely feminine. It is an enticing picture that draws the viewer into the children's world and their personalities shine through (with the exception of Walter, who is still a small baby). Charley appears confident and is the only one looking out at the viewer; Mamie looks good and pensive; and Katey seems to be cheeky and very pretty.

The four eldest Dickens children by Daniel Maclise. Catherine Dickens loved this picture and took it with her while she and Charles toured America and Canada in 1842. (From left to right: Katey, Walter (in a hat), Charley, Mamie, and Grip, the raven.)

Portrait of Catherine Dickens by Daniel Maclise

Charles and Catherine sailed for America on January 4, 1842.[8] On the day their parents went away, Katey was two years old, Mamie almost four, Charley two days away from his fifth birthday, and Walter just eleven months old. To add to the upheaval, Charles had rented out their home. The children and the servants were rehoused in nearby Osnaburgh Street and Fred Dickens, the popular and jovial uncle, moved in, to oversee the servants. Catherine's younger sister Georgina also called to see them as often as possible.

While Fred was at work (he was a clerk in the Treasury Office), his nieces and nephews spent their days at the Macready residence. It was an unhappy situation. In adult life Mamie vividly recalled the regular occurrence of two-year-old Katey sobbing and refusing to be dressed as she hated going. The Macreadys were strict, albeit well-intentioned, parents: "although the very kindest of the kind, [they] brought up their own children with much more severity than the Dickens babies had ever been used to, and they were all certainly miserable in the prim, gloomy, unjoyful house." Unknowingly, the children were also intruding on the Macreadys at a difficult time: William was worried by financial problems at his Drury Lane theater; he was also undergoing a very public trial-by-satirical-press over his ongoing attempt to make theaters respectable.

Back in Osnaburgh Street, there was the amusing presence of Uncle Fred. He was Charles' junior by eight years, a likeable but irresponsible man of twenty-two whom the children knew well. In the early years of Charles and Catherine's marriage, Fred would often accompany Catherine and her sisters to events Charles couldn't attend. Before Charles had married, he had taken the fourteen-year-old Fred to live with him at his bachelor quarters. Uncle Fred was, however, apparently found wanting by Charles' older and more respectable friends. Macready's diary records that he had berated the younger man for his lack of "tact" and "ordinary consideration" for his brother's children. Despite Macready's misgivings, it seems likely the children were fond of their scapegrace uncle; he comes in

---

8 Charles was to prove an almost overwhelming success on this trip, although he was appalled and deeply upset by what one American acquaintance proudly called the country's "domestic situation," i.e., slavery. Charles was outspoken in his detestation of the practice and angered many Americans by writing furiously about it when he went home. He would not return to America until the late 1860s.

for no censure in their later recollections and a letter written by Charles to Forster, before they left the country, states that Catherine "is satisfied to have nobody in the house but Fred, of whom you know, they are all fond." Of course Fred was not really responsible for their welfare, cared for as they were by servants. Perhaps Charles did not yet see how similar to their father Fred was to prove, or perhaps it was his hope that his younger

Portrait of Charles Dickens painted by Daniel Maclise; it is often referred to as "the Nickleby Portrait," as it was completed in 1839, the year in which *Nicholas Nickleby* was published.

brother would learn something about acting responsibly while playing at being master of the house. Swaggering and fun, Fred shared his older brother's propensity for dressing ostentatiously, his sense of adventure and his natural exuberance—though not his aptitude for hard work.

Charles Dickens was renowned for his enjoyment of clothes; his love of the dramatic and his theatrical nature spilled over into his sartorial sense— and was to bemuse many of the Americans he met in 1842. The slightly garish waistcoat or flamboyant cravat, which would not have gone down well in the gentlemen's clubs in St. James's (nor did it in the conventional social scene of Boston), passed as a byword for style in the artistic world in which Charles lived. He was a relatively short, slender man with an enormous personality that he chose to make the most of by dressing to reflect his dandified inner life, not simply to frame his physical features. He also liked to ensure his family was equally well dressed; William Thackeray's daughter Anny was later to recall the envy with which she and her sister Minny gazed at the Dickens girls' pristine clothes, which were always perfectly neat and beautiful, and how their shoes were always shiny and polished and stylish, whereas theirs were always boringly practical brown.

On June 29, 1842, after six months of missing their parents and six months without Charles' famous bedtime singing sessions, Katey and her siblings were alerted to the sound of a coach drawing up outside their house. Charles and Catherine, who were not expected home for several days, had journeyed back early, in secret. Foiling the interest of journalists by this ruse, they reached Osnaburgh Street longing for a private reunion with their children. Mamie remembers looking up from playing with Uncle Fred to see her father leaping excitedly out of the coach before it had time to stop. "Someone lifted me up in their arms," wrote Mamie many years later, "and I was kissing my father through the bars of the gate." There was general merriment and intense overexcitement at the arrival, which culminated in Charley being so overcome with emotion that he fell into frightening convulsions. Once recovered, he and his siblings were overjoyed to have their mother and father home. There would be no more hours spent crying over their absence and, even better, no more daily visits to the Macreadys. As Charles was to write later to a friend, "If we tell them we are going to America again, they all roar lustily."

2
AN ITALIAN ADVENTURE

With their parents back, life for the Dickens children returned to normal. Their father's tenant reached the end of his lease and they moved back to Devonshire Terrace, Uncle Fred resumed his bachelor life, and Katey and her siblings spent hours playing with an American dog their parents had acquired, "a white Havannah spaniel." When he'd been given to the visiting writer as a present, the dog's name had been Timber Doodle; Charles changed this to Snittle Timbery, but back in England he became known simply as Timber. He was one of many such dogs to be welcomed into the Dickens household, each of whom would play a significant role in family life. Charles was a fervent lover of animals, an attitude he took care to instill in his children. He would be seldom happier, in later years, than when walking surrounded by a small pack of dogs. Mamie later wrote that:

> *Timber . . . soon became very friendly with the children, and from this time the home was never without some kind of pet or pets. The second Grip was still alive, and as mischievous and impudent as ever. The children kept a number of rabbits and guinea-pigs in the stable, and whenever a new one appeared, which was a constant occurrence, it was immediately carried to be shown to, and to be admired by, Charles Dickens . . . the children were allowed to keep as many as they liked, provided they looked after them themselves, fed them, and kept their hutches clean and comfortable.*

Now that they were home, Charles and Catherine decided that Catherine's younger sister, Georgina, should come and stay with them. At the beginning of their marriage, another of Catherine's sisters, Mary Hogarth, had come to live with them for weeks at a time. This may sound strange today, but it was quite usual for unmarried sisters to live with their older, married siblings, in the hope that they would meet respectable suitors. Single women of the middle and upper classes were allowed very little freedom, unable to go anywhere without a chaperone (an older woman who was married, widowed, or of an advanced enough age to be considered a respectable spinster). A sister just a few years older than she was must have seemed to Mary an appealing chaperone. Charles had become enchanted with this young sister-in-law, to a degree that one imagines must have been uncomfortable for Catherine to witness (although she was equally adoring of Mary). One evening, when Mary was just sixteen years old, she accompanied Charles and Catherine to the theater. Shortly after their return to Doughty Street, Mary very suddenly collapsed and died from a weak heart. It happened shockingly quickly. She died in Charles' arms, an event that was to haunt him. Mary was to become immortalized in many of Charles' works, the inspiration for the majority of his idealized young women.

The specter of Mary Hogarth haunted the household; it also haunted Catherine and Charles' marriage. Charles spoke openly of his desire to be buried in the same grave as his teenage sister-in-law; after her death he took all her clothes and, instead of returning them to her parents, kept them for himself. For many years he would regularly visit the room in which they were stored, take them out, and hold them. Throughout his life he wore on his little finger a ring Mary had been wearing on the night she died (a ring which remains in the family to this day). It was an odd atmosphere for Katey and her siblings to grow up in, with their mother's dead sister so passionately idolized by their father.

When Georgina Hogarth came to stay, she was sixteen years old. The children adored her, Catherine was relieved to pass on some of the duties she found so arduous, and Charles grew to rely on her as one of his closest friends and advisers. Sadly for Catherine, her husband was seldom content with just her for company. Georgina could not help but fall under the spell of her famous, fascinating brother-in-law. Being so young, unmarried, and childless, it was exciting for her to learn how to keep house—particularly at such an important address—and to help raise her nieces and nephews. Unfortunately, over time, Georgina's youth, enthusiasm, and competence would help to lower Charles' opinion of Catherine, painting her in his mind as a lazy, dull woman who could never be his equal. Catherine, it would appear, had been somewhat confounded by the realities of house-keeping, whereas Georgina was eminently capable, organized, "charming & well & beautifully dressed." Charles, in his unfavorable comparisons,

Charles Dickens and one of his many beloved dogs, from a photograph in Katey's personal photo album (c. 1865)

appears not to have made allowances for the fact that Catherine spent much of her life debilitated by pregnancy and childbirth.

Georgina was to figure largely in the Dickens children's lives. She assisted with their schooling, cared for them when their parents were absent, and became their confidante. Her facial similarity to her dead sister was often remarked upon and, when she arrived to live in Devonshire Terrace, she was almost the same age Mary had been when she had stayed with Catherine and Charles.

In 1842, when Georgina arrived to live with them, Charles and Catherine were happily married. The Dickenses' marriage was viewed by outsiders as one in which fun and frivolity played a large part. Friends described hilarious dinner parties at which riotous games would be played or at which Catherine would deliberately make terrible puns while keeping an innocently straight face, in order to watch her husband writhe in comic agony. They both loved dancing, parlor games, and good food. They enjoyed surrounding themselves with friends and Catherine was renowned as a welcoming, tactful hostess; Charles would seldom see unexpected guests, as they interfered with his work schedule, but Catherine would always receive them graciously and with warmth. She needed to do so with regularity during the American trip, carefully shielding Charles from the overenthusiasm of callers to their hotel. Eleanor Christian said of Charles, "I have never met any one who entered into games with as much spirit and boisterous glee; the simplest of them he contrived to make amusing, and often instructive. His fun was most infectious."

It is unknown how long Georgina's stay was originally intended to be, but before long she had become accepted as a permanent fixture. She joined them on their extended family holiday to Broadstairs and was with them in London when the American poet Henry Wadsworth Longfellow came to stay. Longfellow had met Charles and Catherine on their trip to the United States and the two men had begun what was to be a lasting friendship. He stayed at Devonshire Terrace for a fortnight and was a source of great amusement to the children. In December, Charles wrote Longfellow a warm letter, in which he relates how the children remembered him:

> . . . *After you left us, Charley invented and rehearsed with his sisters a dramatic scene in your honor [sic], which is still occasionally enacted.*

It commences with expressive pantomime, and begins immediately after the ceremony of drinking healths. The three small glasses are all raised together, and they look at each other very hard. Then Charley cries 'Mr. Longfellow! Hoo–ra–a–a–a–a–a–e!' Two other shrill voices repeat the sentiment, and the little glasses are drained to the bottom. The whole concludes with a violent rapping of the table, and a hideous barking from the little dog, who wakes up for the purpose.

At the end of 1842, Katey's paternal grandparents came to live in London (having spent several years in Devon). Charles initially acquired them a home in Blackheath, in the southeast of the city, before moving them to nearby Lewisham. One suspects these locations were chosen carefully, their being not close enough for his parents to intrude on his daily life in the center of town, but close enough for him to keep an eye on their activities. John Dickens was still unable to curb his propensity for getting into debt—and presumably the fact that his son was doing so well made it much easier, as he now knew Charles could always afford to bail him out. Even in America, Charles had been plagued by letters telling of his parents' demands to be eased out of debt.

It is around this time that Charles' letters start to reveal a decided favoritism toward Katey. When writing to his brother-in-law Henry Austin about his children's nicknames, he put Katey's name first although she was the third child:

The childrens [sic] present names are as follows:
Katey (from a lurking propensity to fiery-ness) Lucifer Box
Mamey (as generally descriptive of her bearing) Mild Gloster
Charley (as a corruption of Master Toby) Flaster Floby
Walter (suggested by his high cheek bones) Young Skull
Each is pronounced with a peculiar howl, which I shall have great pleasure in illustrating.

Like her father, Katey experienced emotional highs and lows from a young age. She was given the nickname "Lucifer Box" because of the passionate way her temper flared up like a "lucifer" (another word for a match) or a lit tinder box.

When writing to Catherine while away from home Charles frequently asked her to send his love to the children, listing them all by name, but writing only "KATEY" in capital letters. This role of favored child was a position Katey was to enjoy all through her childhood. Although with each new baby—until it became older and more intrusive—there was a risk of her being overshadowed, Katey remained Charles' favorite child (followed closely by Mamie) until her early teens, when Charles became more enchanted with his youngest son for several years; those years aside, she was never truly eclipsed in his affections and their relationship was one of mutual devotion—and occasional furious arguments.

As the old year moved toward 1843, Katey was at the center of a contented family life. As one would expect from the man who practically invented the way in which the British celebrate Christmas, Charles always made a welcome fuss of his children during the festive season. Each year on December 24, he would take them to a particular toy shop in Holborn to choose their presents (they were allowed one each), and anything they wanted to buy for their friends. Katey later recalled, "At Christmas dinner, when my father had carved the turkey, which he did very rapidly from a side table, and we had all partaken, our glasses would be filled and he would rise from his chair and give the toast: 'Here's to us all—God bless us!'" The festivities would last until Twelfth Night (January 6), which also happened to be Charley's birthday. On that date, a party would take place and a large Twelfth Cake would be consumed. On Charley's sixth birthday, in 1843, there was great excitement about one of his presents, remembered by the family in years to come: a magic lantern. The theatrical nature of this gift was to be echoed on future Twelfth Nights when it became family tradition to put on elaborate plays.

The summer months of 1843 were spent, once again, at Broadstairs. Charles was plagued by the cacophony of amateur buskers, but the children, who were not yet old enough to require daily lessons, enjoyed the delights of a summer at the seaside. That summer, at the tender age of almost four, Katey attracted her first suitor, a young Kentish boy she had presumably met on the beach. On September 2, 1843, her father wrote a letter to his great friend and correspondent Angela Burdett-Coutts[9]—known to the children as Miss Toots, a name bestowed on her by a very young Katey. In it he reported the incident of Katey's very first love-token:

> *Charley is so popular with the boatmen, that I begin to think of Robinson Crusoe, and the propriety of living in-land. I saw him yesterday through a telescope, miles out at sea, steering an enormous fishing-smack, to the unspeakable delight of seven gigantic companions, clad in oilskin. Katey is supposed to be secretly betrothed, in as much as a very young gentleman (so young, that being unable to reach the knocker, he called attention to the door by kicking it) called the other evening, and being gratified in a mysterious, I may say quite a melodramatic, request, to speak with the Nurse, produced a live crab, which he said he had "promised her."*

On Boxing Day, Katey and her two older siblings were taken back to the dreaded home of her godfather. This time, however, it was to attend little Nina Macready's birthday party and Katey's father was to demonstrate a new skill, as a conjurer. The children sat spellbound for an hour as Charles, with John Forster in the role of "servant," performed trick after trick. Charles was not only a perfectionist in his writing; even the task of amateur conjurer for a child's party was one he took tremendously seriously. Evenings like this baby party at the Macreadys' gave Charles a chance to indulge his children as he wanted. One of the guests described the evening as:

---

9 Miss Burdett-Coutts, heiress to the banking fortune and the richest woman in England, was a committed philanthropist and sympathetic to many of the causes Charles Dickens espoused. Together they set up a home for fallen women, Urania Cottage, in Shepherds Bush, then a newly built and not very prosperous area of west London. The house was on Lime Grove—later to be made famous by the film studios in which Alfred Hitchcock began his career and then by the BBC, but at the time an obscure little road, one of many running off the large thoroughfare that led out of London toward Uxbridge. Together the visionary novelist and banking heiress set up a "haven" for former prostitutes and women who had given birth to an illegitimate child. These women were taught domestic skills not the least of which was basic personal hygiene, and then given passage to Australia, where they would be able to start again without the specter of their past life catching up with them (as it undoubtedly would do in England).

the very most agreeable party that ever I was at in London. . . . Dickens and Forster above all exerted themselves till the perspiration was pouring down and they seemed drunk with their efforts! Only think of that excellent Dickens playing the conjuror for one whole hour—the best conjuror I ever saw—(and I have paid money to see several)—and Forster acting as his servant. This part of the entertainment concluded with a plum pudding made out of raw flour, raw eggs—all the usual raw ingredients—boiled in a gentleman's hat—and tumbled out reeking—all in one minute before the eyes of the astonished children and astonished grown people! That trick—and his other of changing ladies' pocket handkerchiefs into comfits—and a box of bran into a box full of—a live guinea pig! would enable him to make a handsome subsistence, let the bookseller trade go as it please!

The party continued with energetic dancing—an activity Katey always enjoyed—and a delicious supper, with Christmas crackers to be pulled and champagne for the adults. It is unlikely Catherine joined in the country dancing with any vigor as she was due to give birth again within a few weeks. Her daughters, however, spent much of the evening dancing; among their partners was the novelist William Thackeray. The author of *Vanity Fair*—another loving and indulgent father—became one of Charles' closest friends and his young daughters were to become long-term friends of the Dickens girls. Although Katey felt quite nervous around Thackeray as a child—she was often shy outside the family, despite her ebullience within it—by the time she had reached adolescence she and Thackeray would develop a special bond. In adulthood, Thackeray and Katey counted each other among their favorite people.

The close of 1843 was one of Charles' finest literary moments. That year, *Martin Chuzzlewit* had been published in monthly installments and, on December 17, *A Christmas Carol* had been released. The latter would bring Charles' own love of the season to the masses and affect permanently the ways in which Christmas was celebrated. It had proved an instant success and by February 1844 three different stage versions of *A Christmas Carol* were being performed at three London theaters, each of which was intended to be the first-ever stage production. John Dickens might have been in debt yet again, but his son and grandchildren were destined for far greater circumstances. The success was welcome—indeed, essential, for an insecure egocentric with depressive tendencies—but the pressure this convergence of praise placed upon the thirty-two-year-old author was causing problems of its own; *A Christmas Carol* would be extremely difficult to follow. Charles determined that he needed a radical change, an escape from the pressures London exerted upon him.

Katey's new brother, Francis ("Frank") Jeffrey Dickens, was born on January 15, 1844. As he was destined to spend his life in far-flung corners of the British Empire, it is fitting that Frank should have been born in the year Charles decided his children should see something of the world. This would not be a year of holidaying in Broadstairs or entertaining friends in Regent's Park; instead the Dickenses were making a temporary move to Italy.[10] Charles had bought a new, extra-large carriage in which to transport them all. It was capacious enough to accommodate eleven people: Charles, Catherine, Georgina, the five children, and three servants.

With Devonshire Terrace rented out again, the family left England on July 2. After a long but relatively easy journey through France, they reached Genoa exactly two weeks later. Charles remarked in a letter how well behaved the children were on the journey, and he seemed very pleased with his decision to bring his entire household away with him. It was not only Catherine who had found the separation from their children extremely hard to bear two years previously.

Charles' first intention had been to write in the same place in which Byron composed some of his works, but the house in which the poet had lived in 1822–23—and where he wrote part of *Don Juan*—was by now overgrown and shabby: not an appropriate home for the obsessively ordered author and especially not suitable for such young children. An old friend, Angus Fletcher, with whom Dickens had toured the Highlands of Scotland three years previously, was currently living near Genoa. It was he who made arrangements for the family to stay at Villa di Bella Vista in nearby Albaro. On first impression, this was a great disappointment. Described

---

10 Living in continental Europe—especially France and Italy—was popular at this date, particularly for those with poor health drawn to a milder climate, for artists who sought inspiration and a less formal society, and for those who could not afford the lifestyle they wanted in Britain.

by John Forster as an "unpicturesque and uninteresting dwelling," it was a source of much embarrassment for the well-meaning Fletcher. Charles also did not think it worth the very high rent he was being charged (presumably on the strength of his celebrity)—and perhaps the villa lost much of its romance when he discovered its owner, Signor Bagnerello, was a "drunken butcher" and that the locals only knew the house as the Villa di Bagnerello. As an expression of his disappointment Charles nicknamed it "The Pink Gaol." Despite this initial setback, however, Villa di Bella Vista proved a pleasant stopgap, a preliminary to the family's move into the much more splendid Palazzo Peschiere, the grandest home for rent in the area. They took over the largest quarters in the *palazzo* in September.

In later years, Katey was to remember their months in Italy as an extremely happy time. Albaro was doubtless a much freer, more exciting place in which to grow up than restricted Victorian London—and she was never content when constrained. The villa may not have been a success at first, but within a couple of weeks Charles was writing to Forster, "When the sun sets clearly, by Heaven, it is majestic. From any one of

Villa di Bagnerello, the Dickens family's first home in Italy in 1844; Charles Dickens nicknamed it "The Pink Gaol."

eleven windows here, or from a terrace overgrown with grapes, you may behold the broad sea, villas, houses, mountains, forts, strewn with rose leaves. Strewn with them? Steeped in them! Dyed, through and through and through." Charles' mood could change everything: If he was happy, the rest of his family would be infected with happiness; likewise if he was depressed, the mood of the household mimicked his lead. After the initial gloom-laden days he began to throw himself into life in Italy. He adored the almost overpowering sense of freedom after the frantic, workaholic months completing *Martin Chuzzlewit*.

For Katey and her siblings this was a fantastic time. All around their Albaro home were new sights, sounds, and smells, unlike anything the children would recognize from London: fresh salty sea breezes, a canopy of vine leaves entwining over their courtyard, the chatter of the Italian servants, the sound of the Mediterranean waves crashing on the cliffs, the vibrant colors of the landscape, the burning heat of the sun, the equally fierce rages of the sirocco and the intensely vivid blue of the sea (which

Watercolor of the Palazzo Peschiere dating from the time the family lived there; this was one of Katey's favorite paintings.

moved Charles to write to Daniel Maclise telling him exactly how the Mediterranean should be rendered in any future paintings). Then there were the cows. In the grounds of the villa, providing a constant supply of fresh milk to the household, was a cowshed with five inhabitants: three cows and a human father and son who cared for, and sheltered with, them. It was a heady wealth of experiences for a four-year-old girl.

A couple of months after the family left England, Katey developed a worrying illness. It began with a dreadful sore throat, which her nurse assumed would pass, but then developed into a pronounced swelling on her neck that continued to grow larger. The bewildered little girl was in a great deal of pain and distress and her screams and tantrums could be heard all over the house. There was no shortage of female servants and relatives able and willing to nurse her, yet despite their attentions Katey could not be pacified. She didn't want the desperate ministrations of her mother, or those of her capable young aunt or the comfortable governess; she wanted her father. Moreover, with a force of character that would remain with her into cantankerous octogenarianism, she *insisted* upon being nursed by her father. On another floor of the pink-stoned villa, Katey's father had appropriated what the previous occupants had known as the master bedroom, a spacious, sun-filled room in which he had created a peaceful office. He had set up his desk precisely as he liked it—exactly as it would have been in London. All was ready for a new work of genius to begin forming itself in his mind. He wrote to Forster that the view from his new office was "a very peaceful view, and yet a very cheerful one. Quiet as quiet can be." The quiet, however, was about to be shattered by the vivid screams of his favorite and very ill child. In a manner that would be repeated throughout their relationship, with one always yielding to the other's will, Charles abandoned his dreams of beginning a new book in favor of nursing his youngest daughter back to health. Katey would never forget her father's selflessness on this occasion and the calming feeling of him sitting beside her bed, holding her feverish little hand in his.

Katey's undiagnosed illness continued unabated. None of the usual remedies—including the use of leeches—worked to bring down the swelling or to soften it and they had little faith in Italian medics. Charles had been dabbling in the newly fashionable art of mesmerism (the precursor to hypnosis) and had had several successes, notably with his wife. He tried to mesmerize little Katey to calm her, but to no avail. He put this lack of success down to his and Katey's temperaments being too similar (it is notable that whenever he tried to mesmerize the more compliant Mamie, he was always successful). To the family's relief, an eminent British doctor, Sir James Murray, was staying nearby; he agreed to examine his famous client's "pet little daughter" and was able to reassure them the illness would not prove fatal. There are several possible diagnoses for Katey's illness. She may have been suffering from scrofula (tuberculosis of the neck), which can be caused by proximity to cows or from drinking untreated milk, both of which Katey was doing every day. This diagnosis could also explain why Katey often suffered from bouts of poor health as an adult. Or her illness may have been diphtheria, which can manifest itself in a condition known as "bull neck." Alternatively, it could have been an abscess, probably a quinsy, also known as a "peritonsillar abscess," which happens when a severe case of tonsillitis leads to infection in the surrounding area. The fact that no one else in the household caught Katey's illness suggests it was a quinsy, but the other two cannot be ruled out.

By the middle of August, Katey was recovering, although she had become pitifully thin and altered in appearance (the use of leeches to drain her blood would have left her even weaker). Not yet strong enough to walk, she was taken out for exercise every evening on a donkey. Charles wrote to a friend of her illness: "She would let nobody touch her; in the way of dressing her neck or giving her physic; when she was ill; but her Papa. So I had a pretty tough time of it. But her sweet temper was wonderful to see." His obvious pride in being her chosen nurse and his willingness to push aside his work schedule to care for her reveal a compassionate, tender side to his character.

When fully recovered, being the age she was and in the sphere into which she was born, Katey spent a great deal of time being cared for by servants. It would have been an intriguing insight into adult ways for the children to watch their English servants settling into Italian life. Charles wrote to Forster, "We have a couple of Italian workpeople in our establishment; and to hear one or other of them talking away to our servants with the utmost violence and volubility in Genoese, and our servants answering with great fluency in English (very loud: as if the others were only deaf, not Italian), is one of the most ridiculous things possible." The Dickenses' cook, however, stunned everyone by quickly grasping the rudiments of the language and capably trading with the locals, refusing to allow them to cheat her. Her ability shamed Charles, who was getting along very slowly with an Italian tutor, spurring him into working harder at the language. No doubt Katey, who was a good mimic, and was to show in later years an aptitude for languages, picked up the Genoese dialect quickly.

When they moved to the Palazzo Peschiere, in September 1844, the children's lives became even more thrilling. Here Charles was in his element. Villa di Bagnerello may initially have dragged up his childhood reminiscences of shabby poverty, but with the move to an Italian palace he was living the life of a wealthy Englishman of a privileged class. The family could not have afforded such opulence in England, but the cost of living in Italy was comparatively inexpensive; as such, it had become a popular location for impoverished aristocrats who wanted to live in style but no longer had the income to do so at home. At the *palazzo*, everything was sumptuous and beautiful. The grounds were extensive, with groves of orange trees, imposing antique statues, and seven fountains, offering an enticing choice of setting in which children could play, hide, or just lie and daydream. There remains in the family a detailed and exceptionally pretty watercolor of the Palazzo Peschiere, which was one of Katey's favorite paintings. It is a fond, much loved remembrance of one of the happiest periods in the family's life, a time when the children felt secure in their parents' contentment and when their pretty young aunt was always on hand to play with them. In the painting, the *palazzo*, bathed in a warm glow, is evocative of easeful, leisured times and long, summery evenings. One can so easily imagine the Dickens children playing joyfully in the sun-dappled courtyard and climbing up, or hiding underneath, the mature trees that partially shade it.

Inside, the *palazzo* was everything Charles could have imagined. The walls were covered in three-hundred-year-old frescoes and the rooms were as large, he boasted gleefully in letters home, as those at Windsor Castle. At night, the glow from Genoa's world-famous lighthouse glimmered on the *palazzo*'s walls at a comfortingly regular pace. The *palazzo* was rumored to be haunted, and Charles said he could feel an atmosphere. It is easy to see how, even at Katey's young age, her artistic mind would have been fed by the rich colors and experiences of her time in Italy.

The Dickens children spent much of their time in Albaro without their parents and aunt, who took off on several occasions to tour the rest of the country and to allow Charles to experiment with mesmerism. Katey and her siblings spent their time exploring the gardens around the *palazzo* with Timber in hot pursuit. The unfortunate dog was plagued so wretchedly by what Charles believed to be the superior tenacity of Italian fleas over English ones that he had to have all his fur shaved off in the hope they would leave him alone.

Of all the adults, Charles was away the most often, as he made business trips to London, Switzerland, and Germany. During these absences he would write the regular letters home in which he inquired about "KATEY." Of the children, Charley, aged seven when the family left for Italy, had been the least enchanted with Albaro, having no boys his own age to play with. This quickly improved when they moved to the *palazzo*, as there was an English merchant living nearby, with a son of a similar age. Catherine helped to keep him busy, organizing dancing lessons for her three eldest children, and Charles arranged to have playing cards and a variety of English and French books sent out, to keep Charley amused and further his education. Receiving books was not as easy as one might imagine; Italian customs officers were notoriously suspicious of foreign books and all were inspected by priests who would burn any book they suspected of being corrupting. Charles' celebrity was to prove a bonus when the priests agreed to let him keep a volume of Voltaire, something he had been told they would be bound to confiscate as Voltaire was so outspoken about the Church.

Katey and Mamie learned the polka with their Italian dance teacher, although Katey's progress was somewhat marred by crippling chilblains (a common ailment in the days before central heating). Mamie was later to describe the lessons as "very funny . . . the children's legs were pulled about, stretched, and turned in the most extraordinary manner," but Charles and their trusted travel courier Louis Roche took great pride in the little girls' dancing abilities and partnered them as often as possible. It seems the five-year-old Katey had made another romantic attachment, this time falling for the son of one of her father's English friends living in Italy. Charles wrote ironically to the boy's father, Charles Black, that

". . . Katey is cut to the heart by your son's devotion—the penknife has penetrated into her soul."

Uncle Fred came out to stay at the *palazzo*, as did the less popular Susan, Mrs. Macready's sister. Charles and Catherine found her somewhat tiresome, but bit their lips in remembrance of how kind the Macreadys had been to their children. Charles, who had orchestrated a temporary escape to Parma for research, wrote pleadingly to an exasperated Catherine: "Remember how much we owe to Macready, and to Mrs. Macready too, for their constancy to us when we were in such great anxiety about the Darlings and do not let any natural dislike to her inanities interfere in the slightest degree with an obligation so sacred." In comparison, Fred Dickens was a most welcome house guest and it was not only the children who looked forward to his arrival; Charles was touchingly excited about it, longing to show his brother the local Sunday "entertainment": Genoese families sitting out on the sunny pavements removing lice from one another's heads.

Fred's visit almost ended in disaster when he and Charles went swimming in the sea and Fred got into difficulties. He had swum out too far and the current was taking him farther and farther away from his terrified brother. Watching from the shore were the rest of the family, horrorstruck by the spectacle of Fred's head getting smaller and smaller among the waves. Katey was convinced the swimmer in difficulty was her father "and her shrieks of despair and fear were something terrible," as Charles Dickens noted in a letter. Luckily Fred was saved by a fishing boat.

Katey celebrated her fifth birthday in Italy, Catherine became pregnant again, and the comical baby Frank had bestowed upon him an even more outlandish nickname than his siblings: He was now known affectionately as the Chickenstalker. On New Year's Eve 1844, after Charles had once more captured the Christmas literary market with *The Chimes* (a story partially inspired by their Italian home and the bells of Genoa), the family celebrated their exciting year with a party in the *palazzo*, attended by the other residents, at which they played charades and danced. One can imagine the *palazzo* lit up with torches and lanterns as the residents danced and drank and laughed together, with all the children running around the darkened gardens, playing hide-and-seek among moonlit fountains.

3

GROWING UP
IN A FAMOUS HOUSE

In the spring of 1845, after nine months abroad, the Dickens children returned to London with the servants; their parents traveled back separately. The family settled back into its traditional pattern of residing in Regent's Park and summering in Broadstairs. Katey and her siblings were enjoying a charmed and privileged life, while their father was busy making plans for them to see more of the world.

By now Katey had been nominated by her siblings as the child responsible for getting treats out of their father. The other children were well aware of her special relationship with Charles and if they wanted him to agree to a favor, or were hoping for clemency after a punishment, Katey was the one to approach him and plead their case. Katey later related how she would be sent into her father's study to do the "asking" while the others waited silently outside the door. Charles' study was sacred, a haven of order and tranquility, into which none of the children would have dared enter without invitation. As Mamie was later to write:

> ... his 'studies' were always cheerful, pleasant rooms, and always, like himself, the personification of neatness and tidiness. On the shelf of his writing table were many dainty and useful ornaments, gifts from his friends or members of his family, and always, a vase of bright and fresh flowers. . . . His study, to us children, was a rather mysterious and awe-inspiring chamber, and while he was at work no one was allowed to enter it. We little ones had to pass the door as quietly as possible, and our little tongues left off chattering.

The novelist Elizabeth Gaskell was invited to dine with the Dickenses at Devonshire Terrace. She met Katey and some of her siblings that evening and wrote an account of her visit:

We were shown into Mr. Dickens' study . . . where he writes all his books. . . . There are books all around, up to the ceiling, and down to the ground . . . after dinner . . . quantities of other people came in. We were by this time in the drawing-room, which is not nearly so pretty or so home-like as the study. . . . We heard some beautiful music. . . . I kept trying to learn people's faces off by heart, that I might remember them; but it was rather confusing there were so very many. There were some nice little Dickens' children in the room,—who were so polite, and well-trained.

Mary Cowden Clarke, who together with her husband, Charles, became friends with the Dickenses, also remembered family life in Devonshire Terrace, with great fondness:

On one of these more quiet occasions, when Mr. and Mrs. Dickens, their children, and their few guests were sitting out of doors in the small garden in front of their Devonshire Terrace house, enjoying the fine warm evening, I recollect seeing one of his little sons draw Charles Dickens apart, and stand in eager talk with him, the setting sun full upon the child's upturned face and lighting up the father's, which looked smilingly down into it; and when the important little conference was over, the father returned to us, saying, "The little fellow gave me so many excellent reasons why he should not go to bed so soon, that I yielded the point, and let him sit up half an hour later."

This gives a cozy view of family life and of Charles as a proud father. In October 1845, he was to become a father yet again.

The birth of Alfred d'Orsay Tennyson Dickens took place on October 28, the day before Katey's sixth birthday. As his name suggests, he had two extremely influential godparents: Count d'Orsay and Alfred Tennyson. Count d'Orsay may be little known today, but in his time he was renowned for being that rare combination: a dandy possessed of an intelligent mind. A bisexual French socialite, he was also a talented artist and sculptor. In his youth, he had been a great friend of the Romantic poet Lord Byron; later he allegedly became the lover of Lady Blessington, one of London's most influential hostesses, whose husband it was rumored Count d'Orsay had also had an affair with. To complicate matters further, the widowed Lady Blessington was stepmother to Count d'Orsay's estranged wife, Lady Harriet (née Gardiner). When he was not at his home in Paris, d'Orsay was a prominent member of Lady Blessington's entourage, spending most of his time at her very fashionable home, Gore House. By the time of Alfred's birth, d'Orsay had become one of Charles' most favored friends and regular correspondents.

With every boy born into the family, Charles' two daughters became even more special to their father. Katey would later relate how "Dickens frequently drove with his girls in a carriage to Hampstead Heath, where they alighted and romped in the lanes around Jack Straw's Castle, or wandered on either side of him—listening to the stories he had to tell from the storehouse of his wonderful imagination." According to his son Henry, Charles was much more reserved around his boys: "He was curiously reserved; he did not like to show what he really felt. He was afraid of 'letting himself go' . . ." This contrasts, however, with a remark made by one of Charles' American friends that Charles "always kissed" his sons as well as his daughters, something highly unusual in a nineteenth-century father. This same observer noticed that not only did Katey resemble her father physically more than did any of the others (although Frank would grow up to look very like him too), but also that "no one of his family seemed to enjoy his *humour* as much as Katie, and in her quick perception of it she was more like him than the others."

Charley was now eight and had begun attending King's College school in London. Mamie, Katey, and Walter were being tutored at home. As was usual in Victorian England, the Dickens boys would be sent to school but the girls would receive a "suitable" education at home from a governess. Katey and Mamie would have learned French and Italian (although not Latin), literature, history, dancing, botany, the geography of the British Empire, singing, and at least one musical instrument, as

Alfred Dickens as a young man. Like his father, he developed a great fondness for fashionable clothes.

well as how to draw and paint. They would have been instructed in the arts of conversation, deportment, and general social skills suitable for girls of their class. Mamie and Katey were lucky to have a father who deemed that girls should be educated well and one who took an interest in their individual tastes and abilities.

During their time at Devonshire Terrace, after graduating from the nursery the two girls were allowed to share a bedroom in the attic, a room that had previously been occupied by servants. They were scared of this room at first, as it contained a "mysterious" trapdoor they entertained ghastly fears about. On discovering this, their father came up to the room, opened the trapdoor and showed them that there was nothing scary inside at all. From this time, they loved the bedroom and turned it into their own special place.

As the children grew older, they became less interested in keeping pets and more interested in running off energy in the garden, so Charles had a swing built for them and joined them in exhaustive games and sport. Mamie would recall that:

Outdoor games of the simpler kinds delighted him. Battledore and shuttlecock was played constantly in the garden at Devonshire Terrace, though I do not remember my father ever playing it elsewhere. The American game of bowls pleased him, and rounders found him more than expert. Croquet he disliked, but cricket he enjoyed intensely as a spectator.

At the end of May 1846, about a year after the family's return from Italy, they all—except Charley, who was left behind at school—went traveling again, this time to Switzerland. There they stayed at the Villa Rosemont in Lausanne, a pretty, rose-covered house with views down to the lake. In July, Dickens recorded how his daughters were thrown into delight at the spectacle of a local girl's wedding. As he wrote to Forster: "One of the farmer's people—a sister, I think—was married from here the other day. It is wonderful to see how naturally the smallest girls are interested in marriages. Katey and Mamie were as excited as if they were eighteen . . ." At the end of August the family attended a regatta at Ouchy.

Here, the family's travel courier, Louis Roche, spent the day boating on the lake with the children and servants. As Dickens once again related to Forster, "I wish you could have seen Roche appear on the Lake, rowing, in an immense boat, Cook, Anne, two nurses, Katey, Mamie, Walley, Chickenstalker, and Baby; no boatmen or other degrading assistance . . ." Baby Alfred was soon awarded his own nickname, Sampson Brass, though also referred to as "Skittle."

By the time of Katey's seventh birthday, the family had moved on to Geneva. Then they traveled on to Paris (the French capital was one of Charles' favorite places). They stayed at the Hotel Brighton before renting another well-appointed home, 48 rue de Courcelles in Faubourg St. Honoré, the property of the Marquis de Castellane. For Charles one of the highlights of the visit was dining with Alexandre Dumas, author of *The Three Musketeers*. For Mamie and Katey (and no doubt for Catherine and Georgina), the highlight was buying Parisian dresses and parading around the apartment in their finery.

The exuberance of the Paris trip was, however, cut short with the news that Charley was very ill with scarlet fever. Leaving the younger children in Paris with Georgina and servants, the worried parents rushed back to London. As their home was being rented out, they stayed at a hotel near Euston station before renting 3 Chester Place in Regent's Park. Matters were complicated by the fact that Catherine was pregnant again, and the doctors would not risk the health of her unborn child by allowing her to visit her son. Charles was also forbidden from visiting Charley, in case he caught the illness and passed it on to Catherine. The frantic parents, tantalizingly close to their son who was by now staying with his grandmother, had to keep up a subterfuge of being still in France. They wrote to Georgina, Mamie, and Katey, asking them to maintain a cheerful correspondence with Charley to keep his spirits up, but not to let him know his parents were so close by. Charles wrote regularly to his daughters, apologizing for missing Mamie's birthday and telling them about Mrs. Macready's birthday party, where "We had some dancing, and they wished very much that you and Katey had been there; so did I and your mamma."

The invaluable Louis Roche, having seen Charles and Catherine safely back to England, returned to Paris to fetch the rest of the family and escort them home. Charley recovered from his illness with no lasting effects and, on April 18, 1847, at the age of ten years and three months, he found himself the eldest of seven children. Sydney Smith Haldimand was born in London and, as always, Charles was enchanted by him. The first flush of new fatherhood aside, however, the author was becoming increasingly irritated by the fact that his family was persistently expanding. He seemed to see the constantly burgeoning number of new arrivals

Sydney Dickens as a cadet in the Royal Navy. As a small child, his family nicknamed him "the Ocean Spectre" because of his large eyes and spectrelike appearance.

to feed, entertain, and educate as solely his wife's fault, famously attributing it in one letter as being all down to Catherine's "perversity" and almost seeming not to understand how she kept getting pregnant. It appears that by this date his love for Catherine was slowly starting to disintegrate and he was beginning to view her as clumsy, slow-witted, and irritating. Of course, the more irritating he found her, the more flustered she became. Their marriage was mutating into a cycle of dual unhappiness. The pretty, flirtatious young girl he had married eleven years earlier had been replaced by an overweight, often disappointed matron who suffered regularly from an irritating condition neither her husband nor the medical profession seemed able to recognize as post-natal depression. To make matters worse, her sister Georgina was a perpetual contrast: attractive, svelte, and intelligent, well able to hold her own in conversations with Charles, charming to his guests, and much adored by her coterie of nieces and nephews.

In the spring of 1847, as Charley was still convalescing and Catherine needed time to recover from a difficult birth, Charles took them to Brighton, for a change of air. Georgina—now nicknamed "The Virgin" by her brother-in-law—went too, to help with the new baby; Katey and Mamie were left behind in London with the younger children and their nurses. The two girls were overjoyed to receive a letter from their father at the end of May.

My dear Mamey and Katey,

I was very glad to receive your nice letters. I am going to tell you something that I hope will please you. It is this. I am coming to London on Thursday; and I mean to bring you both back here, with me, to stay until we all come home together on the Saturday. I hope you like this.

Tell John to come with the Carriage to the London Bridge station, on Thursday morning at 10 o'Clock, and to wait there for me. I will then come home and fetch you.

Mama, and Auntey, and Charley send their loves . . .
Always my dears
Your affectionate Papa

John was Charles' long-serving manservant, John Thompson, to whom the whole family was much attached. The Dickenses appear to have been pleasant employers who valued—and were valued by—their servants. As well as Thompson and Charles' other servant, Topping, Catherine's maid Anne appears regularly in Charles' correspondence, as does the cook and a variety of children's nurses. Anne, who was to cause great consternation by getting engaged, continued to work for the family long after her wedding, even though she might well have chosen to give up working once married, as the majority of women did.[11] The servants were also included in family birthdays and celebrations.

After their holiday in Brighton, the family returned to Broadstairs, where they stayed from June to September. At the end of August, while one of Charles' close friends, the artist Frank Stone, was staying with them, they welcomed into their temporary home a famous visitor. He was Hans Christian Andersen, the nervy, somewhat introverted Danish writer of fairytales, including *The Little Mermaid*. He and Charles had been corresponding for some time and the latter was keen to include Andersen at a family dinner.

Charles often grew bored on family holidays and craved the conversation of other adults, especially literary and artistic men. He surrounded himself with friends and new acquaintances and almost every "family" holiday included a regular stream of visitors, such as his editor, W. H. Wills; Thackeray; the painters Daniel Maclise and Augustus Egg; or Mark Lemon, the first editor of *Punch*. Sometimes these men brought their families, but often Charles would invite them alone.

At the end of 1847, straight after Christmas, Katey's parents left for Scotland, where Catherine suffered an agonizing and humiliating misfortune: She underwent a miscarriage in a railway carriage while traveling from Edinburgh to Glasgow. The overall tone of the letter in which Charles writes of the event to his brother Alfred is irritated and pettish. It

---

11 That the Dickenses' servants were well treated is illustrated by a story one of the parlormaids would relate after Charles Dickens' death. She had been waiting on them at lunch and was using a "dumb waiter" lift to transport the plates and other crockery from the table to the kitchen. The lift failed and crashed down, with a loud sound of breaking china. Charles apparently rushed straight over to the maid, unconcerned about the smashed plates, concerned only that she was all right. She had a bruised arm, so he gave her arnica lotion and made her drink a glass of wine to help her over the shock.

is a few days after the event and he and Catherine have returned to Edinburgh before traveling back down south. The letter focuses on his own embarrassment, first about his wife initially being taken ill in the middle of a crowded street, and continues in irritation, as though Catherine had later chosen to miscarry in order to vex him:

> *Kate was taken very ill on the way from this place to Glasgow, on Tuesday—a miscarriage, in short, coming on, suddenly, in the railway carriage. When we got to the House where we were engaged to stay, she was immediately undressed and put to bed—couldn't go to the Demonstration—and remained in bed 'till late next night. Moreover I was obliged to call in a famous Doctor . . .*

The older Dickens children would have been all too aware that their parents' marriage was no longer happy. Their father was becoming increasingly unpleasant toward their mother, who shrank into her own misery and became more petulant and awkward with every humiliation. During the 1850s, friends of the Dickenses recorded how uncomfortable it was to go for dinner with them as Charles would loudly deride Catherine for her size and slowness of intellect, and laugh at every embarrassing thing she did, almost becoming apoplectic on the occasion her bangles fell down her "fat little arms" at a dinner party and landed in the soup. For Katey and her siblings, this time was unsettling and upsetting. Katey is known to have suffered from depression in adulthood, but it may well have begun in childhood. All through her life, Katey was prey to what she called her "superstitions" (today, they would probably be referred to as obsessive-compulsive disorder). Her brothers would often tease her about her need to touch certain pieces of furniture exactly the same number of times every day and to check under her bed each night before getting into it. On one occasion, she remembered her father putting an end to the teasing by looking up from his book and saying, "I used to do the same," which quelled her brothers' mocking, at least temporarily. This behavior seems to suggest that Katey was troubled as a young child and felt the need to control those things she could—such as the number of times she touched each piece of furniture—as a way of dispelling her feelings about the things she couldn't control, such as her parents' deteriorating marriage and her father's irritation with her mother.

The misery of the failing marriage was compounded in the first half of 1848 by the news that Charles' sister, Katey's godmother Fanny Burnett, was seriously ill. Charles tried everything he could to cure her, sending her an "extraordinarily successful" doctor, who had been recommended to him. Sadly the doctor was unsuccessful in Fanny's case and Charles had to accept that she was dying of consumption (tuberculosis). Katey and Mamie were taken to visit their aunt and Mamie later remembered they "were greatly shocked at their aunt's wasted and worn appearance. Her cough, which had been terrible, and shaking her poor emaciated body almost to pieces, ceased quite suddenly, and when this change came about she knew that she was dying."

Throughout that miserable early summer, as Fanny's health continued to deteriorate and their father's mood grew ever more depressed, the Dickens children tried their best to keep out of his way. Charles was bemoaning his lot as a responsible patriarch and wishing, once again, to be free of his wife and children and all the ties they represented. His discontent with family life coincided with acting success in amateur theatricals. As a young man, he had been desperate to go on the stage and had even secured an audition at a theater company, which he had been forced to miss due to a severe cold. During the tour of America and Canada, he and Catherine had performed in an amateur theatrical in Montreal. Now, he longed once again to be a roaming actor, basking in the adulation of the audience and playing at a new theater every night. He wrote an amusing letter, but one that seems only half-joking, to a friend: "I have no energy whatever—I am miserable. I loathe domestic hearths. I yearn to be a Vagabond. . . .Why have I seven children—not engaged at sixpence a night a piece, and dismissible for ever, if they tumble down, but taken on for an indefinite time at a vast expence [*sic*]." It must have been a relief to his family when they made the annual journey to Kent, knowing he would be spending much of the summer away from them, working in London and visiting his sister.

Georgina took the children to Broadstairs in July, while Charles and Catherine stayed behind, to be near Fanny at her home in Hornsey. Catherine was, however, unwell herself, being, as Charles commented to his friend Bulwer Lytton, once more in "that *un*interesting condition," and soon traveled to Broadstairs, too.

On August 9, 1848, Charles felt able to leave his sister and his work and join his holidaying family. Although it was possible to make the journey by train, he preferred the more picturesque boat journey from London to Margate. Looking forward to seeing him, Catherine set off in the pony cart, together with a footman called John, under whose direction she was driving. As they reached the head of a hill, something spooked the pony and it bolted, careering down the slope with the cart lurching behind. The footman was thrown—according to his own account—although his fellow servants were convinced he took fright and jumped out. His absence left the pregnant Catherine alone (for which he was later much berated in the servants' hall, receiving little sympathy, even though his own injuries were substantial). The reins, having been whipped out of Catherine's hands, became caught around one of the wheels, so she had no option but to hold on and scream for help—probably terrifying the pony even further. Hurtling down the steep slope at speed, the pony managed to break the shaft away from the carriage, tripping itself up in the process and cutting its legs, though luckily breaking no bones. The horse-less carriage came to a halt, leaving Catherine shaken and sobbing but miraculously unharmed. She was taken care of by a couple from the local gentry, who had heard her cries and rushed to her assistance. It is strange to realize, some one hundred and fifty years later, that if the accident had been more tragic, my immediate family and I would not be here today. The baby Catherine was carrying at the time was Henry Fielding Dickens, my great-great-grandfather.

Charles' solicitude for his wife after her terrifying accident (although he could not help wondering why she had gone to the bother of setting out to meet him in the first place) must have improved the family atmosphere. Nor was the pony in any danger. On the following day, in an effort to allay her fears and cure her of any future propensity to bolt, Charles took her back to the spot at which she had shied. After recovering from their fright, Katey and Mamie had an enjoyable summer, including a visit from Charley and Walter (both of whom were now being educated at King's College), let out of school for a couple of days to enjoy the benefits of sea bathing.

On September 2, Katey's aunt Fanny died, devastating Charles and leaving him with yet more financial dependants. He wrote to his brother-in-law Henry, offering to pay Fanny's medical bills and also to take on the financial burden of providing for their disabled son. Money was becoming an increasingly difficult issue, not through its lack, but because of the responsibility it created and the guilt Charles felt when he turned down anyone who asked for his help. Every day he received begging letters from strangers. These overwhelmed him to the point that he had to ask his servant Topping not to pass them on anymore. In addition, around the time of Fanny's death, he discovered that Fred was in debt again. After years of Charles bailing him out, Fred had finally seemed to be in control of his finances and had recently become engaged. On discovering that Fred was as hopeless a case as their father, Charles exploded. He wrote him an angry letter, furious that Fred had been intending to start married life mired in debt. His family's inability to handle money was something that was to plague Charles continually, as he saw the failing pass from John Dickens to Fred and then on to several of his own sons.

When Katey and her siblings returned to London from Kent, it was to find their father miserable over the death of his sister, irritable with his wife, and estranged from their uncle. On October 5, 1848, Charles wrote to a friend that he was in such a vile mood, his children shrank when they saw him coming and quailed at the sound of his voice. Katey and Mamie were comforted during their father's bad moods by the attentions of another adoring father figure, Mark Lemon, the editor of *Punch*.

In 1848, Lemon wrote a fairytale named *The Enchanted Doll*, which he requested permission to dedicate to the Dickens girls. The tale is a moral one, with a main character whose story is not dissimilar to that of Ebenezer Scrooge. At the age of nine, Katey's propensity for independence was coming to the fore: Lemon had written that he would dedicate the book to "Mary and Catherine" and Dickens replied thanking him but adding that his daughters preferred to be known as "Mary and *Kate*, not Catherine." When it was published in 1849, the dedication duly read, "This little book is affectionately inscribed to Mary and Kate Dickens."

The tale is about a discontented doll maker called Jacob Pout and his envy for his neighbor, the kind and good Tony Stubbs. When Jacob meets

Fairy Malice (who is gratified by his miserable intentions), she gives him an Enchanted Doll. At first Jacob is pleased, as he sells it for £100, yet every time he feels envy or discontent the doll returns to him by magic, and on each occasion it has become larger and more cumbersome. The doll haunts him until he manages to mend his ways. The Dickens children are all mentioned in the story. They are at a party (which is similar to the Fezziwigs' ball in *A Christmas Carol*) that Tony takes Jacob to. Even Timber the dog gets a mention:

> *As it is Christmas time there is a table loaded with good cheer, to which all comers are welcome; and those happy-looking folk crowding round the large sea-coal fire are drinking to the good Alderman's health in double ale. . . . Before the huge fire sits the turnspit, dozing and enjoying the warmth after the labours of the morning. Poor dog! he has to work hard at feast-times. He sits up (as our little dog Timber does when he begs). . . . There go the fiddles! The Alderman and a buxom dame of forty lead off. . . . Tony and Dorothy are in the middle of the set and dancing merrily. . . . What peals of laughter are heard every now and then as some blunder is made in the figure, when Charles, who should have turned to the right, wheels round to the left, and bumps against Mary, who nearly tumbles over Kate, who falls into the arms of Walter, whilst Frank, and Alfred, and Sidney clap their hands and declare that Kate did it on purpose. What a shout of laughter! Huzza!*

That the Dickenses were renowned for their real parties, especially those held for the children, was recalled by Anny Thackeray. She and her sister Minny had spent six years living in Paris with their paternal grandparents after their mother, Isabella, was deemed mentally unfit to take care of them and Thackeray himself had needed desperately to earn money to keep them all. The girls, who were of similar ages to Mamie and Katey, had returned to London to live with their father in 1846, when Anny was nine and Minny six (she had left England as a very young baby). Among the inhabitants of their new world were the Dickens family, and the motherless Thackeray girls, whose clothes were always slightly shabby and unfashionable, looked upon Mamie and Katey with a mixture of awe and mild envy. Anny remembered not only the "shining" parties that the Dickenses held, but also the clothes the girls wore:

The Dickens children's parties were shining facts in our early London days—nothing came in the least near them. There were other parties, and they were very nice, but nothing to compare to these; not nearly so light, not nearly so shining, not nearly so going round and round. Perhaps it was not all as brilliantly wonderful as I imagined it, but most assuredly the spirit of mirth and kindly jollity was a reality to every one present. . . . One special party I remember, which seemed to me to go on for years with its kind, gay hospitality, its music, its streams of children passing and re-passing. We were a little shy coming in alone in all the consciousness of new shoes and ribbons but Mrs. Dickens called to us to sit beside her till the long sweeping dance was over, and talked to us as if we were grown up, which is always flattering to little girls. Then Miss Hogarth found us partners. . . . I remember watching the white satin shoes and long flowing white sashes of the little Dickens girls, who were just about our own age, but how much more graceful and beautifully dressed. Our sashes were plaids of red and blue, a tribute from one of our father's Scotch admirers (is it ungrateful to confess now after all these years that we could not bear them?) . . .

As the season of Christmas and parties approached, Charles and Fred Dickens were back on speaking terms in time for the wedding of their youngest brother, Augustus, on December 5, 1848. (It was to prove another disastrous marriage in the Dickens family.) Six weeks later, on January 16, 1849, Henry Fielding Dickens was born. His was an extremely difficult birth, during which Catherine was given chloroform. Although Charles does not relate in his letters what the difficulty was, it seems likely Henry was a breech baby, as the previous baby, Sydney, had been. At first Henry was to be called Oliver, after Oliver Goldsmith, but Charles realized his new son would be forever teased about Oliver Twist, so decided to name him after another of his literary heroes.

Unsurprisingly after such an ordeal, Catherine became ill following the birth, her post-natal depression more pronounced than before. The worried atmosphere in the Dickens household was compounded at the end of January with the news that one of Katey's cousins had died. Henry Augustus Burnett, the disabled son of Charles' dead sister, had lost his fight against tuberculosis of the spine. He was buried in his mother's grave at Highgate. To the post-natally depressed Catherine, it must have seemed a terrible omen: to have a child who shared the name of her new baby die.

In an effort to cheer up his wife, Charles decided that he, Catherine, Georgina, and the two girls should take a holiday in Brighton. They went with the illustrator John Leech and his wife Annie. The two

Henry (standing) and Frank Dickens in the mid-1850s

Dickens girls would never forget the extraordinary events of that week. The family arrived on February 14, having booked rooms in lodgings called Junction House. They spent a few days enjoying the diversions of the seaside town and trying to persuade Mark Lemon to join them; they sent "Uncle Mark" (also known to the Dickens children as "Uncle Porpoise" because of his large, round belly) a poem written by Charles, which included the verse:

Oh my Lemon round and fat
Oh my bright, my right, my tight 'un
Think a little what you're at –
Don't stay home, but come to Brighton!

On the Saturday night, however, their peaceful holiday took a bizarre turn when they heard the sounds of a terrible commotion. The landlord's daughter, who had a history of mental illness, was "becoming much more mad"; in addition, her father was also undergoing a mental breakdown. Together they were shouting, cursing, and creating havoc. It took four doctors, a nurse and several "friends and servants"—like an army of "Mrs. Gamps" (from *Martin Chuzzlewit*), wrote Charles—to restrain them. The two invalids were tied up in straitjackets and taken away. Charles and John Leech immediately whisked their party off to the Bedford Hotel, where it took a while to calm down a badly frightened Mamie and Katey.

They were back in London in time to celebrate Mamie's eleventh birthday on March 6, at which time her father wrote her a touching letter:

My Dearest Mamey,

I am not engaged on the evening of your birthday. But even if I had an engagement of the most particular kind, I should excuse myself from keeping it, so that I might have the pleasure of celebrating at home, and among my children, the day that gave me such a dear and good daughter as you.

As his son Henry was later to recall, Charles found it impossible to make affectionate comments to their faces, so it seems letters such as this were his way of telling his children that he loved them. Charles wrote to his children regularly whenever he, or they, were away. Sadly, none of his letters to Katey survived; they were destroyed in a fire in 1873. There are references, however, in letters to other members of the family, to his writing to Katey "next" or of having written to her the previous day.

That summer of 1849, the Dickenses returned to Broadstairs. Charles left them after a week to travel to the Isle of Wight with John Leech. They were planning a joint holiday to the island if their reconnaissance trip proved successful. Since Queen Victoria had had a residence—Osborne House—built on the island it had become a highly fashionable resort; it had also long been the haunt of artistic types and would soon become famed for its association with Tennyson and Julia Margaret Cameron. From mid-July until October, the Dickens and Leech families stayed at Bonchurch, and Charley was let out of school to join them. The two families were inundated with visitors; these included John Forster, Hablot K. Browne (otherwise known as the illustrator "Phiz"), the playwright Douglas Jerrold, and the ever-welcome Uncle Porpoise. Toward the end of September, the vacationing party suffered a severe shock. While swimming, John Leech was knocked over by a sudden huge wave and smacked his head on a rock. Ironically, for one with his surname, he was treated by the application of twenty leeches to his forehead (which can have had no beneficial effects). He was also successfully mesmerized by Charles, the account of which was to circulate among their friends, told with great awe as it was widely believed that the mesmerism had saved Leech's sanity, and possibly his life. Katey and the other children were terrified by this event, not least because the adults were in such a state of confusion and worry. No doubt the children held Charles in even greater awe than ever, as the adults were hailing him as a miracle healer.

In October, wanting to work alone in London, Charles sent Catherine, Georgy, the girls, and the youngest boys back to Broadstairs. He was becoming increasingly worried about Catherine's health. It was nine months since Henry's birth, but she was still not recovered. Charles consulted a specialist, Dr. Walter, who recommended a course of "very simple medicine." It is unknown what this simple medicine was, but it is unlikely that it included getting pregnant again; however, by the end of 1849 Catherine was expecting her ninth baby.

4

THE LAST CHILD

Every year, at the start of January, Angela Burdett-Coutts sent the Dickens children an immense Twelfth Night cake. She was particularly fond of Charley Dickens, whose expensive education she helped to pay for, and the cake was also in celebration of his birthday. In 1850, the enormous cake arrived on January 5, the day before Charley's birthday; it was placed on a table and he and his sisters performed an impromptu polka of joy around it. Although no reference survives in Charles' letters, it can be presumed they had the usual Twelfth Night party on his eldest son's birthday. Less than a week later, Mamie, Katey, Walter, and the little ones waved their eldest brother goodbye as he left home to begin a new phase of his life, at Eton. He was an instant favorite with his peers and on March 6 Charles was writing proudly that he had received a favorable report from the school, where Charley "is fast becoming one of the most popular boys."

The year that Charley went to Eton, Charles took a short break from his own works and launched a scathing attack on what he saw as a new scourge sweeping the British art world: Pre-Raphaelitism. Disgusted by, in his view, the arrogance of the artists, not to mention nauseating paintings, Charles published an account in his new weekly journal, *Household Words*, of John Everett Millais' *Christ in the House of His Parents* (also known as *Christ in the Carpenter's Shop*):

In the foreground of that carpenter's shop is a hideous, wry-necked, blubbering, red-headed boy, in a bed-gown . . . and . . . a kneeling woman, so horrible in her ugliness, that (supposing it were possible for any human creature to exist for a moment with that dislocated throat) she would stand out from the rest of the company as a Monster, in the vilest cabaret in France, or the lowest gin-shop in England.

Charley Dickens in 1852 by George Richmond. This was around the time that Charley was attending Eton. His education was paid for by the banking heiress and philanthropist Angela Burdett-Coutts.

The wry-necked, blubbering boy was Jesus and the gin-house habitué, his mother, the Virgin Mary.

Perhaps Charles was unaware of how damaging his words would prove, or perhaps he did not care about the consequences; as it was, they caused an outcry about Pre-Raphaelitism and against any artist whose style was in any way similar to that of the movement. Promising young artists counting on selling their latest paintings were ruined by the vitriolic review, having invested everything in finishing them. Several artists were forced to take on other work and abandon painting as Dickens' far-reaching comments caused their very style of art—something most artists would be unable to change easily—to be spurned.

Wilkie Collins' younger brother Charlie had hoped to sell one of his first paintings, *Berengaria's Alarm at Seeing the Girdle of Richard Offered for Sale in Rome* (1850).[12] Following Charles' scathing attack on Pre-Raphaelitism, Charlie's work was equally lambasted. The painting into which he had poured so much of himself was derided by a critic as "an instance of perversion to be regretted," an extraordinary statement about a painting that seems so delicately executed and so very inoffensive; it can only have been made because of the public reaction to the PRB. Those Pre-Raphaelites who were lucky enough to have paintings in the Royal Academy's Summer Exhibition did not manage to sell them that year. After the exhibition, William Holman Hunt temporarily gave up art and, after a year of struggling against the anti-Pre-Raphaelite tide, Dante Gabriel Rossetti, a founder of the Pre-Raphaelite Brotherhood, wrote to a friend declaring: "I am not doing anything and probably shall cut Art as it is too much trouble." It was not until John Ruskin came to the Pre-Raphaelites' defense (in 1851) that the movement began to be saved and, gradually, to be taken seriously—even, in the future, by Charles himself.

Katey, at this age still drawing for pleasure, was happily unaware of the tremors her father had caused in the art world. For her, 1850 was a year of once again holidaying in Brighton—where, this time, she did not encounter any lunatics—and spending her summer months in Broadstairs. She and Mamie were still being taught by a governess, which meant

---

12 The subject matter shows Queen Berengaria, wife of Richard I ("the Lionheart"), terrified her husband has been killed in the Crusades after being offered his belt, or "girdle," for sale by a peddler.

school work and lessons followed wherever they went. The family visited Brighton in March and stayed in Broadstairs from July to October. Catherine did not go with them to Kent, as she was suffering the late stages of pregnancy. Instead the children were accompanied by their father, Auntie Georgy, a governess, and nurses for the small ones. Forster came to stay (and he and Charles had a falling-out), as did the artist David Roberts. As a budding artist, Katey was fortunate to grow up in a household in which artists and illustrators were so often in residence; she had ample opportunity to observe their work and their methods. By now almost eleven years old, she was showing definite promise in her work, following in the footsteps of her uncle Alfred, a talented amateur watercolorist (ten years younger than his famous brother).[13]

One can assume Katey would have learned her artistic lessons by painting still lifes of everyday objects, such as flowers and fruit, and by painting landscapes, such as the family home and garden; it is likely she and Mamie also experimented with painting portraits of each other. Sadly, none of Katey's childhood art survives, perhaps burned with so many of her possessions in the 1873 fire, or destroyed by her own hand. As an adult, Kate regularly destroyed those of her works she considered unsatisfactory; she may have done the same as a child or teenager.

Charles went back to London regularly throughout this summer and was there for the birth of little Dora Annie Dickens at Devonshire Terrace on August 16. He returned to Broadstairs almost immediately afterward to tell the children they had a new sister and to keep working on *David Copperfield*, a novel that was absorbing him even more than usual. Mamie and Katey were no doubt thrilled at the arrival of a sister, after so many little brothers; the boys themselves were less interested—a new baby in the Dickens household was not so unusual an occurrence as to require much comment. Charles wrote a wonderfully witty letter to Catherine about the children's reactions to his news:

Upon the whole I think the baby rather a failure down here. Charley was the most struck last night as connecting it with you. Sydney I

---

13 Uncle Fred and Uncle Alfred were two different brothers of Charles Dickens; Fred's full name was Frederick.

think has been the most reflective on the subject to-day. He was play-
ing the piano after dinner while I was reading and suddenly left off
with, 'I say Pa, can Dora talk?' On my replying No, he seemed to think
that weak on her part and put the question, 'Is she tall?' In answer to
this I measured off about a quarter of a yard on the table and said she
was about that size. He gave her up after that. . . . He is in great force.
Frank is so handsome that he is quite a sight to behold; they all look
wonderfully well.

He went on with minutiae about life in Broadstairs: the town was teeming with people; Mamie and Katey had a new "sworn friend," one Miss Baldwin; and the bathing machine woman—Mrs. Collins—was still wearing the same pink gown as she had been during their previous visits. Perhaps it was because he was unfettered by Catherine's lowering depression, or because his new novel, *David Copperfield*, was going so well, that Charles wrote loving letters to his wife and really enjoyed his time with the children. They played endless games of cricket, went bathing in the sea, romped in the garden and took jaunts to Margate. The would-be artist Marcus Stone (son of Frank Stone) came to join them.

That summer was a glorious one; however, *David Copperfield* was becoming an obsession. Charles was famously to describe the novel as his "favourite child," which was to prove upsetting to his real children. The young Dickenses often felt there was a rivalry between them and the children of Charles' fiction; in later life Katey commented that she thought her father's biggest problem was that he had had "too many children"— and she was not referring only to Catherine's numerous pregnancies.[14]

While writing *David Copperfield*, Charles was exorcizing his own childhood demons. Forster later related that it was around this time he had come to learn the story of Charles' unhappy childhood, something his friend had kept hidden for many years. *David Copperfield* was Charles' way of working through all the problems of his childhood by turning them into fiction. It is his novel of identity, almost a form of counseling.

---

14 Charles' brother-in-law Henry Burnett later wrote that Charles had said to him that "Little Nell was an object of his life—that he mourned her loss for a month after her death, and felt as if one of his own dear ones had left a vacant chair."

That autumn, Catherine and Dora joined the rest of the family in Kent, but the birth of her ninth child had left Katey's mother in an even worse state than before. At the same time, Charles was fretting over the discovery that his brother Fred was, once more, in debt. The carefree holiday atmosphere in Broadstairs must have suffered a considerable slump, coincidentally at around the time Catherine and the baby arrived.

When Catherine proved unable to "pull herself together" even several months after Dora's birth, Charles decided to take her to the famous spa at Malvern. She was suffering regular dizzy spells and blurring of sight, possibly attributable to migraines, in addition to her usual symptoms of depression. Charles had recognized that her problems were ongoing and, presumably, he also recognized that many were connected with giving birth. Malvern was renowned for its success with water cures and he placed great confidence in her being brought back to health by a "rigorous discipline of exercise, air, and cold water."

When examining this period in their life, one feels sympathy for Charles as well as Catherine. Compared with most men of his era, he was remarkably compassionate about her post-natal depression, despite understandably finding it frustrating and upsetting. It has become common in recent years for writers and the media to portray Charles as a bad husband, but he had his very sincere merits as well.

In February, baby Dora became ill with what Charles described as "something like congestion of the Brain," which was probably hydrocephalus or "water on the brain." In all likelihood, she contracted it as a result of meningitis. She recovered, but the extra pressure proved too much for her mother and Catherine suffered a "nervous collapse." In March, Charles and Georgy accompanied Catherine to Malvern, where Georgy stayed to care for her. Charles returned to London, commuting frequently between town and country over the ensuing weeks; no short journey, this would have taken many hours in each direction. The children, including the new baby, stayed in London with their nurses. Catherine had been perfectly willing to go to Malvern, but she wanted a place of her own, not to stay in the spa—which would possibly have felt too much like an asylum to be truly comfortable—so Charles took them to stay at a lodging house (run similarly to a modern "apartment hotel") called Knutsford Lodge.

It seems the spa was as beneficial for Charles as it was for Catherine. He certainly took advantage of the water treatments during his visits to her; doubtless his stress levels were exceedingly high at this time, with 1851 proving a difficult year. Shortly after Catherine went away, Charles' father had become suddenly ill and on March 25 underwent an urgent, agonizing, and primitively executed operation on his bladder. Since childhood, Charles had had a difficult relationship with John Dickens, which made realizing that his father might not survive all the more tormenting. For years, Charles had suppressed the misery of his late childhood and adolescence. All the feelings of anger that he'd been harboring toward his parents had gone undiscussed and now, as his father lay dying, he was starkly aware of how much there was to say. In an uncharacteristically unconfident manner, Charles wrote to Forster straight after his father's death on March 31; his letter sounds confused and uncertain. He tentatively requests that Forster visit Highgate with him to choose the plot in which his father should be buried and adds that he feels he must go to Malvern straight away to ask Catherine and Georgy for advice on the children's mourning clothes.

Auntie Georgy came back to London to take charge of the children at this difficult time, but even her presence was unwanted. Charles could not stand company at this time, preferring to be alone with his grief. The day before his father's funeral he sent Georgina and the girls off to Blackheath, supposedly to go house-hunting (presumably for his widowed mother), but he also instructed them to have fun riding donkeys and enjoying themselves on the heath.

Just ten days later, the family was beset by more tragedy. While Charles was out giving an after-dinner speech, baby Dora went into convulsions. The doctor was called but could do nothing and Dora died quite suddenly, with her mother in Malvern unaware of what was happening to her baby. Forster, who was at the same dinner as Charles, was told the news first. As soon as he could, he broke it to his friend before handing him over to the care of Mark Lemon and heading up to Malvern to fetch Catherine home. Unwilling to tell her of Dora's death until he could speak to her in person, Charles wrote an extremely tender letter for Forster to take, explaining that Dora was very ill and that Catherine must be brave and prepare herself for the worst. Mark Lemon sat with Charles throughout that terribly long and miserable night.

For Katey and her siblings, none of whom have left a detailed record of Dora's death, the year 1851 must have felt like a prolonged punishment. Their grandfather was dead, both their parents were badly depressed, and Katey and Mamie's longed-for sister had inexplicably lost her life. Unusually for a Victorian household, death had not touched them very closely before, but now they had encountered it twice within a fortnight, at the heart of their family. Unwilling to stay in the home where their baby had died, Charles and Catherine decided to let out Devonshire Terrace for a few months and to take on a house in Broadstairs from May to October. Owing to work pressure, Charles spent much of his time in his office in London, pining, as he wrote to a friend, to be with his children; it is noticeable that he did not add that he was pining for his wife. In June, having arrived in Kent, Charles' spirits improved. He wrote to Angela Burdett-Coutts:

> *Broadstairs is charming. The green corn growing, and the larks singing, and the sea sparkling, all in their best manner. When I was in town about ten days ago, I went down to Eton and saw Charley, who was very well indeed, and very anxious to be reported to you. He was much commended by his tutor, but had previously been reported rather lazy for the time being. I had therefore stopped his boat, and threatened other horrible penalties.*

In August, Charles responded favorably to a petition got up by his daughters and delivered to him by Sydney, who had been given the nickname "the Ocean Spectre" (because of his huge eyes, which seemed always to be gazing off into some unseen future). The girls had requested that they be allowed off lessons for the time being, as they had a friend, Rosa, staying with them. Charles acceded to their wishes, telling them that they were "always so good, that I am delighted to do anything to please you. You shall both make holiday, if you like."

While the Dickens children were in Broadstairs, London was playing host to one of the most spectacular events in Victorian history: the

Great Exhibition. This had been the pet project of Henry Cole and Prince Albert, and it took two years to bring to fruition. It was held in the specially built Crystal Palace, which had been erected in Hyde Park—using more than 300,000 panes of glass—and was opened on May 1, 1851.[15] More than 20,000 visitors crowded into the park on the opening day and before the exhibition closed on October 11 an estimated six million people had seen it. Charles went to the exhibition on several occasions—though he found it far too crowded. It is unrecorded whether he took his children or Catherine with him on any of these visits, but it would have been highly surprising if he had not. The Great Exhibition was open every day except Sunday and people traveled from all areas of the country (and from abroad) to view in excess of 100,000 exhibits from all over the world. The exhibition attracted people of every class and every walk of life, and its exhibits, visitors, and architecture would surely have delighted the imaginations of all the Dickens children.[16]

With Charley safely settled at Eton and the girls being educated at home, Charles' attention was diverted to the next eldest, Walter, now aged ten and destined for a career in India. He would not be sent to join Charley—Charles did not consider him clever enough for Eton; instead, he would be joining the school of a Mr. Trimmer, in Putney, southwest London, a master who specialized in training boys for a career in the army and in India. Walter himself quite fancied a career in writing, but his father persuaded him that was a bad idea, probably aware that Walter did not have the aptitude or ambition to work at writing as hard as he would need to do to succeed financially. "He is a steady amiable boy, of a good reliable capacity," Charles wrote to Angela Burdett-Coutts, and his current teacher, Mr. King, was extremely pleased with him. Walter was, along with Mamie in her childhood, the most biddable of the Dickens children, perhaps somewhat overshadowed by the exuberant personalities of Charley and Katey.

---

15 The architect of the Crystal Palace was Joseph Paxton, formerly the Duke of Devonshire's head gardener at Chatsworth House. He also designed the Palm House at Kew Gardens.

16 The profits from the Great Exhibition (over £180,000) were used to purchase land in southwest London on which the South Kensington Museum—now the Victoria & Albert, Natural History and Science museums—was built.

During the family's months in Broadstairs, Charles and Catherine had come to an important decision: It was time to leave Devonshire Terrace and find a more capacious property to house their large family. When the children returned to London in the autumn, they would be living in a new home, Tavistock House in Tavistock Square, Bloomsbury. It was not far from Devonshire Terrace, though not as close to the park. Big enough to accommodate even the largest Victorian family, it also boasted its own gardens. Hans Christian Andersen described the house in a letter:

> *In Tavistock Square stands Tavistock House. This and the strip of garden in front of it are shut out from the thoroughfare by an iron railing. A large garden . . . and high trees, stretches behind the house, and gives it a countrified look in the midst of this coal and gas steaming London. In the passage from street to garden hung pictures and engravings. On the first floor was a rich library, with a fireplace and a writing-table, looking out on the garden; and here it was that in winter Dickens and his friends acted plays . . .*

When Charles and Catherine first went to view the house, it was filthy and in need of renovation. Charles made most of the decisions about what furnishings and fittings they should have, although he asked Catherine to choose the wallpaper, and sent her an enthusiastic letter about how different the house looked once the workmen had removed the faded and dirty curtains and how much light and fresh air could now stream in through the previously grimy windows. He consulted his architect brother-in-law Henry Austin (husband of Charles' sister Laetitia) about the renovations and sent him specific measurements and even a sketch of the type of bath tub he wanted. They hoped to move in October 1851, but the workmen were still in possession. Catherine had joined her husband in London, eager to help with the move, but it seems her presence was irritating Charles:

> *Georgina and the children are still at Broadstairs [he wrote to his friend Richard Watson], until we shall have prepared a pigeon-hole or two into which they may creep. Catherine is here with me and*

sends her kind love. She is all over paint, and seems to think that it is somehow being immensely useful to get into that condition. We sit in our new house all day, trying to touch the hearts of the workmen by our melancholy looks, and are patched with oil and lime and haggard with white lead. We sit upon a ladder. All the doors are always open; and there is no repose or privacy, as Irish labourers stare in through the very slates.

The family moved in in November, at which time Charles settled immediately to writing *Bleak House*.

A friend of the family, and particularly of Charles, was the vivacious Mary Boyle. She was a regular guest at all the Dickenses' homes and occasionally went on holiday with them. Her glowing recollections of life in Tavistock House provide a genial look into the world Katey grew up in:

Tavistock House. . . . The very sound of the name is replete to me with memories of innumerable evenings passed in the most congenial and delightful intercourse; dinners, where the guests vied with each other in brilliant conversation, whether intellectual, witty, or sparkling— evenings devoted to music or theatricals. . . . I can never forget one evening, shortly after the arrival at Tavistock House, when we danced in the New year. It seemed like a page cut out of the Christmas Carol, *as far, at least, as fun and frolic went: authors, actors, friends from near and far, formed the avenues of two long English country dances . . .*

Katey and Mamie had been promised a "gorgeous apartment," but they were not allowed to see it until it was finished. When that great day arrived, Charles "took them up to it himself. Everything that was pretty, dainty and comfortable was in that room." They decorated it with pictures they had painted or cut from papers and magazines. They were very proud of their bedroom and often "dragged" their father "up the steep staircase" to see it. Mamie relates how their father:

encouraged us in every possible way to make ourselves useful, and to adorn and beautify our rooms with our own hands, and to be ever tidy and neat. I remember that the adornment of this garret was decidedly primitive, the unframed prints being fastened to the wall by ordinary black or white pins. . . . But never mind, if they were put up neatly and tidily they were always 'excellent' or 'quite slap-up' as he used to say. Even in those early days, he made a point of visiting every room in the house once a morning, and if a chair was out of its place, or a blind not quite straight, or a crumb left on the floor, woe betide the offender.

Whenever Charles did find some things not to his satisfaction, he would leave behind little messages, which Mamie and Katey called "pincushion notes," because they would usually find them attached to their pincushions. All the children dreaded receiving these notes. Their spirits sank when they saw one, so eventually Katey took it upon herself to ask him not to leave them anymore; she requested that he talk to them instead.

A female visitor to Tavistock House when Katey and Mamey were in their early teens recalled meeting them thus:

I have in my mind still a perfectly distinct picture of the bright, elegant interior of Tavistock House, and of its inmates—of my host himself, then in his early prime—of Mrs. Dickens, a plump, rosy, English, handsome woman, with a certain air of absent-mindedness, yet gentle and kindly—Miss Hogarth, a very lovely person, with charming manners—and the young ladies, then very young—real English girls, fresh and simple, and innocent-looking as English daisies.

The first Christmas after the family moved into Tavistock House was marked by the first family theatrical. The play, acted by the adults and children for an audience of their friends, was a comedy called *Guy Fawkes* (written by Albert Smith). It was performed on Twelfth Night and caused much hilarity. Forster relates a story of Thackeray, at one of the Dickens family theatricals, actually falling off his chair with laughter.

The new house was very near to Mark Lemon's home at 11 Gordon Street, which for Charles was undoubtedly one of the inducements for moving there. Mark and his wife, Helen, had two little girls, Alice (known as "Lally") and Betty, who, although slightly younger than the Dickens girls, were also their great friends. For the next few years the four little girls would run in and out of each other's houses, equally welcome in both.

The Lemons and Thackerays were not the only distinguished people the Dickens children would take tea with. As an adult Katey recalled being taken to the home of Jane and Thomas Carlyle (many years later, she would become friends with Jane Carlyle, often driving out with her in a carriage). On one occasion, when it seems Charles had taken only Katey and Mamie, not the boys, he and Thomas Carlyle enjoyed an exuberant game called Earth, Air, Fire, and Water. Katey remembered that the game revolved around throwing handkerchiefs in the air and that England's greatest novelist and thinker both played with the hilarity of overexcited children.

By the end of 1851, Charles was not the only published author in the Dickens household. Catherine wrote a book, which was brought out in November 1851 by Charles' publishers, Bradbury and Evans. It was entitled *What Shall We Have for Dinner? Satisfactorily Answered by Numerous Bills of Fare for from Two to Eighteen Persons* and was written under the pseudonym Lady Maria Clutterbuck, a pseudonym taken from a character Catherine had performed in a comic play, *Used Up*, at a private theatrical. The book was an unusual and enterprising idea and suggests Catherine had far more intelligence and ambition than she is usually given credit for. In a similar style to that of Mrs. Beeton (whose *Book of Household Management* would be published in 1861), the book was aimed at the inexperienced young housewife who found herself daunted by the prospect of ordering—or cooking—an interesting variety of meals for her new husband. Although Catherine had little cause to cook, having always lived with an ample number of servants, she would have been taught the basics of cooking and household management by her mother. Even those women who were unlikely ever actually to perform the task of cooking needed to know how to do it to be able to instruct new household staff and to ensure they did not get cheated by their kitchen staff. Sadly, despite the book's success, Catherine's literary aspirations seemed to dwindle and she was not to produce any further writings. *What Shall We Have for Dinner?* was well received, going into three editions within the first six months. In 1854 it was still selling well and Bradbury and Evans chose to publish a new edition, for which Catherine was asked to update the menus and add more recipes.

In recent years, it has been popular for Dickensians to claim that it was actually Charles and not Catherine who wrote the book. Although it is more than likely that he helped her with the process, and perhaps he did write the introduction as has been claimed, it seems very churlish to suggest that he penned the whole thing. I also find it difficult to understand why Charles would have been interested in producing a cookbook—and under an assumed name—when he already had so many ideas for novels and too little time in which to write them.

A few months after the move to Tavistock House, Charles met and befriended a young fellow novelist, Wilkie Collins. The two men felt an instant empathy and became intimate companions. Wilkie had grown up in an artistic house, the son of Royal Academician William Collins and the godson of the famous artist David Wilkie. In 1852, Harriet Collins, Wilkie's widowed mother and a superb hostess, gave one of her famous parties. It was a dance at her home in Hanover Terrace, to which she invited around seventy members of London's literary and artistic world; Charles was among the guests. What Wilkie's brother Charlie, then aged twenty-three, thought of this new acquaintance of his brother's—after the pain he had suffered over the PRB debacle—is unrecorded, but they would later become friends. It was perhaps through nights such as Harriet Collins's party, to which Millais was also invited (although he and Charles had not yet become friends, Millais having not forgiven the criticism of his painting), that Charles began to revise his opinion of Pre-Raphaelite art and to become friendly with members of its world. He had always been a lover of art, although his tastes ran mainly to watercolors of landscapes—he was particularly fond of the works of the late William Collins. In her 1903 article "Charles Dickens as a Lover of Art and Artists," Katey would claim that her father regretted publishing his 1850 review of Pre-Raphaelitism.

On March 13, 1852, Catherine Dickens gave birth to the last of her babies, Edward Bulwer Lytton Dickens. He was christened at the age of just six weeks, on May 6, in a ceremony presumably performed early in case he should go the way of baby Dora. Edward, however, was to prove robustly healthy and a source of great delight. Having spent many years entertaining the nation with his books, Charles now decided to write a book specially for his children, *A Child's History of England*. His dedication inside the book reads: "To my own dear children whom I hope it may help, bye and bye, to read with interest larger and better books on the same subject."

This summer, Charles decided his children should visit somewhere other than Broadstairs; he had grown less enamored of the place in recent years as it had become too crowded and less of a hideaway. Ironically, the town's great success was probably directly connected to the fact that Charles Dickens took his holidays there. As a change, from July to

Wilkie Collins, painted in 1853 by his brother, Charles Allston Collins

October 1852 the Dickens children stayed in rented lodgings at Camden Crescent, Dover, the gateway to France. Katey, Mamie, and the youngest boys were looked after by the servants and a French governess while Charles took Catherine and Georgina to Boulogne. Marcus Stone came to stay with the family in Dover, during which time he painted a small

Edward "Plorn" Dickens, the youngest of Charles' and Catherine's children

watercolor of Katey and Mamie. Unfortunately, Stone's painting of the two girls appears not to have survived.

Eighteen fifty-two was also a year of notable deaths for the Dickens family. In July, Richard Watson, a great friend of Charles and Catherine's, died very suddenly; his wife was just two months pregnant. A month later, Charles' friend and Alfred's godfather Count d'Orsay died in Paris. The following month, the country was shocked by the death of the Duke of Wellington, who was "an intimate friend" of Angela Burdett-Coutts. Then, just four days after Wellington's death, Catherine Macready died of tuberculosis. Tragically, the couple's eldest daughter had died a couple of years previously and, at around the time of his mother's death, the Macreadys' son was discovered to have contracted the disease as well. With Catherine and Charles' marriage already in such trouble, these bereavements would have been even harder to bear. With their relationship already strained it seems the deaths served to push the couple even farther apart, instead of drawing them together in their grief. For the children this was a difficult and insecure time; most likely Katey's "superstitions" increased as her parents' relationship became less and less tolerable.

Despite the unhappy situation, the prospect of separation or divorce would probably not have occurred even to the older Dickens children. At that date, very few marriages were legally ended. Until 1857, it was almost impossible to obtain a divorce in England—except for the very wealthy—so it is highly unlikely they would have known anyone who was actually divorced (although separation was less difficult to arrange).[17] Wealthy couples who already possessed more than one home might choose to live separately, but those who could not afford such a luxury were usually bound together for life. In addition, most mothers would not dare leave their husbands, as fathers were automatically given custody of all children over the age of seven.[18] One of the reasons that so

---

17 In extreme cases, such as when it could be proved that a marriage had not been consummated, an annulment might be granted. This was sanctioned by the Church and meant that a person was free to marry again. It was extremely unusual.

18 Until 1873, if a couple separated, children under the age of seven were only allowed to remain with their mother if she was not the guilty party in the divorce proceedings. If, for example, a woman's husband divorced her for adultery, the wife would be denied any access to her children, no matter how young they were.

few couples separated was because it resulted in social suicide. Any form of publicly acknowledged estrangement was viewed with outraged moral indignation. A middle-class woman abandoned by her husband would find it very difficult to retain any kind of social standing in her community. Many such women chose to move to a new area, dress in mourning and re-invent themselves as widows.

The Duke of Wellington was such an important figure in British history that it took two months for his funeral to be arranged—and Charles Dickens had become such an important figure that he was sent a formal invitation to the funeral. It was a very public funeral service and a truly elaborate event, about which Charles would write a satirical article, "Trading in Death," in *Household Words*. The state funeral took place on November 19, 1852, at St. Paul's Cathedral.[19] It was the first funeral on such a scale ever to be held at St. Paul's. Thirteen thousand guests were invited—in addition to the hundreds of thousands of mourners expected to line the streets. The cathedral was closed for six weeks beforehand, so necessary changes could be made, such as the creation of grandstands, the addition of extra tiers of seats, and the hanging of heavy black blinds at every window. The cathedral was lit solely by gas lamps, making the atmosphere suitably—and theatrically—mournful. The already impressive choir had swelled to eighty men and forty boys, as well as "forty additional singers and instrumental performers." Having received his invitation to this grand event, Charles replied requesting a total of twelve seats: for himself, Catherine, Georgina, Mamie, Katey, Charley (who was granted special leave from Eton for the occasion), Augustus Egg, Mr. and Mrs. Wills (Charles' editor and wife), Frank Stone, Mrs. Stone, and Miss Stone. The service was delayed by almost an hour because the procession of the coffin was hampered by crowds of people wanting to pay their last respects. The coffin was carried on a specially commissioned funeral coach that weighed twelve tons and needed to be drawn by nine horses. The theatricality of the spectacle was remarkable to the children and no doubt excited Katey's artistic imagination, but Charles was stirred to write to Angela Burdett-Coutts:

---

19 Traditionally, state funerals were held only for monarchs. In 1806, Admiral, Lord Nelson had become the first non-monarch to receive such an honor; Winston Churchill would also be afforded a state funeral, in 1965.

The Military part of the show, was very fine. If it had been an ordinary Funeral of a great commander, it might have been impressive. I suppose for forms of ugliness, horrible combinations of color [sic], hideous motion, and general failure, there never was such a work achieved.

5

UNREQUITED LOVE

At the end of 1852, Charles made the strange and unexplained decision to take his eldest son out of school early, at the age of sixteen (instead of allowing him to stay, as was expected by Eton, until the age of eighteen). It was a particularly odd decision for a man who had been devastated at the sudden ending of his own education. Originally it had been intended that Charley would go into the army, but he had changed his mind and said he would prefer to become a man of business. Charley was not happy about leaving Eton, but in January 1853 he went to Leipzig, where he was to study German (an important language to know in the business world) under the tutelage of a Professor Müller. Charles sent the principal of the school in Leipzig an interesting letter, which evokes an understanding of how he wished his sons to behave:

> While he is well looked after (as all boys require to be) I wish him to be not too obviously restrained, and to have the advantages of cheerful and good society. . . . I want him to have an interest in, and to acquire a knowledge of the life around him, and to be treated like a gentleman though pampered in nothing. By punctuality in all things great or small, I set great store.

Katey often spoke of her father's obsession with punctuality. She admitted that she alone of his children would ever dare arrive a few minutes late for breakfast. The letter to Charley's tutor bears shades of Magwitch, deciding on a future for Pip, in *Great Expectations*. In addition, Charles wrote Professor Müller "a description of his character and his little weak points," which he read out to Charley before posting. It was excruciating to have the faults he disliked most about himself criticized out loud by his father and then sent off to his prospective tutor.

Charley, a likeable and intelligent boy, seems to have made the most of his travels in Germany, just as he had of Eton. He admitted to his father that he was quite homesick, but nonetheless having a wonderful time. He was, however, somewhat dismayed at how difficult it was to learn German—a language his father had originally intended he should become proficient in within just two or three months.

Charles and Catherine spent early spring 1853 in Brighton, with Charles finding inspiration in the streets around him and making regular trips back to London. Katey and Mamie went to join them and Uncle Alfred also visited. Perhaps Alfred and Katey took their sketchbooks out together and sat in companionable artistic silence, painting the scenes around them. In the same year, Charles decided he wanted to spend some time away from the children and his "pair of petticoats" (as he referred to Catherine and Georgina) and spent several weeks traveling through Switzerland and Italy with the painter Augustus Egg and Wilkie Collins.

The family was back in London by the end of Easter and Edward was a constant source of delight to his father. Angela Burdett-Coutts had recently become an aunt and was inordinately proud of her nephew. Charles wrote to "Miss Toots," when Edward was just over a year old. The letter is one of teasing battle:

> My Dear Miss Coutts,
>
> I think that must all be a mistake about that Suffolk baby your nephew, because (it is a remarkable fact) we have in this house the only baby worth mentioning; and there cannot possibly be another baby anywhere, to come into competition with him. I happen to know this, and would like it to be generally understood.

This banter continues for several letters, with both proclaiming their baby the superior. It seems incredible, therefore, when one considers the admirable and surprisingly hands-on father that Charles Dickens was, that a couple of weeks later it had to be broken to him that his eight-year-old son, Frank, had a pronounced stammer. He wrote to Wills, "I find, to my great vexation and distress, this morning, that they have kept [from] me that Frank ... stammers so horribly as to be quite an afflicted object." One wonders how on earth it had been possible to keep such a thing from a child's father. Charles is particularly disappointed as he knows Frank to be "the cleverest of all the children" and had intended him to become a doctor. A year later, despite the best medical advice available, Frank still had a tendency to stammer. In later life, having suffered much teasing by his peers, his affliction would lead him to give up all hopes of entering the medical profession.

While Charley's education was coming to an end, Katey's was entering a new and exciting phase. For several years Charles had been watching with interest the progress of her drawing ability. When Katey was thirteen, with her talent apparent, he and Catherine decided to send her for lessons at nearby Bedford College. The college at 47 Bedford Square had been founded in 1849 by the remarkable Elisabeth Jesser Reid. Elisabeth was a fervent anti-slavery activist and, like Charles, a proactive philanthropist; they were acquainted and respected each other's work. Bedford College was the very first educational establishment in Britain to make provision for the university education of women. Among its earliest graduates were women who would become Britain's first female barrister, the first female Vice-Chancellor, the first female professor at an English university, and the first female chair of the Trades Union Congress (TUC). As well as these academic honors, Bedford College had an important role to play in the British fashion world—it is credited with launching the scandalous trend for "bobbed" hair into London. It was also the first art college in England to allow women to attend life-drawing classes.

In the 1850s, the college was groundbreaking not only for being concerned with the education of women, but also for allowing the enrollment of girls as young as twelve. Unfortunately, there are very few records for pupils from before the 1890s; fortuitously, however, there is in existence a register of students for the academic year 1852–53, which shows that Katey joined the college in the Easter term of 1853 to take drawing classes. Her fees for the term were £1 11s 6d (approximately £100 today). She is also on the register for the following academic year, when she attended drawing classes for three full terms, at the cost of £4 14s 6d (approximately £300 today). Professor Francis Stephen Cary, described as the "head" of the drawing department, took the drawing classes during the years Katey was a pupil. Although further records have not survived, it is likely that she continued attending classes at the college until around the age of eighteen and that she progressed from drawing classes to learning painting skills. As an adult she worked proficiently with oils, watercolors, and pastels, and the success of her paintings demonstrates that she was taught her craft well.

One can assume that it was at Bedford College that she was taught portraiture. Certainly the idea for holding life-drawing classes was mooted within the college in 1854; it was, however, only intended for "senior pupils," not girls of Katey's age, although it is likely that she attended the classes when she reached seniority.

In the early 1850s, at around the time Katey started at Bedford College, there was a new fashionable pastime in London—the "art" of table-turning. Although in later years Charles was to poke fun at mediums and spiritualism, it seems that at this date he was as affected by this new fervor as the rest of society (either through a genuine interest or as research for his novels). On May 22, 1853, he sat down in his study with Catherine, Georgina, their guests Monsieur and Madame Regnier, Mamie, Katey, and the girls' governess. They attempted to summon a spirit to speak to them. In a letter written the following day, Charles relates how "The Pembroke table in my study gamboled like an insane elephant (with a prodigious creaking!) all round the room!!!" He does not attempt to analyze this or to explain it away. The presence of Mamie, now aged fifteen, and of thirteen-year-old Katey at the table-turning demonstrates that they were becoming accepted as adults; this no doubt provided a welcome respite for Charles from what must sometimes have seemed like a multitude of very noisy little boys.

Throughout 1853, Charles had been working solidly on *Bleak House*, and by the summer he was desperate for a change. His health had been extremely fragile for some time, owing to the recurrence of a kidney complaint he had suffered from since childhood, and Catherine and his friends had begun fearing he would suffer a nervous breakdown. Charles was a Francophile, so when he decided to escape he fled to Boulogne-sur-Mer.

The rented house, in which Katey and her siblings were to spend an exciting summer, was called Château de Moulineaux on the rue Beaurepaire. It was situated on the side of a hill, a fifteen-minute walk from the sea, and had a large terraced garden bursting with roses; there were also vegetable gardens, a coach house, a stable block sufficient for twelve horses, and dense woods at the back. Charles described it as "the best doll's house of many rooms in the prettiest French grounds and the most charming situation I have ever seen—the best place I have ever lived in abroad, except Genoa." Although he did not consider the house very large, by today's standards it would seem palatial. There were eight bedrooms, including "the most ridiculous suite of children's rooms ever imaginable" (but not including the servants' rooms), a huge kitchen, a cellar, and several reception rooms. There was also a large conservatory, a total of five summer-houses to be played in, and about fifteen fountains whose bowls were replete with chubby goldfish (although none of the fountains actually worked). In addition, there was in the garden a separate pavilion, with its own sleeping area; Charles intended this should be kept for Wilkie Collins, who he was hoping would visit them. The only problem with their French home was a treacherous area of the garden, in which Charles feared a toddling Edward might injure himself. In France, as in England, the name Charles Dickens was one that inspired devotion and, within a day, their solicitous landlord, M. Beaucourt-Mutuel, had sent a troop of workmen to barricade off the dangerous area so that no curious children would be able to enter.[20]

Three weeks after Charles, Catherine, and Georgina took up residence in the château, by which time the novelist was back in high spirits, the children arrived by boat from Folkestone. The day before they had been due to depart England there were such dreadful storms that their parents feared for their safety. Two years previously, the first submarine telegraph cable had been laid beneath the English Channel, so when the

---

20 Charles had first achieved fame in France with the translation of *Pickwick Papers* in 1838. Since then his books had been translated almost as soon as they appeared in English and he enjoyed a tremendous popularity in France for a foreign-language author. In 1842 Thackeray recorded having been to see a "hilarious" stage version of Nicholas Nickleby in Paris. It was said that whenever Charles Dickens visited Paris, he could not order an item in a shop and give his name for delivery purposes without causing great excitement to the shopkeeper and his fellow shoppers.

weather stayed stormy Charles dispatched a telegram telling the children and their attendants to delay their journey. It arrived moments too late to prevent their boarding. The crossing was extremely unpleasant and all were horribly seasick. They arrived looking and feeling utterly miserable. A few days later, Charles wrote to Mark Lemon:

> . . . Such miserable objects as the children arrived, you never beheld! they had a very bad passage, and were all manner of toad-like colors [sic]. I was unspeakably ashamed of the whole race. The luggage I had not the heart to look upon—but I am told it over-flowed the custom-house and lay in a sluggish pool upon the wharf. The horse and little carriage came by boat from London. Dimly, in the long perspective of a windy street, I saw the horse swinging in the air, in course of disembarkation—with thirty or forty Natives screeching at him and Cooper [CD's groom and coachman] forlornly exposed to the fury of the populace. I immediately turned, fled into the country, and did not venture home until night, when the animal was—somehow—stabled.

As usual, the family enjoyed a stream of visitors, including the Leeches, Mr. and Mrs. Wills, and Wilkie Collins. It was in France that Charles decided on baby Edward's nickname, the Plornishghenter, to be shortened to "Plornish Maroon" or "Plorn" (the latter was used by his family for ever more).

That summer, Boulogne was alive with activity, although it was also awash with unexpected rain. The children had a marvelous time exploring their new home and getting soaked as they ran round the gardens, dodging the attentions of their nurse. Charles' spirits were, as ever, affected strongly by his surroundings and the weather—a tendency Katey inherited. After what seemed like interminable rain and hail, he wrote gloomily to Angela Burdett-Coutts that although it was July he would not be surprised if it started to snow. When the rain abated, however, there were myriad diversions to enjoy. Boulogne was becoming a popular location for overseas tourists, as well as for the holidaying French. There was a local theater, at which the family saw *A Midsummer Night's Dream*. There was also the annual August fair, which lasted for two weeks, and a fête every

Sunday, which included open-air dancing and fairground rides. Charles strolled around it all, drinking in the atmosphere and sporting a new moustache, which an elderly Katey admitted she had hated. She had also disliked his famous beard.

Charley was unable to join them as he was still studying hard to achieve fluency in German, but reports from his tutors were very promising. Katey's closest brother in age, Walter, was allowed to travel to Boulogne for the summer, also with a glowing reference from his teachers. It is notable that in early September, Walter was being punished for throwing a chair at his nurse—notable because, as his father recorded, it was the first time in his twelve years that he had ever had to be punished! As a child, Walter, like Mamie, seems to have exhibited a placid, amenable temperament, in stark contrast to Katey's fiery personality. This incident of rebellion was probably due to adolescence, but could also perhaps be due to his return to the care of a female nursemaid after so many years of being educated in an all-male school environment. The rain and Walter's punishment aside, the trip to France was such a success that Charles determined his next two sons who were to go to school would do so in Boulogne.

One of the great excitements of that early autumn was an expected visit to the town from the Emperor, which kept being delayed. Bonaparte's nephew Louis Napoleon had proclaimed himself Emperor Napoleon III and presided over a reign that would become known as the "Second Republic." Seemingly adept at public relations, by 1853 Napoleon III had managed to overcome much of the distrust of his family's reputation by promising widespread changes for France's poor at the same time as winning over the upper classes. In this, the year of the Emperor's marriage to a beautiful and fashionable Spanish princess, Eugénie, Boulogne had been lavishly decorated in Napoleon III's honor, richly hung with garlands and evergreen arches, all of which started to wilt and turn brown in the baking sun. Charles wrote scoffingly of them, opining they looked ridiculous, although it is likely his children would have found them quite magical.[21]

---

21 It was during the reigns of Napoleon III and Queen Victoria that the idea of building a tunnel underneath the English Channel was first put forward. The so-called Channel Tunnel was rejected by both leaders in April 1867.

In October 1853, the family returned to London. Charles then set off through Italy once again with Wilkie Collins and Augustus Egg (who proposed to Georgina that year—and was rejected). Charles missed his children greatly and, in his frequent letters, sent each of them his love by name, although by this time "Katey" was no longer written in capital letters. He was away for Katey's fourteenth birthday but sent a letter to say he would be drinking her health. He returned home in late December, via Paris (where he found letters from Mamie and Katey waiting for him), and here he collected Charley and brought him home for Christmas. Katey and Mamie were overjoyed to have their elder brother home, but it seems Charley was growing too like his mother for his father's liking. Charles wrote to Angela Burdett-Coutts:

> *He is very gentle and affectionate, particularly fond of his sisters, very happy in their society, and very desirous to win the love of those who are dear to him. His inclinations are all good; but I think he has less fixed purpose and energy than I could have supposed possible in my son. With all the tenderer and better qualities which he inherits from his mother, he inherits an indescribable lassitude of character—a very serious thing in a man . . .*[22]

For Charley's seventeenth birthday the schoolroom at Tavistock House was transformed into a theater for the performance of *Tom Thumb*, a burlesque by Henry Fielding. The aptly named Henry Fielding Dickens, then aged almost five, played Tom Thumb; his father played the ghost of Gaffer Thumb and Mark Lemon was the pantomime dame. As Henry's recitation skills were not yet well honed, the audience were handed transcripts of his words. As an adult, he still remembered being taken to see his father in costume before going on stage, as the make-up was so realistically ghostly that Charles was worried Henry would take fright when he appeared. Although Katey was a talented actress, she refused to take any part, and no amount of coaxing from her parents or siblings could

---

22 Although Charles would unfairly complain of most of his sons inheriting poor qualities from their mother, this "lassitude" and other qualities that he found so hard to bear were more akin to the behavior of his own father, John Dickens, than to that of the maligned Catherine.

persuade her to change her stubborn adolescent mind. As she watched the others' excitement growing about the play, she began to regret her decision: She was impressed enough by *Tom Thumb* to want to appear in all future family theatricals.

In 1854, Katey was preparing for her fifteenth birthday. As an accomplished artist and an attractive young woman, Katey quite naturally found her thoughts were turning to her future. She lived at a time when little else but marriage and childrearing was expected of a woman, and she had begun wondering who of the many men she met in her father's sociable household might become her husband. Her faith in matrimony could well have been sorely shaken that year, however, with the scandalous announcement in June that Uncle Fred had separated from his wife, Anna. (The couple did resolve their differences—temporarily—and had a reconciliation in 1855, but separated formally in 1858 with Anna accusing Fred of adultery.)

Hoping to escape any ensuing unpleasantness, and with Charles wanting to finish *Hard Times* away from London, the Dickens family returned to Boulogne for an extended holiday in the summer and autumn of 1854, taking with them Betty and Lally Lemon.[23] They journeyed to France in the middle of June and remained until October 17. Apart from a dramatic "strange illness" (as Charles described it in a letter), which affected two of the servants and Georgina that August, it was a very happy summer. Having heard so much about Boulogne from his friend, Thackeray had decided his daughters should also spend the summer there, with their grandparents, and with him visiting as often as work would permit. He rented a villa close to the Dickenses' villa and the two families saw each other almost every day. They often dined together and Thackeray wrote of exuberant games of forfeits and of a game called "buzz." Katey and Minny, Thackeray's younger daughter, discovered they shared very similar, impetuous temperaments, although it seems the girls made friends in defiance of their ages: Anny with Katey and Minny with Mamie. Wilkie

---

23 Mark and Helen Lemon were very concerned about the health of their daughters' feet and discreetly packed in their luggage twenty-four pairs of brand-new stockings. These were discovered by Customs, who gleefully charged duty on them. Charles dryly recorded in one of his letters, "Duty on said stockings, 8 francs."

Collins also came to stay, as did Augustus Egg, Henry Fothergill Chorley (the music critic for *The Athenaeum* magazine and one of Charles' close friends), and Thomas Beard (Charles' oldest friend from his first adult job). For Katey and Mamie it was a gloriously sociable summer; having always been outnumbered by brothers, suddenly there were four girls of their own ages to spend time with.

Once again, Boulogne was festooned with decorations; this time it was because England's Prince Albert was coming by royal yacht to meet Emperor Napoleon III. The town was heavy with celebratory streamers and filled with sailors and soldiers, their uniforms pristine. The families joined in the excitement by filling the villas' windows with candles and oil lamps to rival the fireworks. Charles later related that one day he was out walking when he encountered the two eminent men, flanked by their guards. He raised his hat in salute—and they did the same in return. If Napoleon III had not been sure who this English visitor was, Prince Albert would have been able to tell him: By the mid-1850s, Charles Dickens' face was as recognizable to most British people as that of Albert's wife.

After such excitement and festivity, autumn arrived with a shock when—just a few days before the town's theater burned down in a sudden and uncontrollable fire—Mamie was struck down with what turned out to be "English cholera," a terrifying ailment that could prove fatal within twenty-four hours. Cholera was surprisingly prevalent throughout Europe in the nineteenth century; there were regular epidemics and during the year 1853–54 twelve thousand people died of the infection in London alone.[24] All too aware of the symptoms and effects of the malady, the Dickens family was terrified that Mamie could die. After a horrible couple of days, she recovered, suffering no lasting effects. Equally fortuitously, no one else in the holidaying party had contracted cholera. Charles wrote about it to Wilkie Collins, who had returned home before Mamie's illness. The letter shows he retained his sense of humor, despite the scare:

On the Sunday night after you left . . . Mary was taken very ill. English Cholera. She was sinking so fast, and the sickness and diarrhoea

---

24 It was after this epidemic that the pioneering London doctor John Snow finally started to convince his medical colleagues that cholera was principally spread by water.

were so exceedingly alarming that it evidently would not do to wait for [Dr. John] Elliotson. I caused everything to be done that one had naturally often thought of, in a lonely house so full of children . . . Thank God she recovered so favorably [sic] that by breakfast time she was fast asleep. She slept 24 hours, and has never had the least uneasiness since. I heard—of course afterwards—that she had had an attack of sickness two nights before. I think that long ride and those late dinners had been too much for her. Without them, I am inclined to doubt whether she would have been ill. . . . Plornish Maroon . . . had a fall yesterday—through overbalancing himself in kicking his Nurse.

Henry's chief recollections of the holiday do not include Mamie's frightening illness, which suggests the younger children were kept in ignorance of it. Yet he remembered the theater burning down and the town's futile attempts to save it, as everyone passed water buckets from hand to hand. He also remembered the "very violent gale" in which the family crossed the English Channel on their way home. At that time it was possible to take a "very small" and uncomfortable boat from Boulogne to Gravesend. The storm was so bad that they were not able to land and spent eight hours at anchor being buffeted by it. Poor Mamie, having seasickness so close to her recovery from cholera, felt truly wretched.

Several weeks earlier, while the family had been preparing to return to Boulogne-sur-Mer, Charles had made the acquaintance of an eager young journalist, the twenty-three-year-old Edmund Yates. Desperate to meet the great novelist, Yates used the fact that his father, Frederick Yates, was known by Dickens through the Adelphi Theater and called on him, without an appointment, at Tavistock House. Yates would later write, "There was no one in the world for whom I had so much admiration, or whom I so longed to know." Charles was busy writing and could not see him, but suggested, via Georgina, that Yates return on the following Sunday when he would have leisure to meet him. When writing about this first meeting, Yates claims nonchalantly that he did not push his literary aspirations. However, by the time Charles and his family left for Boulogne just a few days later, Yates had already given him a copy of the book he had been writing, which Charles dutifully took away with him.

Edmund Yates was already married—to Louisa, the daughter of James Wilkinson of Wilkinson Swords fame—by the time he made the acquaintance of the Dickens family. This, though, did not prevent the adolescent Katey from falling in love with him. Many decades later, she recalled the feelings she had had for him, telling her biographer, Gladys Storey, that Yates either did not notice or affected not to notice her feelings. It was a pitiful unrequited love she was to feel keenly, in the all-consuming manner only a teenager with very little else to occupy her mind can do. In an article Katey was to write when an elderly lady, she looked back on her Victorian girlhood and commented, "Many [girls] were thoughtful in those days and greatly given to introspection, a fault no doubt of too much leisure."

If Yates was aware of her adoration, he was probably embarrassed by it. It seems, however, that he was barely aware of her existence, concerned only with her famous father. The one other member of the Dickens family to whom Yates makes any prominent reference in his memoirs is Georgina Hogarth, who had been kind to him on the first meeting. Georgina, however, let it be known many years later that she was not overly fond of Yates (no doubt because she had watched her young niece breaking her heart over him). When Yates was following Charles' earlier advice and undertaking a lecture tour of the United States, Georgina was to write about him to one of her American friends. The lecture tour was in a gossipy vein about great writers Yates had known (by the time of his tour in the 1870s, almost all of them were dead). Georgina commented that she did not think his talks would be in good taste nor would she like to have to sit through them. She described him as "pleasant" and "good" but also as "rash," "not a man to be relied upon," and "very weak, uncertain and easily influenced." Marcus Stone, who remained one of Katey's good friends from childhood onward, said of Yates that he was "superficial" and "no gentleman." Yates played hugely on his association with Charles, flattering the writer obsequiously while using his name as an entrée into polite society, at the same time insidiously causing trouble with Charles' more long-term friends, in particular Thackeray, of whom Yates was exceedingly jealous.

The adolescent Katey, however, was in love with him. When Yates wrote about one of the Dickens family theatricals he had been invited to watch in the late 1850s, Katey is mentioned merely as one of "the ladies of the family." One imagines she had spent weeks dreaming of the moment he would watch her on stage and willing him to fall in love with her too, yet in his memory she was just one of the minor cast members.

6

THE FAMILY THEATRICALS

After their return from Boulogne, the Dickens children began preparing for the next family theatrical—the previous year's performance had been such a success that it was decided to make it an annual event. This time Katey was happy to take part. The play was J. R. Planché's *Fortunio and his Seven Gifted Servants*, which Charles took great pains to rewrite in order to accommodate parts for all his children and any additional actors, such as Lally, Betty, and Mark Lemon, Wilkie Collins (billed as "Mr. Wilkini Collini"), and Catherine and Georgina's sister, Helen. Aunt Helen, the youngest of the Hogarth girls, was only a few years older than her nieces. She was very close to Mamie and Katey and the girls had great fun rehearsing together while the older boys were away at school (no doubt learning their lines in any spare moments). On the playbill, created to look like an authentic theater bill, the play was described as "Mr. Planché's fairy extravaganza, in two acts, with alterations by the dramatic poet of this establishment." The part of Fortunio was played by Henry. His role involved slaying the dragon, played by "Uncle Mark"; Henry would later relate how very tempting Mark Lemon's paunch was to a small boy carrying a sword and how in the slaying scene he couldn't resist taking an unrehearsed poke at his belly.

Baron Dunover, a nobleman in straitened circumstances, was played by Charles; Charley and Mamie played a half-brother and -sister, King Alfourite and Princess Vindicta; and Katey played the part of the Hon. Miss Partina, Baron Dunover's eldest daughter. The playbill was proud to announce the "engagement of Miss Kate, who declined the munificent offers of the management last season!"; two-year-old Edward was listed as "Plornish Maroontigoonter . . . who has been kept out of bed at vast expense." Georgina did not act in this theatrical, as she was providing the piano music. It was a grand affair, with costumes provided by "Messrs Nathan of Titchbourne Street" (real theatrical costumiers whom Charles would use on several occasions) and wigs by "Mr. Wilson, of the Strand." The props manager was a Mr. Thomas Ireland, who worked at the Adelphi Theatre.

Shortly after the theatrical, the family were celebrating the good news of a baby son born to Mark and Helen Lemon. Frank Lemon was born on January 21, 1855—and was fated to die, at the age of just three months, on April 24. That springtime death was a terribly sad time for both families, as Catherine and Charles recalled the death of baby Dora. Remembering what marvelous support Mark had given him on the night of Dora's death, Charles now repaid that kindness with comfort for his grieving friend.

Baby Frank's death, in conjunction with the low moods he had been experiencing since the end of *Fortunio*, served to plunge Charles into misery. He became discontented with his lot in life, with his wife, his family, and his responsibilities. He wrote to Angela Burdett-Coutts that he was suffering "restlessness and worse" and wishing he had a hot-air balloon so he could escape.

This time, however, Charles pulled himself up from his doldrums by deciding to recreate the wonderful feelings he and his children had experienced when acting; he began organizing another family theatrical, to take place in June. He threw himself into the preparations with enthusiasm, deliberately consulting Mark Lemon throughout in an effort to give his friend something other than his son's death to concentrate on. This theatrical would be even more elaborate than before: Tailors were ordered to make special costumes for Katey and Georgina; Augustus Egg was asked to design the costumes; and a policeman was hired to stand at the front door to prevent any gatecrashers from trying to see the play.

A double bill of *The Lighthouse* (a play by Wilkie Collins, in which Mamie and Georgina acted) and *Mr. Nightingale's Diary* (by Charles Dickens and Mark Lemon, in which Katey and Georgina acted) was performed on Saturday the 16th, Monday the 18th, and Tuesday the 19th of

June, 1855, at the specially made theater inside Tavistock House, advertised as "the smallest theater in the world." The marine painter Clarkson Stanfield, one of Charles' good friends, painted the backdrop for *The Lighthouse*.[25] There was even a wind machine—it was Charley's job to operate it and create the storms.

Charles and Mark Lemon's version of *Mr. Nightingale's Diary*, a farce, had been written in 1851. Psychologically, it was interesting that Charles should choose to stage this play at this particular time, as the two men had been in the process of writing it when baby Dora died. The first time the play had been performed was at Devonshire Terrace. Charles, Augustus Egg, Mark Lemon, and Wilkie Collins had all appeared in it. On that occasion, the part of Rosina Nightingale had been played by a "Miss Ellen Chaplin"; in 1855 this was the part played by Katey.

Charles and Mark Lemon had changed the play considerably from the original, altering the characters' names as well as aspects of their roles. In their version, Rosina is the niece of the eponymous Mr. Nightingale (played in 1855 by Frank Stone), a hypochondriac who spends his life seeking a cure for a non-existent illness and attempting to persuade everyone else around him that they are also ill. Mr. Nightingale has forbidden the marriage of his niece to Mr. Gabblewig, a barrister. Through a series of farcical events, Mr. Nightingale is eventually persuaded to give his blessing to their marriage. Though not a particularly challenging part, it was one that allowed Katey much on-stage "disguising" as she and Gabblewig, played by her father, have to pretend to Mr. Nightingale that they are a succession of different people. No doubt this afforded them some hilarious father-and-daughter rehearsal times.

Among the many invited guests were Edmund Yates and his mother, Thomas and Jane Carlyle, the Leeches, the Thackerays, and the playwrights Douglas Jerrold and Gilbert à Beckett. After the last performance of *The Lighthouse* and *Mr. Nightingale's Diary* the family held a splendid party, at which lively Scottish reels were danced until five a.m.

---

25 This eerie-looking painted lighthouse can still be seen in the Charles Dickens Museum in London, and is well worth a visit as it is so evocative of the days of family theatricals, emphasizing just how seriously these performances were taken.

The rest of the summer was spent in Folkestone, where it rained and where Charles grew increasingly despairing of how noisy his sons were and longed for their school holidays to end. He invited his sister Laetitia and her husband Henry to visit them, but advised they delay their journey until the boys had returned to school. Katey and Mamie spent that summer in a fever of excitement and anticipation: Their father had decided that, come the autumn, the family would move to Paris for several months. Part of the reason was that he wanted his daughters to be "finished" in Paris; in addition it was one of his favorite places and he wanted the inspiration of living there; but it was also so that Katey could learn more about art. One can imagine the thrill that ran through the sisters as they discussed the proposed trip. That year, everyone, everywhere, it seemed, had been agog at the famous Great Exhibition, boasting cavernous rooms filled with art and exhibits from all over the world. In 1855 the host city, Paris, was about the most fashionable place there was. Of course, fashion itself was another powerfully enticing reason for visiting the French capital; both Mamie and Katey longed to patronize the city's dressmakers, knowing they would return to London as the most up-to-date of all their acquaintances.

Unfortunately, with the whole world and its servants visiting Paris for the exhibition, accommodation was extremely difficult to find. Charles, Georgina, and some of the servants went as an advance party, to find a suitable temporary home. Although it was not deemed ideal, being somewhat too small, they decided upon 49 avenue des Champs Elysées, "a regular continental abode" as Charles wrote to Catherine, warning her to "be prepared" for it. He went on to say:

> *There is only one window in each room, but the front apartments all look upon the main street of the champs Elysées, and the view is delightfully cheerful. There are also plenty of rooms. They are not over and above well furnished, but by changing furniture from rooms we don't care for, to rooms we do care for, we shall be able to make them comfortable and presentable. I think the situation itself, almost the finest in Paris; and the children will have a window from which to look on the busy life outside.*

The apartment, despite its shortcomings, appears to have been a source of delight and great inspiration to the weary author. In a letter to his editor W. H. Wills he wrote gleefully, "You must picture it as the smallest place you ever saw, but as exquisitely cheerful and vivacious—clean as anything human can be—and with a moving panorama always outside ..."

As promised, Charles busied himself with his daughters' education while they were in France. He hired Daniele Manin, a famous Venetian patriot now living in enforced exile in Paris, to teach them Italian. Manin, a hero of the Italian revolution of 1848, was described by Charles as the "best and noblest" of the rebel leaders. They also took dancing lessons, no longer merely the polka, but sophisticated, adult dancing that would be a credit to them at balls and grand parties during the London Season. Both girls were obviously proud of their ability to dance; many years later Mamie wrote (referring to herself in the third person): "The children *did* get to dance very prettily, and the two little girls as they grew older became quite mistresses of the 'noble art.'"

They were joined in these dancing lessons by Anny and Minny Thackeray, who were coincidentally in Paris as well. Since the girls had spent their earliest years living there with their father's mother and stepfather, returning to Paris was, for them, a little like coming home after a long absence—albeit to a stiff and restricted home. Their grandparents, Major and Mrs. Carmichael-Smyth, lived in the rue d'Angoulême, not far from the Dickenses' apartment. The Thackeray girls' perfect French and superior knowledge of the city would undoubtedly have seemed a great benefit to Katey and Mamie and the four girls greatly enjoyed exploring Parisian life together, though from a strictly chaperoned perspective, of course. When one considers all the Dickens girls' experiences, one realizes what a privileged life they were living.

The family bought new clothes, dined out regularly, and went to the theater. Both of Charles' daughters were proficient in French—having spent many years being tutored by a French governess—and Italian must have been relatively easy for them to pick up, considering their childhood months in Genoa. The Parisian society within which they moved was truly exalted. Charles Dickens was almost as revered a name in Paris as the city's own great writer, Victor Hugo, author of *Les Misérables*. Dickens had met Hugo in the 1840s, but during the months that Dickens was living in Paris, Hugo was partway through his years of political exile, living on the island of Guernsey. In Hugo's absence, Charles and Catherine were lionized by the cream of Parisian society, invited to dine with Alexandre Dumas and to meet the female writer Georges Sands, who wrote "shocking" novels (and whose lovers included the composer Frédéric Chopin), and the artist Ary Scheffer. The latter asked Charles to sit for him so that he could paint his portrait (his brother Henri painted the author at the same time). One evening in November, Ary held a party for sixty guests to hear Charles give a reading from one of his Christmas stories, *The Cricket on the Hearth*.

Charles did not enjoy the experience of having his portrait painted, nor was he enamored of the results, but Katey would surely have been transfixed. It has been suggested that she actually studied under Ary Scheffer at this time, though this seems unlikely, given her gender and the fact that in later life she did not mention being taught by him. She visited the studio on several occasions while her father's portrait was being painted—and marveled to watch the great master at work.

As well as having dancing lessons together, the Thackeray and Dickens girls enjoyed joint drawing lessons. Dickens asked Scheffer if he could recommend a suitable drawing master for them and the lessons were held at the Dickenses' apartment. Anny and Minny loved their grandmother and step-grandfather, but the elderly couple were very rigid and bigoted in their views; Thackeray and his daughters found their opinions frustratingly narrow. Having Katey and Mamie to spend time with and being able to visit the family's Champs Elysées apartment was a relief to the Thackeray sisters. Anny was later to write about their art lessons, reporting that they were taught to draw "gigantic ears and classic profiles" and that their drawing master "never tired of talking [about] and of praising Mr. Ary Scheffer." She also recalled:

On one occasion we all adjourned to Ary Scheffer's actual studio to hear Mr. Dickens read: but I was too woolgathering in those days; life was too brimful of everything; I looked about at the pictures, I watched the company, I admired chivalrous Ary Scheffer's military strides . . . but meanwhile, alas! I carried away little of the reading itself, so engrossed was I with the fact and the scene of it all.

An important aside in Anny's account of their drawing lessons is a comment about Katey: "we had come to settle about a drawing class with our young companion K.E. (who had already found what she liked doing)." ("K.E." was Thackeray's pet name for Katey, the "E" denoting her middle name, Elizabeth.) As a teenager at a time when women of her class seldom worked, Katey had already decided on her path in life and Anny was already convinced that she would follow it.

Ary had by far the superior talent of the two Scheffer brothers. He painted a number of notable portraits, but was also famed for his genre and history paintings, including the powerful *Francesca da Rimini* and the more stylized *Margaret at the Fountain*, in which his Dutch ancestry can clearly be seen. His paintings are grand in style and had a marked influence on the works of the English artist Frederic, Lord Leighton. Although many modern art critics deride Scheffer's work as overly sentimental in subject matter, what cannot be overlooked is his highly honed talent for figure painting and for recreating faces and expressions. Scheffer was a greatly celebrated artist. Tantalizingly, there is no record of Katey's observances at the studio or of her impressions of Scheffer himself.

In what seems a coincidence worthy of a Dickens novel, at the time of painting his portrait of Charles, Scheffer was employing an Italian studio assistant. This young man, who was almost exactly the same age as Katey, worked on the painting, although he does not appear to have met the writer and certainly was not introduced to the great man's daughter. This young painter's name was Carlo Perugini. In later years he would become the most important person in Katey's life—yet at this date she was entirely unaware of him.

In common with all the Dickenses' homes, the Paris apartment was a warren of activity and hospitality. As usual, the family received a stream of visitors, including Alfred Dickens, Wilkie Collins, and Katey's godfather Macready. In addition, all nine children, including Charley, who was just beginning his career at Barings Bank, were with their parents for

Christmas. In a letter to Edmund Yates (whose wife had just given birth to twin sons and who had asked Charles to be godfather to one of them) Charles wrote, "When you represent me at the Font and are renouncing, think that on Christmas Day I had seven sons in the Banquet Hall of this apartment—which would not make a very large warm bath—and renounce my example." Although Angela Burdett-Coutts did not visit, she was there in spirit, via the Twelfth Night cake that she still managed to send on time, despite the distance.

At around this time, Charles achieved a lifelong ambition: He bought himself a house in the country. It is often related how, as a young boy, Charles would take long walks with his father in the Kent country-side. On these walks they passed a large house, Gad's Hill Place (in an area immortalized by Shakespeare in *Henry IV Part I*). Reputedly, John

Gad's Hill Place in Kent, bought by Charles Dickens in 1856. He had wanted to own the house since he was a young boy and was able to achieve his ambition at the age of forty-four.

Dickens told his son that, if he worked hard enough, he would be able to buy it one day. Charles was never to forget that comment. While Charles was in Paris, Wills, to whom Charles had related the story, was at a dinner party, seated next to a woman who told him she had recently inherited a place in Kent and did not know what to do with it. On discovering it was the very same house, Wills informed Charles, who immediately declared he wanted to buy it. It took several months to get the owner to agree to what Charles considered a fair price, but by February 1857 the Dickens family had their very own country residence. A Queen Anne villa with large gardens, near the village of Higham, it was the only home that Charles Dickens ever owned; he only purchased the leases on his London homes, not the houses themselves.

The house purchase was managed mainly from Paris as Charles did not want to return to London too often. He loved the Parisian way of life and particularly enjoyed dining out. One of his favorite restaurants was called Les Trois Frères Provincaux. During the spring, he wrote to Wilkie Collins of having visited the restaurant with Catherine, Georgina, and his daughters. All four of them seem to have annoyed him: Catherine by eating too much and the other three by eating too little. He wrote: "Mrs. Dickens nearly killed herself, but the others hardly did that justice to the dinner that I had expected." It is an irritable, chafing letter suggestive of the stagnant nature his marriage to Catherine was attaining. By this time, she had grown fat and, in his eyes, unattractive, and he was starting to find her very presence claustrophobic. For a man so fastidious as Charles, one who laid such great store by young female beauty, a wife who allowed herself to get as fat as Catherine (albeit aided by twelve pregnancies) started to present what he considered a repellent figure. One imagines that, in the eyes of her husband, Catherine did not shine while surrounded by thousands of Paris's famously elegant women—both natives and those foreigners rich enough to visit Paris purely in order to buy the latest designs. At the beginning of their time in Paris, Charles' distaste for his wife was also being exacerbated by the thought of an old flame. His first love, Maria Beadnell, now called Mrs. Winter and with a teenage daughter, had written to him, after years without any attempt at communication, at the end of 1855. She was the woman who had broken

Charles' heart when he was a young man and he had never quite gotten over her memory. When he had written *David Copperfield* he had used his memories of Maria to create the character of Dora, David's adored young wife. The letter had been forwarded to Paris. In Charles' mind, Maria was still a young, slender coquette, a world away from his dullard of a wife (and equally distant from the reality of the middle-aged matron Maria had become). This letter plunged Charles into discontent and he began corresponding with her as if he were still the ardent young man of twenty he had been when courting her. One wonders how much Katey and Mamie understood about their father's sudden mood change and whether they were aware of who his new correspondent was.

Charles' letters home also record another, quite extraordinary, family incident that occurred while they were in Paris. It was discovered that

A photograph of Catherine Dickens taken in the mid-1850s, showing how she looked after many years of childbearing and post-natal depression had taken their toll.

Walter, now aged fourteen, was "horribly deaf." He was sent to Paris's Deaf and Dumb Institution, where he was fortunate enough to be treated by Prosper Ménière (after whom Ménière's disease is named), who was already a renowned physician, medical researcher, and writer. According to Charles, after three months Walter was "quite recovered." What this so easily cured deafness actually was is difficult to determine, but he was soon well enough to return to school and sit his "India examination."

While the family was enjoying their Parisian adventure, the mood in the city was changeable, with much of the world waiting with bated breath to hear the latest news from the Crimea. The Crimean War, which had begun in 1854, was to come to an end while the Dickens family was in Paris, in March 1856. This particular war had captured the general public's imagination and sense of horror more completely than previous wars, due to the in-depth newspaper reporting—such as had never been read before. The main Crimean correspondent to British newspapers was the groundbreaking journalist William Howard Russell, who sent back his dispatches to *The Times*. It was thanks to Russell's reporting that both Florence Nightingale and Mary Seacole decided they would take their unique nursing skills to the Crimea.[26] Even the children of the Dickens family must have been aware of the terrible reports being sent back from the Crimea. The ending of the war would have been a time of sober celebration as people reflected over the two years of conflict and the realities of the so-called "glory" of war.

After seven exciting months in Paris, in May 1856 the family journeyed to Boulogne for the summer. Cholera was still in evidence, but now there was yet another health scare, diphtheria or "malignant sore throat" as it was known by the English visitors. The disease had been raging around the poorer suburbs of Boulogne, proving fatal to those who were too malnourished or unhealthy to fight it. Although the disease had

---

26 Mary Seacole, a mixed-race nurse from Jamaica, whose medical prowess was extraordinary, had traveled to London to enlist as a nurse. She was refused permission to join Florence Nightingale's staff for no other reason than the color of her skin. Refusing to be daunted, Mary made her own way to the Crimea, where she already knew many of the soldiers from their time in Jamaica. Rejected again by Florence Nightingale, she established her own base, "the British Hotel," at the front line. By contrast, Florence Nightingale's hospital was at Scutari, hundreds of miles away from the fighting. Today, Mary Seacole is finally being given the recognition she deserves.

not made it to the wealthy areas, such as the locality in which the Dickenses were staying, it was taking a frightening hold in the slums—at the end of June, it was recorded that twenty children died of diphtheria in just one day.

The family was joined in Boulogne by their pets, including Timber, the dog, whose life had involved more overseas traveling than most of Victoria's human subjects could even imagine. By now, he was very elderly and the family was distraught when he died that summer. Mamie's much-loved canary, Dick, was also transported out to France and two local cats spent weeks attempting to eat him.[27] These cats, in turn, were stalked with frightening violence by one of the local servants—egged on excitedly by Katey's young brothers. The servant, M. Franche, managed to kill one of the cats, about which there was much rejoicing among the junior members of the family; the remaining cat then became an obsession. Charles found Franche's bloodlust depressing and was convinced his constant gun-laden vigil was going to cause a dreadful accident. He humorously described it in a letter as being like a siege, in which none of the family—except his bloodthirsty little boys—dared go into the garden for fear of being shot at and how the tradesmen entered with trepidation, calling out fearfully to announce their presence in case they be mistaken for a bird-eating feline. As Charles reported, the only being unperturbed by the situation was the wily cat, which remained very much alive. When Charles discovered that Franche, frustrated in his attempts to shoot the cat in the open, had determined to lure her into the coach house with meat and then kill her when she had no chance of escaping, he forbade it, furious about the barbaric plan.

His letters reveal that, like Katey, Charles became gloomy when the weather was bad and that his mood improved dramatically when the sun shone. Charles was a great lover of large windows and mirrors; the latter were not only used to check the state of his hair (he was fanatical about its neatness), but as an essential interior decoration. He had them installed in all his homes. It is quite common to read comments about Charles

---

27 During Dick's lifetime, Charles would not allow any cats to be owned by members of the household. When Dick died he was buried in the garden of Gad's Hill Place and a gravestone was erected stating, "This is the grave of Dick, the best of birds."

liking mirrors because he was a vain man—he was very interested in his own appearance, particularly in his flamboyant clothes and in appearing well groomed—but the abundance of mirrors in all his houses was actually to bring as much light as possible into the rooms, as well as to create an illusion of more space. One must also consider how detrimental to Charles' work bad lighting and lack of sunlight would prove. He was already short-sighted; attempting to write in poor light would have made his eyes much worse. Charles lived before the advent of electric lighting and during his lifetime homes were lit by candles or oil lamps, which gave off relatively little light and could never reproduce the effects of sunlight, as modern lighting techniques are able to do.[28]

Charles' letters home from Boulogne make reference to the "millions of roses" and glorious countryside all around them, and to Mamie being a good little housekeeper-in-training, always taking upon herself the daily task of bringing in and arranging fresh flowers. Surprisingly, his surviving letters make little mention of Katey or of her performing similar household tasks. Perhaps she was excused from them in order to paint and draw; her previous months in Paris must have been a time of great creativity, encouraging her artistic nature and compelling her to record everything she had seen. Her father would have been sympathetic to this yearning, being equally compelled to record all his experiences with his pen.

Throughout the summer, the children basked in the sun, growing brown and getting plump on the "really special" cook's delicious food. These were happy days, but by the end of August the realities of the outside world were beginning to encroach. The curse of diphtheria was coming too close to home for Charles' comfort, particularly in light of the fact that his sons were due to be schooled in Boulogne the following term. He had already sent the boys back to London and now began to wonder about the wisdom of them returning for schooling in September. The decision was made for him after sad news that reached them at the end of August. The English playwright Gilbert à Beckett and his young son had contracted diphtheria and died, very suddenly. The family knew

---

28 Toward the end of Dickens' life, some homes had gas lighting, but this was largely distrusted. Electric lighting began to be used from around 1879 onward, but the majority of homes in England did not receive it until after the First World War.

them well as Gilbert had once collaborated on a play with Mark Lemon and had been present at the performance of *The Lighthouse*. Katey and Mamie were distraught. Charles sent them home as fast as possible (seemingly with Catherine), and he, Georgina, and the servants followed within a few days.

When they reached Tavistock House, it was to discover that Katey had become very ill. The worst, diphtheria, was immediately feared. She was coughing dreadfully and had "lost her usual pretty looks with extraordinary suddenness." As the family doctor, Dr. Watson, was away she was attended to by a Dr. Hastings, who alleviated the family's fears by diagnosing whooping cough and recommended a rest cure. She and Mamie were sent to Brighton, where she could recover her strength.

It was around this time that Katey's parents' marriage really started to unravel. Not long after their return to England, Charles insisted on inviting Maria Winter and her daughter to dine with him and Catherine. Luckily for Catherine, Maria was also matronly and lacking in her earlier, girlish allurements that had led Charles to create the character of the unattainably lovely—though doomed—Dora in *David Copperfield*. After the dinner party, at which he found Maria intensely irritating, Charles lampooned her as the twittering Flora Finching in *Little Dorrit*, whose description included the revealing comments, "Flora, whom he had left a lily, had become a peony. . . . Flora, who had seemed enchanting in all she said and thought, was diffuse and silly." Catherine must have been relieved and perhaps hoped that Charles would begin to understand that age caused every woman's looks to change, just as hers had. Perhaps she even hoped it might make him realize that the passage of time had changed him as well. Sadly, that was not to prove the case and Charles began yearning for the young, beautiful woman he had fallen in love with, desperate to move away from the middle age that seemed determined to claim him. Today, he would no doubt be described as having a mid-life crisis.

It can sometimes be difficult for modern readers, so used to the cult of celebrity, to understand quite what a phenomenon Charles Dickens' celebrity was to the nineteenth-century observer. He was one of the very first "celebrities" in the modern sense. People were fascinated by him, in a manner previously reserved for royalty or the greatest of war heroes, such as Nelson or Wellington. Henry recalls what it was like to be with his father as a young boy and the way in which people reacted when they saw the great Charles Dickens: "To walk with him in the streets of London . . . was a revelation; a royal progress; people of all degrees and classes taking off their hats and greeting him as he passed." It is therefore little surprise that Charles started to believe that he deserved better than what he perceived as his restricted life. He was so constantly lionized, so universally adored, that perhaps he began to feel he was no longer bound by the rules that applied to other men.

At the start of October 1856, while Katey and Mamie were still in Brighton, Wilkie Collins paid a call on Charles. It was to prove an unwittingly portentous evening: Wilkie brought with him the manuscript of the first two acts of his new play, *The Frozen Deep*. This work would prove a turning point in Dickens family history. The play is a melodrama centering on an ill-fated trip to the Arctic and concerned with the plight of two men in love with the same woman who find themselves stranded in the world's most inhospitable land. Dickens helped Collins finalize the play and paid homage to it in one of his novels. The premise of the plot—one man sacrificing himself for the sake of his rival in love—echoes that of *A Tale of Two Cities* (which Dickens admitted was inspired by the play).

The Dickens family loved it, with Charley instantly taking up his father's cry that they must perform it at a family theatrical, and Charles himself teasingly writing to tell Katey that if she didn't get well and hurry back soon he would give her part to someone else. By the time the two girls arrived home just a few days later, the schoolroom at Tavistock House was being transformed back into a theater, with an army of carpenters building the stage and sets. Clarkson Stanfield was busy creating a stunning backdrop, just as he had for *The Lighthouse*.

The family was drawn into hectic rehearsals, with Katey's younger brothers—now back in Boulogne, the diphtheria scare over—being sent out their parts to learn before the holidays. There were three plays being put on, with the farces *Animal Magnetism* and *Uncle John* being performed after *The Frozen Deep* in an attempt to lighten the mood. Katey was playing the part of Rose Ebsworth in *The Frozen Deep* and of Camilla in *Animal Magnetism*. Her Camilla role was similar to that of Rosina Nightingale—a young woman thwarted in her desire to marry the man she loved by an older, controlling man. Henry later recalled that the small children had no parts to play in *The Frozen Deep*, which was a "serious play" for "grown ups," though he was in charge of cutting up paper to make snow.

The performances began on Charley's twentieth birthday, January 6, 1857. There were four performances with breaks in between; the last one taking place on the night of January 14. Acting with the family were Wilkie Collins, Augustus Egg, and Augustus Dickens. The performances were a tremendous success and, after they were over, Charles went into another slump, craving excitement and feeling discontented with his life. Perhaps Katey did the same, as she and Mamie went off to the Isle of Wight for three weeks; they stayed with a family called White, whose daughter they were friends with (and from whom Charles had rented the family's holiday home when they had visited Bonchurch). After their return they kept up the usual social rounds with the Thackeray and Lemon girls—as well as visiting their new home at Gad's Hill, which was currently being made habitable for a large family by an army of workmen. Despite having fallen in love with the place, Charles wanted to make a large number of changes, including building an extension to house a schoolroom for his younger boys and creating a smart billiard room, complete with tiled walls and a lead-lined drawer for storing cold drinks.[29]

While their parents, Georgy, and the youngest boys spent time in Kent, keeping an eye on the progress of their new home, Katey, Mamie, and Charley enjoyed "keeping house" in London, no doubt inviting their friends over to show off their prowess. After a few days, a beaming Walter joined them, fresh from having passed his examinations and being accepted into the East India Office. The four reveled in the freedom afforded them by the absence of all members of the older generation and all the little ones.

---

29 Charles ordered many "improvements" to his new home at Gad's Hill, such as changes to the garden, the addition of mirrors, and the building of a conservatory. Each improvement, he said, would be the "last," and Katey often teased him about it, saying she didn't believe him, that he would keep on "improving" the house throughout his life (she was right). His favorite flower was the scarlet geranium, and many of the flowerbeds and window boxes were planted with them. Katey once said to him, "I believe papa, that when you become an angel your wings will be made of looking-glass and your crown of scarlet geraniums."

By the summer, the whole family was happily dividing their time between Kent and London. While they were at Gad's Hill, Hans Christian Andersen came to stay; he was invited for a few days but remained for five weeks. It seems he had no idea how unwelcome he was, as his letters home show he believed he and Charles were the best of friends. The family found him distinctly odd, but were, nonetheless, very courteous hosts for him to continue outstaying his welcome in blissful ignorance. Lionized in his native Denmark, Andersen had become used to staying in very wealthy houses with a plethora of servants. The Dickens household did not run to spare servants, so Andersen decided that the Dickens children would do instead. Charley—an adult earning his own living—was most indignant on the occasion Andersen ordered him to bring hot water and shave him. From then onward, the coach was ordered every day to drive Andersen to a barber in Rochester. The family would later relate wonderful stories of their guest, such as the day he visited London, which terrified him. On his return, Charles thought Andersen had developed a severe case of corns, because he was walking with such difficulty. It transpired that, convinced his cab driver was going to rob him, he had removed all valuables from about his person and stored them inside his boots.

Andersen had an aptitude for making shapes and small sculptures out of paper and would spend hours contentedly cutting out intricate little designs; the children were bemused by this, unable to comprehend how an adult could take such pleasure in what seemed a very childish occupation. In his *Recollections*, Henry Dickens commented:

> *Much as there was in him to like and to admire, he was, on the other hand, most decidedly disconcerting in his general manner. . . . I am afraid the small boys in the family rather laughed at him behind his back; but, so far as the members of the family were concerned, he was treated with the utmost consideration and courtesy.*

Kate simply referred to him as "a bony bore [who] stayed on and on." On June 15, Katey, Mamie, and Catherine took Andersen to the first Handel Festival, which was held at the Crystal Palace in London. The occasion was a grand one with over two thousand singers and musicians, and the party was thrilled to be seated directly opposite the royal box. Shortly after this successful outing, Andersen wrote to his sister:

Mrs. Dickens I find pretty this time, and the eldest daughter, Mary, is like her. The second, Kate, has decidedly Dickens' face, such as you know from his portrait. . . . The daughters are pretty and unaffected, and seem very gifted.

Andersen seemed to be particularly fond of Catherine, who was always kind to him. One morning, after opening a letter in which he received an unfavorable review of one of his books, he astonished the family by lying on the lawn and sobbing; Catherine went out to comfort him. When he finally left Kent (which was not until the middle of July), Charles went into the bedroom Andersen had occupied and—in the manner of a pub displaying a plaque above a bed announcing that Queen Elizabeth I had slept there—put a printed card above the mirror. It read: "Hans Christian Andersen slept in this room for five weeks, which seemed to the family AGES!" Katey later admitted she had taken it down—the only one who had dared—as she thought it cruel.

During Andersen's stay, Charles had been terribly upset by the news that his friend Douglas Jerrold had died. An author, playwright, and contributor to *Punch*, Jerrold had eked out a living and Charles felt sure that his widow and children had been left in the most straitened of financial circumstances. Charles, Wilkie Collins, and Mark Lemon immediately set about organizing benefit performances of *The Frozen Deep*, with all the profits to be given to the Jerrold family. Jerrold's eldest son was quite vocal about the fact that the family had not been left destitute and objected to them being treated as objects of charity, but the fundraising efforts continued nonetheless. Charles was having far too much fun to want to stop and it seems likely that, despite her son's protestations, the widowed Mrs. Jerrold really was in need of financial help. The money was certainly not refused.

The whole of London was talking about the play Mr. Dickens was going to put on. The atmosphere was electric as people vied for the chance to watch one of the country's most famous men appear on stage—as well as for the chance to see the rest of his family, acting in public. The buzz even made it as far as Buckingham Palace and Queen Victoria wrote to Charles, saying that she would like to see the play. As a result, the first night became a private royal performance, with only very special friends of the cast also present in the audience. This royal gala took place on July 4, 1857, with the same cast as before, at the Gallery of Illustration on Regent Street. Strangely, Katey makes absolutely no mention of this in her memoirs, but it must have been an unforgettable experience. Hans Andersen wrote a letter to his own queen, describing the theatricals; he mentioned that a farce called *Two O'Clock in the Morning* was performed after the melodrama, in which Katey and Mamie took the female leads.

Queen Victoria was highly pleased with the performance and sent a message that she would be happy to meet Charles Dickens immediately afterward. He refused—on the grounds that he was still in the clothes he had worn for the farce and felt it would be disgraceful for him to appear before his queen dressed so inappropriately. She repeated her request after having dismissed his fears, but he refused a second time, on the same grounds. In the end, the Queen acceded to his will and left the theater without having made the acquaintance of one of her most famous subjects and perhaps secretly pleased that someone had stood up to her. Some years later, Charles Dickens would be received at court.[30]

The play was performed to the general public on July 11, 18, and 25. The audience adulation was intoxicating. It certainly proved so to Charles, who now hit upon the idea of taking the play on tour to Manchester. There were problems with this plan, however, the most striking being that women who appeared on stage could say goodbye to their good reputation. Perhaps he was regretting having allowed his daughters to act in public in London; people in polite society were discussing the impropriety of Katey and Mamie appearing as actresses and it would certainly have damaged their reputations. He may have felt exonerated because the London performances had been approved and sanctioned by Queen Victoria herself, but he could never have allowed his daughters to appear

---

30 His court dress outfit, complete with sword, can be seen on display at the Charles Dickens Museum in London and gives the viewer an insightful image of the writer.

on stage in the "provinces." In addition, he knew that the voices of his amateur actresses, not having been trained for the stage, would not carry to the back of a real theater. The male actors could remain the same, but it became apparent that, before anything else could be agreed upon, he and Wilkie Collins had to find replacements for the female roles. They needed to hire professional actresses.

As Katey approached her eighteenth birthday, she would have been thinking increasingly about what the future would hold. She was still breaking her heart over Edmund Yates, but, being very pretty, she was also receiving plenty of attention from would-be suitors. Katey knew she wanted to be an artist—and to be taken seriously, as a professional, despite being female. She was becoming a strong, forward-thinking young woman, used to receiving a certain amount of adulation, yet remarkably unspoiled for one who had been so singled out by her father; luckily, it also seems that none of her siblings resented her or Plorn for their father's obvious favoritism. Until now, she had lived a privileged and exhilarating life and had been looking forward to the future with myriad interesting plans. Katey was ill prepared for the shattering, almost unthinkable changes that were about to take place in her world.

7

"ARISING OUT OF WICKEDNESS, OR OUT OF FOLLY"

Charles Dickens first made the acquaintance of the Ternan family in the summer of 1857. He was introduced to them by a friend of Macready's, Alfred Wigan (an actor and playwright). Wigan suggested Mrs. Frances Ternan, a well-established, respected actress—who had performed with Macready—and two of her three daughters, Maria and Ellen, should act in Manchester (the eldest daughter, Fanny, was currently working). They were asked to play the roles in *The Frozen Deep* and *Uncle John* previously played by Georgina, Mamie, Katey, and Jessie Wills (wife of W. H. Wills).[31] After auditioning for Charles, the three Ternans were engaged with rapidity, and rehearsals began at once. The actresses became regular visitors to Tavistock House, where Charles would rehearse with them in the old schoolroom, and at the Gallery of Illustration, where rehearsals were held when possible. The Manchester performance would be of *The Frozen Deep*, followed by the farce *Uncle John*. Katey's role in the farce was to be played by the alluring Ellen Ternan, who was just a few months older than Katey. One of the stage directions instructed Charles' character to take Ellen's character in his arms, as though she were his daughter.

On August 20, the company of traveling players, with Catherine and Georgina along for the experience, traveled by train to Manchester. The performances were a huge success, selling out and earning extra funds

---

31 The eldest of the Ternan sisters was also called Fanny; she was a promising singer as well as an actress. Charles was to take an active interest in her career, paying for Fanny to receive singing instruction in Italy. She would go on to marry Thomas Trollope, widowed brother of the novelist Anthony Trollope.

for Douglas Jerrold's family. This was the excitement Charles craved. Not only was he intoxicated by the cheers of the audience, but he was also falling passionately in love with eighteen-year-old Ellen Ternan.

On the train back to London, in full view of Catherine and Georgina, Charles innocently inquired of Mrs. Ternan where the family would be performing next; she told him they were engaged to appear in Doncaster.

The actress Ellen Ternan, photographed at around the time she met Charles Dickens

On returning home Charles immediately set about arranging a tour with Wilkie Collins. It would be a travelogue, *The Lazy Tour of Two Idle Apprentices*; one of the places the two idle apprentices would be visiting was Doncaster.

During the Lazy Tour, Charles did a great deal of thinking about his marriage and seemed to come to the conclusion that it was, in fact, intolerable. He and Catherine had been growing apart for several years, but this sudden passion for a young, very attractive woman (who was the same age Catherine had been when he met her) was the spur he needed. The adulation of the Ternans, in particular Ellen, coupled with the adulation of the Manchester audiences, mingled in his mind to show him what he wanted from life and what was missing from his marriage. After twenty years of the realities of marriage, Catherine no longer revered or adored him as he felt he deserved. In addition, she had become unattractive in his mind, whereas Ellen was not only pretty but also extremely sexually alluring, blessed with the type of slim figure Charles so admired.

It appears the Ternans were genuinely surprised when Charles arrived backstage in Doncaster after a performance. Having renewed his acquaintance with them, he set about taking a great interest in their welfare and assisting their careers. Mrs. Ternan, a widow, who had had to contend with the fickleness of the theater all her life, was thrilled that her daughters were attracting the attention of such an influential patron. Charles insisted he was interested in the Ternans purely for philanthropic reasons. Mrs. Ternan can have been under no such illusions, but she must also have seen the very positive aspects of Charles' infatuation with her youngest daughter.

By the end of October 1857, Charles had decided his marriage was over. He did not, at this stage, tell Catherine; instead he set about writing to his friends, creating an opinion about their marriage that he hoped would exonerate him entirely from blame when the separation came. He wrote to his old friend Émile de la Rue, who had come to know the couple while they were staying in Genoa. At the time, Catherine had become jealous of Charles spending a quite unprecedented amount of time with Émile's wife, whom he was mesmerizing in order to "cure" her of a series of hallucinations. Madame de la Rue was apparently infatuated with

Charles, monopolizing his attention by insisting that she could not sleep safely unless she had been mesmerized by him, and constantly writing to him when they were apart, begging him to come and see her and her husband again as she claimed she felt unwell whenever he was away from them. It is understandable that Catherine had become jealous of a woman who was obviously so enchanted by Charles and was able to manipulate him so easily, but he now used this long-ago jealousy as proof that his marriage had become intolerable. In the same way that he constructed the plots of his books, he began to build up a picture of their marriage as one that had been, from its beginning, utterly insupportable, rather than just unhappy and troubled for many years. His passion for Ellen had led him to believe that he had long been feeling the claustrophobia that now assailed him. His letters are a cleverly constructed escape ladder, aimed at allowing him to exit the marriage with his reputation intact:

> *Between ourselves (I beckon Madame De la Rue nearer with my fore-finger, and whisper this with a serio-comic smile)* [he wrote to Émile], *I don't get on better in these later times with a certain poor lady you know of, than I did in the earlier Peschiere days. Much worse. Much worse! Neither do the children, elder or younger. Neither can she get on with herself, or be anything but unhappy. (She has been excruciatingly jealous of, and has obtained positive proofs of my being on the most confidential terms with, at least Fifteen Thousand Women of various conditions in life, every condition in life, since we left Genoa . . .) What we should do, or what the Girls would be, without Georgy, I cannot imagine. She is the active spirit of the house, and the children dote upon her. Enough of this. We put the Skeleton away in the cupboard, and very few people, comparatively, know of its existence.*

From the very beginning of his plot, he determined to paint a picture of Catherine as a bad mother, in order to remove any sympathy for her extended by his adoring friends and public. By portraying her, in addition, as a woman who suffered from jealous delusions, he hoped to keep Ellen's existence a secret from the outside world (and his public in particular). It was an extraordinarily cruel set of moves for someone who was so fierce an advocate of family life. That his children adored Georgina and she was invaluable in the house was undeniable, but it was Charles himself who had handed over most of his wife's responsibilities to her sister, ensuring that Catherine had few opportunities to make herself useful. Reports from friends who had visited the couple suggest that Charles had often made fun of Catherine in company; one even went so far as to say that he stopped visiting because he could not bear Charles' "cruelty" to her (although this comment must be looked upon with skepticism as it was made with many years' hindsight and not fully substantiated). Charles had so often criticized Catherine or made it plain that he found her tiresome that his behavior had helped to turn her into the unconfident, unhappy figure she became.

Quite deliberately, Charles humiliated Catherine in front of the servants and her children by making the decision to have the communicating door between their bedrooms sealed up. He did not discuss this with Catherine, or even tell her of his intention; instead he instructed his staff to see to it and let Catherine find out for herself. One imagines she must have tried the door and then alerted the staff to the fact that it was stuck. One of the servants had the unenviable task of explaining to her the master's instructions.

For Katey and her siblings, this was a bewildering and miserable time. Their father had become so unkind to their mother and so unapproachable to them that the atmosphere at home was desperate. Matters came to a head for Catherine when she was delivered a present from a jeweler used frequently by her husband. Charles had ordered a gold bracelet and, assuming quite naturally that it was for his client's wife, the jeweler delivered it to Catherine. It had been intended for Ellen. Added to the tension within the home was a sense of shame now that their friends and acquaintances were starting to hear rumors of the great Charles Dickens having an affair. Determined to save his and Ellen's reputations, Charles insisted Catherine call on the Ternans and thereby legitimize his friendship with them.

According to the version of events that Katey related many years later, she was passing her mother's bedroom door when she heard the familiar sound of Catherine sobbing; opening the door she saw her mother sitting in front of her dressing table, crying passionately. When Katey asked what was wrong, Catherine told her that she had been ordered to visit Ellen. Katey was incensed and told her mother she must not go; but Charles could be a tartar and Catherine was bullied into it.

Meanwhile, Charles' affection for Ellen was driving him to behave like a reckless teenager. He would decide he could not stand being in the same house as his wife and children, so would set out in the middle of the night to walk the twenty-odd miles to Gad's Hill. He would make every excuse to have contact with Ellen and her family, using his influence within theatrical circles to ensure she and her family were given work. He insisted to anyone who would listen that his feelings for Ellen were platonic, and seemed genuinely to believe that he was beyond scandal—his public adored him and he refused to believe they would stop doing so. He was infatuated enough to risk being seen out in public on his own with Ellen. He was observed wandering romantically across Hampstead Heath with Ellen on his arm; the person who spotted them was his own son Charley.

During the first half of 1858—perhaps as a result of this detection on the heath—Charles wrote a letter to his children, apparently informing them that he would not tolerate any innuendo about Ellen, that she was chaste and virtuous, that he was beyond reproach, and that it was Catherine who refused to understand the simple beauty of his relationship with the actress. This letter—perhaps the most literary example of a man claiming "my wife doesn't understand me"—has not survived the ravages of family editing.

At the start of May, Charles told Catherine that their marriage was over. It seems he had assured himself of Ellen's infatuation and now wanted to rid himself of Catherine officially. Catherine appealed to her parents for help and her mother (also called Georgina Hogarth) moved into the family home to try to negotiate with Charles; he moved out and started living temporarily in the office of his newspaper, *Household Words*, on Wellington Street, Covent Garden.

On May 9, 1858, Charles wrote about the separation to Angela Burdett-Coutts, who would, he knew, be affronted at him breaking up the family. He must have spent a great deal of time agonizing over and perfecting this letter, aimed at appealing to her as a friend and attempting to win her over to his "side." She was an intelligent, shrewd woman, who was fortunate enough to be truly independent. He knew she would not simply take his version at face value, so he included seemingly caring words about Catherine and disingenuously begged Angela not to think the worse of Catherine after reading it. The letter makes for uncomfortable reading and shook many of my own beliefs about Charles Dickens:

You have been too near and dear a friend to me for many years [he begins the letter]*, and I am bound to you by too many ties of grateful and affectionate regard, to admit of my any longer keeping silence to you on a sad domestic topic. I believe you are not quite unprepared for what I am going to say, and will, in the main, have anticipated it.*

I believe my marriage has been for years and years as miserable a one as ever was made. I believe that no two people were ever created, with such an impossibility of interest, sympathy, confidence, sentiment, tender union of any kind between them, as there is between my wife and me. It is an immense misfortune to her—it is an immense misfortune to me—but Nature has put an insurmountable barrier between us, which never in this world can be thrown down.

You know me too well to suppose that I have the faintest thought of influencing you on either side. I merely mention a fact which may induce you to pity us both, when I tell you that she is the only person I have ever known with whom I could not get on somehow or other, and in communicating with whom I could not find some way to a kind of interest. You know I have many impulsive faults which often belong to my impulsive way of life and exercise of fancy; but I am very patient and considerate at heart, and would have beaten a path to a better journey's end than we have come to, if I could.

We have been virtually separated for a long time. We must put a wider space between us now, than can be found in one house.

If the children loved her, or ever had loved her, this severance would have been a far easier thing than it is. But she has never attached one of them to herself, never played with them in their infancy, never attracted their confidence as they have grown older, never presented herself before them in the aspect of a mother. I have seen them fall off from her in a natural—not an unnatural—progress of estrangement, and at this moment I believe that Mary and Katey (whose dispositions are of the gentlest and most affectionate conceivable) harden into stone figures of girls when they can be got to go near her, and have their hearts shut up in her presence as if they closed by some horrid spring.

No one can understand this, but Georgina who has seen it grow from year to year, and who is the best, the most unselfish, and the most devoted of human Creatures. Her sister Mary, who died suddenly and who lived with us before her, understood it as well though in the first months of our marriage. It is her misery to live in some fatal atmosphere which slays every one to whom she should be dearest. It is my misery that no one can understand the truth in its full force, or know what a blighted and wasted life my marriage has been.

Forster is trying what he can, to arrange matters with her mother. But I know that the mother herself could not live with her. I am perfectly sure that her younger sister and brother could not live with her. An old servant of ours is the only hope I see, as she took care of her, like a poor child, for sixteen years. But she is married now, and I doubt her being afraid that the companionship would wear her to death. Macready used to get on better with her than anyone else, and sometimes I have a fancy that she may think of him and his sister. To suggest them to her would be to inspire her with an instant determination never to go near them.

In the mean time I have come for a time to the office, to leave her Mother free to do what she can at home, towards the getting of her away to some happier mode of existence if possible. They all know that I will do anything for her comfort, and spend anything upon her.

It is a relief to me to have written this to you. Don't think the worse of me; don't think the worse of her. I am firmly persuaded that it is not within the compass of her character and faculties, to be other than she is. If she had married another sort of man, she might however have done better. I think she has always felt herself at the disadvantage of groping blindly about me and never touching me, and so has fallen into the most miserable weaknesses and jealousies. Her mind has, at times, been certainly confused besides.

It is a nasty, self-satisfied letter in which Charles takes no responsibility at all for the breakdown of the marriage and even plays the low card of evoking the spirit of the dead Mary against her sister—something entirely belied by Mary's own words just months before she died. Mary had written a letter to her cousin, on January 26, 1837, in which she demonstrates absolutely no belief that anything was wrong between Charles and Catherine; in fact, it suggests quite the opposite: "she has everything in the world to make her comfortable and happy—her husband is kindness itself to her and is constantly studying her comfort in every thing." Mary's letters also show how much she adored her sister. Even Charles' own mother had had no idea anything was wrong in the marriage. When ill, Charles' parents were attended by a Dr. Davey. The doctor's wife was to recall: "Mrs. Dickens was very fond of her daughter-in-law . . . and has often told me that 'there was not another woman in all England so well suited to her son.'" (It has to be admitted, though, that Elizabeth must have been almost alone among Charles and Catherine's acquaintance in believing their marriage still to be perfect.)

In the age of sexual inequality in which he lived, Charles knew he could have had Catherine committed as insane if he chose: After all, there was her history of post-natal depression. There is a sneaking undertone to his letter to Angela Burdett-Coutts—with his comment about her being "confused"—that he is being terribly magnanimous in choosing not to do so. As to Catherine being the only person he had ever been unable to get on with, even his closest friend would have known this to be a ludicrous claim. A brief glance through his letters will come up with frequent—and amusing—comments about people he could not stand to be near, including several of their own house guests, such as the irritating Susan, sister of Mrs. Macready; Hans Christian Andersen; and even John Forster.

For Charles to suggest not only that Catherine's children could not abide her, but also that even her own mother would be unable to live with her was cruel in the extreme. Although Mamie was sadly hardened against her mother (unsurprising for one so easily led that she had been influenced by the father and aunt she adored), this was not the case with Katey.[32]

---

32 Mamie wrote two books about her father, *My Father as I Recall Him* and *Charles Dickens by his Eldest Daughter*. In neither one does she mention her mother except in passing. The only story she chooses to relate about Catherine is one that shows Charles up in a funny light, as an impetuous young man courting her. It is sad to read them and realize how completely Mamie chose to erase her mother from her life.

On May 25, Charles wrote a letter to Arthur Smith, who managed his reading tours and was a fairly recent friend (this latter meant that, crucially, he had loyalty to Charles, not Catherine). The letter was not intended—so Charles said—for publication. It was, he insisted, purely for Smith to show to "any one who wishes to do me right, or any one who may have been misled into doing me wrong." It is very hard to believe that Charles Dickens, the self-publicist and newspaper editor, could possibly have believed that a copy of the letter would not be leaked to the newspapers. Yet, when the inevitable happened, he claimed to be distraught and from then onward referred to it as "the Violated Letter." The name remains to this day. Published in the American papers at once, it took three months to get through to the British press. The letter contains the following passages:

> *Mrs. Dickens and I have lived unhappily together for many years. Hardly any one who has known us intimately can fail to have known that we are, in all respects of character and temperament, wonderfully unsuited to each other. I suppose that no two people, not vicious in themselves, were ever joined together, who had a greater difficulty in understanding one another, or who had less in common.... Nothing has, on many occasions, stood between us and a separation but Mrs. Dickens' sister, Georgina Hogarth. From the age of fifteen, she has devoted herself to our house and our children. She has been their playmate, nurse, instructress, friend, protectress, adviser and companion. In the manly consideration towards Mrs. Dickens which I owe to my wife, I will merely remark of her that the peculiarity of her character has thrown all the children on some one else. I do not know—I cannot by any stretch of fancy imagine—what would have become of them but for this aunt ... who has sacrificed the best part of her youth and life to them.... For some years past Mrs. Dickens has been in the habit of representing to me that it would be better for her to go away and live apart; that her always increasing estrangement made a mental disorder under which she sometimes labors [sic]— more, that she felt herself unfit for the life she had to lead as my wife, and that she would be better far away. I have uniformly replied that we must bear our misfortune, and fight the fight out to the end; that*

the children were the first consideration, and that I feared they must bind us together "in appearance."

This letter seems incredible when compared with one Charles wrote after the death of baby Dora. At that time he wrote to John Forster, "[Catherine] is so good and amiable that I hope it may not hurt her." Katey's later comments about her mother also portray Catherine as a gentle, kind woman who "never rebuked me." "There was nothing wrong with my mother," Katey would recall many years later. "She had her faults, of course, as we all have—but she was a sweet, kind, peace-loving woman, a lady—a lady born." One of the faults Katey remembered was that their mother was too solicitous and too much of a worrier, convinced that any minor scrape or graze might be a life-threatening injury. This could not bear less relation to Charles' version of her.

Mamie, now almost nineteen, was nonetheless her father's dutiful daughter. She attempted to shut out the misery of the separation, clinging ever closer to Auntie Georgy and beginning to shun her mother as she could see her father wanted. It was a dreadful situation for children to be placed in. Katey resisted as much as she could, but even she was forced to back down eventually. She, like Mamie, adored her father; she had always hero-worshipped him and he had made no secret of his adoration for her. She did, however, also love her now-humiliated mother and being made to choose between the two was devastating. Katey's determination not to abandon her mother drove, for the very first time, a wedge between her and her father. Later she would famously comment, "My father did not understand women." Charles was obviously finding it very difficult at this time to understand his younger daughter.

Henry, who was only nine when his parents separated, wrote passionately in adult life that the treatment of his mother was not as bad as the media liked to make it seem: "All I desire to say about it is this: that both in my father's lifetime, with his full knowledge and acquiescence, as well as after his death, I used regularly to visit my dear mother at her house in Gloucester Crescent, Regent's Park, and that we lived on terms of mutual affection until her death." The older children saw it very differently. Charley took Catherine's part most prominently by living with her; Mamie, as we have seen, stayed silent; and Katey later wrote, "we were *all* very wicked" not to take the part of "my poor, poor mother." Katey also said Catherine "was afraid of my father. She was never allowed to express an opinion—never allowed to say what she felt." Katey wished she had "been more kind to her," and Alfred, who was an impressionable thirteen-year-old in that bewildering year, was to write in 1911: "Our dear mother . . . suffered very much." Katey later commented that all her younger siblings were "kept in ignorance as to what was going on" and that Henry "was only a boy at the time, and does not realise the grief it was to our mother, after having all her children, to go away and leave us."

Apparently unaware that he was making a fool of himself over a girl young enough to be his own child, Charles began to fantasize, seeing himself in the role of a knight on a white charger rescuing the grateful princess. Dropping the pretense employed in the letter to Émile de la Rue, he wrote a quite astonishing letter to this effect, to his friend Mrs. Watson:

> *I wish an ogre with seven heads . . . had taken the Princess whom I adore—you have no idea how intensely I love her! . . . Nothing would suit me half so well this day, as climbing after her, sword in hand, and either winning her or being killed.*

To Wilkie Collins, Charles wrote, "I have not known a moment's peace or contentment, since the last night of *The Frozen Deep*. I do not suppose that there ever was a man so seized and rendered."

For Katey and Mamie, the knowledge that their father was sexually attracted to a girl their own age must have been utterly distasteful. Children are never happy to think about their parents' sex life and, in the nineteenth century, sex was a subject seldom discussed between the generations. The humiliation of their mother would also have been increasingly hard to bear for Katey. In a little over fifteen years, Catherine had given birth to ten children, as well as suffering at least two miscarriages. It is no wonder she did not have the energy of her childfree younger sister, nor that she lost the slim figure she had possessed when Charles married her. Toward the end of their marriage he had often made cruel jokes about her size and stupidity while praising Georgina to the hilt as his helpmeet and savior.

Both Katey and Mamie—by dint of being female—would undoubtedly have cringed at the way their father spoke about their mother and the way he made no secret of preferring the company of her sister, of Ellen and, for that matter, almost any other young attractive woman.

When looking at Charles' writing from this time and the way he treated not only his wife, but also several of his closest friends, it seems that he was undergoing an emotional breakdown. His behavior became cruel and unfathomable. In June, Charles wrote an article about the "slander" he claimed people were saying about him. The article was published in *The Times* and *Household Words* (his own magazine) that summer. Both Yates and Forster had advised him not to do so, but Charles was determined. Catherine was not consulted, merely shown the finished article. Her solicitors attempted to delay publication, but it was too late. Those editors who refused to publish the article experienced Charles' wrath; among them were his own publishers, Bradbury and Evans, who also published *Punch* (of which Mark Lemon was editor). As a result of their loyalty to Catherine by not publishing it, Charles left Bradbury and Evans and returned to his previous publishers, Chapman & Hall. This move marked the beginning of a rift with Uncle Mark, too. The article contained the now-famous passage:

> *By some means, arising out of wickedness, or out of folly, or out of inconceivable wild chance, or out of all three, this trouble has been the occasion of misrepresentations, mostly grossly false, most monstrous, and most cruel—involving, not only me, but innocent persons dear to my heart. . . . I most solemnly declare, then—and this I do both in my own name and in my wife's name—that all the lately whispered rumours touching the trouble, at which I have glanced, are abominably false. And whosoever repeats one of them after this denial, will lie as wilfully and as foully as it is possible for any false witness to lie, before heaven and earth.*

The article seems to have done more to fan the flames of suspicion than lay them to rest. It suggested far more than it denied and damaged Charles' reputation, and that of his family, even further. Those who had previously been in ignorance of the scandal—and there were many—now began to discuss it. That autumn, the Violated Letter was also published in British newspapers. For the Dickens children, the contents of the letter and article, as well as the fact that most of the literate world was privy to their family's shame and grief, was horrendous.

Georgina Hogarth's role during this tumultuous time will forever remain a conundrum. When Charles decided to separate from Catherine, the wronged wife's family rallied around her, as could be expected—all of the Hogarths, that is, except for Georgina. It appears that from the start Catherine's closest sister (since Mary's death), who had shared her home and her life for so many years, did not take Catherine's side, nor offer her any form of support. Instead, she elected to stay living with her brother-in-law, as his housekeeper, after he had rejected and humiliated her sister. Why she chose to be shunned by her parents, grandparents, and siblings in order to stay with her sister's husband has never been satisfactorily explained, nor how she could be so deliberately cruel to Catherine. As one of three sisters myself, it is something I cannot understand. When I was a child, it was still maintained within the family that Georgina was Charles' mistress and the reason for the marriage breaking up; but that was before the existence of Ellen Ternan was officially accepted and, with the publication of such books as Michael Slater's *Dickens and Women* and Claire Tomalin's *The Invisible Woman*, any suggestion that Georgina was Charles' mistress was refuted. It is likely, however, that the unmarried Georgina was in love with him, so deeply in love that she trusted him to take the place of her parents and siblings. It must also be considered that, had Georgina left the household, as an unmarried woman with limited income she would have had a particularly dull and miserable life.

Years later, Anny Thackeray was to tell her daughter Hester that there was no doubt in her mind that Georgina had been in love with Charles. Anny, by the time of the separation a very intelligent and observant woman of twenty, had been a regular visitor to the Dickens household since early childhood; she was perhaps better placed than most observers to know what was going on.

Whether what Georgina felt for Charles was sexual love cannot be proved. The fact that she became very good friends with Ellen Ternan seems to contradict the notion that she wanted Charles for herself—although she also knew that, had she not, Charles would have banished her, as he had her sister. There is also the indisputable fact that Georgina wanted desperately to keep hold of the children she had raised for so many years—particularly in light of the fact that she was now of an age when she could no longer have children herself. In addition, she had built for herself a very attractive career: that of housekeeper to one of the most famous men in the world. Living with Charles' family meant she had a very comfortable home in a fashionable part of London with all its attendant luxuries, a house in the country, housekeeping money, a dress allowance, theater trips, dinner invitations, parties, many exciting journeys abroad, and the exalted position of being Charles Dickens' most trusted adviser. It seems that Georgy had begun to believe Charles' version of her sister, to allow his comments to overcome the memories of Catherine and her growing up together.

Or maybe her behavior stemmed from an entirely different source, a childhood resentment or envy, of which we know nothing. The latter would explain a cruel letter Georgina wrote, in May 1858, in the midst of the family's breakdown. It was to Charles' old love Maria Winter, to whom Georgina does not seem to have become particularly close. One cannot help speculating if it was written at the request of her brother-in-law and if he helped her to compose it; certainly it is very similar in tone to the one Charles himself wrote to Angela Burdett-Coutts. It contains the passage:

> Unhappily . . . by some constitutional misfortune & incapacity, my sister always from their infancy, threw her children upon other people, consequently as they grew up, there was not the usual strong tie between them and her . . . in short, for many years, although we have put a good face upon it, we have been very miserable at home.

It is interesting that Georgina chose to write this letter to the one woman who would be expected to have little affection for Catherine, who had only recently come back into their lives, and who had barely any knowledge of the Dickens children. It is a cruel, gloating letter from a childless woman who had observed first-hand the difficulties occasioned by Catherine's constant pregnancies and agonizing births, as well as the way in which her husband had forcibly removed from Catherine the opportunities to spend time with her children. Beginning with their trip to America, he had often insisted Catherine be with him instead of with

Georgina Hogarth, sketched as she looked in character for one of her amateur dramatic performances. The drawing is by Charles Allston Collins.

the children. It was not unusual for a Victorian mother of Catherine's social standing to expect others to raise her children for her; it did not mean she loved them any the less.[33]

One can also imagine that Georgina's own feelings about her family, in particular about her parents and Catherine, underwent a radical change as a consequence of their behavior toward her when the marriage ended. Not only did they accuse her of turning Charles against Catherine, but there was also even the suggestion that it was they who were spreading rumors she was his mistress (although it does seem unlikely that Georgina's family would have chosen to create scandal against themselves).

When a Scottish newspaper wrote an article claiming Georgina was Charles' mistress—and that she had given birth to three children by him—Charles was moved to act. He started organizing a legal case against the paper, and this culminated in Georgina undergoing a medical examination to prove she was still a virgin. She was.[34] The humiliation, pain, and violation of this examination—which would have been carried out by a male doctor—turned her farther against her family, who did not deny the rumors, and who she possibly believed had actually started them.

Despite the impassioned letter Charles had written her, Angela Burdett-Coutts was not won over. She was not as susceptible as Charles believed and refused to take the letter at face value. She must also have been appalled by the Violated Letter, Charles' article, and the very public way in which he was humiliating his wife. She continued to see Catherine after the separation and to plead on her behalf that she be allowed to see her children more frequently. After Catherine (accompanied by several

---

33 This unpleasant picture of Georgy is not, however, a typical portrait. By contrast, her nieces and nephews left several glowing reports of her kindness and selflessness. Charles described her as "the best and truest friend a man ever had," and the majority of her own letters suggest that she was a pleasant, genuine woman who willingly sacrificed herself to overseeing the welfare of her sister's children. While Katey never turned against her aunt, who remained her confidante and friend until death, she did not approve of the way in which her mother was treated and of her aunt's role in it. Toward the end of her own life, she gave her opinion vociferously that a wife's sister should "never, never, never" move into the marital home and she commented to Gladys Storey that Georgina "was not quite straight." For many years there were rumors that Charles sent so many of his sons to live abroad in adulthood because Georgy wanted to get rid of them, but this was furiously denied, after their father's death, by the adult Dickens children.

34 Henry Fielding Dickens was later to tell Gladys Storey that the certificate of Georgina's virginity was among his family papers. The case was never taken to court.

of her distraught children) visited Angela to beg her to plead their case, Angela wrote to Charles, delicately suggesting that it was unfair of him to expect the children to live without their mother and that she could see from their behavior in her home that they truly loved Catherine. Charles replied furiously that they had been acting out a "charade" at Catherine's insistence, purely to dupe Angela.

One wonders if Angela Burdett-Coutts's sentiments would have been more on a par with those of Elizabeth Barrett Browning, who wrote in a letter: "What is this sad story about Dickens and his wife? Incompatibility of temper after twenty-three years of married life? What a plea! . . . Poor woman! She must suffer bitterly—that is sure." Miss Burdett-Coutts's initial reaction upon reading a letter that described his marriage as "blighted and wasted," when she knew well it had produced ten children, is unlikely to have been one of unmitigated sympathy.

While the whole of London was amusing itself with the latest gossip about that moralist and philanthropist Charles Dickens—the man who had set himself up as the standard of family life—Katey was miserably living through it. The tension was indescribable; her father was ripping her mother to pieces and she, a young female not yet of age and with no financial security except her father's money, was powerless to do anything to stop it.[35] She may have stamped her foot and insisted that her mother "shall not go" to see Ellen Ternan, but in reality her furious orders could—and would—always be ignored. In addition, she was pining for the arrogant Edmund Yates and longing to be out of the sadness of her family home.

She must have been extremely grateful to—but equally envious of—Charley. Now aged twenty-one and employed, he refused to accede to his father's demands and had no legal compulsion to do so, unlike all his younger siblings. Instead, he chose to live with his mother and they moved into her new home at 70 Gloucester Crescent, near Regent's Park. Charles was furious about it, although he swiftly turned it to his advantage, telling friends that he had "persuaded" Charley to live with his mother. Charley was doing it, he reported, as "an act of duty." Charles

---

35 The age of majority was then twenty-one.

had referred to the situation in the Violated Letter, keeping face by writing: "My elder children all understand it perfectly, and all accept it as invincible. There is not a shadow of doubt or concealment among us—my eldest son and I are one, as to it all." At the end of the letter he reiterated: "There is not a shadow of doubt or concealment between my children and me. All is open and plain among us, as though we were brothers and sisters. They are perfectly certain that I would not deceive them, and the confidence among us is without a fear."

Behind this bravado, Charles was furious with his son. In December 1858 Charley wrote a piece for *Punch* about the Thackeray/Yates affair—a quarrel between the two men in which Charles had publicly supported Yates. In his article, Charley took Thackeray's side. Charley seems to have despised Edmund Yates, no doubt partly because of Katey's heartbreak, but also because Yates had very deliberately set about creating a rift between Thackeray and Dickens. Incensed by the article, Charles took malicious revenge upon his own son for what he saw as a lack of loyalty: He removed Charley's name from the list of potential new members of the Garrick Club—just as it was about to come up for election. Charley had been waiting patiently to become a member, and membership opportunities were scarce. Charles' step effectively ruined Charley's chances of ever becoming a member; if his name were resubmitted, it would take many years to get back up to the top of the list. One cannot help speculating that Charles' vindictive act had less to do with the Edmund Yates affair than it had with Charley's decision to stand by his mother. A sympathetic and grateful Thackeray wrote a letter to a friend, stating, "the poor boy is very much cast down at his father's proceedings."

Despite his father's vengeful behavior, Charley was a diplomatic and caring young man desperate to maintain good relations with both of his parents. As the months passed he would write dutifully to his father and visit the rest of the family regularly, flattering Charles' ego and allowing him to believe that he still controlled his son's decisions; eventually the rift between them started to heal.

With Catherine residing in London, Charles determined to live mostly in the country, which meant that Gad's Hill then became the family's home. They still spent time in London, but the house in Kent became the base for family life. In Kent, people were more forgiving than the cynics and gossips in town; they were thrilled to have a celebrity—and such an amenable celebrity, at that—livening up their community. Charles and his family were taken to the hearts of the Kentish people as if they and their ancestors had all been born there; in return, the Dickenses took a great interest in local life. The nearest towns to Gad's Hill were Higham and Rochester (a place Charles often used as a setting for his books), and the residents of both towns and the surrounding countryside became used to the sight of the author marching off on one of his many long walks, accompanied by an excitable pack of dogs.

Despite his comments to Angela Burdett-Coutts about Catherine being the only person in the world he could not get on with, Charles soon set about rowing with most of his friends and acquaintances. Mark Lemon was already being seen by Charles as disloyal, because of *Punch's* refusal to print his article about the separation fiasco. At the time of the separation Charles himself had asked Mark to help Catherine by finding her legal assistance, but he suddenly decided that, by helping her, Mark was siding with the enemy and Charles cut him out of his life completely. This was yet another devastation for Katey and her siblings as Charles forbade them to have anything to do with the Lemon family from that day forth. Katey had not only lost her mother, but also now she was to lose Uncle Mark, Helen, and her long-time playmates Lally and Betty. The days of running in and out of each other's homes were forcibly over. She was already defying her father by visiting her mother, and the prospect of being found in the company of the Lemons was too frightening to contemplate.

Then there was Thackeray. The rift caused after the insidious Edmund Yates had begun trouble between the two friends (by getting into an argument with Thackeray and then pleading with Charles to fight his cause) had not yet healed. On that occasion, Thackeray felt understandably indignant at one of his oldest friends siding with someone he must have regarded as an impudent young upstart who had insinuated his way into Charles' life. The dispute still rankled and now, with his life in turmoil and his mental state precarious, Charles became heated over an unfortunate incident. According to Thackeray's version, he had overheard some men at the Garrick Club gossiping about the separation. They were saying Charles had pushed Catherine out of the home so he could carry on an affair with Georgina. Eager to redress the damage and to protect Georgina's reputation, Thackeray confidently said, "No such thing—it's with an actress," misguidedly thinking he was doing Charles a favor. When Charles heard just the latter part of the story, that Thackeray was telling people about Ellen, he became incensed at what he considered Thackeray's rumor-mongering and lack of loyalty. He refused to listen to Thackeray's explanation and ended their friendship. The bewildered Thackeray was left reeling and Charles' children were forbidden to have anything to do with him.

Whether she defied her father at this date or whether her friendship with Thackeray's daughters was rekindled after Katey left home is uncertain. The fact that neither Anny nor Minny would speak to Charles for several years suggests Katey and Mamie had been forbidden to see them also, and they continued their friendship in secret. Since the Thackeray girls happened to be out of London for many months around the time of the separation, there would have been little opportunity for them to meet in any case.[36] Two years later, after moving out of her father's home, Katey would forge a strong bond with Thackeray himself, trying to heal the broken friendship between him and her father.

The atmosphere in the Dickens household was one of turbulence, sadness, and uncertainty. Katey later commented, "My father was like a madman when my mother left home." Of the start of his relationship with Ellen she said, "This affair brought out all that was worst—all that was weakest in him. He did not care a damn what happened to any of us. Nothing could surpass the misery and unhappiness of our home." Mark Lemon believed that "the applause when he acted turned Dickens' head" and several of his former acquaintances, fellow journalists who worked on *Punch* and knew Charles through the Garrick Club, made comments about his "arrogance," saying that he seemed to believe he was God. One such commentator announced, "If he is [God] we are atheists." A few months after Charles had quarreled with Thackeray, the latter wrote to a

---

36 The earliest surviving letters between them date from 1864, so it is not possible to say with certainty what happened to their friendship in the late 1850s.

friend about Charles' mental state: "I'm not even angry with Dickens now. . . . He can't help hating me; and he can't help being a—you know what I daresay. . . . His quarrel with his wife has driven him almost frantic."

For Katey, it felt as though her father was slowly becoming insane and attempting to cut her off from almost everyone she held dear. After hearing rumors that Catherine's family was "slandering" him and discussing his behavior in public, Charles banned his children from going anywhere near the Hogarths, in particular their grandmother and aunt Helen. This was especially heartbreaking, as Helen Hogarth was very close to Katey in age—her senior by only six years—and aunt and niece had been close. Katey's nineteenth year was turning into a nightmare.

To enter the next phase of Katey's life, we must return now to the dinner party held by Wilkie Collins's mother in 1852. That appears to have been the first time that Charles met Wilkie's brother, Charles Allston Collins—known as "Charlie"—the Pre-Raphaelite artist. Since then, Charles had taken an interest in the younger man and for some time Charlie had been an intimate of the Dickens family. Charles had begun actively promoting Charlie's career and the rest of the family had grown exceedingly fond of him. As a young man, Charlie had shared lodgings with John Everett Millais and William Holman Hunt. He was even present at the early discussions about setting up the Pre-Raphaelite Brotherhood, many of which took place at his mother's house. When James Collinson left the group, Charlie's name was instantly put forward by Millais, but it seems Charlie was not viewed so favorably by the rest of the clique and he was never elected a member of the PRB. His mother, Harriet Collins, was a great favorite with Charlie's friends, more than one of whom proclaimed himself in love with her. She had a great enthusiasm for life and reveled in hosting parties for members of London's literary and artistic circles. She was also delighted at a moment's notice, despite her somewhat limited income, to provide a hearty tea for groups of hungry artists, most of whom were living well beyond their means and some of whom often went without food in order to buy painting materials.

At these tea parties, Harriet was more of a draw than her younger son, who seems often to have been made the butt of jokes by the rest of the group. She "enjoyed nothing more than to sit talking and flirting with the boys far into the night, while they smoked and drank their wine. Hunt and Millais pretended to compete for her favors, and all three soon shared 'rollicking jokes.'" In contrast, her younger son was a shy, awkward man whose gawkiness was often seen as standoffishness. He was a good-looking, slender, red-haired man who was often sickly and possessed what seemed to his peers annoyingly ascetic leanings and a tendency to take himself too seriously. William Holman Hunt described Charlie as "slight, with slender limbs, but erect in the head and shoulders, beautifully cut features, large chin, a crop of orange-coloured hair (latterly a beard), blue eyes that looked at a challenger without a sign of quailing." In 1850, he had joined John Millais, his brother William Millais and William Holman Hunt on a painting trip to Surrey, staying in lodgings for several weeks; Millais was painting the background for his famous *Ophelia* at the time. The others found Charlie extremely trying, as he was going through a period of self-denial. He was teased incessantly on the evening he refused blackberry tart, which the others knew was his favorite pudding. Millais' son later recorded the incident in his father's biography:

> *Millais, knowing that [Charles Collins] was very fond of this dish, ridiculed his 'mortifying the flesh' and becoming so much of an ascetic. It was bad for him, he said, and his health was suffering in consequence; to which he humorously added, that he thought Collins kept a whip upstairs and indulged in private flagellations.*

One of Millais' diary entries written on the painting trip recorded an evening on which his brother dozed in a chair, Holman Hunt wrote letters, Millais himself read Shakespeare, and Charlie Collins piously read the Bible. Wilkie Collins came to visit them during this trip and was appalled to see how thin his brother had become from fasting. One of Millais' letters, written once they had returned to London, reveals that he knows Charlie is an "excellent waltzer and polka dancer" but that he refuses to dance anything but "a very solemn quadrille." This type of ascetic behavior, with denial performed as a religious and personal act of piety, infuriated his friends. It was probably for this reason that the other Pre-Raphaelites refused to accept Charlie as a member of the PRB.[37]

Despite this, Charlie was one of Millais' favored companions at this time (although some of the latter's letters reveal his frustration with Charlie's inability to be happy and, on a couple of occasions, he describes him as a "lay figure"—the static wooden model artists used in place of a real model). The less talented artist obviously hero-worshipped his genius friend, and he seems never to have been happier than when the two of them were alone, with no boisterous, sharp-tongued members of the PRB to deride him. In 1850, Millais' witty letters describe how frustrated he and Charlie were becoming by the conditions of painting in the countryside. Charlie in particular, he said, was bothered by "flies and children" and they were both succumbing to an "excess of misery brought on by breathing *pure* country air. We acknowledge to be real London Cockneys and long to imbibe city atmosphere, see smoky faces, square vegetation, dead leaves and green railings." He jokes that they will soon be alcoholics as the inclination to drink is almost insurmountable and that the only way they can find pleasure is by reading *The Pickwick Papers*, which is "*so funny.*" Neither of them could have dreamed at this time how closely allied they would become to the man who had written *Pickwick*.

Charlie had exhibited at the Royal Academy for the first time in 1847—the year of his father's death—and continued to exhibit until 1855. His most famous painting, *Convent Thoughts* (1850), now at the Ashmolean in Oxford, shows a novice nun in a garden, contemplating her future. John Ruskin was particularly enthusiastic about it because of the realism of its botanical details. Charlie's work was exacting and painstakingly created; he was also his own fiercest critic, which meant he was seldom able to finish a painting to his satisfaction. Perhaps it was for this reason that, although he was an extremely talented artist, Charlie had determined to give up painting and set his heart on being a writer instead. By the end of the 1850s, Charles Dickens had started to help him with

---

37 Diana Holman Hunt (granddaughter of William) was told that Charlie was so sure he would be accepted that he made a sketch of Millais and wrote "PRB" alongside his signature. He also signed one of his letters to Holman Hunt in the same way. Diana heard that it was Thomas Woolner, the sculptor, who "fought savagely and successfully against his election" and that Charlie was deeply upset.

this aspiration by commissioning him to write articles for the periodical he edited, *All The Year Round*.

In the early 1850s, Charlie had fallen for the highly principled and deeply religious Maria Rossetti, older sister of the poet Christina and the artist Dante Gabriel Rossetti. He was rebuffed and blamed her lack of interest on his red hair, which he attempted to dye. Holman Hunt assisted him, but they had far less success using hair dye than they did making their own painting colors. Wilkie had hoped that after the break-up with Maria his younger brother would shake off his High Church high-mindedness, but this was not to be. Charlie became even more religious, behaving in a fashion that Millais described as "monkish nonsense."

Over the ensuing few years, however, his religious leanings gradually became less marked, and Wilkie was highly relieved when, toward the end of the 1850s, Charlie discovered a compatibility of mind with Katey,

Convent Thoughts (1850) by Charles
Allston Collins

with whom he became good friends. No doubt Charlie was grateful to find a woman who treated him warmly and admired him for his artistic ability—he had for so long been the butt of "friendly" jokes among his peers (almost all of whom had become a great deal more successful than he). Wilkie later recorded that this friendship with Katey coincided with his brother's belief that he *ought* to settle down. Charlie had passed his thirtieth birthday and many of his friends were now married with children.

For Katey, Charlie Collins was a sympathetic shoulder during her worst times. Added to the misery of her parents' separation was the attendant scandal, which meant that she and Mamie had become social pariahs, derided as unnatural daughters for not staying with their mother. Their new position was all the more keenly felt because, as the daughters of a celebrity, they had until now been so fêted. Just as Katey had been starting to think about marriage, most potential suitors had been turned against the very idea of allying themselves to the name Dickens. Katey and Mamie's great-aunt (on Catherine's side) wrote in a letter of the girls' behavior:

> *they, poor girls, have . . . been flattered as being taken notice of as the daughters of a popular author. He . . . is a caressing father and indulgent in trifles, and they in their ignorance of the world look no further nor are aware of the injury he does them.*

Perhaps as a result of her unhappy family home and her rejection by Edmund Yates, Katey started to look for love elsewhere. She began to develop a reputation as a flirt and was derided as "the fast Miss Dickens." She had many admirers and was not averse to spending time on her own with men, without a chaperone, in an age when such behavior was considered scandalous. She later admitted that she was a practiced flirt who often took delight in making men think she was in love with them when she wasn't. No doubt she hoped that her father, who was by now spending an increasing amount of time with—or thinking about—Ellen, would start to notice her again.

Katey's behavior at this time is interestingly reminiscent of her father's behavior in America. Charles had often shocked straitlaced American society—he "was not refined enough for the best Boston circles," according to one observer (whereas Catherine "showed signs of having been born and bred her husband's social superior"). Charles' overenthusiastic and bawdy wit had appalled his fellow diners at a smart dinner party:

> *In the course of the entertainment a discussion arose among the gentlemen as to which was the more beautiful woman, the Duchess of Sutherland or Mrs. Caroline Norton. 'Well, I don't know,' said Dickens, expanding himself in his green velvet waistcoat: 'Mrs. Norton perhaps is the most beautiful; but the duchess, to my mind, is the more kissable person.' Had a bombshell dropped upon Judge Prestcott's dinner-table it could hardly have startled the company more than this remark.*

It is easy to see from this story where Katey inherited her wild streak and the desire to shock those she felt were already judging her. It seems Charles had felt like a fish out of water in certain elements of American society and that Katey was feeling the same in this new version of London society that no longer revered her as the daughter of a great man. Like her father, she was kicking against the constraints, refusing to kowtow to society's restrictions. She had realized that her card was well and truly marked by her parents' separation and there was nothing she could do to wipe it clean. Perhaps this explains why she took such pains not to conform: She knew she was beaten either way, so she might as well enjoy life.

Mamie seems to have behaved quite differently, retreating into herself and waiting dutifully for her father to come home, so she could be there for him. I think Mamie must have been hoping at this time, as she sided with Charles and did everything he ordered, that she would finally beat Katey to the position of favorite daughter.[38] The views fashionable London held about Katey and Mamie after their parents' separation can

---

38 Sadly, even Mamie had to admit (after her father's death) that Katey was the one who always wore that title. In her book *My Father As I Recall Him* she wrote, "I have been spoken of as my father's 'favorite [sic] daughter.' If he had a favorite daughter—and I hope and believe the one was as dear to him as the other—my dear sister must claim that honor [sic]."

be read in a malicious gossipy letter. It was written to the publisher John Blackwood by a critic named E. S. Dallas:

The great fun I think is to see how Dickens backs up Yates, & how his jealousy of Thackeray comes out. Surely that man will one of these days blow his brains out. With the exception of a few toadies there is not a soul to take his part. They cut him at the clubs. His daughters—now under the benign wing of their aunt, Miss Hogarth—are not received into society. You would be excessively amused if you heard all the gigantic efforts the family make to keep their foot in the world—how they call upon people they never called on before & that they have treated with the most dire contempt. Fancy Dickens & his family going to call on that worthy couple—Mr. & Mrs. Pecksniff, & informing these people upon whom they never called before that they would be happy to see them at Tavistock House. But still better—fancy Pecksniff & his wife in a high moral transport and religious spite informing Miss Hogarth & the Miss Dickenses, that it was with Mrs. Dickens they were acquainted, that if Mrs. Dickens were at Tavistock House they should be happy to call, but otherwise—afraid—very sorry . . .[39]

Katey's life was becoming truly intolerable and she began searching for an escape. For a woman of her time, there was only one option: marriage.

---

39 A Mr. S. C. Hall is the man referred to here, the basis for Dickens' hypocritical character Mr. Pecksniff in *Martin Chuzzlewit*.

8

AN UNSATISFACTORY MARRIAGE

By October 1859, Charlie Collins had resolved his inner turmoil with the decision that it was time to be married. He proposed to Kate (as she now chose to be called) and she accepted, much to her father's disappointment. We do not know how or where Charlie proposed, but he was a regular visitor to Gad's Hill, so he may have asked her to marry him as he walked with her around the picturesque garden. Despite his own encouragement of Charlie and his help in the younger man's career, Charles Dickens did not ever see him as a good match for his favored child. His letters hint that he attempted to persuade her not to accept him, but Kate had always been stubborn and perhaps his attempt to influence her in matters of marriage—when she was witness to the hypocritical way in which he was now living—goaded her into accepting Charlie's proposal in defiance.

As Kate would later admit, she was "not in the least in love with him," but she did love Charlie as a friend, she respected him as a painter, and she was desperate to escape the family home. Perhaps she did, in the beginning, also find him physically attractive—he was tall and slender and his friends all describe him as good-looking—but it seems that his principal attraction for her was his gentle personality. Kate said that she "considered him the kindest and most sweet-tempered of men," and a contemporary description by a female friend suggests that Charlie had a great empathy with women. For Kate he was an escape route out of her plight—her unrequited love for a married man, the "misery and unhappiness" of their family home—and into a position where, as a married woman, she could behave as *she* chose, not as her father dictated.

They made plans to marry the following summer. Charles had not yet given up his lease on Tavistock House and it seems that Kate (presumably with Mamie and Georgina, if not Charles as well) returned to London for the Season. Officially, the Season began after Easter and continued until mid-August, but there would be parties, suppers, theater trips, and other outings taking place as early as February.[40] For Kate there would have been the added necessity of buying wedding clothes. While in London, Kate went to the Collinses' home in Clarence Terrace almost every day, announcing her presence with a deliberately loud knock so that all were aware of her arrival. During this time she began a fond relationship with her future mother-in-law, Harriet Collins. Clarence Terrace was not far from Catherine Dickens' home—the journey between the two was a pleasant walk through Regent's Park—and, occasionally, Kate would defy her father's orders and visit her mother. These visits were infrequent and not as prolonged as Catherine would have wished; in later years, Kate was to chide herself for her selfishness in not visiting her mother more often. Catherine and Kate had an agreement never to talk about Charles; in reality they probably thought about little else as they sat making small talk and seldom broaching the subjects that occupied so much of their private thoughts. The atmosphere must have been strained and awkward as they struggled to come to terms with their new relationship. Catherine, aware that Charles had insisted she not be allowed to attend Kate's wedding, must have longed to hear about the preparations and Kate's thoughts about her forthcoming marriage. Kate would have been equally reluctant to tell, aware that she was not able to stand up to her father and insist her mother be there on the day.

By this time, Kate was starting to be recognized by her peers as a painter. As there are no records left, we have no proof of how long she continued to receive artistic training at Bedford College, but it seems unlikely she would have chosen to give up her beloved art at such a traumatic time as her parents' separation. One can assume that she went to classes at the college up until around 1860. Until her marriage, her father still paid for her expenses, so she would have been able to afford to keep

---

40 August 12 was the official date for the Season to end; it was then that the fashionable and those who could afford it would leave London for the country and the shooting season would begin.

attending. It was probably not expected that she would undertake a career in art; women artists were still seldom seen as professionals and her husband would have been expected to provide for her financially. She was, however, known to be a talented artist and respected as such. Through her engagement to Charlie and through her father's circle, she was in regular contact with other artists, among them John Everett Millais. Not only was Millais one of Charlie Collins' oldest friends, but also he had become friendly with Charles Dickens—the scathing 1850 review of Millais' painting in *Household Words* now long forgiven—and was a regular visitor to Gad's Hill. Millais, a happily married man and father—described by Henry Fielding Dickens as always possessing "the spirits and animation of a boy"—was thrilled to see his soul-searching friend so willing to embrace happiness. He had already become enchanted by Kate and now requested permission from her father to paint her. Although in his early career Millais had striven against the rigid conventions of the art world, he was now one of the most conventional artists of his day. By 1860 he was becoming one of the stalwarts of London's art scene and was well on his way to becoming the highest-paid artist in England. Millais' paintings captured the essence of what Victorian Britain wanted to see in art—scenes of heroism, great moments in history, or chocolate-box pretty images; scenes that the general public could identify with and understand, while admiring the innocent beauty of the female model or the heroic qualities of the male. Happily, for Millais' purposes, Kate was the epitome of what a Victorian woman was expected to look like.

At the age of twenty, Kate had a slim but curvaceous figure, perfectly accented by the corseted fashions of the day. Her hair was a suitably English auburn-brown—not too dark, not pertly blonde, and not red. Her face was pretty, with a high but not overly high forehead, a perfectly sized small nose, and eyes that were neither too big nor too small, not too far apart nor too close together. She was, in short, more than averagely pretty without being unusual-looking or provocatively sexy. She was a world away from the fleshy-lipped, strangely necked, sensuous beauties now starting to adorn Dante Gabriel Rossetti's canvases, but more feminine than the Botticelli-inspired, wraithlike women painted by the young Edward Burne-Jones. In terms of artistic expression, Millais was rapidly leaving his former clique behind him, and he was acutely aware of the importance of commercialism in art. Once he hit on a formula that worked he would strive to recreate it in other works of a similar theme.

One such work that was to prove extremely popular was *The Black Brunswicker*, a conscious evocation of one of Millais' most successful early pictures, *The Huguenot* (1852). *The Huguenot* depicts a young couple embracing. She is a French Catholic, her lover a Protestant (Huguenot). She is trying to persuade him to deny his religion while he is preparing to die for his beliefs during the three days of religious genocide that have become known as the St. Bartholomew's Day massacre of 1572.[41] Millais' son later commented that he thought his father had made more preliminary sketches for *The Huguenot* and *The Black Brunswicker* than for any other picture.

The Black Brunswicker was Millais' homage to the Battle of Waterloo, an event still at the forefront of the public imagination, particularly following Wellington's funeral. The painting shows an English girl and her fiancé, a Prussian soldier—or so-called "Black Brunswicker"—on the eve of battle. The officer in his pristine uniform is about to leave and fight, but his fiancée is desperately trying to prevent his going. She stands between him and the door, making a futile attempt to keep it closed so he cannot leave her. Near her feet is her little dog, attempting to comfort her. On the wall behind them is a painting of Napoleon. It was common knowledge at the time the painting was exhibited that almost every man in the Brunswick regiment was killed in the battle. The painting is expertly executed, with each detail receiving minute attention, such as the creases on the silk of her dress, drawing the viewer's eye and making them feel that they are truly a part of this intimate little scene. The female model was Kate; her Prussian officer lover was modeled by a private soldier in the Life Guards. Some accounts erroneously claim the male model was Charlie Collins, but John Guille Millais—John Everett Millais' son—recorded that it was a man whose name he could not recall, whom his father spotted while visiting a friend in the Life Guards. He chose his model because the man possessed "a splendid type of masculine beauty." Sadly, the soldier died a few months later from consumption.

---

41 As a result of this massacre, thousands of French Huguenots fled to England seeking asylum.

The newly engaged Kate began modeling for *The Black Brunswicker* in January 1860. As this was the age in which a chaperone was always required for a young unmarried woman, she was usually accompanied to the studio by an elderly woman, a friend of the Millais family, who often worked as chaperone when the artist employed female models.

The Black Brunswicker (1860) by John Everett Millais

Sketch of Kate in 1860 by John Everett Millais. It is one of Millais' preliminary studies for his oil painting, *The Black Brunswicker*.

Sometimes, her aunt Georgina would go with her, at other times she was accompanied by her brother Alfred. Charlie Collins was often present as well. This was a time when modeling for an artist was not something most well-brought-up, unmarried women would do. It was the era when to work as a professional model was considered akin to prostitution and was ruinous to a woman's reputation. As Kate was not being paid for her modeling, and as the artist was a friend of both her father and her fiancé, the situation was not scandalous, but many Victorian fathers would not have granted their permission. In order to observe propriety, the two models were painted on separate occasions, with Kate never needing to cling to her fellow sitter, as her character does in the finished painting. Instead she was made to hold on to a "lay figure" (a life-size wooden model) and was never even introduced to the man who was depicted as her lover.

The sittings lasted for three months. Initially, Kate was intimidated by Millais, who could be a stern taskmaster, often becoming so absorbed in his art that his model's welfare was forgotten. A man who, by all contemporary accounts, was charming and effortlessly kind, he could, it seems, become quite caustic when working, furious if a model dared move without permission, even if he or she had been standing absolutely still for hours. Initially, Kate admitted to feelings of "dread" at the prospect of yet another day's modeling—despite the thrill she felt at this up-close chance to watch one of her artistic heroes at work. Kate could often be shy and easily embarrassed at this age and dreaded earning Millais' displeasure. As the sessions continued, however, she began to relax and to forge a friendship with the painter, which was to endure. In his book about his father, John Guille Millais describes the Kate of 1860 as "a handsome girl, with a particularly sweet expression and beautiful auburn hair that contrasted well with the sheen of her white satin dress." When he had been writing the biography of his father, John Guille had written to Kate, asking for her remembrance of the sittings. She replied:

> *I made your father's acquaintance when I was quite a young girl. Very soon after our first meeting he wrote to my father, asking him to allow me to sit to him for a head in one of the pictures he was then painting, 'The Black Brunswicker'. My father consenting, I used to go to your*

mother and father's house, somewhere in the North of London, accompanied by an old lady, a friend of your family. I was very shy and quiet in those days, and during the 'sittings' I was only too glad to leave the conversation to be carried on by your father and his old friend; but I soon grew to be interested in your father's extraordinary vivacity, and the keenness and delight he took in discussing books, plays, and music, and sometimes painting—but he always spoke less of pictures than anything else—and these sittings, to which I had looked forward with a certain amount of dread and dislike, became so pleasant to me that I was heartily sorry when they came to an end and my presence was no more required in his studio.

As I stood upon my 'throne' listening attentively to everything that passed, I noticed one day that your father was much more silent than usual, that he was very restless, and a little sharp in his manner when he asked me to turn my head this way or that. Either my face or his brush seemed to be out of order, and he could not get on. At last, turning impatiently to his old friend, he exclaimed, 'Come and tell me what's wrong here: I can't see any more, I've got blind over it.' She laughingly excused herself, saying she was no judge . . . whereupon he turned to me. 'Do you come down, my dear, and tell me,' he said. As he was quite grave and very impatient there was nothing for it but to descend from my throne and take my place beside him. As I did so, I happened to notice a slight exaggeration in something I saw upon the canvas, and told him of it. Instantly, and greatly to my dismay, he took up a rag and wiped out the whole of the head, turning at the same time triumphantly to his old friend. 'There! That's what I always say; a fresh eye can see everything in a moment. . . . There! get back to your place, my dear, and we'll begin all over again!'

Millais' desire for perfection paid dividends. The artist wrote to his wife, Effie, in May 1860 that *The Black Brunswicker* was "the most satisfactory work" he had exhibited so far, and when the Summer Exhibition opened, the painting was adored by the public (though the newspapers were less enthusiastic, with one sarcastic reviewer claiming that Kate's character showed more interest in her dog than in her doomed lover), drawing enormous crowds. It did not sell immediately, but when it did it was bought by the French collector M. Gambart, who paid the princely amount of one thousand guineas. Millais himself was so proud of the picture that he painted a copy to keep for his family.[42]

Although the majority of modern viewers are unaware of the identity of either model, at the time it was painted Kate Dickens was a well-known name purely on the strength of her father's celebrity. In those days there were no photos in newspapers or on posters and obviously there were no films, television programs, or glossy magazines to bring images of famous faces to the masses. For many, *The Black Brunswicker* would have been the first opportunity to see what one of Charles Dickens' children looked like. The novelist himself was well known from paintings and sketches, but his children were just names currently being whispered around London and mentioned in newspaper articles about their parents' separation. One wonders how much damage the painting did to Kate's reputation among the more censorious elements of society. In 1860, the general public were divided into two camps: those who pandered to Charles Dickens and those who supported Catherine. Most of these people had never met either of the protagonists, but still felt obliged to take one or the other side. Many women were appalled by the treatment Catherine had suffered—for some, their feelings were fueled by fear in case their husbands should choose to treat them the same way—and Mamie, Kate, and Georgina came in for a great deal of censure for their roles in "abandoning" Catherine. The influential journalist Harriet Martineau, an acquaintance of the Dickenses since the early 1840s, wrote to a friend of her displeasure of Catherine's treatment: "such a life. . . . And not a daughter has she with her!—only that weak son." It was a sentiment echoed by many.

While twenty-year-old Kate was being admired as the beautiful girl in Millais' painting, her wedding date was set for July 1860. Yet as the day grew nearer, Charles Dickens became increasingly displeased with the prospect. He was jealous of another man supplanting his importance in Kate's life; moreover, he did not deem Charlie good husband material and

---

42 *The Black Brunswicker* remains one of Millais' best-known works. It can be seen at the Lady Lever Art Gallery at Port Sunlight.

Portrait of Mamie
Dickens as a young
woman

Self Portrait (1883) by
John Everett Millais

he knew, deep down, that Kate had agreed to such a lackluster match only because his behavior had made the last two years of her life so unhappy. He was, however, magnanimous in his treatment of his daughter and future son-in-law. He gave Kate a wedding present settlement of £375 and he gave Charlie regular work as a writer. Since 1859, Charlie had been working regularly for Charles on *All The Year Round*, writing a column under the pseudonym "The Eye-Witness." His articles are witty and show an aptitude for writing, though it is doubtful he would have been given such an opportunity to show off his talent had he not been Wilkie's brother and Kate's fiancé. His articles also display a desperation to write in the same style as his future father-in-law—something he was unable to attain. Charles' lack of enthusiasm for his daughter's choice of husband was made explicit in a letter to his friend W. W. F. de Cerjat in May 1860:

> *My second daughter is going to be married in the course of the summer, to the brother of Wilkie Collins the Novelist. He was bred an artist (the father was one of the most famous painters of English green lanes and coast pieces), and was attaining considerable distinction, when he turned indifferent to it and fell back upon that worst of cushions, a small independence. He is a writer too, and does the Eye Witness in All The Year Round. He is a gentleman, and accomplished. Age 30 [sic]. I do not doubt that the young lady might have done much better, but there is no question that she is very fond of him, and that they have come together by strong attraction. Therefore the undersigned venerable parent says no more, and takes the goods the Gods provide him . . .*

Charlie was actually thirty-two, not thirty, at the time of Charles' letter. It seems unlikely the writer genuinely believed Kate and Charlie shared a "strong [physical] attraction"—perhaps if they had, he would have been happier about the match—but he could see that they had a mental empathy and a great ability to make each other laugh and perhaps he wanted to suggest to de Cerjat that there was something romantic about what, to him, was an obviously unromantic situation. His letter implies that the lassitude Charles deplored so much in his own son Charley was a feature of his future son-in-law's composition as well. Although it is debatable whether Charles would have deemed any man good enough to marry Kate, it seems he was right to have such doubts about Charlie Collins's suitability as a husband.

One can imagine, too, that the sartorially proud Charles was slightly aghast at his daughter marrying someone to whom fashion sense seemed to be an alien notion. Millais charitably described Charlie's fashion mistakes as being down to him wanting to give work to an impoverished tailor, despite the man's obvious lack of ability: "In the kindness of his heart, Collins looked rather to the necessities of his tailor than to his skill, with results quite appalling to worshippers of fashion."

In the weeks leading up to the wedding, Charles' nostalgia for his girls' happy childhood came to the fore, although it also brought back memories of his own wedding day and unfavorable comparisons (see the letter to one of his oldest friends, Thomas Beard, below). Mamie—still unmarried and showing no desire to be so—was to be Kate's bridesmaid. The one member of the family who was not able to join in the enthusiasm, anxiety, and fun of preparing for the wedding was the bride's mother.

Today, most weddings are planned months—if not years—in advance, but Charles' letters of 1860 suggest things were done quite differently then. Guests were informed of the wedding date just a few weeks beforehand. On June 12, Charles wrote to Thomas Beard, whom he had met when still a cub reporter and who had remained a constant in the Dickens children's lives:

> *The girls feel that Katie's marriage cannot possibly come off, without the presence of the ancient friend of the venerable parient [sic]. This is, therefore, to require you to be at this house on the morning of Tuesday the Seventeenth day of July in the present year of Our Lord, to grace the Nuptials then to be solemnized in the parochial church of Higham (N.B. No connection, I hope, with a similar ceremony performed in a metropolitan edifice some four and twenty years ago.). . . . Lord, how the time and Life steal on! It was but yesterday that Katie always had a scratched knee—and it was but the day before yesterday when there was no such creature.*

Beard was one of the first people to be invited—the celebrant was not asked to perform the ceremony until less than a month in advance, on June 19.

The wedding of Charles Dickens' daughter occasioned great local excitement. The night before, a series of loud bangs could be heard in the village—the blacksmith had decided to fire a gun salute in honor of the nuptials (although he had neglected to tell anyone else of his intentions and reportedly terrified them all).

As a propitious start, the day of the wedding dawned sunny, but for Kate it was not to be an entirely happy day. Her mother and all her Hogarth relations (excluding Georgina) had not been invited, nor had the Thackerays or the Lemons, although most of Kate's siblings were able to attend. Sydney—who was now at naval college, where he had earned the nickname "Young Dickens who can do anything"—was allowed leave for the occasion, Charley came down from London, and Plorn was still being educated at home. It seems likely that Frank, Alfred, and Henry were also home from school for the wedding (Charles mentioned "all the boys" in one of his descriptions of the wedding), but Walter was sorely missed, as he was away in India.

At that time, trains could be hired by individuals (or, at least, by those individuals who could afford to do so), so Charles had ordered a special train to bring many of the guests from London. Although there was a relatively small number of officially invited wedding guests, Higham's parish church was packed with local well-wishers, eager for a glimpse of the bride. The wedding ceremony, performed by the Reverend Joseph Hindle, took place at eleven a.m. Afterward, the wedding party walked back to Gad's Hill amid crowds of cheering villagers, who had garlanded their route with arches of flowers and greenery, just as the people of Boulogne had decorated their town for the emperor. Although there are no records of how Kate was dressed, it seems likely that she followed the example of Queen Victoria and chose to wear a white dress. Until the marriage of Victoria and Albert in 1840, a wedding dress could be any color the bride preferred, but by 1860 it had become extremely fashionable for brides to emulate their monarch's example. The decorations at Gad's Hill were certainly all in white: flowers, tablecloths, napkins, candles. Kate had at least two bridesmaids: Mamie and a Miss Amelia Chambers, known as "Tuck" (or "Tuckie").[43] Kate must have been greatly saddened at not being able to include the Thackeray girls in her bridal party.

Charlie's best man was the Pre-Raphaelite artist William Holman Hunt (he had been a founding member of the Pre-Raphaelite Brotherhood and, by 1860, had become a very successful artist). He later recorded that the bride's father had not been in good spirits that day. According to the artist, Charles was argumentative and grew unnecessarily heated during a discussion about art. Overall, the wedding reception was a slightly subdued affair, despite the magnificent decorations and excellent food and wine. There was just one toast and no speeches. The atmosphere was marred by the absence of the bride's mother, an omission embarrassingly apparent to most of the guests; added to which, many of those present were aware that the bride's father was not happy with his daughter's choice of husband. Charles himself later admitted, impishly, that he had found their discomfiture amusing, aware that many of his guests didn't know if they should be solemn or jovial.

After just one hour of the "wedding breakfast," the bridal couple departed for Dover, from where they would travel to France, leaving their wedding gifts stowed safely at Gad's Hill. Fashion-conscious Kate caused a stir by saying goodbye to her guests in a black going-away outfit. Mamie wept bitterly as they said their goodbyes and Charles was visibly upset at Kate's leaving. Her parting from Charley was made even more emotional, as he was about to travel to Asia on a tea-buying and reconnaissance trip and Kate feared for his safety. Charlie is said to have stood white-faced with shock at his new wife's display of misery. Charles was to report in a letter to his sister-in-law two days later: "Mary and all the boys were very much cut up when the parting moment came, but they soon recovered; Mary in particular commanded herself extremely well."

Frederick Lehmann, a close family friend and inveterate gossip, reported expansively on the wedding day in a letter to his wife Nina, even though he had overslept, missed the special train, and arrived in Kent after

43 Amelia Chambers was the sister of Nina Lehmann, one of Kate and Mamie's good friends and someone they often socialized with. Nina and her husband Fred Lehmann were great friends of Charles and were related to W. H. Wills (whose wife was Nina and Amelia's aunt). Not long after Kate married Charlie Collins, Amelia married one of Frederick Lehmann's brothers, Rudolph, a professional portrait painter.

the church ceremony was over. He related how sad Kate seemed to be at leaving her family and how "sweet" she had looked in her wedding dress; he also related that the pompous John Forster, who had known Kate since her birth, exhorted the bridegroom in his "most stentorian voice" to "Take care of her, Charlie. You have got a most precious treasure."

After the departure of the newlyweds, the remaining wedding party played games in the gardens before being driven to Rochester Castle, where they wandered among the ruins; from there they were driven on again to Chatham, where they listened to a military band. They returned to Gad's Hill for croquet, and to see the local children being treated to a special afternoon tea in honor of the bride and groom. At seven o'clock the guests were given supper, after which there was a country dance before carriages arrived to take the visitors to the station to catch their special train back to London.

Having attempted to play the character of genial host for most of the day, Charles let go of his emotions once his house was free of guests. Mamie told her sister that after the party she had discovered their father on his knees on the floor of Kate's bedroom. He was holding her wedding dress and crying into it. Mamie stood in silence, not sure what to do, until he realized that she was in the room, whereupon he sobbed that he knew he was the reason Kate had left home.

9

A CRUISE UPON WHEELS

The newly wed Mr. and Mrs. Charles Collins began their honeymoon—which was planned to last for several months—at a hotel in Dover, before taking a boat to France. They had intended to leave the port town of Calais immediately, to travel to Switzerland, but as Charles Dickens was to note derisively in a letter—with the contempt of a seasoned traveler—they ended up spending several weeks in Calais. The couple was extremely content there, and there was the added bonus—for Charlie—that the cost of living in Calais was very cheap. His letters suggest he spent a large portion of their honeymoon congratulating himself for every penny saved. They did not have a particularly large income, but, in addition to their marriage settlement, Charlie had a small inheritance from his father as well as his payment from the Eye-Witness column, and his obsessive parsimony seems excessive. His letters to his mother are filled with gleeful comments about how cheap their rent was, how good they were at getting by without servants, or how little it cost to buy food.

Kate's expectations of the honeymoon are unrecorded, but there was one aspect that would have been less than pleasing. It seems the marriage remained unconsummated. Throughout the honeymoon they slept in one bedroom (far more economical than a two-bedroom apartment), but in separate beds.[44] After an annoyingly expensive week at a hotel, their first "home" was a rented apartment at 56 rue Royale. They had one bedroom,

---

44 Although there is no written proof that the marriage was unconsummated, it has been rumored for many years: Kate told her father that "Charles ought never to have married" and Frederick Lehmann wrote that it was "an infamy" that Charles Collins had taken a wife. In addition, Kate did not become pregnant.

a small bathroom, a kitchen, and a dining room; their rent was ninety francs a month (the equivalent, as Charlie proudly told his mother, of £3 15s). They also employed a daily maid, at the cost of twelve francs a week, who cleaned and cooked all their meals, except breakfast. Charlie's letters to Harriet Collins are divided into public sections—comments he was happy for her to pass on to their friends—and private sections. The latter consisted mainly of uxorious comments about Kate, such as her health and her housekeeping abilities, as well as how cheaply they were living. This latter, he would stress, must be kept strictly between themselves; neither he nor Kate wanted her family to know. He was obviously worried in case his father-in-law discovered how far Kate's social position had descended since her marriage. Yet, like any Victorian father, Charles would have questioned Charlie closely about his finances before agreeing to the wedding, which suggests that Kate's new husband concerned himself more than he needed to with being frugal.

Kate, however, appears not to have been bothered about carrying out menial household tasks or buying food at the market. On the contrary, it seems to have been a great adventure to her. Charlie obviously treated her kindly and, despite the lack of sex and his constant penny-pinching, they strove to make each other happy and enjoyed one another's company. In a letter home dated July 29, 1860, Charlie told his mother that Kate "has an appetite which it would do you good to see. She takes to housekeeping well is up in good time in the morning and not long at her toilette." He wrote comically of their setting off to market complete with a large grocery basket and pretending to stallholders that they were seasoned food buyers, in order not to be cheated. "It is astonishing," he added, "how quickly and completely one falls into the ways of matrimony. I feel now as if I had been married for ten years. I think it is a good plan to begin housekeeping like this at once instead of going about touring. Besides, I hate living at hotels you are always dreading the huge bill." Whether Kate would have preferred a honeymoon of traveling around and staying in smart hotels is debatable, yet she does seem genuinely happy in her letters to be living in their rented apartment in a quiet manner. After the turbulence of her recent home life, living in peace with a trusted friend with whom she could sit in silence and read and draw all day if she liked must have been blissful.

Charlie's carefulness with money was not purely on his own account. It seems that Harriet Collins was experiencing financial troubles and it's likely Charlie was attempting to save some of his and Kate's money in order to help her out. During the first part of her son's absence from London, Harriet took advantage of a time-honored solution to insolvency: She spent her time staying with a succession of friends, so her food and bills were all taken care of. Then she let out her London home and moved into a tiny cottage in the middle of the Kent countryside.

It is obvious from the postscript to one of Charlie's letters, a postscript written by Kate to her mother-in-law just two weeks after her wedding, that the two women already shared a close and cozy relationship: "My dearest Mrs. Collins. Have you forgiven me yet for going away in black? The fact is I thought you were much too occupied with your flirtations to notice what I went away in. I really think your conduct was disgraceful, *and my respect for you is gone for ever*. I am very happy, and hope to become some day a good wife." Despite Kate's allusions to Harriet's flirting, her attractive mother-in-law did not ever remarry, seemingly preferring to devote herself to her sons and her husband's memory (even though remarrying would have solved her financial problems). In later life Kate would describe her mother-in-law as "a woman of great wit and humour—but a Devil!"

At the end of July, while Kate and Charlie were honeymooning, Kate's young uncle Alfred Dickens died at the age of thirty-eight. His death (from pleurisy) was so premature that his widow, Helen, and their five children—the oldest of whom was just thirteen—were left with no financial security. Once again, the list of Charles Dickens' dependants grew. Kate's aunt and young cousins were brought to Kent, not far from Gad's Hill, where the generous Charles rented a farmhouse for them to live in, along with his widowed mother. Some of the furniture that had once been in Tavistock House was used to furnish their new home.

Kate and Charlie's next few honeymoon letters tell of picnics, boat trips, days spent fishing, and cozy evening meals, including a less-than-appetizing-sounding "chocolate supper with bacon," about which Charlie wrote with gusto. Charlie had thoughts of visiting Lourdes, to write an article for his Eye-Witness column; maybe he also hoped it might help his own poor health.

His column, which had been introduced in *All The Year Round* in June 1859, was a fun project to work on, with "Our Eye-Witness" being sent on a variety of visits to new, exciting, or ludicrous events—from a visit to the zoo to trying out a new German mechanical horse that was the latest sensation in the teaching of riding. His character was given the name David Fudge and his very first assignment had been to visit the "Talking Fish" currently on display in Piccadilly. The so-called fish turned out to be a captive seal, for whom Charlie felt extreme pity. The article begins amusingly,

> *it is not a fish, and it does not talk. In the nine days appropriated to this wonder, no one appears to have noticed this little error in description. . . . Is a seal a fish? Is barking like a dog talking? Perhaps it is.*

It continues in a similar vein until he gives a sad account of the seal itself, writing about it with such sympathy that one can understand why Kate described Charlie as "the kindest and most sweet-tempered of men":

> *The Talking Fish declined to talk. And yet to your eye-witness she did talk, and, oh, how plainly! How plainly as she worked herself round and round, and looked from face to face, how plainly she spoke, not with her mouth, indeed, but with her wistful eyes. 'What have I done?' she said—'what have I done, that this misery should have come upon me? What is this close and stifling room? What are these faces that gaze at me in my prison? Why am I here? Where is the sea that used to stretch around me further than my eyes could follow? Where is the mighty river at whose mouth I lived? Where is the sun, in which I loved to bask? Where is my mate? They have taken him from me, and killed him. Oh that they would kill me too, and deliver me from this dreadful place!'*

Millais was to tell his son that Charlie's kind heart had led him to give up fishing because he had realized it was cruel, even though it was "a pastime he delighted in above all others," and in Charlie's column this empathy for animals comes across on several occasions. This is largely because his column required him so often to visit captive beasts, such as a "performing bull," or the latest sensation to reach London Zoo, a giant salamander—which, initially, he walked straight past as being unworthy of notice. He had expected it to be a huge, fire-breathing, griffinlike creature and was greatly disappointed by a muddy brown, depressed-looking "sort of . . . lizard, of enormous size, bloated, and hideous."

His articles are revealing of his personality and beliefs, from his calling for families of "moderate means" to be given the opportunity to send their children to schools as good as those the upper classes enjoyed, to his views on architecture. In "Our Eye-Witness Among the Buildings" (written just a few weeks before his wedding) he asks for architects to break away from the past and use modern materials, such as iron and glass, instead of stone:

> Let us have no restorations. Mend, if you will, repair as much as you like, but never attempt to return to the past. No more classics, no more medievalisms, no more bran-new [sic] gothic architecture, no more illumination. These things have all been done, done gloriously and perfectly, done once for all. It is wise to do that which you can do better than it has ever been done before. . . . This is an age of glass and iron, why is there no church constructed of these materials?

The columns are a slice of social history, including such topics as a storytelling club where a "professional storyteller" regales illiterate working men, their wives, and children; and a charlatan adolescent performer called the "Infant Magnet." He also visits the Royal Arsenal in Woolwich and the London Docks; attends an Inquiry into irregularities at a local election in Gloucester; and investigates the London Misanthropic Society, Madame Tussaud's (including its Chamber of Horrors), and an annual cattle show, which was held in the unlikely location of Baker Street. One of his funniest articles is about the Serpentine (the lake in Hyde Park), which has frozen over, and the community of amateur skaters who gather there. He identifies eight different methods of falling over—they have names such as "the Smash complicated," "the Stagger victorious," "the Scramble ineffectual" and "the Crash unresisted"—and describes each one in detail. In general, however, the tone of his articles is sententious and overtly moralistic. He tries far too hard to emulate his brother and father-in-law but often fails humiliatingly. The readers of *All The Year Round* appreciated the pieces, but at times Charlie's efforts must have made Kate cringe.

While they were on their honeymoon, Charlie announced that he was going to write a novel based on their travels, and Kate spent much of the time trying to persuade him against the idea. Charles also felt Charlie was making a mistake, although—once the couple was back in England—he did give him help with the craft of writing, telling him, "If you want your public to believe in what you are writing, you must believe in it yourself. I can as distinctly see with my own eyes any scene which I am describing as I see you now; and indeed, on one occasion, when I had shadowed a certain course for one of my characters to pursue, the character took possession of me and made me do exactly the contrary to what I had originally intended."

It is likely that Harriet Collins wrote concernedly to the honeymooners about Charlie's obsession with thrift, for Kate was prompted to write to her, saying protectively, "I hate economy but I am more miserly than Charlie." She then changed the subject to teasing about the weakness of the tea Harriet served at her parties, claiming that she had now learned to be a far superior tea-maker than her mother-in-law. Charlie wrote passionately of his longing to stay in France, of how slowly the time seemed to pass compared with the hectic world of London and what a joy it would be to remain forever in a place where their income placed them in the "rich" bracket, rather than the "poor" (as he seemed to believe they would be in London), and of how difficult it was to "keep pace with people who think of nothing else at all but display."

The newlyweds grew fond of Calais and would have been happy to stay there, but the surrounding factories made the air quality poor and covered everything with smut. By mid-August they had decided to move on to Paris, where they would stay at the Hôtel de Helder. They began their journey by horse-drawn carriage, but the horse grew lame at Amiens. After five days in Amiens attempting to sell their horse and buy another, they decided to stable the carriage and finish their journey by train, something that seemed quite an adventure.

Kate's postscript to their first letter to Harriet from Paris is excitable and girlish, sounding like one of her father's fictional young women:

Charlie says that I may say I am such a dear little thing. My temper is unbearable, he spoils me so, and lets me do whatever I like. He is very good to me and I am very happy. He is such a good man isn't he, no wonder you love him so. I have got the fidgets. Oh!—I can't write any more. Here's a kiss for you.

By the end of September, intending to leave Paris to journey to Lausanne (a new horse having been found for the carriage), both Charlie and his bride were becoming agitated by a lack of letters from either Harriet or Wilkie. Halfway through one of Charlie's missives is an interruption from Kate, which looks as though she had grabbed the quill from Charlie's hand and taken over. It is a petulant, cross letter, in which he chides his mother and brother for not writing and Kate accuses them indignantly of caring nothing for Charlie. There was actually a problem with the post, which was delaying their letters, and, like Kate's own family, Wilkie and Harriet were continuing to write with affectionate regularity. Normally, letters would travel between France and England with surprising speed, meaning Kate and Charlie were able to catch up with family news just a few days after it had happened. Sadly, none of Charles' letters to his daughter survive to tell us what their relationship was like as she moved from being his daughter to another man's wife. Charles would have been aware that, now a wife herself, Kate would be more sensitive to the humiliation her mother was having to deal with. It would be fascinating to be able to read their correspondence; no doubt it was very fond, as they missed each other, but would ignore or gloss over what was really occupying his thoughts—his relationship with Ellen. Unlike Mamie, Kate would never become friends with her father's mistress.

Kate and Charlie's journey to Lausanne took several days of traveling, stopping at Fontainebleau and Auxerre, another excitement. It felt wonderfully liberating to travel across Europe, just the two of them, with no servants, no social restrictions, and no one ready to comment on the "fast" Miss Dickens' behavior. Lausanne, however, was not a success and after a short time Kate began to feel depressed. The weather was inhospitably autumnal and the climate did not suit them. Whenever there was no sun, Kate felt depressed and irritable; she began to blame Lausanne for her unhappiness and determined they should leave as soon as possible. "This place is the coldest in the world I should think," she wrote to Harriet, "and the house is warmed by stoves, such an unhealthy heat, and when we go out we feel the cold so much more than we should were there nice comfortable fires in the rooms." One can't help wondering, though, if the gloss of first being married had begun to wear off and if Kate was now brooding on her fate: marriage for the rest of her life to a man who had no desire to have sex with her. She must have feared that she would die a virgin, and the prospect that there could never be children would have made her deeply sad.

By the beginning of November, Charlie had become ill and was ordered by a doctor to have a change of air, so they decided to return to Paris. Kate overruled Charlie's objections about the expense with a conviction that there *must* be a cheap apartment for rent somewhere in that great metropolis. "I shall be very glad to be settled again and in an appartment [*sic*] of our own," she informed Harriet. She added quixotically, with a sweeping change of opinion from her earlier letters from Calais, "If we stay abroad this winter, Paris is the only place for us. Calais is too dull, in fact all French towns are dull except Paris. In Paris we can be very quiet and Charlie can work as much as he likes, and at the same time if we want any change or gaiety there are always the amusing streets to walk about in and the theatres to visit."

Back in Paris they found a grubby little apartment, 11 rue de l'Arcade. At the beginning of December, Kate wrote an affectionate, witty letter to her mother-in-law, which she signed "Katinka." It seems Harriet Collins moved in the same circles as Catherine Dickens, as Kate was quick to ask her not to reveal anything about their impoverished state to her mother. She detailed their daily life quite happily:

We are quite settled here now, and if the place was only a little less dirty we should be very comfortable. Now I am going to tell you about the queer sort of life we are leading. To begin at the beginning then, we are economising. We keep no servant and we do almost everything for ourselves, not everything though, we pay the cook of the house something to wash up the dishes for us, and the servant of the house makes the beds and does the rooms for us, that is to say pretends to do the rooms, really we do them. Without this help of course we should be obliged to keep a servant of our own, as we shall do if we stay here, when we have a little recovered from the expense of our journey. We have cleaned everything with our own hands and have scrubbed away like two hard working servants. We cook our own food, no one in the world could cook a chop better than Charlie does, and I am very great indeed at boiled rice. In the morning Charlie lights the fire and I lay the cloth, while he fries the bacon I make the tea. After breakfast I clear away, put his writing materials out on the table and he sets down to work while I wash up the breakfast cups in the kitchen, put away everything, sweep up the crumbs and the hearth and get the room neat. Then Charlie goes on working all the morning till about two, and I darn, or mend, or write letters. At two we have our lunch, then a little more work & then we go out for a walk, get what things we want for dinner, come in, cook our dinner and eat it. As soon as dinner is over, we dine generally at a little after six, we get out the Account book and our journal book, Enter in the account book ever [sic] sous we have spent in the day, and write down in the journal book all that we have done in the day. Then comes tea, and then another great tidying of the room, and sweeping up of crumbs and putting away of things. Then we put on our things & go out for a long walk, and look at all the beautiful things in the shop windows and enjoy ourselves as much as we can. If it rains in the evenings we stay at home of course, then Charlie draws and I work. This is our life, this is how we spend our time. Your letters are a great amusement to us so are Mamie's and Auntie's. Charlie received a very nice letter from Wilkie this morning long and amusing.

I am so sorry you have been ill, I trust you are feeling stronger and better again. No one keeps well in the winter, I wish it was over. How many months of cold, and wet, and mud there are to look forward to. Paris is so muddy and no crossings anywhere.

It is not the letter one would imagine a newly married woman would write, but the overall tone is happy and uncomplaining; though it is apparent that the winter is making her miserable. It is also sadly revealing of the fact that, during her honeymoon, Kate painted less and less. No doubt painting materials were too expensive, added to which, without servants to carry their luggage, they would have been reluctant to transport canvases, easels, and other painting paraphernalia around. The letter is doubly interesting for showing Kate in such an unspoiled light. One would imagine that a girl brought up in such a famous household, with people pandering to her and her siblings in an attempt to please her father, could have grown up to be a "celebrity brat." That she remained so grounded, perfectly willing to do her own cooking and cleaning and not complaining about her newly straitened circumstances, is testament not only to Kate's strength and independence, but also to her parents, who brought up their children to have such down-to-earth values, despite enjoying an exalted position.

Kate's letter goes on in a teasing manner about Harriet's dress sense. It seems her mother-in-law was renowned by her sons for wearing hats that were far too big for her and for adding her own details to the latest fashions, so that they all ended up looking exactly the same. Wilkie had written telling them he had bought Harriet a new Parisian hat, and Charlie and Kate amused themselves by writing to her detailing the many ways they'd thought of in which she could have ruined it already.

Perhaps Harriet was filling the space left in Kate's life by her mother's absence. It is notable that Kate writes what a comfort it is to receive letters from Harriet, Mamie, and Georgy, while not mentioning her mother—even though Catherine was known to be a faithful correspondent, writing regularly to her children who moved overseas.

Kate's seasonally affected depression is referred to once again at the end of the letter:

I have not even told any of them at home about the odd life we are leading, for fear that they should fancy we were really frightfully badly off. Now you understand I hope, that we live like this only for a little time, and that we like it, and that we could keep a servant if we liked. You should see Charlie with a gridiron in his hand to see him really happy. As for me I have given up reading, hardly ever sit down, and am happier than I have ever been. The other day for a treat Charlie got me La Petite Comtesse to read. I never was more delighted with any story. It is so beautifully and pathetically written, but so sad that it made me miserable. I shan't read any more books. For a whole day after I had finished my charming petite comtesse, I found I took not the faintest interest in any of my household duties, and wanted only to sit by the fire and read, read, read all through my life. Oh but don't be frightened, I am all right again.

By December 20 Kate's dream of everything going well once they returned to Paris had turned sour. It was a vastly different experience from her previous visit to the city, when she had been fêted as her father's daughter and had dined with the greatest names in Parisian society. She grew sick of keeping house and accounting for every penny and wrote again to Harriet, telling her that they had decided to move to Brussels: "We leave here we hope on Saturday morning. . . . We shall be so glad to get away from here. Papa says Brussels is a charming cheerful little town." A Belgian servant had advised them where to find a cheap apartment and someone they could hire as a maid for just one franc a day. "I hope we shall have her," Kate wrote. "We can afford that. Not that I dislike at all keeping this room neat and washing up the tea-cups etc., but I should be glad and so would Charlie to have someone to cook the dinner, it is so tiring and heating."

Although Kate writes to Harriet that Charlie is "so good and so dear. I never knew anyone so unselfish," reading between the lines of the same letter one can sense an irritation with her husband. He had decided by now to abandon art altogether and become a serious writer. Kate writes loyally of how she is sure he is admirably suited to writing and has every faith in him, but her words do not ring true and her frustration with his attempts to rival his older brother seem to grate. She attempted to persuade him that his articles were so good he should continue with that. "I don't want him to write a novel," she confided to Harriet. "He could not do it nearly so well, and everybody writes novels." Charlie, however, persisted in planning and trying to write it. One imagines it was quite a trial, for someone who had grown up with such a natural and talented writer as her father, to watch Charlie's puffing attempts at his novella. As Kate encouraged him and massaged his belittled ego, desperately trying to steer him from a fruitless course and listening to his constant homilies on economy, she must have pondered on the fact that married life was not at all as she had imagined. She had left her home for a man who would never be able to command her life or take care of her as her father had and for a husband who, as she would later confide cryptically to her father, "ought never to have married."

In addition to the paucity of their finances, Charlie's health had not improved during their time in Paris. His undiagnosed illness was horribly debilitating and led to Kate spending much of her time attending to his needs and nursing him. He suffered from a variety of ailments and exhibited general symptoms of being rundown and unhealthy, such as painful sties on his eyes and mouth ulcers. Their attempts at cooking and housekeeping had taken an obvious toll on the health of both of them and the wintry weather was not helping. "Paris is I am sure very unhealthy," Kate wrote before they set off for Brussels. "It has been very cold indeed here the last two or three days, snow, and mud, and rain and dark cold skies. How I hate winter." The city that had seemed so magical and welcoming to the teenage daughter of Charles Dickens was now miserable for the wife of Charles Collins. Paris had brought out the worst of her husband's obsession with money and her letter is interrupted mid-flow by his calls for her to ask his mother: "Charlie says he wants these questions answered: What is rice a pound in London? What are composition candles a pound? [*scribble*] Here rice 5d or 6d a pound. Mutton chops 11d and candles 1d or 4d." She had never had any cause to think about the price of rice, mutton, or candles when she had lived in the avenue des Champs Elysées and been entertained by the likes of Alexandre Dumas and the famous singer and hostess Mrs. Sartoris. At that time, she had spent her day taking dancing lessons with her sister and learning the piano with the Thackeray girls; now her days were reduced to making poultices for Charlie's eyes, scrubbing the table, and bolstering her husband's esteem with tender wifely comments about what a good writer he was. At the start of their honeymoon, she had had time to paint and draw, but it seems she ceased practicing her art when the autumn set in. She was not yet a commercially viable artist, so she was unable to generate income from her work at this time. Perhaps she felt it was too expensive to practice art purely as a hobby.[45]

In the same letter in which she complains about Paris, she is also concerned for her mother-in-law, who had returned to London but had been living as prudently as possible in order to save funds:

Dear Mrs Collins [she writes for emphasis halfway through her letter], I am very uneasy about something you said in one of your letters. You mentioned unless I am much mistaken that the carpet of the drawing room was up because you wished to keep it nice for us. Unless you immediately have that carpet put down, and unless you have a fire in that room and go and sit there I shall never write to you again. I am in earnest when I tell you that Charlie and I are made unhappy if we think you are making yourself in the least degree uncomfortable. Do you imagine now that a carpet could possibly be hurt by having a fat little woman passing over it every day. Oh please don't always sit in one room and that room the one downstairs. The poor lonely pictures and furniture in the room above will get quite frozen and gloomy unless you have a fire to warm them this horrid weather, the room shut up and cold and dark quite haunts me, I insist upon your inhabiting it or else the idea of its melancholy cold look will drive me mad.

The decision to leave Paris had been a good one and the Belgian capital served the Collinses much better than the French capital. Once in Brussels, they found an apartment where the bedroom led off the sitting room, allowing them to benefit at night from the warmth of the sitting-room fire. Quite what Charles Dickens would have made of this bohemian arrangement and of their being unable to afford a fire in both rooms is uncertain, but Kate was very careful not to tell him. They had engaged

---

45 None of Kate's art from this time survives, and nor do any written descriptions, so it is not possible to say what she was working on then, though one can speculate that she painted portraits of Charlie and scenes from their traveling life. Kate did sometimes paint landscapes, such as *Cottage and Garden at Pinner* (undated), which she would later give to her friend Gladys Storey.

the inexpensive maid recommended by their contact in Paris. She kept their rooms clean, cooked breakfast and lunch, and served their meals. Their supper was sent in every day by a local restaurateur. "Brussels agrees with us both," she wrote to Harriet, although perhaps it was the servant and the lack of cooking that really agreed with Kate, as Brussels no longer seemed to her the exciting place she had dreamed it would be. In the same letter (dated December 31, 1860) she commented without an awareness of sarcasm, "It must be a charming place in the summer." The winter, as usual, was proving depressing and Kate was longing to return home.

By the end of January 1861, Charlie was writing to his mother about the preparations for their homecoming, when they would stay at her home in Clarence Terrace while looking for a place of their own. "We sleep in two beds like sensible people—so will you simply let the bed in the spare-garret be brought down and placed by the side of mine. This will do for the present. No new beds as yet on any account." Whether Harriet thought this something to be concerned about is unknown; many nineteenth-century couples chose to sleep in separate bedrooms, so it is unlikely the desire for two single beds would have provoked much concern.

By mid-February Charlie had forgotten his previous desires to live in France and never return to the bustle of London. Brussels was driving him mad: The stove in their room was stifling and unhealthy, but without it the rooms were freezing; his health was still bad; and he was longing for English cooking "and a glass of sherry." Kate's postscript to his letter was much shorter and more wispy than usual. Sounding once again like one of her father's girlish heroines, she wrote to Harriet just one line: "I dread seeing you. I am always in such a fright at a meeting after a long absence." It may be that she had misgivings as she contemplated the return to living in someone else's home and abiding by someone else's rules after their months of independence. Perhaps it was also the prospect of married life in London and having to endure well-meant familial enquiries about the lack of a honeymoon baby that had her in such a "fright." At this age, only just twenty-one, Kate was still relatively shy with strangers; very likely she also felt nervous about returning to London, because of the rumors and vindictive gossip that had still been in such vicious circulation when she and Charlie had left to be married.

Back in England, during the honeymooners' absence Mamie had spent several weeks hobbling about on crutches after injuring her knee in a riding accident. Sydney had also become ill enough to be hospitalized and then been sent to Gad's Hill to be cared for, but he had recovered by the time of Kate's return and was able to rejoin his ship. Perhaps the most momentous event of all had taken place a few weeks after the wedding, when Kate's father had built a notorious bonfire, on which he burned many years' worth of correspondence from such luminaries as Thackeray, Carlyle, and Tennyson. Several accounts of this bonfire erroneously claim Kate was present and had begged him not to do it. If it is true that she begged him not to do it, she must have written to him from France trying to persuade him against it. Henry would recall how he and his brothers "roasted onions on the ashes of the great." It was symbolic for Charles, signifying that he was entering a new phase of life, unfettered by the past.

While Kate and Charlie had been suffering the cold weather in Switzerland, France, and Belgium, England had been bowed down by an equally grave winter. The temperature on December 25 made it the coldest Christmas for half a century. Charles reported in a letter that one day while he was out walking it had been so cold his beard had frozen solid.

10

THE THACKERAYS AND
THEIR CIRCLE

The honeymooners returned home in early February 1861 and moved in with Harriet Collins, at her house near Regent's Park (not far from Baker Street). Catherine Dickens was now living more closely to her daughter than she had since the separation. Kate and Charlie were back in time to celebrate Charles Dickens' forty-ninth birthday (on February 7), at a party in a house he had rented near Hyde Park. He had taken the house, 3 Hanover Terrace, so that Mamie could be in London during the Season. It was comforting for Kate to come home and discover that her family, especially her sister, would be so nearby. It seems likely she and Charlie also spent time with her mother and Charley. She had apparently written regularly to her mother since her marriage, no doubt promising more frequent visits once she was back in London. In November 1860 (while Kate and Charlie were still abroad), Harriet Martineau had written a letter commenting, "Mrs. D. is now cheerful,—kindly treated by her son, son-in-law, & married daughter. Dickens is wretched, & in an awful temper."

The Thackeray girls and Kate, despite their fathers' estrangement, had retained their close friendship (Mamie had not risked earning her father's displeasure by keeping up a prohibited friendship). Although as a child Kate had been closer to Anny, at the beginning of the 1860s she was especially intimate with twenty-one-year-old Minny, a talented amateur artist. Blanche Ritchie (later Blanche Warre Cornish), a Thackeray relation, who spent summers with the family in the early 1860s, described Minny as having "a complexion of milk and roses ... [with] ... a beautiful and flexible voice, most apt at reproducing comedy but low-toned in a crowd, and especially making itself felt amongst many voices. . . . She had the gift of creating calm." Minny and Anny had been invited to the Dickens family theatricals, until the two authors' estrangement, and they shared with Kate a love of acting and the dramatic. Like Kate, Minny was a very attractive woman, with a train of suitors and a streak of wildness to her nature.

Kate had known Thackeray since she was a small child, but had often been in awe of him. He, in turn, had not been as impressed with her as a child as he had been with Mamie. On discovering from Anny that she and her sister had become intimate friends with the Dickens girls—she with Katey and Minny with Mamie—Thackeray had replied to her letter: "I am glad to think that his girls and mine are friends. . . . I liked the elder best but the pretty one may have the good qualities I liked in the elder, or qualities as good though different." Kate dated her close friendship with Anny's father from shortly after she and Charlie returned from honeymoon. Anny was later to write, "Kate . . . had many friends but few more appreciative than my father." In 1911, Kate wrote an article for *Pall Mall* magazine. She described the beginning of her own adult relationship with Thackeray:

> *My sister and I had known Thackeray's two daughters ever since we were children . . . but it was not until soon after I was married that I came to know their great father. . . . I had been to Palace Green, Kensington, several times before I had any real talk with its master, for notwithstanding my immense admiration for his work, or perhaps, because of it, I felt a little shy and reserved with him, for I too was young and had been brought up with a wholesome awe of men so great as Thackeray; but one morning as I was walking rapidly toward the High Street with head held low to shield my eyes from the sun, I became conscious of a large tall obstacle in front of me and of a cheery voice saying, 'Where are you going to, my pretty maid?' I looked up, startled, and there stood Thackeray. 'I'm going a-shopping kind sir', I said. 'May I go with you, my pretty maid?' And he offered me his arm with a courtly air and led me, not a-shopping, but into Kensington*

Gardens, where, as we walked up and down his 'favourite path', he said, 'Now that I have captured the fair Princess, and brought her to my Enchanted Garden, like the wicked old ogre I am, I want her to tell me about that other ogre she knows who lives shut up in his castle near Gravesend.' And this was the beginning of countless conversations . . .

Thackeray wrote a poem for (and loosely about) Kate, which he called "Mrs. Katherine's Lantern." It was inspired by an antique lantern he had bought for her. The poem tells of a beautiful, mysterious Venetian lady with the initials "K.E." and a man who has become enthralled with the idea of her after discovering her lantern, which has "K.E." etched into one of the panes of glass. He is trying to discover her identity a century after she sat on her Italian balcony and listened to her lovers serenading her from below:

> 'Coming from a gloomy court,
> Place of Israelite resort,
> This old lamp I've brought with me.
> Madam, on its panes you'll see
> The initials K and E.'
> 'An old lantern brought to me?
> Ugly, dingy, battered, black!'
> (Here a lady I suppose
> Turning up a pretty nose) –
> 'Pray, sir, take the old thing back.
> I've no taste for bricabrac.'
> 'Please to mark the letters twain' –
> (I'm supposed to speak again) –
> 'Graven on the lantern pane.
> Can you tell me who was she,
> Mistress of the flowery wreath,
> And the anagram beneath –
> The mysterious K E?
> 'Full a hundred years are gone
> Since the little beacon shone
> From a Venice balcony:

There, on summer nights, it hung,
And her Lovers came and sung
To their beautiful K E.
'Hush! in the canal below
Don't you hear the plash of oars
Underneath the lantern's glow,
And a thrilling voice begins
To the sound of mandolins?
Begins singing of amore
And delire and dolore –
O the ravishing tenore!
'Lady, do you know the tune?
Ah, we all of us have hummed it!
I've an old guitar has thrummed it,
Under many a changing moon.
Shall I try it? Do Re Mi . . .
What is this? Ma foi, the fact is,
That my hand is out of practice,
And my poor old fiddle cracked is,
And a man – I let the truth out, –
Who's had almost every tooth out,
Cannot sing as once he sung,
When he was young as you are young,
When he was young and lutes were strung,
And love-lamps in the casement hung.'

Serendipitously, a strong friendship also formed between Charlie and Thackeray, who was said to like "few people better than Charles Collins." The Collinses spent much of their time at the Thackerays' home in Palace Green.[46] Evidence of this can be seen in an old Thackeray family album, in which a photo of a group including Kate and Charlie is captioned: "some of friends we saw constantly at Palace Green."

---

46 Their home, 2 Palace Green, was a sumptuous villa in the style of a Queen Anne house. Thackeray had bought a Queen Anne property, but it had proved (after purchase) to be unsafe and beyond repair. It was knocked down and their new home built in its place. His family nicknamed it "the Palazzo" because of its opulence.

Many years earlier, Thackeray's much-loved wife, Isabella, had ceased to live with her husband and daughters, having become mentally ill after Minny's birth (which followed closely on the infantile death of another daughter).[47] For years she had lived in a succession of homes in the countryside, cared for by professional "companions." For Kate, the knowledge that someone else among her acquaintance had unusual parental arrangements must have been a source of relief and release. In addition, it seems that Anny and Minny were also apprised of their father's deep but unrequited passion for the wife of one of his friends, Mrs. Brookfield; as such, the Thackeray girls would have been understanding and sympathetic friends to whom Kate would be able to talk about Dickens' infatuation with Ellen Ternan.

Charlie seems to have been widely welcomed by the Thackeray circle, with Blanche Warre Cornish describing him in the most glowing terms: "the chosen friend, though so many years younger, of Mr. Thackeray in his later years. We ... knew him as the delightful humourist ... with chiselled features and searching blue eyes, who always remained grave while others, and especially very young people, roared at his utterances. His delicate humour appealed in a higher way to the lovers of literature." Blanche's memoirs—she herself was one of the "very young people"—indicate that Charlie won her over entirely, as she turns even his "fastidious sensitiveness" into a virtue. It is interesting to read such a glowing female account of someone about whom even his closest male friends' diaries record feelings of irritation and scorn.

It is possible that Charlie Collins was homosexual. This could account for his hero-worship of Millais, his feelings of guilt and ascetic desire to deny himself pleasures, and his early passion for the cold Maria Rossetti, a passion which was never likely to be consummated due to her intense religious fervor. It would also account for Charlie's lack of desire to marry, something that—as his older brother had commented—had needed to be

---

47 Isabella's illness had become pronounced when, shortly after Minny's birth, she attempted suicide by throwing herself overboard while the family was traveling by ferry to visit her mother in Ireland. One of Anny's earliest memories dates from just before this time, when she and her mother were walking on a beach and she was three years old. She remembers her mother picking her up and suddenly hurling her into the surf; the violence of her mother's action and intention was what gave Anny such a strong recollection of the memory.

won over by a great internal battle, and for his impotence when married to Kate, whom he obviously loved dearly. It is impossible to be certain but it is a hypothesis that gathers weight when researching his life. I find it particularly interesting that in his novel, *A Cruise Upon Wheels*, subtitled "The Chronicle of Some Autumn Wanderings Along the Deserted Post Roads of France," the two main characters are men. It is closely based on his and Kate's travels, yet the central characters are two male friends, rather than a honeymooning husband and wife. If Kate knew he was homosexual, it could also account for her later comment to Charles Dickens that Charlie "ought never to have married"; something that could have referred equally either to homosexuality or to impotence.[48] Charlie's impotence was not the well-kept secret it should have been, as Frederick Lehmann was to record that it was an "infamy" that Charlie had chosen to marry at all.

The Palace Green fraternity bestowed upon Charlie the nickname "Colenso," a wry comment on his religious leanings as it referred to the controversial Anglican bishop John William Colenso (1814–83).[49] According to Blanche Warre Cornish, his fellow artist Lord Leighton also had a nickname for Charlie: he called him "Jacques," though she gives no explanation as to why. Kate refers to Charlie fondly as "Colenso" when writing to Anny and Minny and basked in Thackeray's approval of her husband; something especially welcome as her own father was finding it increasingly hard not to judge Charlie for his shortcomings. A couple of months after the couple returned from honeymoon, Dickens wrote to a friend,

> *. . . they seem to get on together admirably. . . . [Charlie] is at work upon a book describing their journey, with illustrations by himself. I ardently wish he were painting, instead; but of course I don't say so. There are no 'Great Expectations' of perspective [sic] Collinses. Which I think a blessed thing, though again I don't say so.*

---

48 It must be remembered that at this date, it was illegal to be a practicing homosexual man in Britain. Homosexual women were more lucky—Queen Victoria refused to believe that women would do such a thing, so no law was passed making lesbian acts illegal.

49 Colenso was the Bishop of Natal, a fervent missionary who wrote several very controversial books questioning long-held principles of Christian belief. In 1861 he had published a new theory about St. Paul's letter to the Romans, renouncing the theory of everlasting punishment in Hell. His Broad Church views caused much controversy and discussion in the Anglican Church.

Kate had left home to be rid of the arguments and atmospheres created by her parents' separation; it would doubtless have been frustrating
and wearing to find herself in the middle of problems once again, this

Mamie (left), Charles Dickens, and Katey in the garden at Gad's Hill Place

time between her husband and father. The situation cannot, however, have been intolerable as, in the spring and summer after their return, Kate and Charlie had begun regularly dividing their time between London and Gad's Hill. As soon as Charles, Mamie, and Georgina returned to Kent, Kate was arranging to visit them, better able to be happy at her father's home now she was a married woman. Henry, who was "still a mere child" when his parents separated, understood little of what was going on. To him, Gad's Hill was a wonderful place where he spent many contented school holidays. He wrote defiantly, as an adult, that he was allowed and encouraged to visit Catherine in Gloucester Crescent regularly, although he does not mention what must have been foremost in the mind of even a "mere child"—that is, why his mother did not live with him anymore and why she was always so sad. Catherine missed her children indescribably. Attempting to compensate for her loss, she would hold parties at her home for all the local children—parties to which her own children never came.

In July of 1861, Sydney was allowed home on leave while his ship was being repaired and it is likely Kate timed her visit so she could spend time with the "Ocean Spectre"—a nickname that must have seemed chilling now Sydney had joined the Navy. At the end of that month, Charles wrote a letter to Mamie, a letter that includes a very interesting comment. Edmund Yates had written to Charles, asking if he could stay at Gad's Hill one Friday night. It was a night on which Kate had intended to stay, so Charles asked Mamie to put her sister off and suggest she arrive on the Saturday instead. It seems the family was aware of Kate's feelings for Edmund Yates—and that these had not been cured by her marriage.

Toward the end of 1861, Charles gained another set of dependants when his brother-in-law Henry Austin died. As with the practice that seems to have been endemic among Charles' relations and acquaintances, Henry left no provision for his wife Laetitia or their children, and the novelist took it upon himself to take care of them. He contacted the late Henry's employers and persuaded them to award Laetitia a widow's pension of £60 a year; in addition, Charles gave her an allowance of £100 per annum, paid for the funeral, and settled all her husband's outstanding debts.

Despite his less than exemplary behavior as a husband, in all other respects Charles was a truly generous man and his munificence was demonstrated not only financially. In spite of his dislike of Charlie as a son-in-law, he did his best to further the younger man's business interests. Realizing that neither he nor Kate could influence Charlie's decision to give up art in favor of becoming a novelist, he wrote to a contact at John Murray publishers, requesting they meet Charlie and talk about *A Cruise Upon Wheels*.

A Cruise Upon Wheels (which would be published in 1862) begins with Charlie's preface that explains:

> *It is an experiment to write the history of a journey in which the interest attaches more to the persons who travel, than to the places which they travel through. . . . It is an experiment to seek to interest the public in a mode of traveling of which it has probably had no experience. It is an experiment to use fictitious characters in a book of travels, and to describe their adventures in the third person.*

His two main characters are Mr. David Fudge—the pseudonym of the Eye-Witness in *All The Year Round*—and "his friend and companion, Mr. Pinchbold." David Fudge is based largely on Charlie, or perhaps the man he would like to be:

> *a personage of simple tastes and of a retiring disposition. He was one who found more pleasure in studying men than in associating with them, one who liked better to be among the woods and fields than in great towns . . . in a word, he was dreadfully unpractical . . . that turn for the romantic with which he was profoundly imbued.*

Francis Pinchbold is not even vaguely akin to Kate and is described:

> *There never was such a strange complication of elements as were brought together to form the character of Francis Pinchbold. If he had not, during the first ten years of his life, been systematically spoilt by a sensitive mother, and frightened out of his wits by a boisterous father, who laughed at him and bullied him by turns, he would have grown*

up a more useful member of society than he was. . . . He was . . .
everything by turns—rash and timid; irritable and long-suffering;
irresolute and determined; and in a thousand other ways inconsistent
. . . [also] conscientious, faithful, and true always.

It seems Pinchbold's character is deliberately very different from Kate's, perhaps in order not to cause any offense or even inspire any scandal about Charlie writing of his own wife in the guise of a man. It would be fascinating, though, to discover if Pinchbold were based in reality, on one of Charlie's male acquaintances. It seems, however, that the friendship between the two men, as described at the start of the book, could refer to Charlie and Kate's relationship during their honeymoon:

When two men ride together on a horse one must ride behind . . .
there is no doubt that in the case we are considering the conduct of the
affairs was mainly in the hands of the older of these two gentlemen,
Mr. David Fudge, and that the other looked up to him, believed in
him, and was ever ready to be guided by him.

The novel is a comedy, trying very hard to be like *The Pickwick Papers,* and proved popular when first published. It was republished in 1926 and seems to have been fairly popular then, over sixty years after being written. One wonders what Kate's true feelings were about her husband's novel. It is something that is not mentioned at all toward the end of her life, although novels by her father, Thackeray, and Wilkie Collins are often discussed. One imagines it proved difficult for her to encourage and praise her husband while thinking, as she had revealed to his mother in her honeymoon letter, that he would be far better to stay with journalism.

The book's two main characters begin their journey in Malaise (very obviously Calais)—staying at the rue Loyale (instead of rue Royale)—about which the author is scathing, seeming in hindsight not to remember any of the initial experiences in the town that made Kate and him write such happy letters home. The hapless duo travel about and encounter various "characters," most of whom are larger than life and provide much of the comic element. They spend some time attempting to buy a suitable horse and carriage and also acquire a highly talented dog, Mazard, who is notably more intelligent than either of his well-intentioned but naïve owners. In the best tradition of Victorian story-telling, the friends undergo a series of small adventures, misunderstandings, and accidents before reaching their final destination, the Alps.

Interestingly, when in 1893 a new edition of the novel was published, the front cover depicted a young woman, who looks remarkably like Kate at the time of her marriage to Charlie, reading a newspaper. Seated nearby is a man who appears to be the woman's husband (though he perhaps resembles Wilkie Collins more than Charlie) and what seems

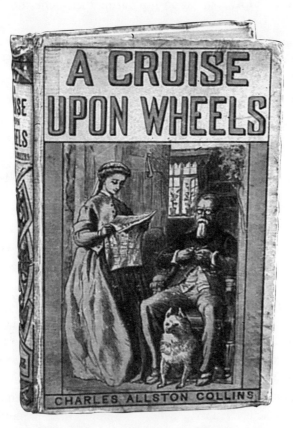

The cover of the 1893 edition of Charlie Collins's novel

to be a Pomeranian dog. (Mamie's much loved dog, Mrs. Bouncer, was a Pomeranian.) It is a very strange cover for a book in which the two protagonists are male; it would appear the illustrator was swayed more by Charlie's real-life journey than his fictional one.

Toward the end of 1861, Charlie Collins's shortcomings as a son-in-law were well and truly overshadowed by the news that Kate's eldest brother, Charley, was to marry his childhood sweetheart, Bessie Evans. Bessie was the daughter of Dickens' old publisher. In the days when the two families were still on friendly terms, the adolescent love match had been welcomed by both sets of parents, but Charles would never forgive the quarrel. It had now become such a point of honor to him that he even refused to attend his son's wedding. To Catherine, this decision must have been a relief, meaning she could attend without fear of reprisals. After the pain of missing Kate's wedding, she had the joy of being mother of the groom. For many years to come, Charley and Bessie would celebrate their wedding anniversary by dining with Catherine.

The wedding date, November 19, 1861, was chosen, but Charles Dickens senior did not tell any of his friends it was happening. His oldest friend, Thomas Beard, was among those invited to the wedding, by Charley. Beard took command of a difficult situation by writing to Charles, explaining that he was going for Charley's sake and not out of lack of consideration for his old friend's feelings. Charles' reply is astonishingly controlling and one hopes that Beard ignored his recommendations:

> *Of course I perfectly understand your responding to any request on the part of Charley, or of his mother, to attend the dear fellow's marriage. But I must add the expression of my earnest hope that it is not your intention to enter Mr. Evans's house on that occasion.*

One can assume Kate and Charlie attended. Kate was very close to her eldest brother, she was living in London, where the wedding took place, and now that she was a married woman her father had no control over her behavior. It was an unhappy time, however, as once again the rift between her parents—and their sets of friends—came to the fore. Not content with boycotting the wedding, a fortnight before it was to happen

Charles wrote to Mrs. Brown (one of his regular correspondents and a friend of Angela Burdett-Coutts, who was in contact with Catherine):

I wish I could hope that Charley's marriage may not be a disastrous one. There is no help for it, and the dear fellow does what is unavoidable—his foolish mother would have effectually committed him if nothing else had; chiefly I suppose because her hatred of the bride and all belonging to her, used to know no bounds, and was quite inappeasable. But I have a strong belief, founded on careful observation of him, that he cares nothing for the girl.

The letter is confused, bitter, and strangely inarticulate. The strain of needing to remain the great Dickens to his public, of no longer being able to confide in his most intimate friends, and of trying to deal with the bewildering force of his feelings for Ellen was beginning to take its toll. Just as he had done about his own separation, Charles started to create a fictional version of Charley's marriage, even before it had taken place. Perhaps this forthcoming wedding, coupled with Kate's disappointing marriage to Charlie, led Charles to feel that he was losing control over his children and this thought exacerbated his deepest fear: that he was growing old. There was no fathomable reason for him to suppose that Charley's marriage would be disastrous—although Charles' sudden feelings about his own may have led him to believe that all marriages were a sham. It seems that his tirade against Charley and Bessie's relationship stemmed from his own selfish desire that his family should not be allied with that of his "enemy." Kate, however, seemed perfectly content with Charley's choice of bride, although she perhaps found her a little lackluster, as they do not appear to have been close as sisters-in-law, despite Kate's fondness for Charley.

Contrary to Charles Dickens' doom-laden prophecies, Charley and Bessie's marriage was to prove a long and very happy one. As their daughter Mary Angela Dickens was to record many years later when writing about her father, "It was a family joke—and also a fact—that he and my mother were engaged when he was seven years old! They were lovers all their lives."

Kate was once more caught in the middle of a family rift, with friends uncertain how to approach the subject, or even if they should mention it at all. It was like her parents' separation all over again; far from being able to celebrate her brother's marriage, Kate found herself treading carefully between both "sides" of her family, so as not to offend anyone. An illustration of the confusion can be found in a letter written by Bulwer Lytton to John Forster. At the end of November he had received a card from "Mr. and Mrs. Charles Dickens Junior," but as Charles Dickens senior had not even told him that Charley was getting married Lytton did not know if he was supposed to make reference to it or not and wrote to Forster asking him for advice.

By December, however, the family's attention had shifted to Kate's brother Sydney, who had been appointed to the *Orlando,* a ship, his father proudly announced to friends, "that every one in the service seemed to be trying for." He sailed for Halifax before Christmas, at the age of fourteen (this was not an unusually young age for boys to start a career in the Navy at that time). By now, Kate had grown used to her brothers disappearing off to all corners of the globe, but little Sydney had always been such a diminutive boy, so deserving of an older sister's protection, and was still so very young, that one imagines his leaving must have been a terrible wrench for her and Mamie. At the age of fourteen, Kate had been happily schooled at home with her sister and attending art classes just a short walk away; at the same age, Sydney was sailing halfway around the world.

Charlie was now a regular columnist on *All The Year Round.* His father-in-law was occasionally scathing about his articles—in correspondence with Wills—but the readers seemed to approve of Charlie. His articles suggest a man of greater personality than his friends' diary entries ever record and he seems to have enjoyed his Eye-Witness job, but he still yearned to be taken seriously as a novelist. It was true that his salary from journalism was much needed, and it seems that Charlie could not be half-hearted about anything, having abandoned his art entirely when the desire to write came upon him, so that he could devote himself to a new muse. He had also suffered several setbacks in his artistic career, finding the seated position he needed to adopt at his easel made him feel ill, as well as experiencing financial problems. He did not necessarily suffer

John Everett Millais' illustration, "Was It Not A Lie?" from *The Cornhill* magazine. It was drawn in 1860, the same year Millais was painting Kate for *The Black Brunswicker*; it seems likely that Kate was his inspiration for the woman in this sketch.

more knocks than any other artist, but he was a deeply sensitive man who took even mild criticism to heart. It was frustrating for Kate, to have married a man with whom she could talk about art and then to see him give up his dreams.

Millais was branching out into book illustration and there are a couple of his drawings that very likely Kate, perhaps unwittingly, was the model for. Both of them illustrations for the same book, Anthony Trollope's *Framley Parsonage*, drawn for the novel's serialization in *The Cornhill* magazine, they are entitled "Lord Lufton and Lucy Robarts" and "Was It Not a Lie?" The latter is the most dramatic, the image of a young girl lying heartbroken on her bed, having just refused the proposal of marriage from the man she loves. Her flounced skirt takes up most of the bed, her face and hands seeming very small and sad in comparison. One little foot in a buckled shoe peeps listlessly out from beneath the hem of her dress. They were drawn in 1860, the same year in which Kate sat for *The Black Brunswicker;* the face of the girl is extremely similar to other pictures of Kate. Although there is no record of Millais consciously making Kate the model for Lucy Robarts, there is also no record of any other model being used and perhaps Millais even drew the pictures unconscious of whose features he was giving to Lucy.

It seems Kate took up painting regularly again as soon as they returned from their honeymoon and that she was now good enough to be considered a professional artist. Although we don't know the names or subjects of any of her works from this date, we know from Georgina Hogarth's letters that she was painting well and was finally starting to make money from her art, selling what she could in an attempt to supplement Charlie's income. In the early 1870s, when the majority of her possessions were destroyed in the storage facility fire, it seems that the paintings and drawings she had completed by then were among them as none have been passed down through the family. Sadly, because of the period, there are no photographic records. Strangely, although Georgina records that some of these early paintings sold, they have not ever come up for auction or been included in any recent art exhibitions. It seems likely that they remain somewhere in a family attic or upon a wall unrecognized for what they are. When I first wrote this book, I mentioned that I knew of no paintings bearing the signature of Kate Collins. I was lucky to be contacted by a couple who, on reading my book, had realized that they owned a painting by Kate, a pretty watercolor painted during her first marriage. They were kind enough to meet me and show me the painting, which depicts a young woman with pale golden-red hair seated at a piano.[50] She is dressed simply in a dark grey gown with white flounced sleeves and collar, looking wistfully into the distance while her fingers hover over the keys, as though the tune she is playing has provoked a melancholy memory. Most excitingly, the painting has a label on the reverse, written in Kate's unmistakable handwriting. The label shows the original title was "Memories of the Past," but Kate has crossed this out and changed it to "A Song Without Words." The label also contains Kate's name and address: "Kate Collins, 10 Thurloe Place, South Kensington" and a price of "£21.0.0." The couple who showed me the painting had bought it in a small art gallery in Bath for £100. The owner told them that he knew nothing about the artist but that she was probably from the local area. It is a pity that nothing more is known of the painting's provenance or of who brought it from London to Bath and how it ended up in the gallery. It is the sole painting I have seen that can be indubitably dated to Kate's career during her marriage to Charlie Collins; it proves that despite the many and difficult demands of looking after a sickly husband, Kate did continue to paint and attempt to sell her work. Charlie's illness placed a great many stresses on Kate and she was unable to pursue her painting career in the 1860s with as much fervor as she was to do in the latter half of the 1870s, but at least we now know she did continue to work and, at times, to sell her paintings. Charlie does not seem to have encouraged his wife and perhaps he was understandably jealous about Kate wanting to pursue a career that he had not felt able to continue with. Although there were not a large number of successful female artists at this time, there were some and the art world was starting to open up to women, albeit painfully slowly, with painters such as Louise Jopling and Kate Greenaway on the scene and the American painter Anna Lea Merrit about to make her way over to London.

---

50 This painting appears on the back cover of *Charles Dickens' Favorite Daughter.*

Despite the many hindrances to her career, Kate remained serious about her art, fully intending to be recognized as a professional artist. She remained very friendly with Millais, who had been fascinated by her since painting *The Black Brunswicker* and wanted to paint her again. Charlie was devoted to his old friend, and the Collinses and Millais saw each other regularly. Much later, Kate would say of Millais, "His was such a beautiful nature, you felt that any little piece of advice he gave you, you would say: 'I am grateful for it and of course I will gladly take it.'"

A few months after their return from honeymoon, the Collinses moved from Harriet's house in Clarence Terrace into their own home, in Kensington, west London.[51] It was a small house with two bedrooms (as well as room for at least one servant) and an attic room, which they used as a studio and for Charlie's writing study. They may have had a cook and a maid—or one servant who worked as both, considering how "very poor" Kate later related she and Charlie had been.[52] There is scant information about their domestic situation at this time, but despite their impoverished finances they could not have lived without a servant.

Kate was a natural interior decorator. With her artist's eye for color and the benefit of having visited many elegant homes, she made their little home very beautiful. Some American friends of the Thackerays, Mr. and Mrs. Baxter, visited London in the early 1860s and were introduced to Kate and Charlie. They found Kate entrancingly beautiful and were "deeply impressed" with how the Collinses' home was decorated and with what excellent "taste."

By moving to Kensington, they had taken their place among the elite of the artistic world. Not far away was Little Holland House—the home of the charismatic Prinsep family—which had become a regular haunt of artists ever since the famed painter G. F. Watts had come to stay for a few days and ended up as a permanent resident. One of Watts's pupils was the son of the house, Valentine Cameron Prinsep, who was also one

---

51 Unfortunately their actual address at this time is unknown; the 1861 census—which was taken on April 7—records them living at Harriet Collins' address and by the 1871 census they had moved house again. We know from Anny Thackeray's records that Kate and Charlie lived in Kensington. The census for 1861 also shows that Charlie no longer considered himself an artist as he gives his profession as "Author/journalist."

52 In the 1871 census, Kate and Charlie are recorded as having two servants.

of the younger devotees of the Pre-Raphaelite movement (in particular, a disciple of Dante Gabriel Rossetti). When the Collinses first moved into their home, the great High Victorian artist and patron Frederic Leighton had a studio in Orme Square, not far from Kensington. In 1866, he would move to live in the area, buying a sumptuous villa on Holland Park Road next door to the Prinseps.[53] The artists who lived in the area have become known as the Holland Park Circle, because of their proximity to Holland House and its grounds. This house no longer stands, having been bombed heavily in the Second World War, but its grounds are now one of London's most beautiful public spaces, Holland Park. Among the group were Marcus Stone and Luke Fildes (who would both become one of Charles Dickens' illustrators).[54]

Kate and Charlie were intimates of Leighton and his circle, as were the Thackeray girls. In the mid-nineteenth century, anyone who wanted to make it in the London art world had to live in London. Today, with high-speed Internet access, airplanes, and telephones, artists can live anywhere and still promote their works, but before the advent of such technology artists needed to live wherever the art collectors found most convenient. As a result, there was a close-knit artistic community in which everyone knew everybody else. Now moving in this circle, Kate found this a time of great excitement, as she took her place in the world as an artist and as an

---

53 Lord Leighton's home, 2 (now 12) Holland Park Road, has become the Leighton House Museum.

54 Edmund Yates wrote an article about Leighton in a series entitled "Celebrities At Home." It is astonishingly sycophantic, suggesting Yates was desperate to be invited into Leighton's elite circle of friends. "In a quiet corner of Kensington, on ground that has become classic by association with the celebrities of many generations, *il pittore felice* of our English shool has built his house. The neighbourhood is a colony of painters, architects, and musicians. On one side rise the noble elms and quaint Jacobean gables of Holland House; on the other the stately studios of many of our best-known artists.... From the windows of his house in Holland Park-road, Mr. Leighton looks, across a bit of sward shaded by ancient elms and cedars, on the studios of Val Prinsep, Watts, Marcus Stone, William Burgess, Thornycroft, Luke Fildes—a little band of honest workers in the same sunny field of prosperous labour. [...] Mr. Leighton is an accomplished linguist, and familiar with the finest works of German, French, and Italian authors, the beauties of which have not been diluted by translation. He is a musician too, and there are few more delightful gatherings in London than the soirees in this house, when the resonant room reverberates with the exquisite tones of Piatti, or Joachim charms all listeners with his wonderful execution of Brahm's masterpieces ..." This article appeared in *The World*, a society journal (the precursor of today's publications such as *Hello!*). It was an article in the same series, about Thackeray, that caused the enormous rift between Yates and Thackeray, and, consequently, between Dickens and Thackeray.

independent young woman, no longer constrained by the house rules of a father who thought two balls in one Season more than enough excitement.

Eighteen sixty-two followed much the same pattern as the previous year, with Charles Dickens taking a house in London, 16 Hyde Park Gate, for the Season and Kate and Charlie making regular visits to Gad's Hill throughout the summer. Kate remained extremely close to her sister and Auntie Georgy, relying on them throughout her marriage just as much as she had beforehand. I am sure the many visits to Kent were due on Charlie's part to economizing—it was much cheaper to let his father-in-law feed them than to do so themselves—but it was not only for this reason that they were such regular visitors. As well as longing to spend time with her family, Kate seems to have been deeply attached to the family home, despite having lived in Gad's Hill for only a couple of years. During one of her visits home she decided to decorate the staircase, anticipating the Bloomsbury Group's painting activities at their summer home, Charleston in Sussex. The designs she painted, an intricate and pretty pattern, can still be seen today. By this date, she and her father seem to have moved beyond their battles over his treatment of Catherine, and Kate was even prepared to tolerate his relationship with Ellen. Just as she and her mother never discussed her father (a rule that was reportedly broken only twice over the years), it seems that she and her father agreed to disagree over her mother. Kate did not ever become as close to or accepting of Ellen as her sister and aunt did, but she did not blatantly shun her and would occasionally stay at Gad's Hill when Ellen was visiting. For the most part, Ellen was not a problem. Charles kept her in her own residence and she did not ever become mistress of Gad's Hill—that position was always reserved for Georgy and Mamie. She seldom visited as Charles strove to keep his family life and his life with her separate, and no visitors to the house would have been aware of her existence. To all outside observers, Charles lived with his children, his sister-in-law; a small staff of servants; and a regular stream of guests.

It was in 1862 that one of Kate's great sadnesses was finally resolved. The bitter estrangement between Dickens and Thackeray had been raging unresolved for several years. Although she and Thackeray would talk, during their "countless conversations," about her father and his works,

Thackeray had never touched upon the argument, until one day when he asked her advice on how a reconciliation could be brought about. Kate replied, hesitantly, that Thackeray would have to apologize, or at least make the first move, as her father was "more shy of speaking than you are, and . . . he cannot apologize, I fear." Thackeray replied instantly that in that case there would be no reconciliation, but then sat and mulled it over. Later in the same conversation, he asked her if she thought Dickens would be kind to him if he did make the first move and she assured him that he would. She described the scene in which the two friends were finally reconciled in *Pall Mall* magazine:

> *Thackeray . . . came to our house with radiant face to tell me the result. 'How did it happen?' said I.*
>
> *'Oh,' he said gaily, 'your father knew he was wrong and was full of apologies—'*
>
> *It was now my turn to look severe.*
>
> *'You know you are not telling me the truth, you wicked man. Please let me hear immediately what really did happen.'*
>
> *Thackeray's eyes were very kind as he said quite simply, 'I met him at the Athenaeum Club and held out my hand, saying we had been foolish long enough—or words to that effect; your father grasped it very cordially—and—and we are friends again, thank God!'*

Although Thackeray and Dickens were now reconciled, it would take longer for Thackeray's daughters to forgive the man who had so hurt their father. Anny and Minny would not be friendly again with Charles Dickens until the summer of 1864. Once more it was Kate who brought about the reconciliation. Her father's last reading of the Season was from *David Copperfield* at St. James's Hall (an important event in the social calendar). Kate secured two extra tickets, then called upon the Thackeray girls, "begging" them to accompany her. She was so persuasive that they finally agreed. After the "unforgettably grand" reading, Kate took her nervous friends around to see her father. Anny recalled that he took their hands in his "with kindest grasps of greeting and comfort."

In 1862, two years after her marriage, perhaps by now resigned to its platonic nature, Kate appears to have been happy and Charles could appreciate that Charlie was a very kind husband. For once, he wrote glowingly of his son-in-law to de Cerjat in Paris (who had met Charlie during the couple's honeymoon). Not all his children came in for such praise:

> *My daughter naturally liking to be in town at this time of the year, I have changed houses with a friend for three months . . . an odious little London box. . . . But we are within a few paces of the Ride in the Park, and of Kensington Gardens, and both Mary and Georgina like the change. . . . My married daughter goes on very happily, and her husband is a most excellent husband and an upright good fellow— clever too, and making his way. They have no family as yet, and (if they would take my word for the fact) are better without one. My eldest boy—married not particularly to my satisfaction—is in business as an Eastern Merchant in the City, and will do well if he can find continuous energy; otherwise not. My second boy, with the High- landers in India, spends more than he gets and has cost me money and disappointed me. My third boy, a good steady fellow but not at all brilliant, is educating 'expensively' for engineers or artillery. My fourth (this sounds like a charade), a born little sailor, is a Midship- man in H.M.S. Orlando now at Bermuda, and will make his way anywhere. Remaining two, at school; elder of the said remaining two, very bright and clever. Georgina and Mary keeping house for me; and Francis Jeffrey (I ought to have counted him as the third boy, so we'll take him here as No. 2 and a half) in my office, pending a vacancy in the Foreign Office . . .*

The "third boy" he mentions is actually his fourth son, Alfred. The "fourth" is Sydney. The elder of the two boys at school is Henry. Plorn is, surprisingly, not given an individual mention or any praise.

In the summer of 1862, Georgina Hogarth became very ill and Kate rushed to Kent to help Mamie nurse their aunt. Georgina suffered from a genetic heart condition; it was this "weakness" of the heart that had caused Mary Hogarth's death and Charles spent much of his life frightened that his own children had inherited it—a fear he kept to himself, not wanting to alarm them. His concern would prove to be well-founded.

—◦—

During this illness, Georgina was examined by Charles' favorite doctor, Dr. John Elliotson (who is remembered as the first doctor to use a stethoscope). He diagnosed an aneurism of the aorta and for several weeks it was feared that Georgy would not live out the summer. Georgina, though, was not the kind of woman to give up on anything and by the end of September she was pronounced "much better." The illness, however, had been a warning and from now on, throughout what was to prove a long life, she would be plagued by an irregular heartbeat and an increased tendency to illness. It seems likely, when reading through his letters, that her illness plunged Charles back into a depression. His fear of losing her was, perhaps, exacerbated by the memories of Mary Hogarth and a sense of guilt that Georgy had become so estranged from her family that her mother and sisters were not there to help nurse her; it was lucky that Kate and Mamie were so devoted to their aunt, or the illness would have been a very lonely one. Although none of Kate's early letters survived the fire, it seems likely that the illness of her aunt and her father's depression would have led to one of her own depressive fits, which came upon her so regularly in later life. Through other people's letters, we know that her health was not at its best at this time, and this may have been due largely to emotional stress.

During the London Seasons of the early 1860s, Kate and Charlie were often to be found in company with the Thackerays at garden parties in Wimbledon or Richmond, picnicking in the royal parks or visiting art exhibitions. In the summer of 1862, London was riveted with excitement about a new exhibition taking place at South Kensington. It had been Prince Albert's idea to build new museums in South Kensington; the first (which is now known as the Victoria & Albert museum) was constructed with large glass domes forming part of the elaborate roof. Although the Prince Consort had died before he could see the exhibition brought to life, it went ahead as planned, in a glorious summer, with the sun streaming through the domes onto the crowds of visitors below.

Among the exhibits was a collection of New British Art. Pre-Raphaelitism was, by now, a leading British movement and, as such, it was well represented. Millais and Holman Hunt were the undisputed stars of the show and no doubt Charlie felt more than a twinge of envy at the knowledge that, had he possessed a private income like Millais, he could have pursued his career as a painter and his works might have been fêted at South Kensington, too.

The exhibition aside, 1862 was a time of great excitement for the Collinses and all their circle. *A Cruise Upon Wheels* was published, as was Anny Thackeray's first novel, *The Story of Elizabeth*.[55] It was the year in which their friend Valentine Prinsep exhibited at the Royal Academy for the first time (a picture entitled *Bianca Capella*) and it was also the year in which Kate became an aunt, when Bessie gave birth to a daughter, Mary Angela Dickens.[56]

By this time, the London art world had welcomed into its circle the artist Frederick Walker, an attractive, fair-haired man, no more than 5 feet 2 inches tall, "with straight features and earnest blue eyes." He moved into a house near Bayswater Road, not far from Kate, Charlie, and the rest of the Kensington artists. A talented man, with a warm, witty personality, often hidden under a welter of shyness, he lived with his mother, sisters, and a large number of cats. Walker was a close friend of Thackeray's, having worked as an illustrator on the latter's novels, and became a great favorite of the novelist's daughters and their circle. He would later illustrate one of Anny's novels (*The Village on the Cliff*). He was a very popular figure. The writer and artist George du Maurier based the hero of his best-selling book *Trilby* (1894) partly on Fred Walker and wrote of his fictional character and its inspiration:[57]

both were small and slight though beautifully made, with tiny hands and feet; always arrayed as the lilies of the field for all they spun and

---

55 Although Anny's name is little known today, during her lifetime she became famous as a novelist and her works were well received.

56 Mary Angela would become a novelist.

57 George du Maurier was the grandfather of the novelist Daphne du Maurier. He also based a character in *Trilby* on Val Prinsep.

toiled so arduously; both had regularly featured faces of a noble cast and most winning character; both had the best and simplest manners in the world, and a way of getting themselves much and quickly and permanently liked.

Despite his closeness to the Thackeray family, Walker became impossibly shy in the presence of women. On one occasion Thackeray, perhaps as an impish form of aversion therapy, tricked Walker into spending time alone with his daughters and their friends. The novelist showed his visitor into a room as if the two men were entering to have a cozy chat; unknown to the younger man, the Thackeray girls and their party were already in residence. Their father promptly left Walker with them, shutting the door firmly behind him as he went. His parting comment to the furiously blushing young man was: "There, Walker, are a lot of pretty girls for you."

Kate was among those who became very fond of "little Walker," as he was usually referred to. In later life, she reminisced about the times Fred Walker would take her out for coffee at a little café on the Embankment that was open late into the night. This was probably one of the reasons she was scorned as being "fast" by sour-faced Society ladies. Fred Walker was certainly captivated by her, although whether his feelings were reciprocated is unknown.

The early 1860s were a happy time for Kate. She and Charlie enjoyed a thriving social life, such as a party the Thackeray girls arranged for their father. Anny and Minny had decided that they and a group of their friends would take over the kitchens and cook dinner; one must remember that at this date young women of their social standing were not necessarily expected to be able to cook for themselves, they had simply to know how to hire a cook and what to instruct them to make. Kate wrote the following account of the evening:

I remember a certain evening when the dinner was to be prepared by his two girls and their guests, who wore white aprons and caps for the occasion. The guests were nearly all young people, and among them were Herman Merivale, afterwards the author of All for Her, *and his pretty sister Ella, who became Mrs. Freeman, and Frederick*

Walker, the young painter, who turned out to be the best amateur cook among us. I should like to think, for the sake of the company, that something was cooked by a professional, though at this distance of time I cannot say, nor do I recollect whether the cooks partook of their own broth, but I do remember that Thackeray tried everything that was set before him, and I am convinced he must have suffered dreadfully, for if ever sacrifices were made to friendship it was upon that evening, and our dear host was one of the kindest and most obliging of victims.

Fred Walker was not the only new face to excite attention in the London art world of this period. A young protégé of Frederic Leighton had arrived back in England after several years in Europe. He was an Italian-born artist, who had spent his childhood in England (and took English nationality), but returned to the Continent to study art. He had met Leighton in Rome and, again, in Paris. There the great artist had employed the attractive young man as a model on more than one occasion and encouraged him with his own work. Eventually, Leighton persuaded him that it was time to return to England and put into practice everything he had absorbed during his years abroad. The name of this bright new star of High Victorian art was Carlo Perugini. It is recorded in Leighton's financial accounts that he made regular payments to Carlo over the next few years. There is no record of what the payments were for, but they were most probably for work as a studio assistant and possibly as a model. We know from Leighton's letters home from Europe that he painted "a head of Carlo Perugini" on more than one occasion.

All the excitement of Kate's married life and her glamorous new circle of friends appears to have left her little time to think about her mother, who remained quietly in her house in Gloucester Crescent, just a short walk from the Collinses' marital home. It seems that at the start of her marriage Kate genuinely had every intention of visiting regularly and rebuilding her relationship with Catherine, but, for whatever reasons, she did so with less frequency than Catherine had hoped for. Years later, Kate admitted that when she did visit it was often only because Charlie had insisted on it. The reasons for Kate's odd behavior are unknown and can only be guessed at: perhaps it was because Catherine's misery could be difficult to bear; perhaps Kate found her own emotions too painful; or maybe it was because Kate was so adoring of her father that his treatment of her mother was more easily forgiven than one might expect. In later life Kate veered between claiming she married to escape her father's house and so that she could visit her mother, and sad outbursts in which she railed that she treated her mother badly by siding with her father and could not forgive herself. It seems the truth lies somewhere in the middle—unsurprising for a young woman who was being forced into an impossible position with estranged parents. There were no counseling services available for the children of separated parents at that time and the subject was not one Kate could talk about outside the intimacy of her own home. She could not even confide in Mamie and Georgina as they were on her father's "side." One hopes that she spoke about it to Harriet Collins and that Charlie was sympathetic.

11

A TIME OF MOURNING

On Christmas Eve 1863, Kate and Charlie Collins were having breakfast when they were interrupted by an agitated servant from the Thackerays' home. The servant brought a desperate message from Anny and Minny, asking the Collinses to come at once. That morning, William Makepeace Thackeray, aged only fifty-two, had been found dead in his bed (after a brain hemorrhage), in a position that suggested he had suffered a great deal of pain. The grieving daughters had sent immediately for a doctor and for their closest friends.

Just a few nights previously, Thackeray had dined with the Collinses and had been in high, lively spirits. Shortly before his death, he had asked Kate to visit him; she hadn't been feeling well so had declined, saying she would come and see him soon. She was devastated she had turned him down and now could never have the chance to talk to him again; Thackeray had been so important to both Kate and Charlie. The only thing that Kate could console herself with was the knowledge that Thackeray and her father had mended their relationship.

Kate rushed to Palace Green while Charlie went to tell his father-in-law before Dickens heard it from anyone else. Later he joined Kate in consoling Thackeray's distraught daughters and mother. Charlie wrote to his brother Wilkie: "I shall never forget the day which we passed at the house . . . or the horror of seeing him lying there so dreadfully changed." Thackeray's grieving valet, Charles Pearman, had discovered the body. He later commented that the anguished wailing of the bereaved women was calmed almost as soon as Kate arrived. She remained with them all day until Anny, Minny, and Mrs. Carmichael-Smyth were persuaded to stay with her and Charlie until the funeral.

The Collinses' house had only one spare bedroom, which was given to Thackeray's mother. It is unrecorded whether Kate and Charlie shared a bedroom (with two beds) or slept in separate rooms. It is likely that Kate slept in one room with Anny and Minny, and Charlie either slept in the other or, if there was no other bedroom, that he slept up in the little attic studio. Anny, who had always been the strongest member of the family, the one whom all the others relied on, was utterly broken by her father's death; it was the usually flighty Minny who proved the steadiest in a crisis. Kate held Anny as she cried heartbrokenly for her father. For the next few months, Anny and Minny were regular guests at the Collinses' house while they picked up the pieces of their shattered lives and searched for a new home.

By the evening of December 24 the news had spread, and London was in shock. On Christmas Day, Millais, apparently spending the festive season alone in London, wrote to his wife Effie:

I am sure you will be dreadfully shocked, as I was, at the death of Thackeray. I imagine, and hope truly, you will have heard of it before this reaches you. He was found dead by his servant in the morning, and of course the whole house is in a state of the utmost confusion and pain. They first sent to Charlie Collins and his wife, who went immediately, and have been almost constantly there ever since. I sent this morning to know how the mother and girls were, and called myself this afternoon; and they are suffering terribly, as you might expect. He was found lying back, with his arms over his head, as though in great pain. . . . Everyone I meet is affected by his death. Nothing else is spoken of.

The Collinses' home was filled with a constant hum of visitors, all wanting to offer their condolences to Thackeray's daughters and mother. Among them was Tennyson, who had heard the sad news while on the Isle of Wight and immediately set off to London to see if he could offer any comfort. Anny was very touched to hear that Fred Walker had come running to her father's house on hearing the news and had been seen wandering aimlessly about the rooms, unable to see properly for crying.

The funeral took place at Kensal Green cemetery, at 12:30 p.m. on December 30. Thackeray had deplored traditionally Victorian funereal "trappings," such as an excess of black clothing and unnecessary ceremony, so his daughters saw to it that his funeral was less formal than was usual. The crowd was joined by many curious onlookers, as desperate to see the expected celebrity mourners as the paparazzi would be today. There were around two thousand attendees. Although the majority had not known the dead man, they were great lovers of his books and felt they had lost a personal friend. It was not yet usual for women to attend funerals, but Thackeray's family was insistent and many of his female fans (and the prostitutes he used to frequent, unknown to his daughters) felt the same way. Millais wrote again to his wife on New Year's Eve, annoyed as much by the lack of aristocratic mourners as he was by the crowds of gawping strangers:

It was a mournful scene, and badly managed. A crowd of women were there—from curiosity, I suppose—dressed in all colours; and round the grave scarlet and blue feathers shone out prominently! Indeed the true mourners could not get near, and intimate friends who were present had to be hustled into their places during the ceremony of interment. We all, of course, followed from the chapel, and by that time the grave was surrounded. There was a great lack of what is called 'high society', which I was surprised at. None of that class, of whom he knew so many, were present. The painters were nearly all there—more even than the literary men.

William Howard Russell, another friend of Thackeray's, wrote poignantly in his diary:

Such a scene! Such a gathering! Dickens, thin and worn, . . . John Leech, Doyle, Millais, O'Dowd, O'Shea, J. C. Deane, Shirley Brooks, etc. The Garrick almost whipped of its cream, but not a swell, not one of the order. Little he cared!

The great novelist was laid to rest alongside his infant daughter, Jane, who had been born in July 1838, in between Anny and Minny, and had died at the age of eight months.[58]

⌐ ⌐

For Kate, Thackeray's was the latest in a sad string of deaths. The previous August her maternal grandmother, Georgina Hogarth, had died; she too had been buried at Kensal Green. The rift between Auntie Georgy and her mother had never been healed. In September, Kate's paternal grandmother, Elizabeth Dickens, had also died after a long and humiliating illness—she had suffered from dementia toward the end—and had been buried at Highgate, alongside her husband and near baby Dora Dickens.

Yet these were not the only deaths to affect the family during those sad few months; even worse news was to come. On December 20, 1863, another of Kate's little brothers had left England to try to earn his fortune abroad. Frank had set sail for India, eager to see Walter, the brother who had been absent for six years. When he arrived, it was to discover that his older brother, aged only twenty-two, was dead. Charles received the news in a letter from a Major R. W. Carter; the letter arrived on his birthday, February 7, 1864. Walter had died very suddenly of the Hogarth family curse, an aneurism of the aorta. His death had taken place in Calcutta, on New Year's Eve. The climate had made it impossible for his body to be returned home for burial, so he had been buried in the Military Cemetery at Alipore. The news was particularly distressing as Walter had been due to come home on sick leave and the family had been filled with excitement at the prospect. Kate wrote to Anny, who was on the Isle of Wight, mourning with Minny. Kate's letter, illustrative of the depression she had been laboring under, is on black-framed mourning paper.

> *My dearest Anny—I am afraid I must have seemed to you to be very ungrateful for not having answered your most kind letter before—I was very glad to get it even in the midst of my trouble—but I could*

---

58 John Leech was to die the following year, 1864, and be buried in Kensal Green, close to Thackeray's grave. George du Maurier recorded: "There were crowds of people, Charles Dickens among them. . . . We all forgot our manhood and cried like women!"

not write somehow. And no one I am sure will understand this better than you—I am quite sure that you and dear Minny sympathise with me, you know how we were looking forward to seeing the poor boy—I suppose one ought to be resigned but it is rather hard at first. . . . My people are in London—in Gloucester Place—near Westbourne Terrace. I hope the change may do Mamie good. She felt dear Wally's death very much—I dont [sic] believe he is dead—I feel as if he must be coming home. Oh I think he might have been allowed to live just to see home once more—This is a horrid selfish letter—You must forgive it—Colenso is better—& Dr de Mussey still comes. Colenso sends his love. . . . I was so glad to get that little greeting from you this morning—We very often think of you and wonder what you are doing—I have gathered together all the little scraps of letters we ever received from your Papa—and tied them up in a pretty little ribbon that I think he would have liked—and you must look at them—for every little word and expression seems to bring him before one again—Goodbye my dear girls.
I am yr most affectionate
K.C.

The letter is particularly interesting because in it, as she was to do throughout so much of her life when depressed, Kate berates herself for feeling unhappy. The reader can see how acceptable—and understandable—it is for Kate to be blaming the world for her brother's death, but she decides, probably because of her friends' own grief, that hers is a selfish letter that needs to be forgiven. Kate was a mercurial mixture of selfishness and self-loathing, at times thinking only of herself and at other times subjugating her own desires in order to please other people.

Another very sad surviving record about Walter's death was written by Sir William Hardman, editor of *The Morning Post*. He wrote:

Poor Mrs. Charles Dickens is in great grief at the loss of her second son, Walter Landor Dickens, who has died with his regiment in India. . . . Her grief is much enhanced by the fact that her husband has not taken any notice of the event to her, either by letter or otherwise. If anything were wanting to sink Charles Dickens to the lowest depths in my esteem, this fills up the measure of his iniquity. As a writer, I admire him: as a man, I despise him.

The misery of Walter's death was compounded by the fact that the true nature of his affairs in India had been revealed, and the family discovered just how badly he had been in debt and how much disgrace he had brought upon his name. During Charley's business trip to India, Hong Kong, and China in 1860–1861, when he had been learning about the tea trade, he had met up with Walter and paid off what he thought were all his debts. Yet within weeks, Walter had run up more debts and was becoming frantic. He had written to his father, who had replied sternly and explained that he had bailed him out enough, he had his other children to think of, and that Walter must learn to live within his means. As a result, Walter had refused to write home anymore, corresponding only once with Mamie, saying that he would not be back in touch with them again until he was out of debt. They had heard nothing for several months, until a short note arrived, addressed to Mamie, explaining that Walter had been unwell and would be coming home on sick leave. As Charles wrote sadly to Angela Burdett-Coutts:

> *He said that he was 'so weak that he could hardly crawl', but otherwise was much better; and he was in joyful expectation of seeing Gad's Hill again. . . . On the last day of the old year at a quarter past 5 in the afternoon he was talking to the other patients about his arrangements for coming home, when he became excited, coughed violently, had a great gush of blood from the mouth, and fell dead;—all this, in a few seconds. It was then found that there was extensive and perfectly incurable aneurism of the Aorta, which had burst. I could have wished it had pleased God to let him see his home again; but I think he would have died at the door. The immediate cause of his death, his sisters and Charley and I, keep to ourselves; both because his Aunt has the same disorder, and because we observe strong traces of it in one of his brothers.*[59]

---

59 It is unknown which brother Charles was thinking about, but it was probably Sydney.

Even more poignant is Dickens' final sad sentence in his letter, dwelling on his own unwitting celebrations at the time of his son's death: "On the last night of the old Year I was acting charades with all the children." Like her father, Kate felt guilt and self-loathing for being alive and for having been happy while the brother who had been closest to her in age was dying.

Just days after the announcement of Walter's death, there was finally some good news: Kate became an aunt for the second time when Bessie gave birth to another little girl, Ethel Kate Dickens (her middle name being in honor of Catherine as well as her aunt). Strangely, it seems Kate did not ever grow particularly close to her nieces. One wonders if her nieces' births, at a time when her circle of acquaintances was no doubt speculating about why she and Charlie had no children, made her too acutely aware of what she was missing out on. Kate loved children and longed for her own, wistfully aware that her best child-bearing years were starting to pass her by.

The year was to continue to be miserable, despite little Ethel's safe arrival. In the spring, Kate and Charlie went to the Sussex town of Hastings, then a popular health resort. It was hoped that both of them would benefit from a rest cure. They had a sociable time as Nina Lehmann was staying at a smart hotel not far from their inexpensive lodgings; Wilkie Collins also came to visit.

Their sojourn in Hastings may have improved Kate's spirits but Charlie, whose health had never been good, was now so ill that he was ordered abroad to seek a spa cure. They spent several months on the Continent, traveling initially to Wiesbaden, renowned as a center of medical excellence, but the doctors there were unable to give them any reassurance. Refusing to give up, they traveled on to Nice, hoping the climate would revive him. Kate spent her twenty-fifth birthday nursing her terribly sick husband, far away from the rest of her family, and she was soon to hear that, on the day of her birthday, the loved family friend John Leech had died. It was a dreadful year.

Nice did not revive Charlie. In fact, as Kate wrote to Minny Thackeray, he was "so ill" there that they decided it would not be wise to stay and moved on to the Hôtel d'Angleterre in Menton, where they spent an unhappy Christmas. On December 22, after three weeks in Menton, Kate wrote a witty but peevish letter to Minny, telling her about their "dull" life in France:

> There is a great decoration of the Church going on at this moment. The High Church here consists of a very low white washed room with chairs which we all knock down when we try to take our seats. Dreadful girls in very sanctimonious and consequently ugly dresses are illuminating texts which are impossible to read when finished—and they all look very good and self satisfied. Tell Anny with my very best love that she will look so when she has founded the Establishment for the Bilious Sick at Ramsgate—Yes Minny, District visiting does breed conceit. Thats partly why I dislike it—and why should you ruin your temper and health by going out on muddy wet days—and if you remember it always rained on your visiting days, to see cross old men who dont want you. If you really want to be charitable write to your dull friends at Mentone. . . . Now Minny collect every scrap of news you can think of and write at once—ask Anny to write also, [but] I am afraid she is too much occupied with the Bilious Sick. This letter ought to reach you on the 24th a day on which you will be even more in our thoughts dear Anny & Minny than you are on other days. I cant wish you a Merry Christmas—but I may wish you a happy New Year and do from my heart and so does Colenso. . . . Goodbye—write at once—
> Yrs Kitty C.

Despite all the doctors and spas the Collinses visited, it seems this trip was not to provide them with a diagnosis. What neither Charlie Collins nor his wife was aware of was that he was suffering from stomach cancer.

12

A CELEBRATED BEAUTY—
AND "A LITTLE HUSSY"

Kate would spend much of the next decade nursing an ill and under-standably difficult husband. The pain of enduring stomach cancer without effective treatments would have been dreadful. The accepted treatment for any such extreme pain would have been an opiate, such as laudanum, or opium itself. Most invalids, especially those experiencing the kind of pain Charlie must have been in, became addicted, needing ever more of it to get the same results a few drops could achieve at the beginning. If Charlie had become addicted (and very few people did not), he would have suffered from frightening mood swings and exhibited unreasonable, angry behavior. As his addiction grew, the medicine would have been less effective in pain control; likewise, as the cancer grew stronger, so would his pain. Few family letters from this period survive, and those that do were subject to heavy editing—often with portions cut out altogether and destroyed—by Mamie and Georgina, who took it upon themselves to sanitize history. It seems, however, that Kate was deeply unhappy and often ill herself; no doubt the strain of constant nursing and the unhealthy air of the sickroom played havoc with her own health. For someone who was to live to such a robust old age, reaching a greater age than any of her siblings, Kate was a surprisingly sickly young woman.

At this time, patients from the middle and upper classes would invariably be cared for at home; hospitals were disease-ridden, unhygienic places that only the most unfortunate would be sent to and the nursing profession had not yet been regulated. Women would tend to their sick relatives and friends, perhaps with the help of a paid nurse, but very seldom would a nurse be trusted to look after a patient on her own. Kate and Charlie could not afford a nurse.

Mrs. Beeton's *Book of Household Management* and Dr. Buchan's medical "handbook" were the most popular guides to be used when caring for a patient. Typically, the patient would be in a room devoid of furniture except that necessary for holding medicines, drinks, and so on. If the bed had curtains, they would be removed. Fresh air was vital, so windows would be kept wide open in order that the carer would not catch any infections the patient might be suffering from. Nursing was exhausting work, made even more so by the lack of modern facilities such as washing machines and tumble-dryers; the simple requirement to wash, dry, and air bed linen would take hours.

Despite her own ill health and emotional sadness, Kate remained a celebrated beauty and, after she and Charlie returned to London in spring

Kate Collins (née Dickens) in 1865 by
Marcus Stone

1865, family friend and fellow artist Marcus Stone painted her portrait. The picture reveals a pretty young woman, pensive but with her lips starting to shape into a slight smile. She fulfils all the ideals of the many women depicted in her father's books as the epitome of feminine beauty. Her hair is thick and well styled, her features, including her exposed left ear, are all ideally proportioned—not too big, the ideal shape, and all carefully defined. Her neat, straight nose, prominent cheekbones and eyebrow

Kate photographed at Gad's Hill Place in 1865, during her marriage to Charlie Collins

bones highlighting her expressive eyes and the small but prettily shaped mouth may perhaps have been idealized, but, if so, all paintings of Kate, by several talented artists, must have been similarly idealized. In photographs taken during this period of her life, she seldom looks as pretty as in paintings, but one must remember that posing for a photograph in the mid-nineteenth century took several minutes of standing absolutely still. Quite often, in photographs, Kate looks bored or irritable. Photographs taken toward the end of her life, by which time photographic technology had improved vastly, show her to have been commandingly attractive even in advanced old age.

After Frank Stone's death in 1859, Dickens had begun to treat nineteen-year-old Marcus Stone as another son, making him fully welcome into the family home. Marcus had long been a regular member of the Dickenses' family life, performing in the amateur theatricals, along with Frank, and being encouraged by Charles to keep drawing. As he had with Katey, Charles had noticed Marcus's artistic talent when the boy was just twelve years old, after Marcus had drawn a picture of one of Charles' own characters, Jo, the crossing sweeper from *Bleak House*. Charles was extremely impressed and asked if he could have the picture, which he hung on the wall at Tavistock House. After the death of Marcus' father, Charles had taken it upon himself to aid the young artist in his career, recommending him to reputable book publishers as an illustrator. This was to lead to a lucrative career. Marcus had his first painting accepted by the Royal Academy at the age of seventeen; it was the very first picture he had submitted to them and he was never to have a picture rejected. By the early 1860s, Marcus had become Charles Dickens' own illustrator, taking over from "Phiz" (Hablot K. Browne) and making his debut with the frontispiece for the Cheap Edition reprint of *Little Dorrit* (1861) before going on to draw all the illustrations for *Our Mutual Friend* (1864–65).

By 1865, Marcus was a well-respected and successful artist, working freelance for magazines and newspapers, as well as earning money through book illustrating. He and Kate sat and talked about art for hours; he was a positive influence on her, encouraging her to keep going with her own works and, most important, taking her seriously as an artist.

Their individual experiences are indicative of the marked gender gulf in nineteenth-century British art: Marcus was a year younger than Kate and both had been artistically trained from an early age, but while he could command respect as a career artist, she was expected to be content with dabbling in art as a hobby. Georgina's letters no longer make reference to Kate selling her paintings, perhaps owing to the fact that she no longer had the time to paint, with Charlie needing such constant care, or perhaps her works had not proved as popular as she had hoped they would. In addition, she and Charlie were living in a small home, where the smell of painting equipment would have been quite overpowering and probably deeply unpleasant for an invalid trying to get better.

It is interesting that Marcus chose to make a portrait of Kate at the same time as he was illustrating *Our Mutual Friend*, because her father was also using facets of her personality for his portrayal of the willful Bella Wilfer. Many people have suggested that Ellen Ternan was the inspiration for Bella, but I concur with the view of Dickens expert Michael Slater that the character of Bella was drawn largely from Kate. This is not to suggest that Kate's personality was akin to the spoiled, selfish, materialistic girl that Bella is for most of the story; it is in Bella's adoring relationship with her "Pa" (Rumpty Wilfer or "R.W.") that Dickens drew upon his relationship with his own favored daughter. "Pa" was what Katey called her father; when she was a child Charles would ask her to "come and k.p." which meant to "come and kiss Pa."

The scene in *Our Mutual Friend* in which Pa's "lovely woman" invites him to be the sole witness at her secret wedding could not have been further from the reality of Kate's wedding to Charlie, but is perhaps suggestive of how Dickens wished it had been—simply him, his daughter, and a son-in-law worthy of being her husband. Just as Catherine was banished from her daughter's wedding, Mrs. Wilfer is kept in the dark about Bella's plans to marry.

In the novel, Pa's lovely woman lives a perfectly contented married life with a virile young man who adores her and is in the peak of health. Despite Bella's belief that they will live in relative poverty, John inherits a fortune and he, Bella, and their children live a privileged life in a magnificent home, surrounded by friends and family.

In reality, Charles Dickens' lovely woman and her less-than-virile husband continued to suffer from poor health throughout the 1860s. On occasion, one or both of them would be rushed to Gad's Hill to be cared for by Mamie and Georgina. At the end of 1865, Charles Dickens wrote to de Cerjat, "Katey and her husband are going to try London this winter, but I rather doubt (for they are both delicate) their being able to weather it out." Telling his friends that Kate was as "delicate" as Charlie was perhaps also a good way in which to deflect questions as to why the couple had no children.

At the start of 1866, when the Collinses were returning to London after a memorable and happy festive season in Kent, Charles recorded that Charlie was "on the whole, much better" but Kate was still "very delicate." She remained unwell in February, although Charlie's health continued to improve; her poor health was notable when she attended a party but was too ill to join in dancing the Scottish reels she normally so enjoyed. Her father worried that she was suffering from the weakness of the heart that so plagued Georgina, but there are no medical records to support this. Depression can manifest itself physically in a distressing variety of symptoms. Throughout her life, Kate's depression was exacerbated by cold and miserable weather. She would often mention in letters that she was feeling low because of the weather. I believe she suffered from the condition now known as Seasonal Affective Disorder (SAD) and that her continuing illness was brought on by this.

Kate's poor health during the autumn and winter of 1865–66 may have been further exacerbated by the nervous shock that had assailed the family a few months earlier, when the world almost lost its favorite author and Kate nearly lost her father in a terrible train crash. The Staplehurst accident had taken place on June 9, 1865; it occurred when a train traveling toward London had gone off the rails in Kent. There were some 110 people on board, of whom ten were killed and fourteen seriously injured; of the surviving passengers, most suffered minor injuries and all must have suffered from shock. The accident was caused by a train worker loosening the plates that held the tracks together and then not tightening them again in time for the express train's arrival—he had misread the timetable and not realized the train was due to come through that afternoon. (Because the train connected with the boat from France, its timetable varied according to the tides.) The loosened rails were, catastrophically, on a bridge over the River Beult and several of the first-class carriages hurtled over the edge of the bridge—and dangled there. Charles Dickens and his two companions, Ellen Ternan and her mother, were in the first of the carriages not hanging down into the river. The back half of their carriage remained, precariously, on the bridge, but the front half stuck out into the abyss. Luckily all three were able to escape the wreckage, whereupon Charles joined an army of other survivors, helping to pull injured and terrified people out of the mangled carriages.

After hearing about the crash, Kate, Mamie, and the rest of Charles' children would have been horrified to realize how even more tragic the outcome could so easily have been. It must have made Kate frighteningly aware that, one day, her father would no longer be around. The difficulties of her marriage were made far more bearable by the knowledge that her father could always help compensate for her husband's financial and emotional shortcomings. The fear that one day she would be alone, trapped in a sexless marriage with no omnipotent father to help her escape from reality, could well have led to a severe depression.

One of Kate's younger brothers, twenty-year-old Alfred, remained in blissful ignorance of the Staplehurst accident; he had set sail for Australia on June 5, just four days before. Like his brother Walter and his grandfather before him, Alfred had found himself in debt before leaving. It seems he was following his father's example in becoming something of a dandy: Charles was required to pay his son's tailor's bills for numerous items, including eleven pairs of kid gloves, eight silk scarves, three pairs of trousers, scarf pins made of cameos and onyx, a silver-mounted cane, a bottle of scent, and a traveling rug.

Alfred, complete with his silver-topped cane and multiple numbers of the finest kid gloves, set sail on the SS *London*, bound for Melbourne. He was to become a moderate success and to remain in Australia until the early years of the next century. By the time he returned, life in England would have changed forever. It was fortunate that Alfred did not delay his passage in order to pay off his debts: On the *London*'s very next outward journey to Australia, leaving Plymouth on January 1, 1866, she was wrecked in the Bay of Biscay. Out of a crew and passenger list of well over three hundred, there were just nineteen survivors.

In the summer of 1866, another brother, Sydney, completed his cadetship in the Navy, to the immense pride of his family. He soon set sail again, this time for West Africa on board the *Antelope*. A slight, seemingly fragile boy, the "Ocean Spectre" had always been a strange-looking child, with his too-slender frame made even more striking by disproportionately large eyes. A picture still owned by the family, painted by Frank Stone, shows Sydney as a young boy, dressed in ghostlike white, standing beside a garden trellis. He appears nervous, ready to bolt, as if the viewer has come upon him unexpectedly. He clings to a part of the trellis, holding on to a child-size spade, his eyes peering out worriedly, as if trying to lose himself among the greenery. It is a world away from the brave young man of just a few years later who, having overcome all the physical hurdles of military training, at the age of nineteen set sail for three long years away. The family was deeply saddened to see him go. For those children left at home, it may have seemed that their father was determined to send them all away. Quite why Charles was so keen to scatter his much-loved sons around the globe is a question that has never been satisfactorily answered. His letters show that every departure hurt him dreadfully, but he persisted in doing so. This was not an age when a child in Australia could be easily visited; he knew perfectly well that every time one of his sons left he might never see him again. For many decades, quite astonishing rumors were spread about Catherine Dickens, in order to exonerate Charles' decision to separate from her. As well as the whispers that she was an alcoholic or was illiterate, there were even claims that it was she who insisted her sons be sent abroad and that Charles could only obey. These claims are frustrating not only for their inaccuracy but also for their stupidity. What they fail to explain is how Catherine, already denied the right even to visit her own children in London, could possibly have wielded enough power to insist her estranged husband send their sons abroad. Catherine missed them desperately and one assumes she dwelt on the fact that, had they remained in England, she could have rebuilt a relationship with them as adults, becoming as close to them as she was to Charley.

Catherine was assiduous in writing to her sons, always ensuring that she did so in good time for them to find letters awaiting their arrival in their new country. Kate, on the other hand, was surprisingly lax in writing to her brothers, despite the genuine sadness she felt at their leaving home. It is a strange part of her personality, akin to the way she treated her mother, always meaning to visit but seldom doing so. It seems to suggest a shallowness of character, as though out of sight really did mean out of mind, but that is in opposition to the comments made about her by those who knew her well. Her friends and close family all insisted she was a wonderful friend, extremely good at keeping in touch and always there to listen. I can only imagine that Kate's seemingly unfeeling behavior in terms of her brothers overseas stemmed from the fact that, in missing them, she did not like being reminded of their absence and chose to try to forget them.

Meanwhile, neither Kate's life nor Mamie's was running as either sister would have wished. They drew ever closer, one in a sexless marriage and one apparently determined to remain independent and never change her beloved father's name for that of any other man. There was more than a whisper of scandal about the Dickens girls at this time. In 1866, Kate and Mamie went to a dinner party at Henry Chorley's house that was also attended by Fred Lehmann. Nina was unable to go, so Fred sent her a letter describing the party ("Kitty" was a pet name for Kate that many of her family and friends used):

My dear, anything more demented and awful I never witnessed. We were fourteen, ten at one table and four at a side table. Chorley, Mamie, Mrs. Vivian and Mr. Underwood at the side table, from which Mamie kept darting distressed and furious glances and shaping her mouth all the time for the word 'beast' whenever Chorley looked away from her. . . . Kitty looked a spectacle of woe and between Prinsep and me was quite distracted. She told me that Mamie, who looked round and matronlike, was to be pitied and she could not lead such a life, but added mysteriously, 'she takes her happiness when she can, and a few visits to town lately have given her all she cares for'. She added, 'Of course, it will come out. Sure to.' My dear, these two girls are going to the devil as fast as can be. From what I hear from third parties who don't know how intimate we are with them, society is beginning to fight very shy of them, especially of Kitty C. . . . Mamie may blaze up in a firework any day. Kitty is burning away both character and I fear health slowly but steadily. When she smiled something of her former pretty self reappeared, only to make the pained and woebegone expression that would follow more distressing . . . these two girls, for both of whom I have an old kind of affection, gave me to think . . . [the others] behaved like a set of maniacs, especially the society women . . . the Dickens and Collins faction was at one end of the drawing-room and Society at the other and when I came up Mamie said the Society women were beasts and the little rooms were suffocating and I was not at all sure I wasn't in Bedlam.

It was around this time that Mamie had a sudden burst of independence and bleached her hair, something considered very shocking at that date. As Fred noted in his letter to Nina, it was now "the fashionable colour yellow with a dash of auburn red" (auburn was the hair color shared by Charles, Kate, and Frank Dickens). Kate's behavior was becoming ever more worthy of comment and in 1867 even Lehmann himself, usually one of Kate's biggest fans, described her as "a little hussy" after Kate had appeared to slight him at a party held by Leighton.

As Lehmann's letter suggests, Kate was in poor health in 1866 and this continued throughout the 1860s, which may explain why there are no records of paintings done by her at this time (although it is possible that she destroyed them). In December 1866, Wilkie Collins was dining with the Lehmanns and told them that his sister-in-law was seeing the doctor "again." It seems she was stressed to the point of exhaustion. By mid-December, Mamie and Georgina had rushed to London to take care of her. She is recorded as having been suffering from "nervous fever" and was "seriously ill." The family's Christmas plans were thrown into disarray. By Christmas she was "slowly getting better," although she was unable to travel to Kent and missed all the spectacular festivities that Charles had organized for his guests and the local villagers (these included Boxing Day races and other sporting events, at which Charles gave out prizes). On December 27 she, presumably accompanied by Charlie, was transported to Gad's Hill by a special coach and horses, a tormenting journey when so unwell. There her sister and aunt continued to nurse her assiduously, fearing at times that she would not recover.

In her book of recollections, Anny Thackeray writes of a time when Kate was "dangerously ill," which was probably this occasion, before Kate was taken down to Kent:

> *I remember Mr. Dickens . . . when his daughter . . . lay dangerously ill of a fever in a house in Sloane Street. We had gone to ask for news of her. It was an old house, panelled and with a big well staircase, on a landing of which we met Mr. Dickens coming away from the sickroom. He was standing by a window, and he stopped us as we were going up. 'K.E.' has told me since then, that in those miserable days his very coming seemed to bring healing and peace to her as she lay, and to quiet the raging fever. He knew how critical the illness was, but he spoke quietly and with good courage. . . . 'When she is better,' he said, 'We must carry her off to her old home in the country to recover.' And then he asked us with great kindness to come and stay with him at Gad's Hill where he was living at that time.*

It is fascinating that, just as had happened in Genoa so many years ago, Charles' presence was able to soothe Kate's illness unlike that of anyone else.

Meanwhile, Charles' health was also failing. He had never been quite the same since the Staplehurst accident and had become understandably phobic about rail traveling; he was also suffering from attacks of faintness and nervous exhaustion. Charlie's health was also poor of course and by the end of January 1867 Mamie and Georgina must have felt as though they were running a home for invalids. Nina Lehmann wrote to her husband from the south of France on January 23:

> *I had a very loving sweet letter from Mamie to-day. Charlie is very very ill. I hope he is not going to take Kittie's illness. I trust they haven't lead pipes in their house. However, De Mussy is in close attendance, so it's sure to be all right.*

Nina's letters are not overwhelming in their concern and make amusing reading for their unintentionally ironic juxtaposition of serious news and frivolities. Her letters show us that the Collinses were back at Gad's Hill in March, that Kate was better, but Charlie still very ill. At one time, still in France, Nina wrote petulantly to her husband, asking *why* Kate had not sent her a letter, to which the answer must surely have been, because Kate was so busy nursing her frighteningly ill husband. Kate also had to nurse her sister back to health after Mamie succumbed to whatever fever it was Kate had been suffering from.

In March 1867, Charles (who was away from home, on a reading tour of Ireland) replied to a letter from Georgina in which she had commented how beneficial the air at Gad's Hill was proving to Charlie's health. Charles gave her his own considered opinion of what was wrong with his son-in-law: "It seems to me that nothing is more likely than that all Charley Collins's miseries do really originate in that diffused gout. It stimulates all sorts of disorders, and unquestionably is his inheritance. I am afraid, therefore, that Gad's may not do him permanent good." This letter is interesting because it shows that Charlie's cancer had not yet been diagnosed. Some sources claim that Charlie was given the grim news in Wiesbaden in 1864, but this letter makes it clear that in 1867 the cancer remained unrecognized.

Throughout all this illness, Kate was cheered at the news that in the spring of 1867 her father had made up his argument with Mark Lemon. It happened after the death of Clarkson Stanfield, their mutual friend. Stanfield is said on his deathbed to have begged Charles to patch up the quarrel. The two estranged friends reportedly shook hands as they stood mournfully together while the coffin was lowered into the grave. Their friendship would never be as close as once it had been, but the breach had been bridged at least.

Another piece of good news was that Minny Thackeray was to be married on June 19, 1867. Her fiancé was Leslie Stephen, who would go on to edit the *Dictionary of National Biography*. In the 1850s, he had been ordained as a church minister, but religious doubts had led him to leave the Church and become a "man of letters." Four years after his marriage to Minny, he would become editor of *The Cornhill*—the magazine that Thackeray himself had founded. Leslie was eight years older than his bride, who was twenty-seven when she married. Anny had celebrated her thirtieth birthday just days before her sister's wedding. She remained unmarried but very happy as a successful author and had become the adopted "mother" to the two bereaved daughters of one of their cousins, whose mother, Amy, had died in India. The two little girls, Margie and Annie, had been shipped back to England in 1865 to live with Anny and Minny. Their father, Edward Thackeray, visited his daughters, but his career in the Indian Army meant he was unable to keep them with him.[60]

Minny and Leslie had become engaged at the end of 1866, but had delayed the wedding until they had been able to sort out their complicated home life. It was decided that Leslie and Minny would not move into a home of their own; instead, they would all live in the house that Anny and Minny had bought after their father's death, 8 Onslow Gardens, in the area now called South Kensington (but then known as "Brompton"). It was within walking distance of Kate and Charlie's home. After Minny and Leslie left for their honeymoon, Kate tactfully spent time with Anny, helping her sort out the numerous wedding presents and keeping her company in her sister's absence.

The Collinses spent much of the first half of 1867 at Gad's Hill; their finances were in a dreadful state after months of Charlie being unable to earn money. At the end of May, Wilkie Collins noted that Charles had just "doubled" Kate's marriage settlement, and the banking records at Coutts show that Charles wrote a check to C. Collins for £150 at around this time.[61] Having just returned from his tour of Ireland—where he apparently spent much of his time trying to uncover Fenian atrocities—Charles was considering another trip to the United States. He was desperate to make more money and an American tour seemed the best way to achieve a large sum: He anticipated it earning him £10,000. A

---

60 In a few years' time, Edward would remarry and he and his wife set up home in north London. He had the girls to live with him then, but his attempts at family life were sporadic and the girls still spent a great deal of time living with Anny.

61 This must have been a first payment as Charles had given Kate £375 when she married.

letter to Wills, in which he complained bitterly about his sons, shows why he felt so in need of money. The letter is written on headed paper mono-grammed with the letters "E.T.," indicating it was written from Ellen Ternan's home. It is dated June 6, 1867.

> ... *my wife's income to pay—a very expensive position to hold—and my boys with a curse of limpness upon them. You don't know what it is to look round the table and see reflected from every seat at it (where they sit) some horribly well-remembered expression of inadaptability to anything. . . . My worldly circumstances (such a family considered) are very good. I don't want money. All my possessions are free, and in the best order. Still, at 55 or 56, the likelihood of making a very great addition to one's capital in half a year, is an immense consideration.*

After a short spell in London, the Collinses were back at Gad's Hill during late August and September. The family party was a happy one, with regular visits from London friends, including Chorley, who, the family had realized, was in love with Mamie, despite his being some twenty years her senior. After moving to Kent, the Dickens boys had set up a cricket team with local players, and matches with visiting teams became a regular fixture in the field behind Gad's Hill Place; any members of the Dickens family not playing might be roped in to do the scoring. At the very least they would be expected to attend and offer support. That summer, Charles remained in Kent longer than he had intended to, specifically to act as scorer for a match held on August 30. The Collinses cheered on the Gad's Hill cricketers from the sidelines. A couple of days later, Kate was thrilled to discover that her brother Sydney had been promoted to Lieutenant. The family found out the news when he appeared home unexpectedly and stood proudly in front of his father "with the consequent golden garniture on his sleeve. Which I, God forgive me, stared at, without the least idea that it meant promotion," wrote Charles.

On November 8, 1867, a group of well-wishers—interestingly including both Kate Collins and Edmund Yates—traveled to Liverpool to see Charles Dickens safely onto the *Cuba*, a ship bound for Boston. A dejected family party returned south, with promises to meet again in

December. The Collinses and Chorley would be among the guests at Gad's Hill that Christmas.

In January, according to Kate, she and Charlie moved into "a tiny, tiny house" at 10 Thurloe Place, South Kensington. Shortly afterward, Charlie and Wilkie discovered that their mother was dangerously ill. For two months, Harriet Collins remained in great pain, suffering from what was described as "internal neuralgia," with her doting sons taking turns to

An engraving of Charles Dickens giving one of his famous readings, from a photograph taken in 1861

stay by her bedside. Meanwhile, Charles Dickens' health was also causing concern; he had been below par ever since arriving in America and
became ill in February. He remained incapacitated—though still, remarkably, continuing to work—until he left the United States on April 22. He
was weak and could barely eat anything solid. On April 7 he wrote the
following quite astonishing paragraph in a letter to Mamie:

> *I cannot eat (to anything like the ordinary extent), and have established*
> *this system: At seven in the morning, in bed, a tumbler of new cream*
> *and two tablespoonsful of rum. At twelve, a sherry cobbler and a biscuit.*
> *At three (dinner time), a pint of champagne. At five minutes to eight,*
> *an egg beaten up with a glass of sherry. Between the parts the strongest*
> *beef tea that can be made, drunk hot. At a quarter-past ten, soup, and*
> *anything to drink that I can fancy. I don't eat much more than half a*
> *pound of solid food in the whole four-and-twenty hours, if so much.*

Perhaps if she too had followed this interesting diet, Harriet Collins
might have regained her strength; as it was she died on March 19, greatly
mourned by her sons. Both Wilkie and Charlie became ill after her death.
Wilkie suffered from what sounds to be an agonizing complaint, "gout in
his eyes," but Charlie's health was far worse. It seems his cancer had still
not been diagnosed, as on May 15, 1867, Charles Dickens, now back in
Kent, wrote to Alfred, in Australia: "Charley Collins, I am sorry to say, is
very ill. Besides having spasmodic asthma badly, he has some mysterious
illness (originating in the brain, I fancy) which weakens him with con-
tinual sickness. He is in bed at present, but is to be got down here as soon
as he can be moved." A month later, Charles was writing to Kate's godfather, Macready, "Katie's husband is still ill, and I begin to doubt his ever
recovering." Wilkie Collins refused to believe that his brother's illness was
life-threatening and Charles' regular comments along these lines were
to create problems between him and Wilkie. For several years, Wilkie's
friends had been trying to get him to take Charlie's illness seriously, but
he refused to believe how ill his brother was.

In the middle of June, Charlie's own doctor, still unable to work out
why he was suffering, advised his patient to see another doctor, but Charlie

stubbornly refused. Throughout the summer, Kate nursed him tirelessly, but his condition continued to worsen. On July 7, Charles Dickens wrote to his friend and American publisher J. T. Fields:

> *Charley Collins is—I say emphatically—dying. Only last night I thought it was all over. He is reduced to that state of weakness, and is so racked and worn by a horrible strange vomiting, that if he were to faint—as he must at last—I do not think he could be revived. My man came into my room yesterday morning to say 'Mr. Collins, Sir, he is that bad, and he looks that awful, and Mrs. Collins called me to him just now, that brought down by his dreadful sickness. As it has turned me over Sir.' And last night we all felt (except Katie before whom we say nothing) that he might be dead in half an hour.*

Despite this agonizing experience, Charlie recovered and, just twelve days after his letter to Fields, Charles was able to write to Millais and report his old friend was "decidedly better" and able to venture outdoors. By the end of July, Charlie seems to have been much recovered, so the family was shocked to receive a letter from de Cerjat in Paris, offering condolences for his death. He had seen in a newspaper the obituary for another Charles Collins and had assumed, after all Charles Dickens' assurances that his son-in-law was dying, that it must be Kate's husband.

Throughout this worrying summer, Kate's youngest brother, Plorn, was away from home, attending Cirencester Agricultural College, in preparation to join Alfred in Australia. While Plorn was just beginning his career, poor Charley was forced to swallow his pride and beg his father for help when the company of which he was a partner failed. Although slightly gloating—he had warned Charley against this particular business venture and had still not forgiven him for marrying against his wishes— Charles came to his aid, offering Charley a regular position at *All The Year Round*. It was not purely nepotism: There was an opening as replacement for a colleague who was on extended sick leave and unlikely to return. Charley was to succeed at this position and finally make his father proud.

On October 2, 1868, sixteen-year-old Plorn set out for Australia, clutching the "rifle of his choice" (a present from his father) purchased from the London Armory Company and a box of cigars—a present Georgina had asked Charles to buy on her behalf. It is unrecorded whether he left with quite so many fashionable clothes as Alfred, but he did take with him "an immense dog." His closest brother, Henry, went with him on the train and reported back that Plorn had been very pale and crying a great deal, although he had tried to conceal it. Plorn sailed from Plymouth to Melbourne on board the *Sussex*, a 1,000-ton ship, which was delayed from leaving for several days due to bad weather. His departure left the whole family, particularly his father, miserable. Charles appears to have felt guilt-stricken about banishing the adored boy and makes several references in letters to losing his "youngest and favourite little child," "the last little child you can ever dearly love" and "the pet." Again, one wonders why, as the parting caused Charles such immeasurable grief, he persisted in sending Plorn away, rather than choosing to keep him at home with Henry and Charley.

In the same month as Plorn's departure, Henry Fielding Dickens, the academic star of the family, went up to Trinity Hall, Cambridge. This happy occasion was unfortunately followed almost at once by the shocking news that Uncle Fred had died an ignominious death at the house of a friend, a retired Yorkshire innkeeper; his death was probably the result of alcohol abuse. As Kate's letters and diaries for this period were all destroyed by fire, it is impossible to know how Fred's death affected her, but no doubt she reflected on the time her parents were in America and Fred lived with them. Charles wrote to Forster, "It was a wasted life, but God forbid that one should be hard upon it, or upon anything in this world that is not deliberately and coldly wrong."

The next few years continued for Kate in a miserable routine. Her husband's health was erratic: Some days he would feel fine, but at other times she would be scared he was dying. As her father wrote to a friend at the end of 1868, "Charles Collins continues in the same state and his pretty young wife's life is indeed a weary one." Although it is impossible to be certain, it seems very likely that Kate had at least one affair during her marriage. Fred and Nina Lehmann's many letters hint that Kate was "intensely eager . . . to find other lovers." Fred Walker may have been a lover, or he may just have been a friend who took her out for romantic walks on the Embankment late into the night. A more likely candidate as Kate's lover is the artist Valentine Prinsep. This idea was mooted by Caroline Dakers in her fascinating book *The Holland Park Circle*. There is no definite proof (how does one find proof of an affair when, by its very definition, it is something the two participants struggle to keep secret?), but Prinsep was a close friend of the Thackeray girls and Kate, and it was said that he was in love with her and she with him.

Although not a handsome man—in fact he was "quite odd looking," as his descendant Sue Meynell was the first to admit to me—Val Prinsep appears to have been physically attractive and a truly interesting personality, as well as a talented artist. As mentioned earlier, he had been tutored in art by G. F. Watts, and encouraged and assisted by Dante Gabriel Rossetti—both of whom were great artists whose works Kate would have known and admired. Val was unusual in that he was an artistic chameleon: He could—and frequently did—change his artistic style depending on which influences he was currently inspired by. This ability must have been tantalizingly seductive for one who was still struggling to create her own distinct style. Val was very tall for a man of his era, about six feet two inches tall, and his extremely well-muscled physique was so well regarded that it would even be commented on in his obituary. One cannot imagine a man less like the ascetic Charlie Collins and—unlike Charlie—Val was only eighteen months older than Kate. In addition, he was passionate about art and fascinating to spend time with. He had grown up in an Anglo-Indian family and was connected, either by blood, marriage, or sympathy, to many of the most famous names of the day. His family was allied to the Kiplings, the Tennysons, and those who were to become known as the Bloomsbury Group. He spent holidays with Julia Margaret Cameron, G. F. Watts, Tennyson, and the Thackeray girls. Anny Thackeray recalled going regularly to the Prinseps' second home on the Isle of Wight; on one occasion she wrote in an amusing letter to a friend, "We then went on to the Prinseps' next door. . . . Everybody is either a genius, or a poet, or a painter or peculiar in some way, poor Miss Stephen says is there *nobody* commonplace."

That Kate was in love with Val Prinsep was confirmed by Lady Lucy Mathews, one of Kate's oldest friends and one of the few who lived almost as long as Kate did. In 1925, Lucy revealed that Kate had been so "deeply in love with Val Prinsep" during her marriage to Charlie that "it made her very ill." This could explain her debilitating poor health around Christmas 1866.

Another indicative factor in the assumption that Kate and Val had an affair is that he did not get married until relatively late in life. Not until

Valentine Cameron Prinsep by Alphonse Legros. Kate was in love with Val Prinsep during her marriage to Charlie Collins.

1884, by which time he was in his mid-forties and Kate was no longer available, did he marry. An eligible bachelor, wealthy and with exalted family connections, Val would have been sought after by many match-making parents. He had no aversion to the wedded state, so perhaps he married so late in life because until then he was in love with Kate and didn't want to marry anyone else.

In 1872, Val would exhibit at the Royal Academy a painting entitled *The Harvest of Spring*, depicting two young women picking flowers. One, probably a servant, is dressed plainly in light colors with no hat or bon-net; the other is more richly attired but in somber mourning-style clothes, suggesting she is a young widow. The latter is seen in side profile, a sad contemplative look on her face, accepting the flowers being handed to her without looking at them. She bears a great similarity to Kate. It may be coincidence, but this was being painted at the time Val and Kate were in love and it could have been a wish fulfilment: Like Charles Dickens, Val must have been expecting Charlie Collins to die at any time.

During the late 1860s, while Kate's emotional life was in turmoil, her family remained a source of great strength, helping her care for Charlie when necessary and providing a second home at Gad's Hill, a spacious escape from their "tiny" house in Thurloe Place. Christmas 1868 saw a large party gather in Kent. Kate and Charlie, Henry, Charles and Bessie with the children, Marcus Stone, Chorley, and the archaeologist Sir Henry Layard had all arrived at Gad's Hill by Christmas Eve.[62] That Christmas, Charlie was "no better and no worse," but at least had a healthy appetite; Kate had recovered her health and her spirits and was looking "very young and very pretty." Perhaps she and Val had resolved the problems that had made her so "very ill" and she was happily enjoying being in love, even if it wasn't with her husband. Maybe Charlie was aware and even accepting of it; he must have known that his wife would need to make love to someone else, considering he was not capable of doing so. If he was homosexual, he would have felt guilty for marrying her under false pretenses and perhaps he would even have been happy that Kate, who was by now his closest friend, had found love. The Collinses stayed in Kent well into January,

---

62 Sir Henry Austin Layard (1817-94) was the archaeologist who excavated Nimrud, the supposed site of the biblical Nineveh.

enjoying their time with Mamie and Georgy, but Charles went back to Ireland soon after Christmas. He coped alone, without his daughters or Ellen to comfort him, as yet another family scandal broke out, this time in America.

Many years earlier, Charles' brother, Kate's Uncle Augustus, had left his wife and children and run away with his mistress to America. They had lived for some time in the countryside of Illinois before moving to Chicago. Augustus had died a couple of years previously, most probably from tuberculosis exacerbated by alcoholism. Now his mistress, Bertha Phillips, who understandably had been calling herself Mrs. Augustus Dickens, had also died. The city's *Daily News*, enraged already with Charles for canceling the Chicago leg of his US tour in 1867 (due to ill health), launched a blistering written attack on him for leaving his brother's widow to die in what they described as a poverty-ridden suicide, leaving behind three orphaned children.[63] The story had also been covered in the more respectable and widely read *New York Times* and the English papers were quick to report on it. After an internal struggle, Charles wrote in person to the editor of the *Daily News:*

> *I am required to discharge a painful act of duty, imposed upon me by your insertion in your paper . . . a paragraph . . . respecting the death, at Chicago, of 'Mrs. Augustus N. Dickens, widow of the brother of Charles Dickens, the celebrated English novelist.' The widow of my late brother in that paragraph referred to was never at Chicago; she is a lady now living, and resident in London; she is a frequent guest at my house; and I am one of the trustees under her marriage settlement.*

Charles had been forced to do the very thing he had spent the last couple of years attempting to avoid: His declaration in the newspaper

---

63 In 2010, I researched Augustus and Bertha's time in Illinois and was amazed to discover that, far from dying in poverty as is usually claimed, Bertha left an estate of over $7,000 for her children. It also seems extremely unlikely that her death was a suicide; she was not distraught over the death of Augustus, who had not been a particularly good "husband." She was happy and content with her children and home and had been making plans for a family Christmas. It seems much more likely that Bertha, who suffered from debilitating and agonizing neuralgia, took an accidental overdose of painkillers.

meant that he was exposing his brother's children as illegitimate in order to save both his and the abandoned Harriet Dickens' reputations. He sent money out to Augustus and Bertha's children, something the US newspapers declined to report.

What Kate felt about yet another family scandal is unknown, but it would have been another nail in the coffin where London's gossips were concerned and no doubt had yet more unpleasant consequences for Kate and Mamie's social standing. It must also have made them even more worried about a journalist discovering their own father's secret. That the newspapers had been quiet on the subject of Ellen Ternan—although many of the editors would have known of her existence and their affair—is a testament to Charles' own reputation. The editors were fully aware that the vast majority of the British public did not want to read anything untoward about their national hero. Decades after his death, well into the twentieth century, when newspapers did start to print articles about Charles having a relationship with Ellen Ternan, most people still refused to believe it. Even in the 1930s and 1940s, Charles Dickens remained a heroic figure whose reputation for morality no one wanted to believe was tainted.

By the middle of February 1869, Kate was once again nursing her husband back to health; she was also spending increasing amounts of time with Nina Lehmann and her set of friends. Several of Nina's letters from this period tell of parties at which the Collinses, or at least Kate, were present.

By September, Charlie Collins had recovered enough to start taking an interest in art once again. He did not intend a return to oil painting, but was following Millais' lead in offering himself as a book illustrator. His father-in-law ignored his own misgivings—and the advice of Millais himself—and told his publisher that Charlie would illustrate his latest book, which was going to be published, as usual, in installments. The title of the book was *The Mystery of Edwin Drood*. Charles had written to his publisher on the Friday; yet by the Sunday, Charlie had discovered that the position he needed to sit in in order to draw was the very position that made him ill. He was forced to resign after being employed on the project for just one weekend. His father-in-law was entirely unsympathetic and equally unamused. In the end, Charlie was replaced, again on the advice of Millais, by the young artist Luke Fildes.

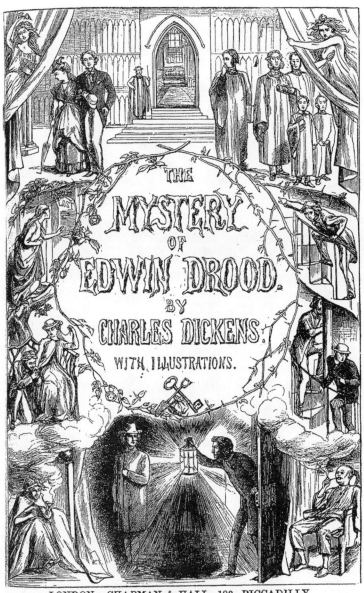

Charles Allston Collins's design for the frontispiece of *The Mystery of Edwin Drood*, 1870. This design was not chosen by Charles Dickens.

Poor Charlie remained in agonies for several months—in addition to which, he was most definitely relegated once again to *persona non grata* by his father-in-law, as Bessie Dickens had been grudgingly accepted after providing Charles with grandchildren. Charles was extremely touchy on the subject of his age. He hated to feel old and was not pleased to be acknowledged as a grandfather; as a result he instructed that his grandchildren call him "Venerables." On December 27, 1869, Charles wrote to Macready: "Harry is at home ... Charley is here, and Mary, and Georgina, and Katie, and Charley's wife, and a grandchild . . . (relationship never permitted to be hinted at)"; as an afterthought he added, "Charles Collins is here too . . ."

Although Charles was reluctant to be reminded of his advancing age, he was as delighted with his grandchildren as he had been with his own babies. Kate had fond memories of seeing Charles taking the small children on a tour of his house and garden, sitting with them underneath the large mulberry tree, with at least one on his lap, and chatting away just as he had done so happily to her when she was a little girl. In particular, Charley's eldest daughter, Mary Angela, remembered her grandfather with reverent affection. She recalled how she had been badly scalded after playing close to a pot of boiling water while staying at Gad's Hill. She remembered her aunt Mamie being very gentle and kind, but her overwhelming memory was of her grandfather sitting beside her bed, holding her hand and promising he would make her well. From that night onward, she fervently believed that as long as he was nearby, no harm could come to her. She wailed bitterly when he went away. The story has a great symmetry with that of Katey's illness in Italy—she had been of a similar age to Mary Angela at the time of the scalding—when Charles' presence was the only thing to soothe her.

Just a couple of weeks after his letter to Macready, Charles wrote a letter that is unusual for mentioning Kate's work: "Katie has made some more capital portraits and is always improving." The letter demonstrates that not only was Kate concentrating once again on her art, but that she had decided on which direction her art would lead—into portraiture.

13

"SUCH AN UNCANNY GENIUS"

Eighteen seventy was a turbulent year for Europe. War raged between France and Germany; the Siege of Paris resulted in many thousands of people starving to death. Residents of neighboring countries were nervous of being drawn into the fray and they worried too about their friends living in the warring nations, friends such as those Charley had made in Leipzig and all the family's friends in Paris and Boulogne.

For the Dickens family in England, the beginning of the year was marked by Henry turning twenty-one, in honor of which a small family party was held at the rented house in Hyde Park Place. Henry was working hard at Cambridge and becoming popular with his fellow undergraduates as well as the teaching staff. Unlike most of his brothers, he was also earning his father's respect—except on the occasion he chose to redecorate his rooms expensively and send the bill home; for this he received a stern written rebuke. Charles was obviously dreading the possibility that Henry would follow so many of his siblings into the Mr. Micawberlike world of debt. It seems the letter worked: Henry was to become the most financially astute of all the Dickenses.

The start of the year was also marked by the death of Kate's maternal grandfather, George Hogarth; he died a few weeks after falling down the stairs at his workplace, the office of *The Illustrated London News*. Georgina must have suffered a good deal—if in silence—over the death of her father. With both her parents dead, she could never be reconciled to them.

In February 1870, Kate and Charlie attended a party at the Forsters' house, to celebrate Charles' birthday.[64] Unusually, Mamie was staying with friends outside London, and missed her father's birthday celebrations. Despite his relatively young age, on his fifty-eighth birthday Charles was not in the best of health. He had still not recovered from the shock of the Staplehurst crash more than four years earlier, and his unpredictable illness had continued to plague him after his return from the United States. The novelist decided it was time to abandon the more exhausting aspects of his career. On March 16, he gave his very last reading. Kate attended, together with several of her circle of friends. It was an emotional evening, at the end of which Charles symbolically gave his specially designed and commissioned reading desk (a type of lectern covered with red velvet and tassels, made to be portable, so he could take it with him around the world) to his younger daughter. Kate cherished it and kept it to the end of her life.[65]

Although he was winding up many of his more stressful business affairs, 1870 was not to prove a restful year for Charles. On April 1, Daniel Maclise died; he was followed to the grave within weeks by Mark Lemon, Kate's much loved "Uncle Porpoise." The family was distraught. In addition, Kate's brothers were once more proving problematic. Charles was concerned about Plorn; he wrote to Alfred for news, asking him to find out if his youngest brother was unhappy in Australia. It is no surprise they were worried: Plorn had been the most cosseted child in the family; he had grown up with an army of people taking care of and helping him; he had not even been made to attend the same school as his brothers, as he had found it too large and frightening. Suddenly he was adrift in Australia, a land entirely unknown to all of the family except for Alfred, and he was only eighteen years old. Charles must have been berating himself daily for his decision to send such a young and favored child to the antipodes.

---

64 Forster had married in 1856, at the age of forty-four.

65 Charles' reading desk is now in the Charles Dickens Museum in London.

Even more worrying was Sydney. All should have been well, as his career had continued successful and he had been promoted to "1st Lieutenant"; he was currently on board the HMS *Zealous*, stationed in the South Pacific. Unfortunately his career was not the only thing Sydney was zealous about. He had—in true Dickens family fashion—begun drinking heavily and leading a riotous lifestyle, ending up in debt. On May 20, Charles wrote despairingly to Alfred that Sydney was "much too far gone for recovery, and I begin to wish that he were honestly dead . . ." It was a deeply distressing letter for Alfred to receive from his father.

The Collinses' finances were also in a deplorable state. Charlie could not work at all and Kate could not earn enough from her painting to support them both. She hated asking her father for money and usually refused to do so, especially as the responsibility of "keeping" her should have been passed to her husband at their marriage. In desperation she looked for other ways to supplement their income. She still loved the theater and she and Mamie continued to act in private theatricals held at friends' houses. Such theatricals were very fashionable at this time and at the start of June 1870 Kate and Mamie performed in a play at the home of a Mr. and Mrs. Feeke, who lived not far from Kate, in a house just off the Cromwell Road. The sisters were performing in *The Prima Donna*.

According to Percy Fitzgerald (a friend of their father's who had often contributed to *Household Words*), Charles was actively involved in the production, coaching his two daughters in their parts and "supervising" them on stage. Charles attended the performance, on the night of Friday, June 2, but insisted no one should know he was there and made sure his seat was away from the audience and obscured from view. After the play was over, his seat was found empty and his worried family began to search for him—his health had not been good and his behavior erratic. Charlie Collins found his father-in-law, who was thoroughly confused and in a "dreamy state," erroneously believing himself to be in his own home. It seems he was persuaded not to make the long journey back to Gad's Hill, so he stayed the night in the *All The Year Round* office and carried on the next day as though nothing had happened.

At around this time, perhaps after seeing her in *The Prima Donna*, or perhaps having seen her in another private theatrical, the actor-manager

Horace Wigan offered Kate a contract to become an actress in his company. Interestingly, Kate chose to talk over this opportunity not with her husband but with her father. On June 4 she traveled to Gad's Hill, where she and Charles talked long into the night. It was one of the most intimate times they had ever shared, with Charles telling Kate secrets he said he had never told anyone else. In later life, she claimed that after that evening she knew things about her father that no one else, not even her sister or Georgina, would ever know. This suggests, perhaps, that Charles had finally confessed to one of his children the truth about his childhood, as well as about Ellen. When she was in her eighties, Kate recalled that evening during a conversation with her friend Gladys Storey:

> *I shall never forget that talk . . . with great earnestness my father dissuaded me from going on the stage. 'You are pretty and no doubt would do well, but you are too sensitive a nature to bear the brunt of much you would encounter. Although there are nice people on the stage, there are some who would make your hair stand on end. You are clever enough to do something else.' . . . He went on to speak of other subjects—with regret. He wished, he said, that he had been 'a better father, a better man' . . . he was not a good man, but he was not a fast man, but he was wonderful! He fell in love with this girl, I did not blame her—it is never one person's fault.*

She was later to comment about her father's behavior with the simple sentence, "What could you expect from such an uncanny genius?" In 1898, she wrote with regret about refusing Wigan's offer, to her friend and correspondent George Bernard Shaw: "I took it to my father, but he was more severe on the subject of the profession than you are. I had to refuse it to my sorrow."

That night, during their long talk, her father promised that he would "make it up to her." How he intended to do so is uncertain, although it is quite probable he intended to give her an allowance, or lump sum of money, to help her and Charlie through the financial slough they had found themselves in.

The following day, Kate returned to London. Before leaving, she went to see her father in his writing chalet. A present from the actor Charles Fechter, it was a genuine Swiss chalet, built in the grounds of Gad's Hill. She had asked her aunt to say goodbye for her (knowing her father hated protracted farewells), but something made her change her mind, something she described as "an uncontrollable desire to see him once again." She went into the chalet, where, as she described it:

> *His head was bent low down over his work, and he turned an eager and rather flushed face towards me as I entered. On ordinary occasions he would just have raised his cheek for my kiss, saying a few words perhaps . . . but on this morning, when he saw me, he pushed his chair from the writing-table, opened his arms, and took me into them . . .*

Later that day, Charles wrote letters to both of his daughters (Mamie had gone to London with Kate). Georgina later wrote to Annie Fields in Boston that for the last couple of days he had been very uneasy about Kate, worrying about her unhappiness and her "dreary unfortunate fate" in being tied to the morose invalid Charlie had become. The following day Charles collapsed; according to John Forster (and others), he fell into a coma at 6:10 p.m. on June 8.

Following his collapse, Charles Dickens remained in a coma for twenty-four hours and never regained consciousness. It was reported that, just before he died, a single tear ran down his cheek. After his death, Kate traveled back to London to break the news to her mother and then returned to Gad's Hill on the same day, to be with the rest of her family. Poor Henry's journey from Cambridge to Kent took a long time and he was to arrive too late. He never forgot how terrible it was to be greeted at the station with the blunt news that his father was dead.

Kate later recalled that she and Mamie had been resting at her house in London on the afternoon before their father's death, in adjoining rooms, with the door between them open. She suddenly had a premonition that "something was going to happen" and called out to Mamie. Her sister asked her if the something was good or bad and Kate said only that she didn't know. That evening, Mamie was dining with friends when Kate came rushing to find her, as she had received the telegram to say their father was very ill. The sisters hurried to Gad's Hill together and—in company with their aunt and eldest brother—sat with Charles as he lay breathing stertorously on the sofa that had been brought into the dining room, next to the conservatory of which he had been so proud and which was newly finished. The local doctor, a Dr. Steele, had been summoned at once, and a telegram dispatched immediately to a London specialist, Russell Reynolds. On arriving at Gad's Hill and seeing his patient, Reynolds is recorded as having said "He cannot live." Charles died, aged fifty-eight, exactly twenty-four hours after first becoming ill. The time of his death is recorded as being 6:10 p.m. on June 9, 1870—five years to the day since the Staplehurst accident. In the pocket of the coat he was wearing was found the last letter Kate had written to him.

There have been claims of a mystery surrounding the death of Charles Dickens, most notably whether he was really taken ill at Gad's Hill or whether he became ill at Ellen Ternan's home and was moved.[66] There is, however, so much evidence of Dickens being at Gad's Hill when he collapsed, that I don't believe there is any mystery to it at all. Had Dickens died at Ellen's home and been moved after death, that makes all his children complicit in a very complicated lie, apparently all pretending to have been there when he died. Had he been taken ill at Ellen's home and moved while still ill, I feel they would have been compassionate enough to have transported him not to Gad's Hill, which was farther away from her home than central London, but to his magazine offices. It would have been far kinder and less painful to have taken a dying man on a shorter journey than would have been required to take him to Gad's Hill.

The children's testimonies all point to Charles being taken ill at home and it seems unlikely they would all have been willing to fake these testimonies. Kate and Mamie were summoned to Gad's Hill as soon as their father was taken ill, as were Charley, Henry, and Ellen Ternan. Kate later related how she and Charley sat anxiously together on the steps to the garden as others took their turn to be alone with Charles. Mamie related

---

66 In *The Invisible Woman*, Claire Tomalin propounds the theory that he actually collapsed at Ellen Ternan's home and was brought back to Gad's Hill by carriage.

how they sat around the sofa on which he lay and that she attempted to warm his feet. Another piece of evidence that refutes the idea Charles was taken ill anywhere other than his home was given to me in 2012 by an audience member at one of my lectures at the National Portrait Gallery in London. A woman came to talk to me after I had given a lecture on Dickens. She told me that her great grandmother was the maid at Gad's Hill "and when Dickens collapsed she was told to run and get the doctor." Sadly, someone else came to talk to me at that point and when I turned back to ask for any more information and her contact details, she had already left, unfortunately without leaving her name.

On June 10, George Dolby, Charles' manager, having heard rumors that his friend and client was dead, rushed to Gad's Hill, where he was met by Kate and Georgina. Luke Fildes, who had been invited to visit that day, arrived to find the house in mourning. In the one way he felt he could express his grief, he painted what is now one of the most famous images in the Dickensian world, *The Empty Chair*, a picture of Charles' writing chair pushed out slightly from his desk, as he had left it just before he collapsed. Millais, who had also been invited to stay—perhaps in honor of his birthday on June 8—arrived to discover his friend's body lying waiting for the undertakers. As was the practice, the deceased's face was bandaged, to prevent the jaw from falling open. Expressing his grief in the same way as Luke Fildes, by drawing, Millais made a tender pencil sketch of the great man in death. He later gave it to Kate, who wrote to him on June 16:

My dear Mr. Millais,—C[harlie]—has just brought down your drawing. It is quite impossible to describe the effect it has had upon us. No one but yourself, I think, could have so perfectly understood the beauty and pathos of his dear face as it lay on that little bed in the dining-room, and no one but a man with genius bright as his own could have so reproduced that face as to make us feel now, when we look at it, that he is still with us in the house. Thank you, dear Mr. Millais, for giving it to me. There is nothing in the world I have, or can ever have, that I shall value half as much. I think you know this, although I can find so few words to tell you how grateful I am.

Despite this fervent letter of the time, she remarked in later life that she wished Millais had removed the bandage so she could have remembered her father as he looked in life and not in death. She felt that in death his face had appeared calm and serene, but in the sketch the bandage made it look uncomfortable. Kate herself often wished she had painted a portrait of her father. "It somehow never came off. I feared not to do him justice," she admitted.

Queen Victoria sent the family a telegram expressing her sympathy. Thomas Carlyle wrote a letter of condolence to John Forster, in which he compared the death of his friend to that of his much-mourned wife, Jane, who had died four years previously:

> *I am profoundly sorry for you, and indeed for myself and for us all. It is an event world-wide; a unique of talents suddenly extinct; and has 'eclipsed', we too may say, 'the harmless gaiety of nations'. No death*

Charles Dickens shortly after his death, sketched by John Everett Millais at Gad's Hill Place, 1870. Millais gave the sketch to Kate.

since 1866 has fallen on me with such a stroke. No literary man's hith-
erto ever did. The good, the gentle, high-gifted, ever-friendly, noble
Dickens,—every inch of him an Honest Man.

The death of Charles Dickens also caused an outburst of public mourning, akin to that observed after the death of a loved monarch. Henry Dickens was later told a touching story of when the news of Charles' death had been announced: One of Henry's friends had been in a tobacco shop when "a working man" came in and said miserably, "Charles Dickens is dead. We have lost our best friend." That story sums up the mood of the country at the time. People really did believe that Charles had been a personal friend; he was adored by readers of every social class and all ages. Another story often related is of a little girl who, on being told Charles Dickens was dead, asked if that meant Father Christmas would die, too. Perhaps it was a comfort for Kate and her family to be surrounded by such a tremendous outpouring of public grief, echoing their own feelings.

The funeral took place on June 14, 1870. One of Charles' last requests was that he be buried in his beloved Kent, but this was overruled by the will of the government and Queen Victoria, who decreed he should be laid to rest in the area of Westminster Abbey known as Poets' Corner. His desire for a quiet funeral was, however, respected and just after nine o'clock in the morning the family and a few select friends gathered at the Abbey for an understated service. Later in the day huge crowds of mourners arrived at the grave, which had to be kept open for two days, owing to the number of people who wanted to pay their respects.

Many years later, in 1906, Kate wrote an article in *Pall Mall Magazine* about her father's death and the unfinished book he had been writing when he died, the aptly titled *The Mystery of Edwin Drood*:

That my father's brain was more than usually clear and bright during
the writing of Edwin Drood, *no one who lived with him could pos-*
sibly doubt; and the extraordinary interest he took in the development
of this story was apparent in all that he said or did, and was often
the subject of conversation between those who anxiously watched him
as he wrote, and feared that he was trying his strength too far. For

although my father's death was sudden and unexpected, the knowledge that his bodily health was failing had been for some time too forcibly brought to the notice of those who lived with him, for them to be blind to the fact that the book he was now engaged in, and the concentration of his devotion and energy upon it, were a tax too great for his fast ebbing strength. Any attempt to stay him, however, in work that he had undertaken was as idle as stretching one's hands to a river and bidding it cease to flow; and beyond a few remonstrances now and again urged, no such attempt was made, knowing as we did that it would be entirely useless. And so the work sped on, carrying with it my father's few remaining days of life, and the end came all too soon, as it was bound to come, to one who never ceased to labour for those who were dear to him, in the hope of gaining for them that which he was destined never to enjoy. And in my father's grave, lies buried the secret of his story . . .

She also hints at her father's premonition of his death.

[He spoke] among other things of Edwin Drood, *and how he hoped it might prove a success—'if, please God, I live to finish it' . . . what greatly troubled me was the manner in which he dwelt upon those years that were gone by, and never, beyond the one mention of* Edwin Drood *looked to the future. He spoke as though his life were over and there was nothing left. And so we sat on, he talking, and I only interrupting him now and then to give him a word of sympathy and love. The early summer dawn was creeping into the conservatory before we went upstairs together, and I left him at his bedroom door. But I could not forget his words, and sleep was impossible . . .*

One of Kate's most interesting comments—and one that would provoke furious reactions from her father's many fans—was made about her father's death in Gladys Storey's book *Dickens and Daughter* (1939). From a distance of many years, looking back on that period of her life, she commented: "If my father had lived he would have gone out of his mind." She had been watching with concern as her father's health deteriorated and she felt that the "madman" he had been when her mother was told to leave home had never fully disappeared.

After Charles' death, Georgina, Mamie, and Henry rented a house in London, 81 Gloucester Terrace, Hyde Park. In accordance with Charles' will, Gad's Hill Place was to be sold. It was bought by Charley and, for the first time since the end of her marriage, Catherine Dickens became a regular and welcome visitor, spending many happy days there with her grandchildren.

A few months after Charles' death, Kate's brother Frank arrived back in England from India, where he had been a member of the Bengal Mounted Police. He was to remain in England for several years (and managed to go through his entire inheritance from his father in record time) as, after neglecting to return to India at the end of his official amount of leave, he was dismissed from his post. Frank had grown into a lovable but dissolute young man, exemplifying the scathing criticism in his father's letters about his sons' "lassitude" and of their having a "curse of limpness" upon them. For the next few years, Kate, Mamie, Henry, and Georgina would spend much of their time worrying about Frank's future.

In December 1870, the family was cheered by the news that Minny Stephen (formerly Thackeray) had given birth to a daughter. Minny had already suffered the death of one premature baby and when she had gone into labor again prematurely, it was feared she would lose the second, too. Tiny though she was—weighing less than three pounds—the baby survived and was named Laura Makepeace Stephen. Disaster seemed to have been averted, but a few years later it would be discovered that Laura had learning difficulties and other health problems (probably caused by the prematurity and complications of her birth). For the moment, however, the Stephen and Thackeray family, as well as the Dickenses, had reason to be joyful.

After the death of her father, Kate found her life grew less and less tolerable. Charlie was increasingly ill and by 1872 had become bedridden. By now, they knew that what he was suffering from was cancer of the stomach. Charlie would never get any better, they realized; the stark reality was that he would continue to deteriorate until the extremely painful end came. Gladys Storey wrote that Kate's life at this time was "divided between painting pictures and tending her invalid husband." The loss of her father and favorite confidant had been constantly preying on her mind. Fred Walker would regularly take tea with the couple in an attempt to cheer them up and no doubt offered Kate advice about her paintings. In September 1871 he sent a letter to a fellow artist written from the Collinses' home. He had, he said, been working on a poster for the play of Wilkie Collins's *The Woman in White,* which Wilkie, Charlie, and Kate all approved of. He was asking for help in engraving it—the poster needed to be about five feet high, almost as tall as Walker and Kate themselves. The poster design was extremely modern, a black-and-white swirling design of a young woman dashing out of a door and into a vividly starry night. It is reminiscent of the style made famous by Aubrey Beardsley in the 1890s. One can imagine Walker animatedly drawing Kate and Charlie into his excitement as they planned and then watched him making up the design, he trying to enthuse his friends and give Kate a brief artistic escape from both the drudgery her life had become and her husband's constant bad temper.

In 1872, Georgina wrote to Percy Fitzgerald, a friend of Charles' who had wanted to marry Mamie. It is a sad letter, in which Georgy related that Charlie Collins was so ill he was unable to get out of bed and Kate was extremely depressed as a consequence. Charlie seems to have become even more neurotic and extremely demanding as a result of his relentless illness and Kate's life was very tough.

Although the family was cheered by Henry's attainment of a law degree at the start of 1872, this achievement was soon to be overshadowed by distressing news from the Navy. The family had all been looking forward to being reunited with Sydney, whom they knew had been ill and was granted sick leave. In a sad echo of the death of his brother Walter, Sydney had died, while traveling home on board the hospital ship *Malta.* His death was seemingly caused by the same inherited heart condition that had killed Walter. Sydney died less than a month after his twenty-fifth birthday, on his way to see his family for the first time in five years. The "Ocean Spectre" was buried at sea.

One of the few amusements Kate had at this sad period in her life was that afforded by living close to Lord Leighton's house and being invited to his parties. Leighton's spectacular home was decorated in the most up-to-date aesthetic style, complete with stuffed peacocks. Fred Lehmann was also a frequent guest at these parties and wrote to the absent Nina after one such occasion that he found the cliquey atmosphere unsettling. He described it as being like a "court," with the ordinary, non-favored people left out of the central action. Prominent among the members of this "court" were Kate and Val Prinsep. Another member of the elite was Mrs. Adelaide Sartoris, one of Leighton's closest friends. He once described her as a "true painter"—despite the fact she was not an artist—because of her great feeling for art and understanding of composition. Mrs. Sartoris was the sister of the renowned actress Fanny Kemble and a famed singer who had performed at the Opera House in Covent Garden. She was a generation older than the Dickens and Thackeray girls, who had first met her as children. In the winter of 1855–56, Anny had grown very close to the older woman, who chaperoned her and Minny on their journey to Paris.[67]

It was presumably at one of Leighton's sumptuous parties that Kate became acquainted with his protégé, Carlo Perugini, whom it is known she met for the first time at Leighton's house and who would later play a significant role in her life. Carlo's history before this time has been difficult to unravel. It is known that he was born in Naples, in 1839 (the same year Kate was born), to Anglophile parents and that he had one older brother, Edward C. Perugini. They all moved to England at some time before Carlo's eighth birthday; reports range from claiming that he was brought up in England from infancy, to those that state he arrived in the UK at the age of seven. His obituary in *The Times* asserted that his parents had moved to England before he was born and that Carlo was born in Italy simply because his parents were holidaying there. His parents, Leonardo and Concetta, do not seem to have been particularly well off and, by the time Carlo was in his early thirties, he was supporting both of them. Leonardo was a singing teacher and Carlo's brother would become a bank clerk.

---

67 When Henry was older, he would also attend Leighton's parties, with his wife. He was obviously in awe of the painter and wrote about "his handsome figure, his elegance of mien and the polish of his language."

What we do know about Carlo is that he was educated in England before traveling to Continental Europe as a teenager, in order to learn more about art. It is known he studied under Ary Scheffer in Paris in 1855, as previously mentioned, and that he assisted the brothers with their portraits of Charles Dickens. He was also said to have studied under Giuseppe Bonolis (1800–51) and Giuseppe Mancinelli (1813–75); if this is true, he must have been very young when he was taught by the former. In 1855, Leighton was also in Paris and the name Carlo Perugini starts to appear in his letters home. He wrote to his father:

Dear Papa . . . I have, after great trouble and manifold enquiries, taken the only studio that at all suited me, and for that I give unfurnished 150 francs a month. . . . It is the dearth of studios and the great demand for them that makes the price so high. Those who have had studios some time of course pay very much less, others put up with little holes far too small to paint a picture of any size. Carlo Perugini is painting in the studio of a friend, and that is a strip not large enough for one person . . .

In September, Leighton was writing to his father again: "I have nothing whatever to tell you, except that I have just finished a head of Carlo Perugini (for myself) which is the best thing of the kind I ever did." A letter to his mother, dated a month later, made me wonder if there was some kind of family connection between the Leightons and Peruginis, although the records at Leighton House and the Kensington Library do not throw any light on the matter. Leighton wrote to his mother that October saying:

Carlo Perugini, whom I saw to-day, sends 'tante cose' to his cousin. He is a charming boy, most gentlemanlike, and has that peculiar childlike simplicity which belongs to none but Italians.

It was during this time in Paris, and again when the two men met in Rome in around 1856, that Leighton persuaded the younger man to move back to London and pursue his career in earnest. Carlo began enjoying the camaraderie of London's artistic world, having been introduced to the several young artists that Leighton gathered around him and often assisted financially. In around 1858 Carlo was sitting as a model to William Blake Richmond (a protégé of Millais). In 1860, the year in which Kate married Charlie Collins, Leighton was writing again to his parents, this time about the Artists' Rifle Corp, which he had recently joined: ". . . I was yesterday raised to the rank of Captain; I command the 3rd Company. . . . One of the ensigncies has been given to Perugini, contingent on its being lawful for him to hold such a commission." Doubt over Carlo's eligibility arose on account of his having been born Italian, despite being a naturalized Briton.

The setting up of the Artists' Rifles seems to have been viewed by the military as something of a joke. In around 1860, Britain feared invasion from France once again and many volunteer corps were set up by workers from all walks of life, including railwayworkers, firemen, miners, and bakers. The Artists' Rifles, expected to be a somewhat half-hearted regiment, was surprisingly successful. It would go on to become, by the start of the First World War, one of the most well-organized volunteers' corps in the British Isles. Their motto, *Cum Marte Minerva* (meaning "Mars with Minerva"), evoked the ancient god and goddess of war (as well as the classical themes of many of the artists' paintings). By 1914, the men were so well trained that it was decided they would not fight as a regiment; instead they would be promoted to officer ranks and sent to take command of a variety of other regiments. Throughout the so-called "Great War," the ranks of the Artists' Rifles provided well over ten thousand officers. The only time the regiment fought as one body was at Passchendaele; it was massacred. After the end of the war, it was decided that the Artists' Rifles should continue as an Officer Training Corps. It proved highly effective during the Second World War and, after 1945, was merged with an elite fighting force that had been set up during the war: the SAS. Today the Artists' Rifles, whose records begin with the signatures of some of Britain's most distinguished artists, shares its archive with that of the SAS. The original album that details who joined the regiment, and when, reads like a *Who's Who* of the art world. Frederick Leighton, Valentine Prinsep, John Everett Millais, G. F. Watts (an honorary member only):

They are all there amid a number of those whose names are sadly no longer remembered. Here and there a name has been rendered illegible by an overenthusiastic line placed through it on resignation—or, occasionally, after its owner has been dismissed for tantalizingly unrevealed behavior.

The records show that Carlo was allowed to join. He signed up in 1860 and served for twelve years. There are also a couple of remaining letters, sent to a less than eager member of the corps, in which Carlo gently but firmly reminds him that his presence is required at the next drill session. It is apparent that he took his duties very seriously, unlike the many who were only interested in the social life. It is no coincidence that Leighton was a very early member of the regiment that was to become renowned for holding the best and most lavish parties. Many new recruits reportedly joined solely because membership offered the opportunity to mix with some of society's most flamboyant and charismatic figures. Perhaps it is for that reason that Carlo spent his time chasing up recruits unwilling actually to learn the art of soldiering. That should not suggest, however, that Carlo was averse to socializing with the rest of the troops. One of his great friends during his Artists' Rifles days was the amateur painter Arthur Lewis. A member of the corps, a part-time artist and a full-time textiles expert and manufacturer, Lewis found time to host an exclusive men-only club where London's literary, artistic, and musical cliques could mingle and drink together. As well as Carlo, the club's many members included Leighton, Prinsep, Watts, Fred Walker, Millais, Edmund Yates, and, occasionally, the Prince of Wales. These male-only evenings were a regular social event until 1867, when Lewis married. From then onward, his parties were open to men and women.

In 1863 Carlo exhibited his first painting at the Royal Academy; he would continue to exhibit almost annually until 1914. From at least 1870 onward, Carlo was receiving regular payments from Leighton. Val Prinsep was among the other artists who received similar payments, and although there is no definitive record of what these payments were for it is assumed the artists were working for Leighton, probably as studio assistants. The payments were largely motivated by philanthropy. Leighton was an extremely generous man who went out of his way to promote the careers of struggling artists.

By the end of 1872, Charlie Collins had recovered enough to go on a restorative holiday. Holman Hunt mentions in a letter that he was joined in Brighton—a popular destination for invalids—by Millais and Charlie, though there is no mention of Kate. Perhaps she herself was too ill to leave London, or perhaps she had gratefully allowed Millais to take care of her husband while she had a well-earned rest from her grouchy spouse. It seems that by this date she would have been less inclined to spend time alone with Val, as she had a new suitor.

A few months later, the family was saddened, though presumably little surprised, to hear of the death of Chorley (whose extraordinary looks had once led to his being described by a friend as the missing link between a chimpanzee and a cockatoo). He had long been in bad health owing to his excessive drinking, about which pathetically funny stories abounded. With no family and few dependants, he left to Mamie—the object of his unrequited love—a lifetime annuity of £200. If Kate had been afforded any time to reflect, she might well have pondered the fact that her finances would doubtless have been much more stable if she had also remained unmarried. She was, however, kept constantly busy by the demands of an increasingly ill husband.

By spring 1873, she knew Charlie had reached the end of his life. The marriage may not have been a love match, but she loved him very much as a friend and watching his suffering, while unable to alleviate it effectively, was almost unendurable. On the first Saturday in April, she realized death was very close and refused to allow anyone else to take her place, nursing him constantly and not sleeping. She kept up this loving and dedicated vigil until his death, five days later, on Wednesday April 9, 1873. He died at their home, after twenty-four hours in a coma. Wilkie was also at his bedside. Kate was in a state of exhaustion after five days and nights without sleep.

The previously uninterested Wilkie began searching for a religious belief he could cling to in the hope that he would see his much-mourned brother again one day. He later wrote an entry about his brother for the *Dictionary of National Biography* that included the words:

His ideal was a high one; and he never succeeded in satisfying his own aspirations. . . . The last years of his life were years of broken health and acute suffering, borne with a patience and courage known only to those nearest and dearest to him.

Several weeks after Charlie's death, Holman Hunt wrote a letter about the friend he had known since adolescence:

One of my confessors is gone. Charles A. Collins, who had often listened to my [scrapes?] and was in many respect [sic] a good rein to me, being timid and therefore sure to put on the curb, and who was one of the men I valued in life as thoroughly fearing and loving God through all of his rather eccentric changes in faith. He might now be a better advisor but must not be so. In this world it is evident that the Father would rather we stumbled than walked with leading strings forever.

14

THE SECRET MARRIAGE

After the death of her husband, Kate left Thurloe Place to move in with her family. She placed the vast majority of her possessions in storage. Shortly afterward, the warehouse in which her items were stored—a famous storage facility in London's Belgravia, known as The Pantechnicon, which specialized in storing fine art and furniture—burned down. Among the many possessions Kate lost was every letter she had kept from her father. This is why volumes of Charles Dickens' letters do not contain any that he wrote to Kate. She also lost many of the books her father had bequeathed to her and it is likely that Kate's paintings were also lost in this fire as, although we know she was doing well and had begun painting portraits, none of her commissioned works dating from any earlier than the mid-1870s has so far come to light. The loss of hers and Charlie's possessions, as well as so much that she had inherited from her father, was deeply upsetting.

In the same year as Kate was widowed, the family heard from the other side of the world that Alfred had married an Australian girl named Jessie Devlin.[68] It was also the year in which Henry was called to the Bar. At least someone in the family was likely to make enough money to support himself (and perhaps his widowed sister, if need be). Henry was now living in London with Georgina and Mamie at 81 Gloucester Terrace and it was to this house that Kate retreated when she left Thurloe Place.[69] Henry and Mamie seem to have become very close around this

---

68 Tragically, Jessie was fated to die after just a few years of marriage, having sustained fatal head injuries when her pony carriage overturned. She and Alfred had two young daughters, Kathleen and Violet.

69 The 1871 census lists that the household kept three servants: a cook, a housemaid, and a pageboy, who had previously been in the employ of Charles Dickens.

time and, from 1872 until 1876, went regularly together to the Monday Popular Concerts, known as "The Pops." These were, as their name suggests, a weekly occurrence, held at St. James's Hall, Regent Street, one of London's most prominent concert halls during the latter half of the nineteenth century. One imagines that, as soon as a respectable period of mourning had elapsed after Charlie's death, they included Kate in these weekly outings. Although they had never been very close as children, owing largely to the age difference, Henry and Kate now started to forge a close relationship that would endure to the end of their lives. Before Charlie Collins' death, Kate and Henry had seldom lived in the same home, as Henry spent so much of the year away at boarding school, and by the time he was old enough to be taken note of Kate had married and moved away.

Shortly after Charlie's death Kate received several proposals of marriage, including one from Val Prinsep (who had good reasons for believing he would be accepted) and another from Fred Walker. Both of the artists' marriage proposals were declined. It was fortunate for Kate that she did not accept Fred. If she had done so, her life would have returned to the rounds of nursing yet another very sick husband; Fred was to fall fatally ill just a year later.

It seems that neither Valentine Prinsep nor Fred Walker were accepted for a very good reason: Kate had already fallen in love, with Carlo Perugini. Precisely when their relationship began and when he proposed is unknown. Georgina Hogarth later said that Kate would not allow her family to announce the engagement to Carlo until a year had passed after Charlie's death, although she was engaged to him some time before this first anniversary. When writing to Annie Fields to tell her the news that Kate had married a second time, Georgina described Carlo as "a most sensible, good, honourable and upright man, and *devotedly* attached to Kate. Every one likes him—he is so *perfectly* unaffected, simple and straightforward. . . . [He will be a] good and tender guardian [of her] future life and happiness"; she added how much she longed for Kate to be happy after the "many dreary years of her youth" while being married to Charlie Collins. She also commented how pleased with his new son-in-law Charles would have been, had he been alive to witness it: "This blessed change in her existence would have greatly eased and brightened him, I know—and he would have much liked her Husband who I know would have appreciated and loved him."

Millais, who had become close to Kate and continued to be one of her best friends until the end of his life, was obviously thrilled by the young widow's chance at happiness. Having married the former wife of John Ruskin, he was all too aware of the miseries a sexless marriage could cause. Effie Ruskin had remained a virgin throughout her first marriage (which had eventually been annulled on the grounds of non-consummation). Millais had saved Effie from this miserable existence and now he could experience the pleasure of seeing Kate passionately in love with a man who was in love with her. As a wedding present, Millais offered to paint Kate's portrait. Although he began the picture in 1874, it was not to be finished until 1880, and there are sections of it that still appear to be in need of extra attention. Millais himself was never fully satisfied with the way he had portrayed her and it was said by Kate that he used to shake his head over the painting when he went to visit the couple and saw it hanging on the wall.

The wedding of Catherine Elizabeth Macready Collins and Charles Edward Perugini took place on June 4, 1874, at St. Paul's Church in Wilton Place, Knightsbridge. It seems to have been arranged in something of a hurry as Charley Dickens was away at the time of the announcement and could not get back in time for the wedding. Frank, complete with a fetching golden moustache, took his older brother's place and walked Kate down the aisle. Once again, Catherine Dickens was not invited to her daughter's wedding. Kate's explanation to her mother was that they did not want Carlo's parents to attend, which meant that they could not invite Catherine either, but that seems spurious. It is more likely that Kate could not cope with the awkwardness that would ensue if Catherine, Mamie, and Georgina were all in the same room. The only guests at the ceremony were Georgy, Mamie, Frank, Henry, and Millais. Carlo's brother Edward and his wife Florence do not seem to have been invited (or at least did not attend). Kate wore a dress made of pale grey silk with a white patterned veil and carried a "perfect bouquet." John Forster—who gave the bridal couple £150 as a wedding present—and the family's solicitor, Frederick Ouvry, were invited to attend the wedding breakfast, at

Gloucester Terrace. Mamie had decorated the room with arrangements of white flowers and there was a "pretty wedding cake" waiting in the center of the table. Poor Catherine was not invited to that intimate wedding reception either. She had, however, already met Carlo and liked him "very much indeed."

After they had eaten, Kate wrote a couple of short letters, one to her mother and one to the Thackeray girls, written in a bold, excited hand:

> *My dearest Annie & Minny,*
> *I write you one line to say I have been married about two hours!—and*
> *before I go away I must write and ask you to come and see me as soon*
> *as I return to town.*
> > *Your loving Kitty*

While she was thus occupied, Carlo talked business with Ouvry, who had brought papers with him that needed to be signed. Georgina was most impressed that Carlo refused to allow any of Kate's money from her father to be signed over to him, insisting that her money be kept for her and the children they hoped to have.[70] With the letters written and dispatched, the wedding party left the house to pay a visit to Westminster Abbey to see Charles' grave. The newlyweds then had dinner with Carlo's parents (one assumes that the Peruginis had been told they could not attend the wedding as the couple did not want Catherine to be there) before setting off for a honeymoon in Paris. Sadly they did not call on Catherine as well.

That description of their marriage is, at least, the official version. While researching at the Family Records Centre in London I made a quite extraordinary discovery: Kate and Carlo married each other twice, within a period of nine months. The first wedding took place on September 11, 1873, barely five months after she had been widowed. The minimum mourning period—during which time widows were not even

---

70 A few years before Kate and Carlo's wedding, one of the first great reforms in British women's rights had taken place: The Married Women's Property Act had been passed in 1870. This new Act meant that the money and property belonging to a woman did not automatically pass to her husband's control when she married. The Act was vitally important to the position of women in society and was a prominent stepping stone on the road to female emancipation.

supposed to socialize—was one year, and widows were expected to wear full mourning dress for two and a half years. Getting married after such a short period of grieving was more scandalous than anything the fast Miss Dickens had ever done before. This first wedding was at a register office and was witnessed by Henry Thomas Mitcham and Ernest Edward Earle, who apparently were strangers. The wedding was not announced and they did not live together until after their second wedding; Carlo remained with his parents at 4 Westbourne Place and Kate remained at 81 Gloucester Terrace. Georgina, Mamie, and Henry may have been aware of the wedding, which would explain Georgy's slightly cagey letter that Kate had not allowed the family to announce the "engagement" until a year after Charlie's death. However, it seems more likely—as none of them was invited to the register office—that Kate and Carlo kept their first wedding a secret from everyone.

This secret marriage could also explain why neither Carlo's family nor Catherine were invited to the church wedding, in case the first wedding was known of by the celebrant and mentioned at the service. The celebrant seems, however, to have been in ignorance, as there are two distinct marriage certificates from the two different dates, both of which claim Carlo to have been a bachelor and Kate a widow. The second wedding was a full marriage, not just a blessing service. Neither Forster nor Ouvry could have known about the first marriage.

The most plausible reason for their clandestine marriage is that Kate was, or thought she was, pregnant. A pregnancy seems to be the only possible reason why they would have chosen to get married so soon and with such secrecy. If she had undergone a miscarriage, her aunt and sister at least would have discovered their secret.

—◆—

This secret marriage is something that has never before been alluded to, nor mentioned in any family tree. For the rest of her long life, Kate only ever referred to her wedding as having taken place in June 1874, and never mentioned it actually being their second wedding.

On their honeymoon, Kate and Carlo picked up bad colds from "sleeping in a damp bed"; note that this time there was no thought of sleeping in separate beds. On their return, the new Mr. and Mrs. Perugini moved into 141 Warwick Street, in Belgravia (not far from Kensington). Although over the next few decades Kate and Carlo would continually worry about money, they kept three servants: Sarah, the cook, Emily, the parlormaid, and Susan, Kate's "lady's maid." They would never be as impoverished as Kate and Charlie had been, but it does seem that Carlo, like his deceased father-in-law, was responsible not only for himself and his wife, but for his elderly parents and their household (which also included three servants). It is from this time that Kate's career as an artist can truly be counted.

Kate threw herself into her new life with Carlo with a passion, spurning acquaintances she found boring or did not have time for and living selfishly and happily for the moment. In winter 1874, Georgina wrote a very embarrassed letter to Annie Fields and her husband, who had sent Kate and Carlo a painting as a wedding present. The painting, by an American artist, William Morris Hunt (1824–79), had arrived while the couple were on their honeymoon, but four months after it was sent, and long after the honeymooners had returned, the Fields had still not received a thank-you letter. In her letter to Annie, Georgina commented, "Katey is a very naughty girl not to have written to you, and I have not a word to say on her behalf! The only thing to be said is that I think she has behaved equally ill to every one she knows, almost."

Surely Kate can be exonerated for her behavior: She had spent so many years repressed, both sexually and emotionally, stifling her youthful impulses and freedom in order to stay at home and nurse a man she was not in love with; finally she had a chance to be impetuous and to enjoy being in love. It is not surprising she chose to embrace her new life and revel in the wonderful things it had to offer, nor that she forgot about things like writing thank-you letters, when the time could be better spent with her new husband or in painting.

She did, however, write to Plorn in October 1874, from Sevenoaks. In the letter she—and Carlo, in a postscript—thanks him for his wedding present and gives an endearing portrait of her new married life, as well as a revealing insight into the world of the Dickens family at this time:

My dearest Plorn,

I have to thank you for a charming letter and a beautiful present. I cannot tell you dear, how very kind and good I think it is of you to make us a wedding gift. You being so far away. I hope you and Carlo (Bob I have christened him in preference to so happy peasanty and Newfoundlandy a name)[71]—will some day be very good friends. I am quite sure you and Ally will like him, he is so very nice, and good. H[enry] and he are capital friends, and Frank was constantly with us and I know is very fond of him. My dearest Plorn how very good of you and dear Ally to join us in wishing to help Frank to a new start. I feel quite sure that Frank's future life will repay us for any kindness we can do to him now, at this very moment I expect he is starting. H. like a dear is with him to the last, and as soon as H. himself comes from Liverpool he is coming down here and we shall hear all about the final departure. These goodbyes are so painful! It is better to say how do you do! and I hope dear Plorn we shall have to say that to you before many years. It will be so pleasant to see your nice little old face again and dear Ally too. How much I should like to see him, and his pretty wife and little girl. But I hope they will all come to England some day. Ally's photo is quite imposing I think, and he seems to have more whiskers than all the rest of the Dickens family put together. By the bye, Plorn, how do you get on in that way? Tell me when you next write, also if your dear noble nose is still a little on one side? Perhaps it has gone over to the other, or do you lie flat on your face in order to keep a symmetrical front view? Tell me all particulars, also exactly how tall you are. Mamie and I are still very small. I am afraid we don't grow with years, except in wisdom of course. H. is not tall, but he is slight & nicely formed and is a very good looking young fellow I think and in his wig, is truly beautiful. You will see the photograph, it is a lovely creature. Frank had always a handsome face and has now, a nice little very light golden moustache, he is going to let his beard grow. Bob is handsome, everyone says. I know his face so well that I don't know whether it is handsome or not, but I am quite sure it is the very best

---

71 Carlo was the name of one of the performing dogs in *The Old Curiosity Shop*.

and goodest face in the whole world. Mamie is staying with us which is a great delight to me. She & I are always devoted to one another. She is simply an angel. I wish you could see your present which she has chosen. Now Plorn if you forget to give my dearest love to Ally & Jessie I'll never never never forgive you.

Your loving Kitty.

My dear Plorn, We are so pleased with the beautiful present you have sent us through Mamie and think it so kind of you from so far to think of us. I hope I shall see you and know you some day and that I shall get on with you as well as the rest of your brothers. Kitty says you are like her so from that I shall like you. Yours afftely 'Bob'.

The new start in life that Frank Dickens' siblings had helped to bring about began with a journey to Ottawa, where Frank joined the Canadian Northwest Mounted Police (now the Royal Canadian Mounted Police). Throughout the remaining years of the 1870s and into the 1880s, he was stationed in the areas that became the provinces Alberta and Saskatchewan, where he and his fellow troops often encountered fierce attacks from Cree Indians.

There are not a great many examples of Carlo's handwriting in existence, but in most of them, as in this postscript to Plorn, he exhibits a spidery, small, well-formed hand—often quite challenging to decipher—but with a larger, flamboyant signature at the end, as though all the previous lines were written by a different person. Interestingly, in a surviving letter of Carlo's written in Italian, his handwriting is much more expansive and florid, as though his real personality can be given free reign in his mother tongue. As Kate spoke Italian, perhaps they conversed in both languages in their home, but only in English in public.

There are many periods of Kate's and Carlo's life unaccounted for. Very few holidays are ever mentioned and none abroad, but presumably such holidays were taken; perhaps they even visited Italy together. The Charles Dickens Museum has a small photo album that once belonged to Kate. Inside it are several Italian photographs (professional shots, sold as postcards are today). These may indicate that they visited Carlo's homeland together, or they may simply have been collected as a reminder of the country they both knew.

Given the highly conventional and often xenophobic world in which the Peruginis lived, Carlo would have found himself putting on an act in public, trying to be as correct and English as possible so as not to be discriminated against. When I first began researching, I found that he was never listed as Carlo in artistic records; instead his name is always Anglicized to Charles Edward Perugini. For some time I assumed that he was a confirmed Anglophile who had changed his own name, given that he had lived in London for most of his life and was flawlessly fluent in English. Yet when I began reading contemporary references to him in letters written by such intimates of his as Kate or Leighton, I saw that they wrote about him as Carlo. Perhaps to avoid any confusion, Carlo tended always to sign himself on letters and other documents with his initials instead of Christian names: "C. E. Perugini." His paintings are signed with a stylized monogram in which the letters C, E, and P are intertwined. It seems that Kate and he devised a very similar monogram for her, as almost all her surviving works are marked with a K and P placed one on top of the other in emulation of Carlo's monogram. It is lovely to see the two monograms placed beside each other and to wonder when they came up with the idea—perhaps on their honeymoon or while discussing the wedding. One can imagine the newly happy Kate practicing her married "signature" before feeling confident enough to place it on a finished canvas.

After their marriage, Carlo painted Kate regularly, but frustratingly few of the pictures are dated. In the year of their official marriage he exhibited a portrait of her, entitled *A Labour of Love*, at the Royal Academy (now on display in the Sunderland Art Gallery). She stands beside an arrangement of roses, looking down, her attention absorbed in her task. It is a beautiful painting and remains one of the museum's most popular exhibits. A small watercolor painted by Kate is of Carlo painting *A Labour of Love*. It gives an intimate portrait of their married life, with Carlo absorbedly intent on his easel and Kate's image. His hair is dark and neat, his beard a slightly lighter color, the kind of subtle difference noticed by someone in love with her subject. He uses a wooden stick as a hand rest as he paints in the flowers, preventing him from smudging the paint already on the canvas. In his mouth is a half-smoked cigar (one of Carlo's favorite indulgences). Although he is dressed somberly in a pale-colored jacket, the ends of a vivid green cravat peek out jauntily. One can imagine how many happy hours they spent helping each other with their work or painting separately in companionable silence.[72]

Carlo also painted a stunning scene entitled *Doubt*, for which the sitters were Kate and Mamie. Kate sits at a desk, having stopped pensively while writing a letter. Mamie leans over her. Both sisters look exceptionally pretty—with Mamie coming across as far more attractive than she is depicted in other paintings or photographs. Their features are expertly defined, with the facial expressions of both suggesting a complicated story behind the letter that is being jointly composed. The painting is also striking for the way in which Carlo recreates the rich fabric of their clothes, with elaborate sleeves and skirts that billow out in a lustrous profusion of detail and artistic skill. It is one of his best remaining paintings.

Another of his portraits (probably from the late 1870s) shows Kate wearing a chocolate-brown dress with an ornate shawl collar and a matching mob-cap in ivory. A black velvet ribbon encircles her neck, matched by another that circles her cap and secures a perfect pale-pink rose and several delicate rosebuds.[73] Attached to the central V of her shawl collar is a slender stem of a bluish-tinged white flower, which appears to be a forget-me-not captured at the moment before it turns blue. Both Carlo and Kate studied the history and language of art, which hold that a forget-me-not is a symbol of love. This is one of the few pictures of Kate in which she is looking directly at the viewer, her face not turned to either side. It is a very loving, intimate picture. The roses, both in bud and bloom, and the simple wild flower suggest how varied her personality was. The rose was also a symbol of Kate as it was well known to be her favorite flower.

---

72 This painting was presented at the end of her life by Kate to her much-loved maid Ellen Eakins.
73 This portrait is featured on the book cover.

Artistically, 1875 was a good year for Kate. Her paintings were starting to sell at last and she was beginning to gain a reputation as a professional artist. In the summer she exhibited two paintings at the Suffolk Street Gallery. Not only did both sell, but also there were several buyers clamoring to purchase them. Georgy related proudly that each of the pictures could have sold "four or five times over!"

Sadly, Kate and Carlo's first wedding anniversary, on June 4, 1875, was deeply marred by the death of Fred Walker, aged just thirty-five. He had been ill for most of the previous year and his health had deteriorated after the death of his beloved mother in November. His funeral took place in Cookham, where he was buried in the same grave as his mother and one of his brothers.

Nothing, however, could take away Kate's happiness at this time: She had discovered she was pregnant. To conceive a baby in her mid-thirties was a major achievement and something Kate had longed for. (This may,

A Summer Shower (1888) by Carlo Perugini

of course, have been her second pregnancy.) In September 1875, the Peruginis made the decision to leave London and bring their baby up in the lush county Kate had grown to love. They rented a cottage at Sevenoaks, in Kent, although they chose to remain in London for the birth, probably unwilling to trust an unknown doctor. Blissfully happy in preparing for the arrival of their baby, it was a dreadful shock to learn at the end of November, when Kate was a contented eight months pregnant and thirty-six years of age, that beautiful, vivacious Minny Stephen had died after going into premature childbirth at the age of thirty-five. The baby had died, too. Her grieving widower, Leslie, was left with their five-year-old daughter, Laura. Anny Thackeray, unmarried, fatherless, and now without her only sibling, was devastated. She had been away on the night her sister died and wrote to a friend, "One day I went away for a night . . . & she was dead when I came back next day." Minny's death brought Kate and Anny much closer, as they drew comfort from each other. For Kate, the misery of losing her friend was compounded by the terrible fear that she,

Green Lizard (1902) by Carlo Perugini

too, might die in childbirth. If Minny, who was a year younger than Kate, and who had already borne a child, could die, so could she, a first-time mother in her mid-thirties. The last month of her pregnancy must have been extremely frightening.

Kate went into labor on December 28 and Auntie Georgy was summoned to help (Mamie was staying with friends in Hampshire). Perhaps due to a physical characteristic Kate shared with her mother, who had always suffered greatly in childbirth, the birth was not easy. After a traumatic and difficult time she gave birth to a son. They named him Leonard Ralph Dickens Perugini, after Carlo's father Leonardo, but he was always known as "Dickie." How long Kate was in labor for is unknown as his birthdate is unrecorded and the birth certificate merely states that it was "the end of December 1875"; Georgina later wrote that Kate "had suffered very long and very much."

Dickie became the center of the family's attention, adored by his parents (and, no doubt, his grandparents) and the darling of his aunt Mamie and great-aunt Georgina, who described him as "everyone's pet." He was an alert, intelligent, happy baby whom Georgy predicted great things for, hoping he would grow up to be a genius, like his maternal grandfather. By the time he was a few months old, Georgina was telling her friends that he was starting to look very like Charles Dickens; she wrote in a letter: "I am always thinking HOW proud and pleased her Father would have been—and how delighted with Katey's little Boy!" Apparently Dickie always kept "a bright smile" for Mamie and Georgy, and Kate was a "most excellent and practical little mother." She was utterly devoted to him; life seemed wonderful. Just a few years before, griefstricken by the death of her father and the terrible illness Charlie was having to endure, she very likely felt she would never be happy again. Now, in her family home with her handsome husband and beautiful baby, enjoying a blossoming career, she could but rejoice in her change of circumstances.

15

"A POWER OF LOVING SHE DID NOT KNOW SHE HAD"

For some reason, Kate and Carlo had chosen to stay in London after Dickie's birth, perhaps to avoid a country winter and perhaps also in response to pleas from Mamie and Georgina to keep Dickie near them. After several idyllic months of parenthood, Kate and Carlo were unprepared for tragedy, but at the age of seven months Dickie became suddenly and violently ill. He began vomiting and suffered from constant diarrhea. His body, being so tiny, weakened with terrifying rapidity. The doctor diagnosed a bowel inflammation, but nothing he, Georgy, or Dickie's frantic parents tried was of any use. A much-loved baby, doomed never to grow up, Leonard "Dickie" Perugini died after just two days of illness, in July 1876. His minuscule coffin was lowered into the ground at St. Nicholas's Church, Sevenoaks, in a plot that Kate and Carlo purchased for a family grave. His death certificate states only that he died in July; no date is given. Georgina wrote to Annie Fields:

> *I cannot express to you what grief it is to Katey. . . . Her love for the child was a revelation to herself, of a power of loving she did not know she had in her. . . . [Dickie was a] fine, noble engaging creature—with the sweetest nature—so patient in his suffering! I think he was one of those children who are not meant to live. He looks so pretty in Death.*

After the funeral, Kate and Carlo began concentrating intensely on their art, trying to work away their grief. They divided their time between

London and the cottage in Sevenoaks, where they could be near the grave of their son, and they made sure they were in Sevenoaks for the first anniversary of Dickie's death. The house in London now felt so terribly sad, as the bereaved parents could not overcome the memory that their son had died there.

They may have been in London for Henry Dickens' wedding on September 25, 1876, but, as they were grieving, possibly they did not attend. Henry's bride was Marie Roche, a Catholic girl of French extraction (but born and brought up in England). Marie came from a musical family: she was the granddaughter of the composer Ignaz Moscheles, her mother had been taught by Chopin, and one of her great friends was the composer Charles Gounod. As a wedding present, Gounod composed for Henry and Marie their very own *Wedding March,* a beautiful piece of music that is still performed at family weddings today. Like Kate and Carlo, the newlyweds moved in artistic, musical, and literary circles. As well as being musically talented, Marie was extremely pretty. Even in old age, photographs show her as an attractive and elegant woman.

What Kate thought about her brother's wedding at this date is unknown, but when she was an old woman she was deeply upset about a sale of family letters, which included one written by Georgina Hogarth claiming Kate did not like Henry's wife "at all." At the time of the sale, Kate said the letter—written in around 1882—was untrue, but although by the end of their lives the two women saw each other regularly and were apparently perfectly amicable it seems there was not a great deal of love lost between them. Kate was particularly irritated by Marie's Catholicism, which was passed on to all Henry's children, and even in the late 1910s she was writing scathingly about the Catholicism of a family memorial service.

—✦—

Henry was not the only person to fall in love at this time. In May 1877, at the age of thirty-nine, Anny Thackeray announced her engagement. It had long been assumed that the older, less pretty Thackeray girl would remain a spinster, so London was doubly shocked not only that her engagement was announced just a month before her fortieth birthday, but that her fiancé, Richmond Ritchie, was seventeen years her junior. He was one of her second cousins—and her godson. Society was scandalized, although Richmond's siblings were happy about it and even his mother didn't take it too badly, having always been very fond of Anny. When one of her friends asked Anny if she truly loved Richmond she reportedly replied, "Yes, but not well enough to refuse him."

As can be imagined, Kate and Carlo's friends were divided in opinion about the wedding; Kate, one hopes, was simply glad that her friend had managed to find happiness after so much sadness. John Millais was not at all pleased, however, and railed about it to his children, shouting angrily that it was "preposterous."[74] Anny's brother-in-law Leslie Stephen was also appalled. On the day they announced their engagement, he walked into a room, discovered the couple kissing, and walked out in a revolted fury. Despite Leslie's and Millais' disapproval, the couple was married on a sunny Thursday in early August 1877. The wedding was a small one, with a service that lasted for only four minutes; Kate and Carlo may not have attended, as the majority of guests appear to have been family members and Lionel Tennyson (son of the poet), who was Richmond's best man. Anny had just one bridesmaid, one of her cousins. Accompanying Leslie was his new fiancée, the beautiful Julia Duckworth (niece of the photographer Julia Margaret Cameron), with whom Anny had become very friendly and who had been instrumental in persuading Leslie to accept the couple's engagement.[75]

Like Leslie, Julia had been married before and widowed. Her husband, Herbert Duckworth, had died seven years previously, but Julia still wore deep mourning at Anny and Richmond's wedding. Her first marriage had resulted in three children, Stella, George, and Gerald. Together, Leslie and Julia would go on to have four more children and, in doing so, directly affect the history of English literature and art. Their two sons were Thoby (born in 1880) and Adrian (born in 1883); but it was their daughters who would become household names. Vanessa Stephen (born in 1879) went on to become the painter Vanessa Bell; her sister, Virginia Stephen (born

---

74 It is worth noting that Millais would not consider Val Prinsep's marriage "preposterous" even though Val was twenty-four years older than his wife.

75 That Leslie Stephen was fourteen years older than his fiancée also did not bother Millais, despite the fact that he found the seventeen-year age difference between Anny and Richmond so offensive.

1882), was the writer Virginia Woolf.[76] While the collection of eight children—including Minny's daughter Laura—were growing up, the Stephen family lived at 22 Hyde Park Gate, very close to the house that Charles Dickens used to rent to keep Mamie happy during the London Season.[77] Poor little Laura suffered sadly in this household of clever, sometimes bullying children and Anny was always concerned about her (and a constant visitor). Despite being one of the eldest, Laura could not keep up with the younger ones' quick-witted activities, as she suffered from an unspecified and debilitating learning disability. It made Anny deeply sad to see her sister's child so unhappy and left so far behind her precocious half-siblings. In later life, Virginia Woolf intimated that she and Vanessa had been sexually abused and constantly bullied by her half-brother Gerald, who assumed control of the Stephen children after they were orphaned in 1904. It is, sadly, possible that he treated Laura in the same way.

Eighteen seventy-seven was not just a year of weddings, it was also a momentous year for art. It marked the opening of the controversial Grosvenor Gallery[78] and the lead-up to the Ruskin v. Whistler libel suit, which was on everybody's lips.[79] It was also the year in which Kate Perugini was accepted to exhibit at the Royal Academy. Nine years previously, the Academy had moved to its present location in Piccadilly, the imposing Burlington House—a fitting home for the country's most distinguished art gallery and school of art. Having a picture accepted by the Royal

---

76 Virginia was very fond of Anny and immortalized her as the character Mrs. Hilbery in her novel *Night and Day.*

77 Leslie had already bought 22 Hyde Park Gate before Anny's wedding and it was from this house that the new Mr. and Mrs. Richmond Ritchie were married.

78 The Grosvenor Gallery, opened by Sir Coutts Lindsay and his wife Blanche, was designed to be an alternative to the conventional Royal Academy. It was the most progressive gallery in Victorian London, showcasing new artists and styles of art as well as established painters. Gilbert and Sullivan immortalized it in their operetta *Patience* and Oscar Wilde praised it for having revived London's culture.

79 The art critic John Ruskin had published a scathing letter about one of J.A.M. Whistler's paintings after seeing it on display at the Grosvenor Gallery. The painting, entitled *Nocturne in Black and Gold: the Falling Rocket,* now accepted as one of Whistler's finest works, was then an entirely new style of art. Ruskin accused Whistler of "flinging a pot of paint in the public's face." The case was tried in 1878. Whistler won—but was only awarded one farthing in damages, which caused him to become bankrupt, unable to pay his legal fees. It was one of the most important legal cases in art history, indicative of how the art world was changing. One can only imagine wryly what Ruskin would have thought of Surrealism had he lived to experience it.

Academy was the pinnacle of an artist's career: Kate was finally a genuine member of London's artistic elite. Her picture was entitled *An Impartial Audience* (this painting isn't traceable today). Carlo's paintings were not doing well at this date and Georgy fondly noticed how selflessly happy he was for Kate, despite his own misfortune: "as proud as if the success were his own," she told Annie Fields.

With the anniversary of Dickie's death safely behind them, the winter of 1877–78 was a happy, sociable one. The Millais family arrived in Kensington, moving into 2 Palace Gate. According to the painter's son, John Guille Millais, his father's "old friend" Carlo Perugini was a regular visitor to the family home, where he and John Everett Millais would play cards and talk long into the evening. They visited each other's studios regularly, and Millais would give Kate tips on her pictures before she sent them off to be judged at the Royal Academy. Anny recorded that that winter she and Richmond lived in a social whirl of seeing their friends.

In May 1878, after residing at a couple of temporary homes in the Kensington area, Anny and Richmond Ritchie moved to 27 Young Street, just a few doors away from the house in which Anny and Minny had grown up. Anny later described their marital home in her journal: "[it] was the prettiest old house with a long garden at the back, and an ancient medlar tree with a hole in it. There was also a lovely acacia tree."

Less than a month after moving to Young Street, Anny surprised her circle of acquaintances yet again by giving birth to a healthy baby girl, mere days before her forty-first birthday. The baby was named Hester Helena Thackeray Ritchie. Hester was to become very important in Kate's life and the two women would grow close, but at the time of Hester's birth, with the second anniversary of Dickie's death just a month away, Kate must have been suffering very mixed feelings. On June 5, however, she wrote Anny a touching, loving letter:

> *I saw today in the Times that you had a little daughter, and my husband and I went to your house and heard with great pleasure that you were going on well and the dear little one too. I have been thinking so much of you lately dear and I am so thankful that it is all over—and*

well over!—and I am so happy to think that you are feeling all the wonder and delight of having a dear little creature of your own to love and watch over—There is no greater happiness in the world, and no one who could appreciate it so much perhaps as you dear Annie, who have so much love to give—God bless you and It. and oh I am longing so to see 'It'. Do let me come soon—as soon as you may receive friends?—I send you a kiss for the dear little tiny thing and for yourself & many kind things to your husband[.]

from yr loving
Katie

If the tone of the letter can be believed as real and not bravado, Kate was on her way back to happiness. In the following year, 1879, she exhibited *A Little Woman* at the Royal Academy. (Unfortunately, there are no records at the Royal Academy about this painting.) It sold on the very first day and, most important, it sold to a stranger, not to a well-intentioned friend or acquaintance of her father. At around this time, she was beginning to receive commissions to paint children's portraits. It had long been fashionable among the rich and titled to commission portraits of their children, many of which depicted a Victorian ideal of childhood, rather than a true glimpse at how these children lived.

Carlo, whose own style of art was very similar to that of Leighton, usually painted large-scale genre paintings and pictures of beautiful women in the Classical style, draped in sensuous fabrics, leaning against marble columns or resting beside scenes reminiscent of ancient Greece or Rome. At times, Carlo would also turn his brush to portraiture. Among these paintings is *Miss Helen Lindsay* (1891), daughter of Sir Coutts Lindsay, founder of the Grosvenor Gallery (and also a pupil of Ary Scheffer). The identity of the sitter for Carlo's witty *Portrait of a Lady in an Aquamarine Dress* has not survived history. It shows a miserable-looking woman, swathed in furs, with a dog leaping up at her; the dog is wearing a bow of the same aquamarine as her dress. Carlo also painted a commanding portrait of John Forster, remarkable for its photorealism.

Among his works are several paintings of young women who bear a resemblance to Kate. An example of this is *Dressing Up*, dated 1877, a striking picture of a woman of Kate's coloring wearing a wine-colored dress, in the act of placing a white fur cloak around her shoulders. In addition, the Sunderland Art Gallery possesses several sketches of Kate by Carlo, all of them beautiful and some with a suggestion of the influence of Edward Burne-Jones upon his work. In one, she is seated beside an arrangement of flowers, but looking wistfully beyond them, her hands occupied automatically but her mind elsewhere. Her dress and figure are recreated perfectly by just a few delicate strokes.

Although life for the Peruginis was becoming happier again, 1879 was not without its heartache. Catherine Dickens had been diagnosed with cancer and it was apparent to Kate that she was in the last stages of the disease. Kate attempted feverishly to make up for the years of neglect, visiting Catherine with much greater regularity and allowing her mother to talk about Charles—a subject that had long remained taboo between them. Just as she had once done with her father and Thackeray, Kate also helped to bring about a reconciliation between Catherine and Georgina. The sisters had not spoken to each other in two decades. After their reconciliation, Kate told a friend that the meeting had been very "emotional" but that they had managed to put all their bitterness and feuding behind them. Mamie was also making a concerted attempt to end the feuding between herself and her mother.

On one of her visits, Catherine gave Kate a package. It contained all the letters from Charles that Catherine had kept, many of which dated back to their courtship, and a lock of his hair. She told Kate she must decide what to do with the letters, but that her wish was they be placed in the public domain, so that the world could know that her errant husband had loved her "once." Kate was to spend many years agonizing over what should be done with the precious little bundle, a decision she would not feel able to make until the century was almost at an end.

As the cancer moved into its last grasping stages, Kate and Mamie took turns in caring for their mother, assisted by a nurse. For Kate it was a dreadful return to the helplessness she had felt while watching Charlie die. Among the friends who called to discover how Catherine was faring, one of the most regular was Wilkie Collins. He had always been fond of Catherine and perhaps, like Kate, he felt guilty for not standing by her when Charles ended the marriage.

Catherine died on November 22, 1879. She was buried at Highgate Cemetery, in the same grave as her baby daughter, Dora. One wonders if Catherine had truly forgiven Georgina for all those years of hurt, as Kate believed. In her will Catherine deliberately bequeathed to her sister a ring in the shape of a serpent (which had been given to Catherine by Alfred's godfather, Count d'Orsay). The dying woman wrote that she wanted Georgina to have "my snake ring." Perhaps it was an item she knew Georgina admired; on the other hand, there are grounds for believing that the snake emblem was Catherine's poignant comment on how she viewed her younger sister.

16

THE PURSUIT OF PAINTING

After a dreadful decade in which Kate had lost a husband, a brother, several very close friends, both her parents, and her only baby, the 1880s started on a much more cheerful note. In March 1880, Anny Thackeray gave birth to a son. He was named William Makepeace Denis Ritchie, and known as "Billy." Later that year, Kate and Carlo went on a holiday to Erigmore in Scotland, with John and Effie Millais and a group of friends. There is a photograph of the group in which Kate's features are all but obscured behind a fashionable veiled hat and Carlo's are in the shadow of his hat's large brim and partly hidden behind his considerable beard. Thankfully, Millais wrote everyone's name beneath the photo. Kate and Carlo stand on Millais' right, emphasizing the closeness of their friend-ship. Kate's stance is confident and suggests she is well aware of how attractive she is. She looks far less stern than the other women in the party—all of whom appear vastly uncomfortable—and through her veil can be perceived a smile. It is interesting that Carlo is standing deliber-ately behind her, as it is indicative of the relationship he and Kate seemed to enjoy: She the outgoing exuberant one, pleased to be in the limelight, and he more reserved and happy to remain in her shadow. Millais and his family holidayed in Scotland—his wife's home country—every year; it is possible Kate and Carlo joined them regularly.

At about this time, Luke Fildes made a sketch of Kate sitting on the balustrade at the top of a small flight of steps. Originally one of Charles' friends, he was closer in age to the Dickens children and had remained a family friend since Charles' death (after which he had given Kate his painting of *The Empty Chair*). He saw Kate, Carlo, Henry, and Marie regularly in London and was friendly with Charley and Bessie. Kate also became very friendly with his wife, Fanny, who would later recall the time the two of them had decided to try their hand at needlework and attempted to make together a "grey silk dress. . . . It went in and out of fashion, but it was never finished." At the time Fildes made this drawing (dated June 13, 1880), Kate must have been staying with Charley and his family, as the sketch is apparently outside the room that used to be her father's study at Gad's Hill Place. It is a charming though unfinished drawing of a pretty woman who looks slightly apprehensive upon her perch, as if she's trying not to fall off. Although Kate was by now forty, in Fildes' depiction she looks half that age. Fildes described Kate, in this summer of her forty-first year, as being "beautiful—like thistledown."

A painting that Kate produced in 1880 was also brought to light, when I was contacted by Brigitte Berg, who inherited a painting from one of her ancestors. It is unknown who the sitter was, but the person who bought it

Kate sketched by Luke Fildes in 1880. She is shown sitting outside at Gad's Hill Place, now owned by her brother Charley. Fildes described her at this time as "beautiful—like thistledown."

was a German merchant named Gustav Christian Schwabe (1813-1897), who is recorded as having bought the painting in 1886. Interestingly, the painting seems to have been created as a genre scene, rather than a commissioned portrait, which suggests that either the commissions had temporarily dried up, or that Kate had the time and money to allow herself to produce a painting that wasn't a portrait of a "spoilt child," as Kate would sometimes describe her sitters. The painting depicts a young girl wearing an unusual white, red, and brown dress and cap, with a black ribbon tied around the girl's neck. The dress seems to have more in common with a dirndl than the current British fashion for young girls, which suggests the subject might have been inspired either by overseas travel or perhaps by observing foreign visitors to London. The little girl, who has brown hair and large brown eyes, is gazing out of the canvas, her eyes looking into the distance as though she is lost in thought. In her right hand is a slender piece of chalk, in her other hand, resting on her lap, is a slate. The painting was entitled *Multiplication*. Although her skin is very pale, the girl's notably dark eyes suggest she might have been Italian, which could be indicative of Kate sharing models with her husband, who, like his great friend Lord Leighton, often hired Italian models to sit for him. The painting's gilt frame is richly decorated and ornate, reminiscent of the types of frames made famous by Kate and Carlo's friend G. F. Watts.

The new decade began with good news about two of Kate's brothers overseas. Despite his father's worries of so many years before, Plorn was now fully settled and happy in Australia. In 1880, he announced that he was getting married, to a girl named Connie Desailly, from a "good Melbourne family." The wedding took place in New South Wales in July.

It was also a good year for Frank. Having joined the Mounties as a Sub Inspector six years before, in 1880 he was promoted to the rank of Inspector.[80] The situation between the Mounties and the so-called "Indi-

---

80 The North West Mounted Police had been set up in 1873, largely in response to the appalling treatment fur traders from America had been meting out to the people of Canada's First Nations. Unfortunately, rather than protecting the native people from the unscrupulous fur traders and other adventurers, the government—like most of the new settlers—seemed to think that all they needed to do for Canada's original inhabitants was to permit them to remain in their own small areas, or reservations, of a land that had once been theirs. By the early 1880s the troops of Mounties and tribes from the First Nations were on increasingly unfriendly terms.

ans" had become inflamed following the assassination of a North West Mounted Policeman, Constable Grayburn, in November 1879. Over the previous few years, relations between Canada's First Nations, in particular the Cree tribes led by legendary chief Big Bear, and the settlers had become increasingly hostile. In 1880, Inspector Francis J. Dickens and his troops were moved to a frontier area known as the Blackfoot Crossing.

Meanwhile, as Georgina explained to Kate's brothers when they complained that she never wrote to them, Kate was kept very busy painting and exhibiting. It was not until February 1883, almost three years after their wedding, that Kate finally remembered to post a wedding present to Plorn and Connie; she and Carlo sent them a set of salt cellars accompanied by a short letter. It was true she was kept very busy, but she was not yet making anything like enough money—and neither was Carlo.

Doubtless Kate's professional reputation was aided by the public's knowledge that she was one of Dickens' daughters, but she was not receiving much income from his estate. Charles had had so many dependants that the money he left was divided between a great number of people. In addition, copyright laws were very different then from today's. At the time of Charles' death, royalties were paid for only forty-two years or the life of the author plus another seven years, whichever was the longer. Within a decade after his death, his early works went out of copyright.[81] Kate did have an annual income from Catherine's will, but there were also the needs of Carlo's parents to be taken care of.[82] The younger Perugini couple needed to make money from painting, so Kate's works were deliberately devised to be as commercial as possible and her father's name was a great help.

In 1881, in a blatant attempt to improve her commercial standing, Kate decided to paint a picture whose subject matter she took from *The Old Curiosity Shop*. She displayed *Little Nell* at the Royal Academy (and then again in an exhibition given by the Institute of Water Colour Painters

---

81 Although Charles' books sold even more copies in America than Britain his family did not receive any royalties from these sales, as there was no protection for authors under US law until 1881.

82 In his will, Charles Dickens had left his wife an annuity, which was divided among their children after her death.

in 1885). In 1882 she repeated the experiment with *The Doll's Dressmaker* (from *Our Mutual Friend*), which was also exhibited at the R.A. In later years she would paint *Nancy* (Society of Lady Artists, 1886)[83] and *Brother and Sister,* whose subject was taken from *Dombey and Son* (Royal Academy, 1893). She also experimented with book illustrations, producing five woodcuts (all pictures of children) to accompany the text in *The Charles Dickens Birthday Book,* published in 1882. In the same year, a train named "The Charles Dickens" made its inaugural journey, between Manchester and Euston: Twelve years after his death, Kate's father remained one of the most popular celebrities Britain had ever known.

Sadly, by the time Kate's wedding present reached Plorn and Connie, it must have appeared a terrible irony to the recipients. In 1883 no one in the family had heard from Plorn for over a year; what they were unaware of was that the young couple was in dire financial trouble. Kate's pretty little salt cellars must have mocked them—English gentry silverware sent to a despairing Australian family about to lose everything. It seems likely that Plorn pawned them as soon as they arrived. Perhaps it was Plorn's refusal to respond to any of the family's letters that had prompted Kate to send her present at last. No doubt she felt guilty that he had already been married for three years before she got around to posting it; maybe she thought she had upset him, especially as he had been so thoughtful about organizing a wedding present for her and Carlo. Before he had left for Australia, she and Plorn had been very close; the family hoped she might receive a response where the rest of them had failed. Still they heard nothing. Then, at the end of May 1884, Plorn sent two distressing telegrams. They are no longer in existence, but from the tone of Georgy's answering letter it seems they were desperate—perhaps aggressively worded—pleas for a large amount of money, but with no explanation of why he needed it. The station his father had bought for him, far from making him rich as it had been hoped, had failed, with all the livestock dead from the vagaries of the harsh Australian climate. It left him mired in debt. He and Alfred had set up a land agency together, but that was also failing and, although his wife came from a "good Melbourne family," it seems there

---

83 This painting is unknown today. I assume it is of Nancy from *Oliver Twist,* but it could be a commissioned portrait of a child named Nancy.

was no money available from that quarter. Australia was undergoing an economic depression (which would really take hold in the 1890s, leaving very few families unscathed). The harsh realities of life in Australia must have hit Plorn all the harder because he was so ill-equipped for hardship, having always been the petted baby of the family. Georgy's agitated reply is revealing of exactly what was happening in the family at the time and discloses that Kate and Carlo were also in financial trouble:

My dear dear Plorn,

I hope you can imagine the dismay and grief which we all felt when we received those distressing telegrams from you. We had had no news from you, not a line for nearly two years, except one sweet little note from Connie which I received about a year ago. . . . Your last letter was full of hope about the sale of your station, and about your new business. Then we never heard whether your station was sold or not, never one word as to how the new business was going on. But we always hoped and believed that you were as prosperous there. . . . The two telegrams came to me and exploded upon us like a bomb shell. . . . Of course, neither Mamie nor I could do anything. If we had had the money, God knows how gladly we would have lent it: but we have nothing but our incomes, and out of these, you may well believe, there is no possibility of sending a big sum of money. We require every penny we have to live, and to provide for some claims which we have upon us. . . . My dear boy, we have not one now, on whom we have the smallest claim. Those who might wish to help cannot, and those who could and might have helped, are dead. If Mr. Ouvry or Mr. Forster had been still living I could have applied to them for help and assistance. But there is not another soul. The Peruginis have a very precarious income depending entirely on the sale of pictures—the last two years have been very bad, this is very bad, and they are in great anxiety and trouble themselves about money. Charley is of course out of the question. He has an immense family. . . . Dear Harry is the thriving one of the family, thank god, but he has a large family, so though his income is increasing, his expenses increase too, year by year. . . . I went to him of course directly I got your first telegram, and he has written to you, I know, a long letter, telling you how impossible and how useless he thinks it would have been for him to sacrifice that large sum of money probably to do you no good at all. . . . Of course we are quite in the dark as to the notion and causes of your difficulties and we are hoping that a letter may be now, on its way, . . . to give us some light and explanation. For God's sake, do write fully, dearest Plorn. I cannot tell you how anxious and unhappy we all are about you. . . . We are all pretty well. Mamie is staying with Mrs. Lehmann on the Thames near Maidenhead just now. Of course she is most anxious and most unhappy about you . . .

It seems incredible that, less than fifteen years after Charles Dickens' death, his family was suffering such financial problems. Despite Georgy's words and his ever-growing family, Henry Dickens, the closest in age to Plorn and a man who felt very deeply the responsibility of family, came to his brother's rescue. He sent him as a loan the large sum of £800, which was apparently the amount Plorn dictated. Plorn, perhaps eaten up by guilt and embarrassment over his need of the money and envy of Henry, did not even bother to thank him or let him know that the money had arrived safely. For decades to come, Henry would remain greatly upset by Plorn's treatment of him. Many years in the future, after Plorn's death, Connie visited England, but Henry refused to meet her. It seems he blamed her for Plorn's behavior, refusing to believe that the brother he was so fond of could have been so unkind. I have often wondered if the other Dickens boys resented Henry and Charley for being allowed to stay in England, with their sisters and parents, while they were all shipped off abroad, and whether they especially resented Henry for having been supported through university. Plorn's behavior seems to suggest that he did; perhaps in a twisted way the very fact that Henry could afford to send him the much needed £800 made his resentment even stronger. Plorn may have felt that the family—and Henry, in particular, who had enjoyed such an expensive education—owed him the money.

As Georgina's letter confirms, the mid-1880s were a difficult financial period for the Peruginis. Neither Kate nor Carlo is recorded as having exhibited or sold much. In the previous year, Val Prinsep had finally married. A man with considerable wealth of his own, he had married

Florence Leyland, the heiress daughter of a rich art collector (already deceased). One wonders if Kate felt a pang with the realization of how much easier her life would have been had she accepted Prinsep's pro-posal. Her marriage to Carlo, however, appears to have been solid and loving and there are no rumors of extramarital affairs this time. Sadly, it seems there were no more pregnancies either. She may, of course, have become pregnant again and suffered a miscarriage—such things were sel-dom discussed and would probably not have been recorded in letters or other family memorabilia—but by now Kate was in her mid-forties and very possibly no longer able to conceive. Her many illnesses and regular depressions during her marriage to Charlie would have placed a great strain upon her body. In addition, with a very different diet and lifestyle from that of today, many women reached menopause at a much younger age than happens in twenty-first-century Britain.

In 1885, after a year of family misery about Plorn, some welcome news arrived from Canada. The formerly wayward Frank Dickens was being hailed as a hero. It happened after he and twenty-two of his men were encamped in a fortification known as Fort Pitt, near Great Sas-katchewan. An army of three hundred Cree, led by Big Bear, descended on the fort and ordered them to surrender. Frank and his troops knew that white settlers allied to the Hudson Bay Trading Company had been massacred at nearby Frog Lake. As the Inspector in charge of the troops, Frank managed to lead his men to safety, with all twenty-two still alive, to the town of Battleford, ninety miles away. It took six days to make the journey by river, on a quickly constructed boat (or "scow"), leaving their personal possessions behind. Big Bear gave his word they would not be fired on, but nonetheless it was a grueling and terrifying trip during which all suffered from frostbite. They were all believed dead, so Frank and his men arrived in the town to an ecstatic heroes' welcome. Sadly, though, the six days battling with ice floes and the elements took their toll on Frank's health and he was never to recover fully. He left the Mounties in the spring of 1886.

Toward the end of the 1880s, Kate and Carlo's finances, it appears, finally took an upward turn. Since the 1860s Carlo had continued to receive regular payments from Leighton, but these came to an end in 1888.

The payments had been averaging £100 to £200 a year, and were probably made more from philanthropy than from any real need to keep Carlo working in the studio. There are no explanatory records of precisely what Carlo's work for Leighton involved. However, one must presume that the payments were ended because Carlo felt he was able to make it on his own and no longer needed to accept financial help from his friend.[84]

Kate's own status was assured in 1886, when she was accepted as a professional member of the Society of Lady Artists, whose number included fellow portrait painter Louise Jopling. This organization had been set up in the mid-1850s, as the Society of Female Artists, because women were finding it so hard to be taken seriously as artists and therefore to obtain commissions or sell paintings. It changed its name to the Society of Lady Artists in 1873 and then, in 1899, to the Society of Women Artists, the name by which it is more commonly known. For Kate, membership was a very positive step, as the Society held exhibitions every year. An excellent showcase for her work, it was also an organization that someone seeking an artist would approach for recommendations. Unfortunately many of the Society's archives prior to 1920 have been lost or destroyed, which means that there may well be more of Kate's works that we do not know about. Although the Society's catalogue for 1886 does not include her name, other archive sources claim that the Society showed two of her paintings that year, at an exhibition held at the Egyptian Hall in Piccadilly. Her works were called *Fastening the Plait* and *Nancy*. The latter sold; whether the former did after the exhibition, or had already been sold beforehand, is uncertain. In the same year, an exhibition of Millais' collected works, including his portraits of Kate and Louise Jopling, as well as *The Black Brunswicker*, was held at the Grosvenor Gallery.

The previous year, Millais had written Kate a moving letter after the critics had panned what he had thought was one of his most "important" paintings. The tone of the letter and the fact that it was Kate he chose to write to on the subject demonstrate how close their friendship was, as well as his admiration for her as an artist. The picture that the critics were so harsh about was Millais' portrait of the recently deceased

---

84 Records show that between the years 1871 and 1888 Lord Leighton made payments totaling more than £2,100 to Carlo Perugini.

John Gould (1804–81), the English ornithologist who became known as the "father" of Australian ornithology after visiting the antipodes in the 1830s, accompanied by his wife, and returning with what seemed to be a comprehensive study of the country's birdlife. The portrait is a stunning work that most viewers today would appreciate more fully than paintings such as *Bubbles,* the portrait of a young boy blowing bubbles through a pipe (which became globally famous after being used to advertise Pears soap), or *My First Sermon,* in which a very beautiful tiny girl listens attentively while seated on a hard church pew. (Millais also painted *My Second Sermon,* in which the same little girl—modeled by one of his daughters—is seen fast asleep in the pew.) In the letter, Millais explained to Kate sadly, "I don't think I will trouble the critics and the public any more with 'an important picture.'" Even Millais had had to conform: He was not immune from the requirement to produce commercially popular art. As a young artist, family money had allowed him to live a carefree life, but by the 1880s he and Effie had eight children and Millais had developed a fondness for an increasingly expensive lifestyle. Like Kate, he needed to paint portraits of people who could pay well for them.

During this time, Kate and Carlo seem to have become quite reclusive together. Although the accepted image of Kate is one of being vivacious and sociable, she admitted in one of her frank letters that she did not like going out—which may perhaps have been because Carlo preferred them to stay at home. Gladys Storey wrote of them, "Although Mr. and Mrs. Perugini enjoyed the friendship of many, it may be said that they lived a somewhat cloistered though happy life, devoting themselves to the art they loved so well." Wrapped up in her new career and happy to be sharing that love of art with her husband, it seems Kate withdrew to some degree from the whirling sociable world of which she had always been such a central part.

While her sister was making a name for herself in the art world, Mamie was making a bid for freedom. The Mamie who twenty years before had shocked her acquaintances by bleaching her hair was now barely ever at home and had become very secretive about, and protective of, her new life. In 1878, she had left her social circle to live in the suburbs of Manchester with a clergyman and his wife, who worked at

St. Thomas' Mission Church. She seldom returned to London and none of her family, in particular Georgina, to whom Mamie had previously been so close, were at all pleased about her decision. Family history from this time is patchy, with comments about Mamie obscured or cut out altogether. What actually happened in Manchester remains shrouded in mystery, but as well as allegations of heavy drinking there have been suggestions that Mamie was sexually involved with either the clergyman or his wife. Obviously none of this can be proven. We know that Mamie grew particularly close to Mrs. Hargreaves, the clergyman's wife, who remained her devoted companion until her death. The Reverend Hargreaves was reportedly a boorish, unpleasant husband who intimidated his partner. It seems unlikely that Mamie, who had resisted the advances of several eligible suitors, would have been at all tempted by the dubious charms of the Reverend Hargreaves, at least not those as experienced by Kate and Georgy when they finally made his acquaintance in 1896, but she obviously found him charismatic. Mamie made the decision to live with the couple, moving around as they did and working for the mission. The rumors of an affair may just have been malicious gossip, spread by people who could not understand an intensely felt friendship between the two women.

In January 1886, Georgy wrote to Alfred about Mamie. She begins the letter by begging him to get Plorn to write to "Harry," who is miserable because he has heard nothing from him and waits anxiously for the post every morning. Then she goes on to let off steam about Mamie's strange behavior and her friendship with the Hargreaves couple:

> *I have let my house in Strathmore Gardens on a lease, to some very good and nice tenants I am happy to say. Mamie so seldom came there, even from the very first. . . . I have now taken a flat which is a much easier and more independent way for me to live alone. . . . She seems to have quite 'cast in her lot' with that clergyman and his wife with whom she has been staying constantly for 8 years. We are all dreadfully sorry, she seems to have quite given up her own family and her old friends, and I must say that we have a very bad opinion (and with reason I know) of the people with whom she lives. I know she spent all her money upon*

*them and upon his church wherever it may be. She is constantly mov-
ing about, and has no settled living anywhere. . . . Mamie is of course,
entirely her own mistress, and has a right to choose her own way of living. Katy and I have both remonstrated with her many times. But we
can do no more, she chooses this life and prefers it, and I can only hope
that she may continue to get satisfaction out of it . . .*

Mamie is a shadowy figure, who grows more fascinating the deeper
one delves into history. Ostensibly, and by popular opinion, she was the
quiet, conventional, eminently dutiful daughter of Dickens, while Kate
was the wild, rebellious one. According to contemporary reports, Kate
was certainly the prettier, cleverer, and more vivacious of the two, but
Mamie was an interesting and enigmatic character. When Kate left
home, Mamie made the most of having her father to herself and said
that she was proud she had never exchanged his name for that of another
man. She made herself popular locally and, as a minor celebrity in her
own right, she was once asked to launch a ship at the Chatham docks.
She astonished the locals in Higham by acquiring a bicycle and being the
first woman they had ever seen riding one. In a letter to George Bernard
Shaw, written in 1897, Kate makes the tantalizing promise, "Some day I
will tell you about Mamie and myself—it will help you to a better understanding of our old home life." Sadly, if she ever wrote that letter, it does
not survive and whatever it was Kate was going to reveal about her sister
remains a mystery.

Mamie may have never married because she was emotionally scarred
by her parents' marriage; she may have preferred to emulate her aunt
Georgina, who had enjoyed a successful single life. There are, however,
several circumstances that suggest Mamie could have been a lesbian and
not merely because of the rumors of her liaisons in the "provinces" of
Manchester. There is a letter from Nina Lehmann to her husband Fred
in which Nina describes, in a quite astonished manner, a greeting she
received from Mamie when she went to visit her; the latter greeted her
like a "lover," records Nina, constantly kissing and caressing her. Nina was
obviously deeply embarrassed by it. It did not, though, affect their friendship and the two regularly went on holidays around England together.

There is also Kate's cryptic comment to Frederick Lehmann in 1866 about Mamie coming up to London and taking "her happiness where she can" and the worried addition, "Of course it will come out. Sure to." Kate's comments suggest not only that the secret was something scandalous but also that it was something sexual. (She may have been having an affair with a married man, although no one has ever been suggested.) In addition, Mamie showed a marked aversion to being courted by men, not only—understandably—to the unwelcome attentions of the intoxicated, elderly Chorley.

During her father's lifetime, Mamie was content to remain his housekeeper (jointly with Georgina), enjoying the status the role afforded her and needing no other man in her life, but after his death, as she began to drift unhappily from the life that had once made her so content, it is surprising that she did not succumb to marriage. Gladys Storey asserted in her book that in her early twenties Mamie had been in love but her father did not approve of the suitor, "so that was the end of it," but no other information has ever been discovered about this and Kate never seems to have mentioned it to anyone else. Perhaps she made the throw-away comment to Gladys as a foil, to stop her asking questions about her sister. Charles himself wrote to a friend, "You would not recognise Gad's Hill, I have changed it so since I bought it. And yet I often think that if Mary were to marry (which she won't), I should sell it and go vagabondizing over the face of the earth."

It was unusual for a woman of Mamie's time to resist marriage so strongly and there can have been no shortage of suitors for an attractive woman with such an illustrious father. Percy Fitzgerald wrote glowingly of her, "It would be difficult to find a more attractive girl than Mamie Dickens . . . decidedly pretty . . . curious spirit of independence and haughty refusal of submission. . . . She was of a petite figure, small well-shaped features." Throughout the 1860s, while Kate was earning a reputation for being "fast," Mamie was shunned equally by society for being the child of separated parents and for not choosing to live with her mother, but not through any rumors of wayward sexual behavior, as Kate was. She does not even appear to have been berated for mild flirting, despite the influence and proximity of her coquettish sister. Henry Dickens wrote contemplatively toward the end of his life, "I have wondered, sometimes, why my sister never married. She was very attractive, clever and an experienced housewife."

I wonder if Kate's second, successful, marriage had anything to do with Mamie's erratic behavior. During her marriage to Charlie, Kate had needed to, and did, spend a great deal of time with her sister; at this stage, their relationship seems to have changed little from when they were teenagers. After her marriage to Carlo, Kate needed her sister less and spent less time socializing with her. Throughout her life, Mamie had always been depended upon, whether by her father, her sister, or one of her many brothers. She and Georgy had always been the ones who fixed things and made life easy for the rest of the family. Perhaps she began to feel useless and redundant after Kate married a second time, or perhaps she embraced this new-found freedom with excitement. No correspondence remains between her and Kate to provide any clues to their adult relationship (which is not surprising given that Kate regularly burned private papers). As Mamie died three decades before her sister, Kate inherited the bulk of her papers. An undated letter from Anny Thackeray suggests that she had also felt pushed out of Kate's life since the arrival of Carlo. She refers to a letter Kate had sent her and comments, "I am perfectly certain the zealous Perugini stood over Kitty as she wrote."

While Mamie was in Manchester and out of favor, Georgina grew much closer to Kate. She wrote to Alfred:

> *Kitty comes to me very often, and I go to her ... I shewed her your letter ... [she] was much touched by your message to her and says you and Plorn are not to think because she does not write that she does not love you and think of you as much as we do. But she is a bad correspondent, and besides she is always at work, painting, so she has a good excuse for not writing. .... She is becoming a very well known artist, and paints children most charmingly. She gets lots of commissions now. She is looking very well now and I think she is as pretty as ever she was.*

At around this time, the family was distressed by a series of bizarre and voracious rumors that had begun circulating about Charles Dickens.

Just as people regularly question how Shakespeare could possibly have written all the works attributed to him, journalists had begun to question whether Dickens had genuinely written all his. *Macmillan's* magazine published an article entitled "Who Wrote Dickens?" in June 1886, which began years of speculation, with people from all walks of life claiming it would have been impossible for one man to produce so much. Since most of his children were still alive, and very much witnesses to the terrific volume of work he had penned, it seems incredible that the story gained such force, especially in an age long before typewriters, when the manuscripts were all in Dickens' own very distinctive handwriting. It was frustrating and upsetting for the remaining Dickens children that the newspapers constantly put before the public such ridiculous speculation.

In the same month as the article was published, forty-two-year-old Frank Dickens, who had gained quite a degree of fame in North America, traveled to Moline, Illinois, to give a speech about the 1885 rebellion. Just moments before he was due to speak, his body was racked by chest pains; within a very short time, he was dead. It seems that he too had inherited the weak heart so prevalent in the Hogarth family and that the problem had been exacerbated when he was given a glass of iced water to drink. His death was accredited to the water being so cold it shocked him. How ironic, that the man who clung to a raft on an icy river for several days could be killed by drinking a glass of iced water. The community of Illinois raised the money for a funeral themselves and he was buried there without any of his family present. There is no record of Kate's feelings about Frank's sudden and shocking death, nor of the fact that he had, like Walter and Sydney before him, managed to get himself into severe debt in the few years before he died.

17

AN IMPASSIONED
CORRESPONDENCE

During the late 1880s, Kate was not able to see Anny as often as before, as Anny, Richmond, and the children had moved to Wimbledon (at that time quite a journey from central London). The Ritchie family would not return to living near the Peruginis until 1898, but the two women's friendship remained strong. With Mamie also absent, Carlo's company became even more important to Kate and at times they barely left the house, working hard and preferring to spend their free time together rather than out in society.

Throughout the last years of the decade Kate painted feverishly and exhibited regularly, both for the Society of Lady Artists and the Royal Academy. It was after the 1887 exhibition for the Society of Lady Artists that Kate began what was to become an extraordinary friendship and correspondence. To the Society's exhibition, again held at the Egyptian Hall in Piccadilly, Kate had contributed two works: *Peggie* and *There's a Sweet Little Cherub that Sits Up Aloft*. (The latter, whose title was taken from a well-known nautical song often cited by Kate's father, was priced at £140.)[85] The exhibition was reviewed for *The World* magazine, whose editor was Kate's former unrequited love Edmund Yates. The review of the exhibition contained a scathing piece about Kate's work, in which she was accused of merely copying Millais' style. Its author was an Irish writer by the name of George Bernard Shaw.[86]

---

85 Neither of these paintings is known today.

86 At this date, Shaw's writing was already relatively well known. He had also helped to found the Fabian Society in 1884.

On April 12, Kate was moved to write to Yates:

Dear Mr. Yates—I could not help feeling a little aggrieved when I read the criticism of a picture of mine now being exhibited at the Egyptian Hall. Pray do not think I am sufficiently thin skinned to quarrel with G.B.S. for finding fault with my work—I know too well all its shortcomings but at the same time I do beg to assure him that in doing my utmost to paint what I see, I have difficulty sufficient to contend with—without adding to it all the complications arising from trying to imitate anybody's work. Much as I admire Sir John Millais's pictures and the pictures of many another great man I do most positively deny that I have the slightest intention to endeavour to imitate them—I have always maintained the opinion that a woman's work is nearly always in many respects at least inferior to a man's and that is the reason perhaps that I would never try to be anyone but myself in what I aspire to do.

You would do me a favour if you would forward this letter to G.B.S. of course I do not wish him to take any public notice of it but I do venture to hope that his opinion of my work—or rather the aim of my work may be a little altered. I remain dear Mr. Yates
Yours sincerely
Kate Perugini

It was a letter that Kate regretted almost as soon as she had written it and attempted to get back before Yates gave it to Shaw. Today, one would hope that Kate regretted the letter because of her comment about a woman's work being nearly always inferior to a man's, but sadly that was not the case; she regretted it because, after the heat of her fury had faded, she accepted that critics were entitled to their opinions and she had made a fool of herself by complaining.

The letter that Kate had sent to Yates to pass on to Shaw was to begin a long-lasting friendship. Her furious letter sparked, initially, a row—shortly afterward, Kate and Shaw were invited to the same dinner where they had a caustic exchange of words before deciding they liked each other. This marked the beginning of an intense correspondence, one that is sometimes painful to read because of Kate's quite desperate attempts to cultivate their friendship more completely than Shaw was interested in doing in the early days. Very few of the letters remain, as, toward the end of her life, Kate requested that Shaw return all she had written to him and—despite his entreaties not to destroy them—she burned them in her drawing-room fire as soon as he had left. She also burned the letters she had received from him. Most of her letters that survive date from early on in their correspondence; perhaps Shaw forgot he had them, which is why they escaped being destroyed.

Although Shaw seemed initially reluctant, they did become good friends and Shaw respected her opinion. After a few years, he was regularly sending her signed copies of his latest works for her comments. One cannot help wondering what Carlo made of this frequent and impassioned correspondence. The self-confessed bad correspondent, who was far too busy to keep in touch with her brothers overseas, was writing long and intense letters almost every day to a man seventeen years her junior who, it seems, did not have time to reply to her with anything like the regularity with which she wrote to him. Her letters are often embarrassingly flirtatious, begging him to come and visit her or scolding him as though he were her lover or a lifelong friend. Even before they had met each other, she was writing to him as though they had a flirtatious understanding. After a while, she begins describing him as her "youngest brother," but the tone does not seem sisterly and bears little comparison with the few remaining letters that she wrote to her real brothers.

The letters are acutely revealing of Kate's personality. Many demonstrate the fiery and violent temper that earned her the nickname "Lucifer Box." When one reads some of the pompous content of Shaw's surviving letters, it is unsurprising that there are times when Kate flies into a fury and writes such lines as "Nothing at this moment could afford me such supreme satisfaction as to see you writhe in anguish." At other times she is coquettish and seductive, proving Gladys Storey's later assertion that Kate had told her she had been from a young age a successful flirt who enjoyed making men think she was in love with them, even when she wasn't. The letters reveal a woman who is used to using her charms to get what she wants—and who usually succeeds.

Kate's letters to Shaw also reveal a great deal about her life over the next few years. She writes to him about her impressions of life, her marriage, her feelings of depression, his writing, and her paintings. In April 1889, two years after her first letter to him, Kate sent one of her most interesting letters. Although she begins by telling him she has been feeling depressed, she goes on to write a superbly witty and clever letter,

Dear Mr. Bernard Shaw,

I have been very busy, very poorly and in such low spirits that art & literature—the world—and every body and every thing in it— even Socialism—have all seemed to me but 'vanity and vexation of spirit'. To-day I am a little better, so I will try and answer your letter, which with the article you so kindly sent me, I read with a great deal of interest,—and not a little amusement. You dont [sic] in the least frighten me by describing yourself as a Socialist, although I confess I have very vague ideas as to what Socialism really means.

I take a Socialist to be a kind of Radical philanthropist, who wishes to do all the good he can in the world, but who in so doing would also like to take away from the lives of people all that makes life beautiful and worth having—and who would reduce the world at last to as dull a level as—as Gower Street on a cold spring day, with dust flying and cold pale yellow oranges being cried and sold! I also imagine a Socialist (for some inscrutable reason of his own) to have rather ungracious manners and to wear creaky boots, but no doubt I am wrong. The only Socialist I know is indeed very unlike this, he has a pretty house, gives charming dinners—and rumour has it, that he rides in the Row every morning on a very handsome horse—but I suppose my Socialist has not the courage of his opinions—or he would live on a crust, would he not? and cut up his horse into mincemeat to divide among his poorer friends? But as I have already said, I have vague ideas on the subject—I should like to see a real thorough going young Socialist in the flesh, I would therefore most gladly repeat my invitation to you—only of one thing I am most horribly afraid. I am afraid of boring people—I consider it should be a punishable crime to bore anyone, and as you seem to think it might bore you to come and see me, I have nothing for it, although I regret it very much, but to beg you to stay away. Your startling assertion that you hate all artists is a little sweeping is it not for even a Socialist to affirm? I imagined a Socialist was a very large minded individual indeed—but again I fear I have been wrong in my estimation of him, but in this case, as I was born and bred among artists as it were, I suppose I cannot be expected to agree with you. My husband is an artist, my father was one—and although a humble wretched little painter I try to be one myself. I therefore cannot hate artists—although I do not think that art will save the world—but will Socialism? Both have some good in them surely—and might ought rather to walk hand in hand—doing all the good they can together—than sulk off separately and make themselves disagreeable.

Yrs. very sincerely
Kate Perugini

During these years, Kate had been exhibiting regularly and her works were selling well. Carlo's works were continuing to gather some interest, though this was sporadic and never reliable. When he did sell a painting, it commanded a higher price than one of Kate's—but it was the regularity of her sales that kept them from financial ruin. The catalogues for the Society of Lady Artists' exhibitions suggest that almost all Kate's works were paid commissions, as most of the portraits she exhibited were not priced for sale. Yet she remained uncertain of herself and at the end of April she was writing again to Shaw, this time agreeing to a criticism he had made of another of her paintings. It is a strange letter, in which she seems jokingly not to care anymore about his comments, yet in common with most artists Kate could be her own most scathing critic. In this letter she seems to believe she deserved to be taken down a peg, an overly self-deprecating attitude that Kate seemed to veer toward and away from in all areas of her life.

Yes that boy of mine is the worst thing a would be artist ever produced I know he is, and you are quite right to say so and would have been right to publish your opinion had you thought it worth while I should not have been offended. I was only offended when you said I imitated Millais—a thing of which I am guiltless because I am not clever enough to imitate anyone. I know the boy is very bad & I ought not to have exhibited him.

In the very next line she is teasing him and joking about her relationship with Carlo. It is written in a easy manner that suggests the correspondents have developed a jovial relationship over the previous two years:

Now let me ease your mind on one point. Mr. Perugini treats me very well thank you, and does not beat me—although perhaps you will think that is not a subject for much thanksgiving—but I assure you I am the meekest of women & if only you knew me I think you would acknowledge this. Why won't you come and judge for yourself? also it would be such a triumph for you to compare the horrors of Warwick Street with the delights of Gower St. But there, no, I will not give in about Gower St. I do know that street very well alas, and when I was particularly naughty as a child, it was always after a walk up or down that—to me—hideously dull and eminently respectable thoroughfare. It is its respectability I think which makes it so dreadful to me.

Her letters also give an interesting insight into the kind of life she and Carlo lived and her attitude toward some of her sitters. In a letter from June 1889, she writes:

I have been very busy—painting all day—and going out every evening (which I hate) that I have not had a moment for letter writing and indeed at all times I am considered by my friends to be one of the worst correspondents in the world and can hardly ever be brought to write a line to anyone—having a perfect detestation of note writing. Today two rich, pampered 'robber' children who are sitting to me are to come a quarter of an hour later than usual, so I seize upon the opportunity to answer your questions.

It seems the need to paint "pampered" children grated quite considerably on Kate; she felt trapped in her particular sphere by the need to earn money, and painting children was considered the correct thing for a lady to concern herself with. She did, however, have a great love of children and those who were well behaved she adored with the wistfulness of a bereaved mother. In 1893, she painted a genre painting of a young girl holding a basket of blackberries; although the name of the painting is *Blackberries,* the little girl is definitely the main focus of the painting. She looks out directly at the viewer, her gaze compeling and thoughtful. Kate's love of children would come through in 1904 and 1905 when she painted the two young daughters of Sir George Lewis, Jr. (the friend and lawyer of Oscar Wilde), Elizabeth and Peggy. She and Elizabeth struck up a fond friendship and Kate promised the girl that the finished portrait would be addressed to her not to her parents so that Elizabeth could enjoy the importance of receiving a large parcel. When Peggy arrived to sit for her, Kate was astonished by the child's looks and wrote to Lewis:

> *I am perfectly amazed at the beauty of little Peggy. She is far prettier even than she was and has a lovely expression too. I want the little pale blue frock she wore kept for the sittings. It does perfectly and the coral beads. I hope to finish in four or five more sittings. She is a darling—and what a colour! She is like some brilliant flower. And I love her, as I do my pretty sweet Elizabeth. You are certainly lucky in your children. Ever very sincerely K.P.*

Kate also painted landscapes on occasion. She may have yearned to paint large-scale works like her husband did; certainly she enjoyed helping him with his works.

As Kate's letters to Shaw continued, their friendship developed and her letters start to sound more confident. On one occasion she gives him her opinion of the celebrated actress Mrs. Patrick Campbell, whom she and Carlo had been to see play Ophelia:

> *I saw the new Hamlet at the Lyceum on the first night. Mrs. Patrick Campbell I confess did not please me, not because she was good or bad, or conventional or unconventional, but simply because she did not convince me that she was out of her mind. Perhaps on a 'first night'*

people on the stage are too sane, too much thinking of the effect they are making to 'let themselves go'. No doubt she has improved. I have only seen two insane girls in my life. They were not at all like Mrs. Patrick Campbell on the stage as Ophelia—or like any other actress simulating madness I have ever seen.

Mrs. Patrick Campbell was one of Shaw's most intimate friends, but Kate's critique of her acting was something he took great pleasure in. He later gave this review as a historic reason why Kate should not burn all the letters she had written to him; it is perhaps no coincidence that he saved this one from the fire.

When Shaw married the wealthy Charlotte Payne-Townshend in 1898, Kate sent him a witty letter about his engagement, saying that she sent her congratulations to Shaw, but wasn't at all sure that she should congratulate Charlotte on choosing to marry him.

18

LIFE IN OLD KENSINGTON

The year 1889 was not a good one for lovers of English literature, as it marked the deaths of two of the country's greatest writers. One was Kate's former brother-in-law, Wilkie Collins, who died at his home, 82 Wimpole Street. Kate and Mamie sent wreaths to the funeral. In his will, Wilkie requested that his much loved portrait of Charlie Collins, painted by Holman Hunt, be returned to the artist. The other much lamented death of 1889 was that of Robert Browning, a good friend of Anny's and Val Prinsep's. His funeral was a grand affair held at Westminster Abbey.

In the same year, good news reached Kate and Henry from Australia, where Edward "Plorn" Dickens had dragged himself out of his financial quagmire and been elected MP for the constituency of Wilcannia, in New South Wales. Kate must have found herself pondering over the very different lives she and so many of her brothers had found themselves living. In common with her parents and the majority of her siblings, Kate was never to visit Australia; she could have had little, if any, understanding of the ways of life Plorn and Alfred experienced.

While Plorn was winning over voters, Kate was continuing to paint exhaustively and exhibiting regularly. Among other paintings she was working on was a picture entitled *Flossie* (1892), hung in a wide, delicately patterned gilt frame (of the style made popular by G. F. Watts). It was a portrait of Flossie Broughton, niece by marriage of Mr. Broughton, a Royal Academician. That Kate was being recommended by members of the RA demonstrates how well respected she was, and this was thirty years before the first female Royal Academician of the twentieth century would be—somewhat grudgingly—allowed to be appointed.[87]

Flossie is a stunning painting, the image of a girl who seems only recently to have entered adolescence. She looks out boldly at the viewer, attempting to act stern and grown-up, but with the flicker of a smile just catching at the edge of her lips. She is dressed in claret-colored velvet: a demure, high-necked dress, with a self-patterned bodice in a criss-cross style, lightly puffed shoulders heading the long sleeves, and a matching velvet hat, with a stiff brim and large velvet bow above it. Around her neck and draping over her right shoulder snakes what appears to be a black feathered scarf. The ends of the girl's fair curls can be seen just beneath the brim of her hat and curling behind her ears. The color of the velvet contrasts perfectly with a slubbed green background and the delicate fair skin tones of Flossie's face. The most arresting aspect of the portrait, however, is the sitter's eyes. They are a rich dark brown, with just a suggestion of thick dark lashes and carefully shaped eyebrows. Flossie's eyes gaze directly at the viewer, giving the impression that this was a forceful young woman who would not be cowed by experience. Though not a large painting, it is truly eye-catching for its clarity and intensity; Leighton himself openly admired it.

What happened to this painting after it was exhibited at the Royal Academy is unknown; it seems most likely the Broughtons commissioned it, yet there is a slight mystery attached to it, as toward the end of Kate's life it hung on the wall of her Chelsea flat. Most probably it was returned to her, perhaps in accordance with Mr. or Mrs. Broughton's will (as had been the case with Wilkie and Holman Hunt's painting). She would later give it to a friend and admirer, Lord Leverhulme. In June 2001, Sotheby's held an auction of the Leverhulme estate, at which *Flossie* was among the items. The sale catalogue predicted it would sell for between £8,000 and £12,000, so art collectors were astounded when it realized £107,000. It was bought by a London art gallery who later sold it on for an undisclosed sum; I was able to ascertain only that it was sold at a profit.

---

87 There had been two female Academicians in the eighteenth century—Angelica Kauffmann and Mary Moser—but none since.

Kate herself was now fully confident in her career. In the 1891 census, for the very first time the "occupation" box near her name is filled in; in all previous censuses the field has been left blank and her status confirmed solely as "wife." Interestingly Kate didn't just call herself an artist: It was recorded that she was an "artist/sculptor." There are no surviving sculptures by Kate, but perhaps she was experimenting with the medium at this time. There are also no surviving sculptures by Carlo, but I have known two references to his also being a sculptor: one in Winifred Gérin's 1981 biography of Anny Thackeray and the other was in a conversation I had with Belinda Norman-Butler, Thackeray's great-granddaughter, who remembered my great-great-grandfather Henry Fielding Dickens and whose father often spoke to her about his friends Kate and Carlo. She told me Carlo was a sculptor as well as a painter. Leighton produced several very beautiful sculptures and Carlo, who was so often at Leighton's studio, would have been involved in the process, whether directly or simply by observation. It is notable, however, that Carlo never included the word "sculptor" when he wrote about his profession on any official documents; nor are there any records of sculptures among his works.

The census for 1891 may offer some answers as to why the Peruginis' finances had been so troublesome in the 1880s. It seems Carlo had lost both parents during that decade, which means he would have been actively supporting the bereaved parent and probably losing a great deal of studio time, as well as paying for medical expenses and funerals. His brother, Edward, also died in December 1888. The death certificate records that Edward died following an operation for gangrene. Carlo was present at his death. By the time of the 1891 census, Edward's wife, Florence, was living with their three younger children, Mark, Laurence, and little Stella. They were living in Chiswick, a suburb to the west of London, in reduced circumstances, with only one servant. The eldest daughter, also called Florence, had married a musician named Harry Campbell in 1887. Carlo's sister-in-law, to whom in earlier censuses no profession was ascribed, is now recorded as being an "actress," suggesting she is struggling financially and having to work. Local historian Laurence Duttson kindly sent me the information that Carlo's eldest niece, Florence, had also become an actress and was acting under the name Mrs. Campbell

Perugini. Carlo's nephew, Mark, would later record that both his parents had been on the stage; although there is no definite information that Edward was ever a professional actor. No doubt Carlo would have taken on the responsibility for his brother's family just as Charles Dickens had needed to do on several occasions.

Kate and Carlo must, however, have started enjoying a measure of financial security in the early 1890s, as in 1893 they moved into a new home. Perhaps it is no coincidence that 1893 was the year Carlo's eldest nephew, Mark Perugini, was of an age to leave school and start work, which means the care of his mother and siblings would have passed to him. Georgina Hogarth had long been worried about Kate remaining in the house in which Dickie had died, so the move was a relief to her and it brought them much closer to their circle of friends. Their new address was 38a Victoria Road, a large terraced town house a few minutes from the top end of Kensington High Street.[88] Inside the house they created a double studio with huge windows to let the morning sunlight flood in. Victoria Road was very close to Anny and Richmond Ritchie's home and near Leighton and Millais. No doubt Millais enjoyed the peace and quiet of their child-free home, while Carlo and Kate must have envied him his large affectionate family. They would not, however, have envied Millais' health. For many years, he had seldom been seen without his pipe; in 1892 the gentle father of Pre-Raphaelitism was diagnosed with throat cancer.

Even during these happy years of her second marriage, Kate remained prone to depression, an instance of which is shown in an undated missive to Anny Ritchie, sent from 38a Victoria Road (at which address the Peruginis would live until 1905). It is a short note that reads: "My Annie—I *loved* the sashes—and everything you do—but I hate myself—and everything I have done, that is all. Your ever loving Kitty." Despite these periods of depression, which probably assailed her every year around the anniversary of her baby's death, the Peruginis lived together contentedly. They

---

88 In 1905 the council changed the street numbers and the Peruginis' home became number 32 Victoria Road. This made research confusing and seems to be the reason for some earlier muddle about Kate and Carlo's address. It is often claimed that they lived on St. Alban's Grove. In fact, their house stands at the corner of Victoria Road and St. Alban's Grove and was originally numbered as part of the latter, but not during the time the Peruginis lived in it.

would sit for days at a time, painting happily in their studios, luxuriating in the fact that they had such an overwhelming interest in common. In 1892, Kate painted a little girl named Marie Strauss, who was the daughter of hers and Carlo's friends, Alphonse and Hedwig Strauss. The painting is still owned by Marie's descendants and has always been known in the family as *Poppies* because Marie, whose facial expression makes her looks older than the seven years old she was in 1892, is carrying a mass of poppies caught up in her apron and has a garland of poppies in her long dark hair.

Despite the fact that they would both live to an advanced age, neither Kate nor Carlo enjoyed robust health, although the reasons for their regular periods of illness do not appear to be attributable to any particular ailment. It seems likely that their bouts of ill health were caused by overwork and stress over money. Kate's family had nothing but praise for Carlo and how happy he made his wife: Their relationship seems to have been playful and caring, they shared a sharp sense of humor, a love of the unconventional and a genuine desire to please each other.

Kate's childhood "superstitions" (or obsessive-compulsions) continued until the end of her life. How Charlie Collins viewed them is not related, but they were kindly tolerated by Carlo and, when Kate was too ill to carry out her usual superstitious routine, Carlo would always check under the bed for her so that she would be able to sleep in peace.

Although little concrete evidence can be discovered about Carlo at this time, it seems he was happy to remain slightly in the public shadow of his vivacious, sometimes controversial wife, while remaining at the forefront of Kate's world in their own home. Kate needed a man she could look up to and she adored Carlo with a similar intensity to the adoration she had shown her father and, according to Lucy Mathews, to Val Prinsep, an intensity of feeling that she had been unable to pour into her first marriage. Contemporary reports of Carlo are glowing: as a friend, a husband, and a painter. The Royal Academy's archives contain two photographs of him. One shows the sombre, serious side he presented to the outside world, in an attempt to overcome the handicap of being an Italian—and, therefore, deemed in some way untrustworthy—in a xenophobic English society. It appears to have been taken for an official calling card and presents an eminently respectable, correctly and

A more serious-looking Carlo Perugini, photographed at the studios of John and Charles Watkins in c.1860s-70s. This is the side of Carlo that casual observers and acquaintances would have seen and was presumably intended to be used as a calling card.

Carlo Perugini apparently dressed up for a fancy-dress party, photographed by
David Wilkie Wynfield in c.1860s. This picture reveals Carlo's flamboyant side
and embraces his Italian ancestry.

carefully dressed gentleman leaning casually back in a velvet and gilt chair. His thick hair is gleamingly lustrous, but kept under strict control by being parted severely and hair-oiled into submission. His beard and moustache are equally thick and well ordered. He looks sternly at the photographer, in the accepted fashion (smiling for photographs was not yet the norm). It is somewhat difficult to see the "handsome" man written about by Kate and her family in this picture, but Victorian photography did not allow for photogenia.

The second photograph in the Royal Academy's collection is by David Wilkie Wynfield and shows Carlo's flamboyant side. It's a side-profile portrait of Carlo in fancy dress. He is wearing a floppy hat, complete with large white feather, a white artist's smock–style shirt, and an embroidered coat or jacket. He is, again, looking serious, but in this instance it is a theatrical pose; he stands with his chin tilted high and his right hand (which seems oddly well manicured for an artist) held to his chest in dramatic attitude. Perhaps it was taken to commemorate one of Leighton's flamboyant parties. Fancy-dress parties were extremely popular in the nineteenth century; the archives at London's National Portrait Gallery are well stocked with photographic portraits of revelers in elaborate fancy dress. In this particular photograph, taken at a side angle, one can see Carlo's extremely well proportioned facial features: straight nose, high cheekbones, prominent browbone, even a well-shaped left ear. If one can envisage away the bushy beard, it is easy to see why people described Carlo as handsome. We know from his army records that Carlo was five feet ten inches tall, above average for a Victorian European man. He would have towered over Kate's diminutive brothers and over Kate, who had described herself to Plorn as "very small."

That Henry Fielding Dickens and his wife, Marie (known as "Pupsey" and "Mumsey" to their descendants), were so diminutive has been recorded for posterity. In 1926 an amateur film was made of their golden wedding celebrations; in it their small stature is highlighted by the fact that their children, grandchildren, and other relations all look like giants by comparison. When my great-uncle Eric appears on the scene—a tall, slim, long-limbed man in his early twenties who dances an impromptu Charleston, much to Henry's annoyance—he could be wearing stilts, the way he towers above them. One can imagine Carlo standing out hilariously whenever the Peruginis and Dickenses met.

In 1893, Kate seems to have been at the peak of her success. In that year alone, she exhibited a total of nine paintings: at the Society of Lady Artists, at the Royal Academy, and as part of the British Women Painters' Exposition. These paintings were: *Brother and Sister* (depicting Florence and Paul Dombey), three portraits of children, including *Flossie* and *Portrait of Dorothy de Michele*, one portrait of Mrs. Benjamin Charles Stephenson and four genre scenes, all of children. Her output during this time and over the next couple of years is prolific; sadly, few of her paintings have been in the public domain in recent history, so they are unknown and even descriptions of them are difficult to find. Her works do not appear to have been photographed while on display, so we have very little knowledge of them, except for their titles. I have been grateful to receive new information about Kate's paintings since my biography was published in the UK and perhaps this updated edition will bring yet more of her works to light. It is disappointing that few if any of Kate's works are ever seen in public collections (there are a couple of galleries that own paintings by her, but seldom seem to choose to display them), though perhaps that is also testimony to the fact that the paintings are still enjoyed by the families whose ancestors commissioned the paintings or sat for them.

Of those we do know, and which were displayed in 1893, *Portrait of Mrs. Benjamin Charles Stephenson* is an unusual example of Kate's work, in that it portrays an adult. It is a beautiful, oval painting in an elaborate gilt frame, reminiscent of portraiture from an earlier era. I was lucky enough to view this painting, as the current owner contacted me after reading my book. It is a captivating work of art and it is easy to understand why the owner was moved to buy it despite knowing nothing about the artist, purely "for the love of the painting." As is usual with her portraits, Kate seems to have captured the sitter's personality, showing Mrs. Stephenson to be a warm, smiling young woman, perhaps suppressing a laugh at a joke she is sharing with the painter. A portrait of the young Guy Colin Campbell, later to be the 4th Baronet, painted in the same year, shows a beatific-looking child with gleamingly brushed fair hair, wearing a white smock complete with pink bow necktie and holding the hilt of an ancient sword, presumably one that belonged to the 1st Baronet. The little boy was one of Nina and Fred Lehmann's grandchildren, the son of their daughter (also called Nina). The picture, however, seems just a little too perfect, the child a little too angelic. One can't help but wonder if Guy was one of the spoiled "pampered" children Kate so detested painting and had written so scathingly of to Shaw in 1889.

Portrait of Mrs. Benjamin Charles Stephenson

Portrait of Eric Hawksley painted by Kate Perugini

Flossie is the third portrait and the fourth is entitled *A Portrait of Dora Critchett*. It is a very pretty, full-length picture of a young girl holding a skipping rope as if in readiness to start jumping. At her feet are other discarded toys including a racket and shuttlecocks. Dora, her pale brown hair shiny and neat, is dressed in a blue velvet dress with long sleeves and delicate lace collar and cuffs. On her feet are slender dark pumps. She stares directly out at the viewer, in a style reminiscent of *Flossie* except that this child is younger and perhaps a little timid. I particularly like this painting as it is so similar to one that Kate painted of my great-uncle, Eric, as a child. In it he is seated, wearing a blue velvet sailor suit and looking every inch the angelic Edwardian child. Not surprisingly, it was a portrait he hated as he believed himself to be far from angelic and, according to his wife Eleanor, he wanted to destroy it. He objected vehemently to the Little Lord Fauntleroy style of the painting (one assumes that several of Kate's other sitters may have felt the same). Luckily, he did not destroy it and it remains in the family. It was painted several years after Dora Critchett's portrait, but could easily be a companion piece. I wonder if Kate was particularly pleased with her portrait of Dora and therefore chose to emulate it when painting her great-nephew. Both are stunning for their clarity and realism of expression, especially of the eyes.

Of the four genre paintings exhibited in 1893, three are still known. *Tomboy* depicts a young girl, in disheveled clothing, who appears to have been caught in the act of scrumping apples. One can see that she started the day in a neat dress and hat, but her dress has been rumpled and torn, her hair is wild, and the ribbons of her hat hang limply undone. *The Flower Merchant* is one I believe to have been inspired by Carlo and his works. Italianate in style and color, it depicts a very young girl selling flowers at a market stall. She has Mediterranean looks, with dark skin, eyes, and hair, and wears a peasant-style outfit of pinafore, patterned blouse, and shawl. She stands, looking sideways at the viewer, surrounded by pots of blooms, some of which are taller than she, showing how very young she was to be working. It is the attitude of a canny, working-class child, sweet but wary, very different from the upper-class children Kate usually had to idealize in commissioned portraits. The colors Kate used in this, and which overflowed into many of her very British portraits, are imbued with the light techniques and hues of Italianate art and are perhaps informed by her formative happy year surrounded by the sights, sounds, and colors of Genoa.

In addition to these were *Happy and Careless,* of which I have no knowledge, and *Feeding the Rabbits.* This latter was probably commissioned, as the sitter's name is given as Agnes Phoebe Burra and it is similar in style to Kate's portraits. In it, Agnes—who looks about eight years old—is holding out her apron, which is filled with salad leaves, and behind her is a hutch, through the bars of which can be seen a rabbit, sniffing out the leaves. Agnes stares straight at the viewer; she wears a simple dress, with her bonnet tied by its ribbons and slung casually over her shoulder, leaving her head bare. It is a three-quarter-length portrait, in which her head is positioned in the top third of the canvas, yet as is common with Kate's work the girl's eyes are so intense that the viewer's gaze is drawn immediately up the canvas to look at them.

The Flower Merchant by
Kate Perugini

In the same year as the British Women Painters held their "exposition," England went into mourning over the death of its Poet Laureate, Alfred, Lord Tennyson. Anny Ritchie attended his funeral at Westminster Abbey and related how the actress Ellen Terry sobbed on her shoulder as the coffin went by; he was buried in Poets' Corner not far from

Untitled portrait by Kate Perugini

Kate's father. It was also the year in which Kate's aunt Laetitia died, at the age of seventy-six. The Dickens children were very fond of her and Henry was to write in his *Recollections* that Laetitia had been "a dear good soul"—whom he compared to his father's character Betsy Trotwood (in *David Copperfield*)—who had been "a constant visitor" to Gad's Hill and took great care of her blind, abandoned sister-in-law, Harriet Dickens.

Eighteen ninety-three was not a good year for Anny Ritchie. Not only did she lose her great friend from the Isle of Wight days, Tennyson, who had been a pivotal figure in helping her to recover from the death of her father, but there was bad news about her husband. Richmond Ritchie, so many years her junior and expected to outlive her by at least a decade, was diagnosed with the condition known as Ménière's disease. Their marriage had not been the great romance that Kate and Carlo seemed to have found, Richmond was often unfaithful, but they had two adored children and they loved and respected each other.

Ménière's disease is a debilitating condition that affects the sufferer's inner ear, causing hearing loss or distortion, problems with balance, and attacks of vertigo, which can lead to sickness and disorientation. Having watched Kate live for so many years with an ill husband, Anny was well aware how much her and Richmond's life would change. Of course the condition was not as serious as Charlie's cancer, but the attacks were frightening and left Richmond feeling increasingly weak and incapable. A few months after this diagnosis, Anny's mother, Isabella Thackeray, died at the age of seventy-six; there followed, in 1895, the death of Julia Stephen, the stepmother of Minny's daughter Laura. Anny, feeling very much alone, turned to Kate at this time. It was natural for her to call on the closest person she had to a sister, while so many of her relatives were dying.

19

ANNUS HORRIBILIS

Eighteen ninety-six was one of those years that must have made Kate shudder whenever she looked back on it; I imagine she and Carlo lived through it in something of a daze as relentless tragedies followed one after another. At the end of January, the Peruginis were shattered to hear of the death of Frederic, Lord Leighton, at his home in Holland Park Road. He was only nine years older than both Kate and Carlo and had just celebrated his sixty-fifth birthday; his death certificate states that he died of a bronchial cold and heart disease. Leighton had given his last party in March 1895, before becoming too ill to host another. The sad ceremony of his funeral was held at St. Paul's Cathedral. At the time of his death, Leighton was President of the Royal Academy; this honor now passed to John Everett Millais, by now a very ill man himself.

While they were still reeling from the shock of Leighton's demise, Mamie became ill. It was apparent from the start that her condition was serious and Georgina and Kate rushed to Surrey, where Mamie was staying, to help Mrs. Hargreaves nurse her. For several months, Charley had also been "hopelessly ill," with what seems to have been a recurrence of the family heart problem. He had been suffering for some time, but his death on July 20, at the age of fifty-nine, came as a shock. He left behind a large family for whom—in typical Dickens fashion—he had made no financial provisions and left, as Georgina wrote, "*no* money."[89] Devastatingly, on the

---

89 Charley had not done well out of *All The Year Round*, which never attained its earlier popularity after his father's death. He had used much of his own money in an attempt to keep the magazine afloat, with disastrous results for his widow and daughters.

day of Charley's funeral, Mamie died. She was only fifty-eight, the same age their father had been at his death. Kate and Georgina were with her until the end.

Georgina wrote to Plorn's wife, Connie, after the deaths of her niece and nephew within three days of each other. Although the two women never met, they kept up a regular correspondence and Georgy often revealed to the unknown Australian very intimate family secrets. Her letters seem to have been her way of dealing with grief or disappointment; perhaps the knowledge that she was unlikely ever to meet Connie made it easier to confide in her. The letter Georgy wrote after Mamie's death is highly revealing and doubly sad when one considers how close Mamie had previously been, both to her aunt and sister.

My love for Mamie as you know was most true and tender—so was her sister's and Harry's—But the loss—out of our lives—is not so great as it would have been years ago—For it is a long time since she ceased to be my companion. She had not lived in London for nearly 18 years—She was always dearly beloved whenever she came to see us—and stayed with us on special occasions. But she had given up all her family and friends for those people whom she had taken to live with her—Mr. Hargreaves is a most unworthy person in every way—and it was always amazing to me that she could keep up this strong feeling and regard and affection for him to the very end of her life. Mrs. Hargreaves has kept true and devoted in her attentions to Mamie during her long illness—and Kitty and I were very grateful to her—I don't know what we could have done without her help at the last—we were thankful to have our darling Mamie all to ourselves—as both Mr. and Mrs. Hargreaves went away before she died—Kitty and I had been staying close by her for some time—and finally were always in her room—I dont [sic] know—and I dont [sic] care! what has become of Mr. Hargreaves—I never want to meet his kind again—and I only hope and pray I never see him alive! She poor woman has been living since Mamie's death with some friends in the country and has two sisters who are very good to her—she is trying now to get some casual service as housekeeper or Companion and if Kitty or I can help or recommend her we shall be only too glad to do so—she has had a sad life—and will be much better without her detestable husband.

Georgina also relates some of the particulars of Mamie's will. Mamie had made the will in 1871 and written a letter to accompany it. She wrote: "I wish Plorn to have Kitty's sketch of my room in the dear old home. Tell him how I love the little picture." Georgina duly posted the sketch out to Australia, although what became of it is a mystery.

These three deaths were not the only tragedies to hit the Peruginis in 1896. On August 13, the Royal Academy was deprived of its second president within a year when John Everett Millais lost his battle with throat cancer. The kind, passionate genius of an artist, whose studio had played host to the very first meeting of the Pre-Raphaelite Brotherhood; who together with Dante Gabriel Rossetti had dubbed the venerated Sir Joshua Reynolds "Sir Sloshua"; the man whom Anny Thackeray fondly remembered shaking his fist at the Raphael Madonna when they visited the Royal Academy together, was dead at the age of sixty-seven. Within a few months Kate and Carlo had lost so many of their most intimate friends. Kate "never forgot the sadness of her last visit" to Millais and referred to it often toward the end of her life.

Millais' funeral took place in the crypt of St. Paul's Cathedral on August 20; among his pallbearers were William Holman Hunt and the actor Henry Irving.[90] Kate, and perhaps Carlo as well, sank into a very deep depression and throughout 1897 she did not exhibit anything either at the Society of Lady Artists or the Royal Academy. A few years previously, Mamie had published *My Father As I Recall Him*. It is an adoring—and extremely idealized—depiction of Charles Dickens, which demonstrates Mamie's deification of her father and is overtly saccharine to a modern reader. After her sister's death, Kate experienced a burst of fury; she went through the book like a woman possessed, making sweeping, bitter changes.

She annotated the book on more than one occasion (at times, she wrote comments in the margin, which were later obliterated). Some of

---

90 Henry Irving was the greatest actor of the Victorian stage; he was the first actor to be knighted and is credited with having made the theater "respectable."

the alterations are rational, straightforward editing—changing the odd word, inserting pictures, moving pieces of text around. Others involve crossing out chunks of pages with thick black crosses. Anything that gives Mamie too much credit or seems to push Kate out of the picture is deleted (though, to be fair, Kate also deleted Mamie's comment about Kate being the favorite daughter). One of the first sections that Kate expunges is one of Mamie's most adoring comments:

But in what I write about my father I shall depend chiefly upon my own memory of him, for I wish no other or dearer remembrance. My love for my father has never been touched or approached by any other love. I hold him in my heart of hearts as a man apart from all other men, as one apart from all other beings.

The paragraph can be read as an aspersion upon Kate herself, as if by marrying she had betrayed her father. Many passages in the book indicate to the reader that, of all the children, Mamie had the closest bond with her father and Kate deleted these. She also struck out a paragraph in which Mamie describes herself dancing with her father but gives no mention of Kate, who was presumably at the same party and dancing as well:

I was thoroughly worn out with fatigue, being selected by him as his partner, I caught the infection of his merriment, and my weariness vanished. As he himself says, in describing dear old 'Fezziwigs' Christmas party, we were 'people who would dance and had no notion of walking.'

Kate took out all reference to a New Year's Eve party at Gad's Hill that Mamie recalls as the evening that "stands out in my memory as one of the merriest and happiest of the many merry and happy evenings in our dear old home . . ." Strangely Kate also deleted all Mamie's comments about their childhood Christmases. She defiantly inserted a request for a photograph of their mother, who had been almost completely eradicated from the family's life story by Mamie.

Mamie frustratingly wrote her book in the third person, so when she makes mention of "one of his daughters" it is not always clear whether the reference is to her or Kate. One story, which is about Mamie but is written in the third person, relates how she had been very ill as a child and Charles had insisted she spend the day in his study with him. The way it is worded is ambiguous, suggesting that this special treatment was always given to her when ill. Kate inserted into the text quite caustically the word "once."

The passages that came in for the heaviest censorship, however, relate to their father's death and obviously angered Kate. In the book, Mamie makes herself the central figure and the following deletions are the most heavy-handed of all Kate's corrections; whereas other passages are crossed out or simply ruled through, these have been scribbled over until the words are almost illegible (and would have appeared illegible to Kate's short-sighted eyes in an ill-lit room). The offending passages included: "my sister (on one side of the couch), my aunt (on the other) and I (keeping hot bricks to the feet which nothing could warm) hoping and praying that he might open his eyes and look at us, and know us once again." The words about Mamie holding hot bricks to his feet are the most heavily deleted of that sentence. Kate also inserted her brothers Charley and Henry, whom Mamie has excluded from the death scene altogether. The most heavily scored-out lines in the book are Mamie's words "I made it my duty to guard the beloved body as long as it was left to us."

In December 1897, the same month in which Effie Millais followed her husband to the grave, Kate wrote a flurry of letters to George Bernard Shaw. They are indicative of the wild mood swings to which she was prone and suggest her depression was not yet alleviated. On December 9, she sent him a letter about her dead mother, an outpouring of her feelings about Catherine that were so raw and exposed that she later requested him to burn it. He did so, leaving only the envelope and a note explaining why.

> *I burnt this letter at Mrs. Perugini's request. It contained an account of her mother, shortly before her death, giving her a box of her father's love letters and asking them to read them when she was dead and consider whether they could not be published, to show the world that Dickens once loved her. When Mrs. Perugini read them they proved*

to her exactly the reverse of what Mrs. Dickens gathered from them—
convinced her that Dickens, even before his marriage, had given up
all hope of finding adequate companionship in his wife's limited sen-
sibilities & outlook. Mrs. P's conclusion was that she had better burn
them. I energetically dissented & advised her to leave them to the
British Museum with a memorandum stating how they came into her
possession.

Mamie's death had encouraged Kate to start looking into her family's history and spurred her on to make a decision about what she should do with her mother's letters. She must, at this time, have become startlingly conscious of her own mortality and greatly concerned in case she and Carlo should die as unexpectedly as Charley, Mamie, or Leighton, and the letters entrusted to her by Catherine be passed on to another. This question of what to do with the letters was something she worried away at, like a child with a scab. She wrote repeatedly to Shaw, sadly seeming to prefer his counsel to her husband's. The letters are so mercurial and so repetitive that one imagines Shaw found it quite difficult to keep his temper; every time he replied with a solution, she wrote again posing more problems. From the beginning, Shaw gave her his opinion that the letters should be handed over to the British Museum. Yet even after Kate had been finally persuaded to do so, she wrote to him several times asking him how she should word the letter that would accompany them and how many years she should insist upon elapsing before the letters be made available to the public.

Just two days after first writing to Shaw about her mother, a letter that suggested a great degree of trust and intimacy, she was writing to him in a rage. In response to his apparently having made a comment about Mamie and her mother's letters, she reveals that she had never told Mamie of the letters' existence (something that does not seem so strange when one considers how distant she and Mamie had become). The intriguing letter begins with the following words:

I will burn you with the greatest of pleasure if you will allow me.
Nothing at this moment could afford me such supreme satisfaction as

to see you writhe in anguish; mental agonies I would prefer, because you seem rather to enjoy bodily pain. O for another smart writer and critic to take your scalp and the worst of it is that my feelings of hatred towards you are increased rather than otherwise by the conviction that from your own point of view you are right.

Yet the long letter concludes, after a stream-of-consciousness-style narrative, with Kate making a joke and closing with the words "Believe me always yours very sincerely." It seems the act of letter writing has assuaged Kate's anger and by the end she is trying to lighten the mood. Nevertheless she still chose to send the letter.

On December 19 she wrote to him again. The letter begins:

My irritability having quite evaporated I write a few words to which I shall not expect an answer until you have a little time to spare. . . . The next time I tell you anything of the smallest interest I intend telling it in the baldest, dryest, coldest, least sentimental manner my manner can ever aspire to, and if I see any little bit of sentiment looming in the distance, I promise to give you fair warning so that you may shut your eyes and swallow it down quickly like a pill.

The overall tone throughout the letter is sarcastic, but witty and even flirtatious. She describes him as looking like "a benevolent Viking," with the air of one bestowing a pet name upon a favorite friend. She ends the letter flippantly:

I remain yours very as sincerely as the circumstances of my life and my own nature permit me to be. Kate Perugini. [PS] If you could make the public understand that my father was not a joyous, jocose gentleman walking about the world with a plum pudding & a bowl of punch you would greatly oblige me.

On New Year's Eve of 1897, Kate responded to a letter from Shaw in the way one would expect an eager lover to write; her first paragraph is so keenly alive with the excitement of having received his words:

Your last letter arrived with a batch of Christmas Cards, idiotic 'Greetings' and all the rest of it I seized upon the one real live thing in that mass of unreality and it gave me as I knew it would real satisfaction to read your letter. Thank you. Yes, I have often noticed the curious affinity there is between us in what we feel. Are you quite quite sure you don't happen to be my youngest brother? Or do you think I have a little Irish blood in my composition? That I could ever attain to your accuracy of mind even remotely, or to your knowledge of human nature or to your power of thinking about what you feel is I fear extremely doubtful. I have never trained my mind to think and no one ever trained it for me. I always trusted to a quick throb or jump of the brain to arrive at any conclusion about any subject which puzzled or distressed me. This jump or throb almost like a physical sensation, has helped me often through many difficulties, it is I suppose what nine women out of ten are conscious of possessing; it is what we call instinct when we recognize it in animals.

The letter, another long and involved one that must have taken some time to compose, makes one sad for Carlo. Was he aware of the intensity of Kate's feelings for another man? No matter what her words claim, her feelings toward Shaw at this time do not seem sisterly. Perhaps Carlo was wise enough to see it for what it was, an excitement that Kate so badly craved after eighteen months of depression, but it must have been very difficult for him, and a letter Kate wrote the following month shows that their relationship was experiencing unprecedented problems. In general, the letters suggest she saw Shaw as her main, if not her only, confidant, that she felt unable to talk to her husband at the time. The situation was perhaps exacerbated for Carlo by the fact that his own great friendships were no longer possible; he could not choose to play cards with Millais, or smoke and chat with Leighton by the fountain in his famous Arab-inspired room, in order to while away the hours Kate spent writing long, impassioned letters to a man so many years her junior. Acutely aware, herself, of this age discrepancy, Kate began her next letter (sent on January 14) by referring to herself as an "elderly lady." She was in fact only fifty-eight, but since both her sister and father had died at that age it would have seemed a perilous landmark. This is, perhaps, illustrative of why Kate's depression continued well into her fifty-ninth year and why she and Carlo were not getting on. With everything they had been through over the previous couple of years, it is not at all surprising they had reached what seemed like an impasse. The only indication we have of a rift between them is in the letter written by Kate to Shaw on January 14, 1898. It is a melancholic, reflective missive in which she dwells on her childhood, her brothers and her parents' relationship, as well as her own. She becomes very depressed about Dickie's death and realizes that she is proving unbearable to live with, although it is apparent she still loves Carlo and all his "good points," in stark comparison with her own "faults." She also seems very concerned about her mental state. It is, I think, the saddest of her remaining letters and illustrates so much of her muddled, complicated personality.

O the poor children of a man of genius! There is only one lesson they should be taught early in life and that is: to face death bravely, and to do away with themselves as soon as they can make up their minds to commit suicide. If they could learn that lesson there would be an end to a great deal of misery in this world! Out of our large family of nine children, there was only one who seemed to me to be really quite sane. That was Harry my lawyer brother, and I have wondered for years whether his sanity is to last through his life! I don't mean to say that we are, or were raving lunatics, but something worse. Apparently sane but each of us with a crack somewhere. There are four of us left. Two men in Australia from whom we never hear a word, Harry and myself. I am so thankful my one child died. At any rate my faults will die with me. He might have inherited his father's good points, but I am positively certain he would have had my bad qualities. Men of genius therefore ought not to be allowed to have children. Yet who is to decide whether a man is a Genius or not! And who could prevent a man of genius from marrying! It's all a muddle. And why should people marry at all, why should they spoil one another's lives, when they could be so happy in occasional meetings? There seems something all wrong some where.

It is also highly revealing that Kate begins this letter with the words "On these awful dark days there is no work to be done; so this morning after answering notes and paying bills and doing everything I hate doing, I sat down in a very depressed state of mind to read." Many of her most miserable surviving letters, at all periods in her life, make reference to gloomy weather—one must remember that as an artist she needed strong light to work by. She continued in a state of seasonally affected depression throughout the remaining winter months, suffering from migraines and general low spirits, but her mood seems gradually to have lifted by the start of spring 1898, and she and Carlo began enjoying their social life, inviting friends over to dinner and visiting the theater. Lawrence Alma-Tadema was, at this time, heavily involved in painting theatrical scenery, of which he was very proud, and the Peruginis were often guests at the ensuing performances.

Kate also began painting again, although it was unfortunate that the first picture she attempted to exhibit was rejected by the Royal Academy. Even before the Committee viewed it Kate was describing it in a letter as "a bad picture," but the Academy's rejection threw her back into a state of dejection, though this time she seems to have been cross and upset, rather than genuinely depressed. The spring weather was having a positive effect on her emotions and she was back to jokily criticizing Shaw, finding fault with his dress sense and asceticism; their friendship seems to have settled down at last into just that—friendship. That April, she finally managed to get Carlo and Shaw to speak to each other. They had met previously but on that occasion Shaw had appeared to snub Carlo and had needed to write to Kate afterward to explain that it was unintentional. Kate's reply is tender about Carlo, protective and defensive on her husband's behalf, in a manner that suggests the couple had resolved their problems.

My husband did not think you rude. He merely thought you did not know him. He is, as many Italians are, a little formal and conventional in manner, but in manner only; and he is so modest a man that he never forces himself upon any one, indeed I think this same modesty has been much against his getting on in his profession as modesty is a quality which is neither appreciated nor wanted in these days!

Their eventual meeting, unexpectedly while at the theater, was not everything Kate had hoped for. It seems the two men were polite but little impressed with each other—not surprising when one considers their very different personalities as well as the unspoken rivalry that had grown up between them. The following day Kate wrote to Shaw wistfully, "I was very glad too that you and my husband spoke a little together. You are as unlike one another as you can be; and yet I am certain you would be good friends if only you had the time to become friends."

Although it is not possible to be certain, given the large numbers of letters Kate destroyed, from those that remain it seems that her passionate feelings for Shaw abated as quickly as they had arisen. Their friendship remained constant, but her letters (at least those in existence) are more tempered and less painful to read. She continues to write regularly and to be hurt when he does not respond as quickly as she would like, but her affection now seems to be more in keeping with the feelings she has always exhibited for her friends and family. It seems Kate genuinely did begin to look on Shaw more as a "youngest brother," especially welcome after so many of her real brothers had now died. Shaw certainly continued to anger and frustrate her as much as a sibling would, as well as cheering up her gloomy days by sending letters or birthday telegrams. His earnestness and superiority, which sometimes delighted her by its wit, often infuriated her. It is perhaps telling that, while talking of him one day to a friend, she—possibly unintentionally—referred to him as "Shernard Bore."

20

LITERARY PURSUITS

During the final years of the nineteenth century, Kate became increasingly preoccupied with two problems: She was still dwelling upon the destiny of her mother's letters and she was wondering how to help Charley's impoverished children find work. Their mother, Bessie, had been left with a small income, but it was not enough to support herself and five grown-up daughters. The most resourceful of Charley's girls were Ethel, who set up a typewriting agency, and Mary Angela, who made a name for herself—though sadly not much of an income—as a novelist and journalist. When possible, Ethel gave work to her sisters and to an impoverished aunt on their mother's side. Kate recommended her nieces to her influential friends and did everything she could to help them achieve financial independence. Although Shaw declined to assist Mary Angela in finding writing work, despite a direct plea by Kate, he did help Ethel, using and recommending her typewriting agency. W. S. Gilbert (one half of Gilbert & Sullivan) also used Ethel's agency, as did J. M. Barrie; both were friends of Kate's. It was a sad irony that the Dickens family had hit such a financial slough while the rest of the world believed them to be living in the lap of luxury thanks to the continued success of Charles Dickens' novels.

In the matter of her mother's letters, Kate finally acceded to Shaw's suggestion and gave them to the curators at the British Museum (which was, then, still home to the British Library). On June 1, 1899, the letters were handed over to Mr. Garnett and Mr. Scott, a pair of curators whom Kate had kept in a state of scholarly anticipation for over a year. The letters were placed in a box, at the front of which was put a note: "With the consent of the Trustees of the British Museum, this box is not to be opened—except by myself—until June 1925. Kate Perugini 1st June 1899." The lack of Henry's name signifying he was an authorized visitor suggests that Kate continued to keep her siblings in ignorance of her mother's gift. The date restriction also suggests that Kate did not expect to be alive in June 1925, a fair assumption as she would have been almost eighty-six years old by then.

The twentieth century dawned with the deaths of John Ruskin and Oscar Wilde, and with the Siege of Mafeking. The Boer War, which had begun in 1899, was still raging and people in Britain were becoming increasingly uneasy. Tens of thousands of British troops were being slaughtered while fighting a people who once had been their friends and allies. The army was in a dreadful state and funds were desperately needed. While the younger generation was beginning to kick against the idea of war and even the idea of Empire, Kate was of the age group that believed fervently in the authority of the generals and the superiority of British rule.

In 1900 she painted a portrait of her niece, Henry's daughter Enid, who had recently become engaged to a solicitor, Ernest Hawksley. Enid was twenty years old at the time, but in the portrait she looks as though she could be about fourteen. She sits on the grass, absorbed in reading a book, with her hair carefully arranged on top of her head and her white and lilac-colored dress neatly splayed around her. It is a charming picture, which, unusually, Kate signed with her full name, not her monogram. Across the bottom are written the words "Kate Perugini War Fund 1900." Although the painting is now in the family, it was intended to be sold to raise money for the fund—which suggests that it was bought by Enid's fiancé. The fact that she wrote her name in full suggests Kate wanted people who did not normally go in for buying art to be aware of who the artist was. Her name was very well known at this time and since Mamie's death Kate had taken to styling herself, in a somewhat macabre fashion, "the only remaining daughter of Charles Dickens," which made her signature even more valuable.

At around this time, Henry and Kate received word from Australia that Plorn was very ill and unable to work. Although his siblings in England were probably unaware of it, Plorn was back in dreadful debt and had become a serious gambler. He had still never thanked his brother for, nor repaid him, the £800 loan given in 1884, now worth a considerable amount more through lost interest. Henry had at one time attempted to get Plorn simply to pay the interest. Taking advantage of a business colleague, a solicitor who happened to be traveling to Australia, he wrote Plorn a very fair letter suggesting that he merely for the moment pay the money Henry had lost on the loan and repay the £800 itself when possible. Plorn had resisted even this, not bothering to acknowledge Henry's letter. All these years later, however, Henry swallowed his anger and, full of pity for their brother, he and Kate scraped together £100 to send to him. Plorn had moved to a town called Moree, in New South Wales, where he hoped to find work. He was unsuccessful and died in Moree in January 1902, at the age of forty-nine; Connie was with him at the end. The £100 arrived too late to give him the "comfort" his siblings had hoped it would provide. It is a pathetically sad end to the story of the adorable Plornishmaroonghenter, "The Baby who defies competition," who dominated so many of Charles Dickens' letters in the 1850s. In Henry's *Recollections,* he sums up Plorn's life in the following words (making no mention of the unpaid loan or the anger that had sprung up between brothers living on opposite sides of the world):

> *my brother Edward, [my father's] youngest and best-loved son . . . my father bought a sheep 'run' for him on the River Darling. There was a heavy drought one year and the sheep died like flies and his business was entirely destroyed. He then joined my brother Alfred in a land agency in Melbourne, which was never very successful I am afraid. He was at one time a member of the Legislative Assembly. . . . He married in Australia and died without issue in January, 1902.*

The dawning of a new century, the last of the millennium, as well as the death of Queen Victoria in 1901, had brought about a nostalgia for the "old days." While the young were eager to usher in a modern world, thrilled with the advent of a new king, many others were fearful of this fast-paced age and hankered after the erroneously perceived safety and security of the heyday of Victoria's England. As a result, there was a renewed interest in the reputation and works of Charles Dickens. No longer were people so interested in articles about his private life; nor did they question whether he had written all his books. Instead, there were laudatory articles nostalgically yearning for the golden age when authors such as Dickens were alive (and neatly ignoring the fact that the miseries Charles had written about so heartrendingly were just as prominent a part of Victoria's England as the books' more romantic aspects). On July 23, 1902, Kate wrote a letter of gratitude to the author of one such article, the poet Algernon Swinburne; the letter is on black-edged mourning paper for Plorn:

> *. . . I have just finished reading your article 'Charles Dickens' and I cannot refrain from writing to thank you most earnestly for the eloquent, beautiful, and wonderfully sensitive and acute appreciation you have written on my father's works. That you should understand him so perfectly—and value his books so highly is not of course surprising; and every word of your praise and admiration finds a glad echo in my heart. Nor am I less keenly alive to the truth of your criticism on certain of my father's literary faults—faults that must always be of immense interest to those who love him as being perhaps inseparable from his virtues, and without which he probably would not have been what I venture to think he was: a great genius; a man of singularly simple and direct a nature—eminently human—and with a largeness of character and an intuition so complete as to appeal to all those who looked upon him and his works with 'an eye above the level and beyond the insight of a beetle's . . .'*

At this time, Kate was also aspiring to fulfill literary ambitions of her own and in 1903 her article "Charles Dickens as a Lover of Art and Artists" was published in the *Magazine of Art*. It coincided with the opening of a museum at her father's birthplace, in Portsmouth. At around the same time, she decided to write a biography of her father and approached Shaw on the matter. His reply is astonishing. Irritated by what he considered the sycophantic tone of Swinburne's popular article and impatient for the world to move on from Victorian sentimentality into twentieth-century modernity, Shaw wrote back a letter pompous in the extreme and deeply insulting to Kate's father's memory. Scrutinizing the letter and

Kate's furious reply, one is surprised not at Kate's vituperative response, but that a man as intelligent as Shaw would have sent such a letter to Dickens' own daughter. He begins with pompous advice:

> *The question whether you ought to write a book about your father is not an easy one. As a rule a daughter's biography is even less trustworthy than a widow's; and that is saying a great deal. But on the other hand the most violently prejudiced books are often the most useful; for though it is true that there are many things which a prejudiced person cannot see and which a surviving relative musnt [sic] say, yet it is equally true that there are things that only a strong feeling can discover and only a surviving relative gracefully admit.... So if you want to say anything about your father, say it. The one thing I implore you not to do is to write a book about him and to leave out all the things you want to say. This is the usual course; and it is a most disloyal one...*

Unfortunately, Shaw goes on into his own little world and starts writing what appears to be a self-congratulatory treatise on his own superiority to authors including Dickens and Thackeray. Of Kate's father he says:

> *At the same time ... all his stories, as stories, were failures; and those which are pure stories and nothing else are not good enough for the Strand Magazine.... All I can tell you is that your father was neither a storyteller like Scott, nor a tittle-tattler like Thackeray: he was really a perplexed and amused observer like Shakespear; and if he had frankly borrowed his stories as Shakespear did, instead of laboriously inventing them for himself, his books would have been all the better.*

Incredibly, Shaw seems to think that Kate will agree with him and he does not appear to expect she will take offense. He even adds a genial postscript: "P.S. Will you come to lunch someday. Say yes; and I'll fix up a date—or rather Charlotte will." Whether Kate accepted the lunch invitation is not recorded, but the tone of her ensuing letter suggests she did not:

I have been reading your last letter over again, and have noticed something in it which made small impression upon me at the time I received it because I looked upon it as a mere absurdity which you scarcely intended to be taken seriously, but which read again seems to bear another interpretation so I feel bound to make my protest against it.

You say, in talking of my father's works 'A few centuries hence all the really able critics will agree that these stories are interpolations by an abysmally inferior hand', you speak of the stories introduced in Pickwick and elsewhere. Believe me Mr. G.B.S. whatever 'the really able critics' may say now, or hereafter, all the bad in my father's work is as entirely his own as all the good. He was a man who worked for others but who would not have tolerated others to work for him. If you had known the man you would have been as aware of this as I am. This theory of yours is unworthy [of] your very clear sighted mind. Just consider this: There is so much of indifferent [sic] in his work that had it been written by another hand it would have struck him as being very inferior work indeed and unfit for publication, but having been written by himself in moments of fatigue or in what people call his 'uninspired' moments he let it pass as worthy to be placed with his best. This is visible in most of his books. He would have been as clear sighted as your—usual self—had those stories been written by any other hand than his own and would have put his [word illegible] upon them. He could not have been the man he was without his weaknesses in his writing, as in his character. They explain the man.

You might as well argue that because I sometimes send you letters that might have been concocted by a child of five, I am incapable of writing you the letters of a woman of sense which I have also sometimes sent you Sir. But I am the same individual in my moments of idiocy as in my moments of a slightly higher enlightenment and my most silly letters are not written by the char-woman round the corner whom I have invited in to write for me.

No, no Sir—you are wrong. My father was . . . 'a very clever man' but like all clever people he wrote and talked nonsense at times. But that nonsense was his own.

Any letters that followed in this period of their correspondence no longer survive; the next letter in the collection was not written until 1919.

In this same year, 1903, Kate exhibited a portrait entitled *Sybil*. A picture of a very young girl, the daughter of Mr. and Mrs. Frederick D'a Vincent, it was shown at the Summer Exhibition at the New Gallery. Unusually, Kate signed her name in full, as she had done on the painting of her niece Enid. These are the only two known instances of Kate painting her name on a picture, rather than using her usual monogram, though there may, of course, be other examples that are unknown. *Sybil* bears other similarities to the portrait of Enid: In both paintings, the sitter is seated outside, on grass, and in both Kate makes use of pastel colors and muted tones suggestive of innocence. Unlike Enid, whose eyes look down at her book, Sybil ignores the flowers she has been picking and looks directly out at the viewer. As with *Flossie*, Sybil's eyes are the most striking aspect of the painting, and are almost exactly in the center of the canvas.

At around this time, Kate began contacting publishers about the possibility of publishing her book about her father; it appears she was not doing so in order to make a large amount of money, as she was interested solely in a deal in which she could stipulate the book be published only after the deaths of both herself and Henry, who was ten years her junior. She began working on the manuscript, in which she proposed to "tell the truth" about her father and mother (as opposed to what her sister had written and what gossip-mongers had spread) and, in doing so, attempt to exonerate Catherine and save her much blighted posthumous reputation. Over the years Kate had listened to scores of rumors about her mother: The public still could not bear to hear anything untoward about their favorite author, so Catherine had had to be made the guilty party. All were designed to sanctify Charles and excuse his behavior of separating from her; all carefully refrain from suggesting that Charles remained anything but celibate after his wife's enforced departure. These ridiculous rumors were to persist well into the mid-twentieth century, although the gossip about Charles' love life was not entirely forgotten. In February 1905 Kate wrote Anny a wry letter about a book that mentioned both their fathers in a somewhat scurrilous manner.

I am amused and irritated by Mrs. Lyne Lynton [sic]. How did she know who were our father's loves? Of this I am certain; that neither of them ever loved her, and what she says of my father seemed to imply that he did! But I am always angry with Mrs. L.L. since reading what she had to say about George Eliot to whom she ought to have been on her knees! Forgive therefore this burst of impatience.[91]

As the public was looking nostalgically back at the Victorian way of life, many of those who had made it so artistically rich were passing away. In July 1904—the same year in which J. M. Barrie published *Peter Pan*—G. F. Watts, such a pivotal member of the Victorian art world, died at the age of eighty-six. His death was followed tragically by that of Val Prinsep on November 11th. The robust younger artist, who had been expected to live on well into his eighties, as his father had done, died as the result of an "unsuccessful" prostate operation at the age of sixty-six. He was buried in the Brompton Cemetery, the same graveyard as Charlie Collins. His obituary in *The Times* lamented the loss of such a talented and popular man, extolling him for "his genial nature, his fine physique, and his real gifts as an artist." Kate must have felt his death keenly.

The following year, during which Carlo was unwell for some time, Kate exhibited her last painting for the Society of Women Artists before terminating her membership. Why she chose to break away is unknown, but it seems likely she was now able to make a good enough living without needing to remain a member of the Society. (Unfortunately there are no records available from that date explaining members' resignations or reasons.)

Kate continued to work on her manuscript about her parents; she had developed a taste for writing and it was proving a beneficial way to supplement their income from painting. In 1906 she published a book entitled *The Comedy of Charles Dickens*, in which she collated her favorite

---

91 Mrs. Lynn Linton's memoirs were published posthumously in 1899. She had been at least an acquaintance of Charles and they shared mutual friends. Her writings about Charles in the memoirs were veiled but darkly hinted at scandal, guaranteed to get gossipy tongues speculating as to what she had intended.

comic passages from her father's works and wrote the introduction. She was aware that reading standards had fallen since her childhood and that her father's books were now seen as inaccessible and "difficult" by many; in her introduction she remarks that she wants to bring his works to a new audience. In the same year she wrote an article for *Pall Mall Magazine* about *Edwin Drood,* which book's lack of an ending continued to tantalize readers and historians. In 1911 she contributed to the magazine again, an article entitled "Thackeray and My Father." She also made regular public appearances, for the Dickens Fellowship, at schools and organizations such as the Ladies Lyceum Club. The latter was one of the first members' clubs for women and was aimed at female writers and artists.

In between such Dickens "industry" engagements and her painting, Kate also wrote a large number of poems, most of which, unfortunately, are dreadful. She was very proud of them and often composed them as little extras in letters she sent to friends. Sometimes she would send off a poem, only to make a small change to it and send off a second or even third copy, requesting that the original be burned—this was, of course, in the days when post was collected several times a day. Enviably, Victorian and Edwardian Londoners could write a letter and have it delivered within a couple of hours of posting. An example of one of Kate's poems can be found in a somewhat despondent letter to Anny Thackeray, written while Kate was ill. (Unfortunately there is no date on the letter, but it was written after 1905 and, judging by its tone, before the outbreak of the First World War.)

> *. . . here we remain—placid indeed though rather invalided but with windows open to let in sun and air where there is any, and from these we watch the people go up and down bent upon the busy, important— or unimportant trivial things of life, just as though they all mention something necessary for their salvation—as I suppose they do—in a way. But I can't help thinking at moments, how much more necessary it is to stop and stare and try to understand than to hustle and bustle through life seeing nothing, not even a clump of trees with the hills beyond! 'A yellow primrose' sort of thing. I am indeed old to think like this, though I remember being of the same mind when I was very*

young, before the fight of life really began. No doubt, that was distinctly morbid,—for it is so wholesome to fight and conquer—and I am not sure that when I am feeling quite well and extremely sane I shouldn't love to begin life all over again—with just a few regrettable incidents omitted! . . . However . . . I must try and be contented with what is . . . in spite of not feeling very strong.

So Very Obvious
Unlucky 'tis to have a face
That tells a tale when we are ill, –
Of suff'ring we would hide each trace
Yet these 'tis writ in letters still.
Unfortunate to own a voice
That drops two tones when we [?] down
And brings to him, we love the best,
A wrinkled brow and anxious frown,
Ah, – should kind health return once more
And smooth that brow to placid smile, –
We'll treasure it as ne'er before
and bask in sunshine for a while!

And I am getting better. The Doctor was here the other day and said so. Carlo gives me my medicine regularly like a good Nurse and brings me home chocolate and good things to tempt the appetite. All goes well and thank Heaven he is no worse.
Your K.E.

Kate's literary persuasions may have come about as a result of her greater involvement with the Dickens Fellowship, which had been founded in 1902. In 1906, as a result of her dedicated involvement with the Fellowship, as well as her parentage, she was asked to become one of the Vice-Presidents and in 1912 was named President. She was later made Life President, an honor that was also bestowed on Henry. Kate's relationship with the Fellowship over the years was turbulent, in particular with two of its leading lights. The first of these was Percy Fitzgerald, one-time unsuccessful suitor for Mamie's hand in marriage and one of

Dickens' former colleagues; Kate felt that he was trying too hard to be the central figure on the Dickensian stage. The other was the very earnest F. G. Kitton (who died young in 1904). Kate had found him highly irritating, though she admitted he was actually very inoffensive and kind and that she was being intolerant. She and Shaw referred disparagingly to him in their letters as "the kitten" and made jokes about saucers of milk. These two aside, Kate forged close friendships with members of the Fellowship, holding regular "At Homes" at Victoria Road—at one time every Saturday and Sunday in order to accommodate the overwhelming number of people who applied for invitations—and corresponding regularly with Dickensians in North America. She would also take the time to meet and befriend these overseas Dickensians if they traveled to London. The Dickens Fellowship in Chicago still proudly proclaims on its website that their charter was signed by Kate in 1923.

By 1908 Percy Fitzgerald was so out of favor that it was extremely fortunate he had never become Kate and Henry's brother-in-law. He delivered a speech at a Dickens Fellowship event that criticized Thackeray. Kate was incandescent with fury and her infamous "Lucifer Box" temper led her to write in a passion to the Fellowship, berating Fitzgerald's behavior. Kate related the incident to Anny:

> *I left the Guildhall in such boiling indignation that I could not simmer down until I had written and sent off a letter*
> > *To/The Committee*
> > *'The Dickens Fellowship'*
> > *Etc. Etc.*
>
> *which I hope by now has reached its destination. I should have gone straight to the wretched man himself, but for the reason that, we are none of us 'on terms' with him, for in spite of his pretended devotion to my father, he wrote so offensive an article about him some little time ago, with such an utter disregard of truth in it, that Harry had to call upon him for an apology. I know, I shall be told by the Committee, that he is absent-minded, irresponsible and so on, but if these are excuses for what seem too like malicious folly, all I can say is, that, such a poor fool should not be placed upon the Guildhall platform . . .*

when I think of your great father, with his splendid and immortal genius—his delightful presence—and the smile with which he would have listened to my anger on such a subject, the whole thing seems too trivial even for mention; yet I am glad I wrote to the Committee! When one is hotly indignant (and in many many other moods) there is such an immense satisfaction in the mere act of writing and I certainly let off steam in my letter, although it was done in a collected and passionless manner, I trust.

Judging by similarly furious letters written to Shaw, Kate's belief she had written in a "collected and passionless manner" was unlikely to be true.

At around this time, Kate began friendships with two great literary figures: G. K. Chesterton (and his wife), who was a prominent member of the Dickens Fellowship, and J. M. Barrie. Strangely, biographies of Barrie do not make any mention of this friendship, yet their relationship was enduring and compassionate and was obviously important to both of them. Frustratingly, little remains of their correspondence, no doubt a victim of Kate's obsessive burning sessions, except a couple of birthday telegrams Barrie sent toward the end of her life and a letter in which Kate tells a friend how thrilled she was to receive a book from him when he knew she was ill and depressed. There is also a letter sent to Anny (in which Kate reveals again a deprecating view of her own gender). Kate has apparently mentioned a visit from Barrie in her previous letter and Anny has responded with a fascinated query as to how Kate came to know him:

You seem very much interested in the Barrie incident. I should tell you he is not a new friend but a dear old one, and there is nothing new in his coming to see me. He is invariably most interesting when he speaks, but he is very often silent; I suppose I understand his moods, for we get on capitally well together and I am very fond of him, he has all the noble qualities and the virtues we most admire in men with really few of their faults, and those few faults, are the lovable ones we always forgive. He talks a good deal if he talks at all and says the most delightful things full of humour and kindness, that make his company exactly the thing required. I don't suppose he cares much for very clever women,—no offence meant dear Annie,—what I really mean is, they must be simple and kind before they are clever, with a touch in them of something—just a little more stimulating than barely water, something more like the Grand Marnier we wanted to press upon you the other day; but the clever women who bore pensively and pose and prose (you know the kind I mean) don't attract him in the least and who shall say he is wrong! We none of us have any use for them have we?

Both Kate and Barrie were prominent figures in London's artistic society and Barrie lived nearby, so it seems feasible they were introduced by a mutual acquaintance.

In her other literary correspondence, with G. K. Chesterton and his wife, Kate seems eager to set the world straight on one rumor that had obviously long rankled: that of her father being in love with her long-dead aunt Mary Hogarth. Popular belief, originating with Charles himself, held that Mary was seventeen when she died. In a letter to Chesterton, Kate asserts Mary was in fact only "sixteen and four months." In another letter, in case she had not stressed clearly enough the first time the impropriety of a man of Charles' age falling for a girl barely out of the schoolroom, she further emphasizes the difference in age, looks, and sympathy:

At the time my father was 'courting' my mother the Hogarth family consisted of George Hogarth, his wife, and several boys and girls. Of these, my mother was the eldest and was between eighteen and nineteen. She had three sisters. Mary, aged between fourteen and fifteen, very young and childish in appearance. Georgina aged eight and always in the nursery, and Helen aged three, also in the nursery. My mother had no sister at that time with whom it was possible to fall in love, or no doubt my father, being young and, quite likely, very impressionable, might have done so. As it was he sincerely loved my mother or thought he did, which came to the same thing for he married her and as you know, they did not live happy ever afterwards, although, I fancy, they had several years of very great happiness indeed before my poor father found out his 'mistake' and before my poor mother suffered from his discovery. They were both to be pitied.

Chesterton was a leading figure of the Dickens Fellowship and Kate was fast becoming the family oracle, lionized for being the repository of Dickens family memories. Accompanied by Carlo when his now fragile health permitted, at other times by Georgina or Henry, Kate spent a great deal of time attending official Dickens Fellowship functions. Her father's popularity refused to wane and she was influential in keeping that memory alive and revered. The great theatrical couple Joseph and Marion Comyns Carr were good friends of the Peruginis and the couples often dined together. Marion Comyns Carr (née Terry) was the sister of one of the Victorian theater's most popular actresses, Ellen Terry, who, at the age of sixteen, had been briefly married to the much older G. F. Watts, adored mentor of Val Prinsep and regular guest on the Isle of Wight, moving in the same circles as the Thackerays. When Joseph Comyns Carr's stage version of *Oliver Twist* opened in September 1905, it is more than likely that Kate and Carlo were among the opening-night audience. In the same month, a bust of Charles Dickens was unveiled at the Pump Rooms in Bath—even though Charles had requested in his will that no monument be made to him.

In 1907, Kate's father was honored with an exhibition about Pickwick, in Piccadilly. It was declared open by the Irish MP T. P. O'Connor, a Dickens fan; he was to become one of Kate's most trusted and adoring friends in old age, but they had not yet been introduced, although their paths must have crossed on more than one occasion. Then, on February 7, 1908, to coincide with Charles' birthday, there was the dedication of the National Dickens Library at the Guildhall. It was here that Percy Fitzgerald made his ill-chosen speech. February was always a busy time for Kate as she was expected to be in attendance, often with her husband, at the annual "Boz Club Dinner," at which she occasionally made speeches. The Boz Club had been set up shortly after Charles' death and comprised a group of men who had known Charles well; the original members included Charley and Henry. Women were denied membership and were not usually permitted to attend the dinner. Kate and Georgina were notable exceptions by the start of the twentieth century, though it seems they may have been allowed in solely for the purpose of delivering speeches, not participating in the dinner itself.

Through the Dickens Fellowship Kate grew closer to one of her cousins, Edmund Henry Dickens, son of Uncle Alfred. He was also a Vice-President of the Fellowship and named Kate's book *The Comedy of Charles Dickens* the one he always kept beside his bed. Their closeness was to be short-lived, as he died in May 1910, a few months after two more of Kate and Carlo's friends had passed away. The first was the poet and writer Algernon Swinburne. The other was a fellow artist, Laura, Lady Alma-Tadema, wife of one of Carlo's remaining closest friends, Lawrence Alma-Tadema. Their social circle was rapidly depleting. Fortunately, Kate still had two very close friends remaining, women who had known her for many decades: Anny Thackeray Ritchie and Lady Lucy Mathews, wife of the director of public prosecutions, Sir Charles Mathews.

21

A DIFFERENT WORLD

Ten years into the new century, Kate and Henry Dickens were to be reunited with a brother they had not seen for almost exactly forty-five years. Alfred d'Orsay Tennyson Dickens had departed England for Australia on June 5, 1865, aged nineteen; he had lived there ever since. On June 10, 1910, he returned to England, planning to undertake a lecture tour of countries including Britain, Canada, and the USA, before going home. Kate was very happy to welcome her brother back into her life, and Alfred, she and Carlo spent time getting to know one another. Henry, it seems, was less enthusiastic and he and Marie did not join in the celebrations. Perhaps Alfred took Plorn's side against Henry or maybe even at this mature time of life Henry felt jealous at being usurped in his sister's affections. Kate and Alfred had an obvious affinity, despite the years apart, since their birthdays were just one day apart and they must often have shared their celebrations. The estrangement between the brothers may have been caused by an unresolved rift dating back to before Alfred left England as a teenager. Whatever the reason for the estrangement, in Henry's memoirs there is absolutely no mention of Alfred's return to London—even though Alfred stayed until the autumn of 1911. Kate was keen to encourage him in his lecturing career and in April 1911 she presided over a meeting of the London Dickensians, to whom Alfred gave a talk about their father's life and works. It appears Henry did not attend.

Alfred's American tour began in Boston on October 1, 1911. He was made as welcome in the United States as his father had been and the tour looked set to be a success. Tragically, just three months after his arrival in the country, Alfred died very suddenly. There is no mention of the cause of Alfred's death, but its sudden nature suggests that he had succumbed to a heart attack. It happened on January 2, 1912, while he was staying at the Hotel Astor in New York. His tour manager cabled Kate, asking whether his body should be returned to England for burial; she said no and Alfred was given an elaborate funeral service at Holy Trinity Church, New York. None of his family was able to travel the distance to be present at the funeral—neither his siblings in England nor his family in Australia, to whom Kate would have had the terrible job of telegramming with the distressing news. As with both Frank's and Plorn's funerals, the expenses were paid for entirely through the generosity of the people among whom Alfred had been when he died. It is sadly ironic that Alfred was buried on Twelfth Night, January 6, 1912, the date that would have been Charley's birthday and had been, for so many years, the hallowed date of family parties.

Henry's book merely states baldly (and incorrectly), "Alfred went to Australia in about 1867 . . . remained there continuously until 1911, when he went to America on a lecturing tour and died there in January, 1912. He had been quite a stranger to the family from the time he went to Australia. He left two daughters, who came over to this country some years ago, and remain great favourites with all of us." Despite his behavior toward Henry, Plorn gets a much more compassionate mention than Alfred in Henry's *Recollections*. Equally interesting is Alfred's obituary in the *New York Times*, which mentioned him being survived by "his sister, Kate Perugini," but made no reference to Henry.

In the meantime, Charley's now orphaned children (Bessie had died in 1908) were so financially troubled that they were forced to resort to appealing for public donations. It seems incredible today that anyone would imagine the public would give them money because their grandfather had been famous, but amazingly this appeal seemed to work. One must remember that, at this date, there was no such thing as unemployment benefit or a free health service; those who failed to find work could not rely on anything except the kindness of wealthy benefactors. Ethel, who wrote the begging letter, must have been desperate. She sent the letter to Lord Alverstone, Lord Chief Justice of England, via the *Daily Telegraph*, who printed it as follows:

My father died 15 years ago. . . . My mother was subsequently granted a government pension of £100 a year, which on her death—three years ago—was continued to my four sisters . . . £25 a year each. Of these four sisters two (who are not at all strong or fit for work at all) are just barely making a living—one as a kindergarten teacher, and the other keeping a home for Indian children. The third is at present out of a post altogether, and while trying to find fresh work has nothing at all but her £25 pension, and the fourth is one of the secretaries at the National Health Society.

I myself, who am supposed to have been fairly successful—I have a copying office—have been working excessively hard for over 20 years. I have had one or two bad attacks of overwork illness, and the doctor now tells me that I have overworked for so long that six months' complete rest is imperative. . . . Poverty, through absolutely no fault of one's own, cannot possibly be regarded as a disgrace, and I am perfectly sure that my grandfather himself would not, were he now alive, be ashamed of us, and of any acknowledgement of our pecuniary position.

Donations for the sisters were requested to be sent to either the *Daily Telegraph* or Coutts Bank. Kate and Henry were humiliated in the extreme as their brother's children were reduced to begging from strangers. Henry was financially secure, but he had a large family and there would not have been enough to spare to keep five grown-up nieces. Georgina Hogarth, who was now in her eighties, had enough to keep herself tolerably comfortable, but not enough to share around. The girls' begging letter caused a family rift that lasted—between the families of Charley's and Henry's descendants—for many years.

At this time, Kate and Carlo were also in financial difficulties, again. In June 1911, Carlo wrote a letter to the recently widowed Lady Gilbert, apologizing for not yet having been able to pay back a £200 loan her husband, W. S. Gilbert, had made to him and requesting more time. Gilbert had been a friend of the Peruginis as well as one of Carlo's patrons. Kate and Carlo had often visited the Gilberts' home, Grim's Dyke. On one occasion Gilbert and Kate had an argument; as usual, she flared up and then stormed off. When she went to find him to apologize, he was in the middle of choosing a cigar—one of his favorite pleasures. As she stood embarrassedly apologizing, he turned around to her with a twinkle, shoved the cigar he was holding into her mouth and told her to "smoke that and think no more about it!"

Gilbert had died of a heart attack while swimming in the very cold lake at Grim's Dyke. He had been trying to rescue one of their visitors, a sixteen-year-old girl, from drowning (she survived unharmed). Carlo's letter is charmingly worded, very tactful, and quite formal. It demonstrates genuine grief on the side of the writer and genuine sympathy for the widow. Although he is asking for a favor, there is no sign of "toadying." He does, however, employ a little emotional manipulation, by making reference to the generous bequest W. S. Gilbert had left him—some expensive cigars—calculated to remind Lady Gilbert of the close ties of friendship, not just of patronage, between Carlo and her late husband. He also adds, ". . . dear Sir William—who ever since I had the honour and delight of knowing him never ceased as you have never ceased—to show kindness and goodwill to me and Kitty in every possible way." The letter is interesting because, although Gilbert was known to buy Carlo's work—a large C. E. Perugini painting was among those of Gilbert's effects placed in a sale after Lady Gilbert's death—the letter states that the money was a "debt," apparently a loan, not part payment for a picture commissioned but not yet finished.

Gilbert was not the only one of the Peruginis' patrons to be a friend as well. Letters sent by Kate to and from Sir George Lewis and his family demonstrate that they were close; Kate received a personal letter from Sir George's daughter Gertie to announce her engagement in 1902. Kate's reply is one of genuine friendship and she signs herself "Mrs. Peru," a nickname a few of her friends knew her by:

My dearest Gertie—I don't think you can really be a bit more happy than you have made me by your pleasant news. I am delighted; for you are one of the few girls who ought to marry. You are unselfish, good, gentle and kind, and would make any man happy. I hope he knows my dear that you are a Pearl; if he doesn't please tell him so, with my kind love. And mind you bring him to see me as soon as you can.

But my Gertie, I must know all details. How long have you been engaged. How and where did you meet. Does Katie approve—and are your father and mother pleased? All these questions including, of course, when are you going to be married must be answered as soon as possible by my dear friend Betty—or yourself—or my dear little Katie. We are here for the next ten days—Is he dark or fair? We are having a nice time only the weather is wretched, of what profession? . . . Is he tall or short? There is also here a high wind and clouds of dust and hats flying in all directions. Is he an Englishman? Oh for goodness sake do write and tell me what he is and all about him. Carlo sends you most affectionate messages and says I am to say that he thinks Mr. Birnbaum a very lucky man!

One of her letters to George Lewis Jr. shows that she felt confident enough to express her irritation at his meddling with her methods of finishing off a picture:

Dear George, The pastel must take its chance. All pastel painters differ as to the way of framing and glazing their work. I have tried your painter's way several times; but have always found the pastel drops away! If any thing goes wrong with this particular work, you must hold me responsible and I will do you another for the love of Peggy. But I will ask you to do two things to prevent accidents: one is, to recommend your housemaid never to use a cloth to clean the pastel, and never to move the pastel from the wall. She should flick the dust off it with a feather brush. The other thing I ask you to do is to hang it on a dry wall as pastel suffers from any damp! These two things remembered I think and hope that all will be well.

Around 1911 there are a few references to Kate attending social events, such as the celebrations for the centenary of Thackeray's birth on July 16, but Carlo is not mentioned as being present. His health was beginning to deteriorate and he had been diagnosed with angina. He had never been as sociable as his wife, so perhaps it was something of a relief to Carlo not to have to attend every function the couple was invited to.

The death of W. S. Gilbert had prompted a group of artists and writers to form a Gilbert memorial committee, of which both the Peruginis and T. P. (Thomas Power) O'Connor were members. It is probably from around this time that Kate and T. P. began their friendship. The year was 1912, and while the artistic world was still mourning Gilbert, Lawrence Alma-Tadema died; the last of Carlo's close group of friends. It seems neither of the Peruginis was enjoying the best of health at this time, perhaps because life was just too depressing. Kate was suffering from influenza, so it seems likely that Carlo would also have caught it. That she was feeling depressed was made explicit in some interesting letters that were brought to my attention by family historian Simon Bowring. He discovered that his great grandmother, May Hagborg, had enjoyed a brief correspondence with Kate in 1912 and 1913. May and her husband Otto Hagborg seem to have been a fascinating couple. Otto was an artist (and the brother of a relatively successful Impressionist artist, August Hagborg, who lived in Paris). Otto came from Sweden, but had trained as an artist in Paris before moving to London in 1890, where he remained until his death in 1927. He was also a celebrated Olympic diver. His wife May (née Hannah May Posener) made jewelry and in 1912, Kate sent May some of her own designs and asked her to make them into jewelry. The first commission Kate sent to May was for a turquoise and diamond pendant, which she wanted for "a dear friend." Kate sent a sketch of what she wanted and described her design as "Large turquoise with one of the four large diamonds above it. The other three diamonds in center of three silver flowers—the other turquoise below withe [sic] tiny turquoise at the end of little silver chain, all the chains in silver." This first letter was sent on May 14, 1912, and perhaps May Hagborg responded unfavorably to Kate's design, as on May 16, 1912, Kate sent another letter explaining "I have determined on having my own design carried out as far as possible as the pendant will be for a dear friend who would prefer it to any other— imperfect though it may be—so please do not send me any other designs."

It appears May responded immediately and explained she had another commission to finish first and Kate replied (also on May 16, 1912), "Dear Mrs. Hagborg, By all means do Mrs. Newcomer's work first, I am in no hurry. I scarcely ever do feel sad or lonely unless I have influenza, but

I shall be *very* glad indeed to see you at any time you can manage to come in for a cup of tea." These first letters are written on black-edged mourning paper, presumably for Alfred Dickens. By the time of the next surviving letter to May Hagborg, at the end of November 1912, Kate had reverted to her usual, non-mourning paper, sending May a short note inviting her to visit ("please come any day except Saturday, at 4.30. Very glad to see you.").

In June 1913, Kate wrote to thank May for the pendant, which she likes "very much indeed. The work is beautifully done, fine and delicate. The stone doesn't seem to me to be quite set in the middle of [the] setting, but that is a small matter." Despite finding the stone's setting off-center, Kate enclosed a check and commissioned May to make her two "tiny" diamond pins, which she wanted "to fasten the piece of black tulle I wear across my head." She added, "But I can't go to any more expense just now so, if you will keep the diamonds for me, and come to tea one day when you can, you will be able to tell me exactly how much they would be and if the cost would not be very great I hope to have them. In an undated letter, Kate thanks May for her "beautiful work, which I like better and better each day" and sends her two guineas, presumably to pay for the diamond pins. She also adds, "Hoping you will not forget your promise to come and see me sometimes."

Perhaps the "dear friend" referred to in Kate's letters about the pendant was Anny; she certainly had reason to need cheering up. Her husband, Richmond, became very ill in the early autumn of 1912 and died on October 12. Anny was surely one woman who had felt certain she would die before her husband, but he had cheated the age difference between them. By the time of his death, Richmond had become a very successful man. He was Permanent Under-Secretary of State for India and had been knighted. The bereaved Anny was now known as Lady Ritchie.

The world was becoming a very different place from the one in which Kate and Anny had grown up and Kate was not happy about the changes. Although as a child she had longed for more freedom than girls were usually permitted and later sought desperately to be taken seriously in her career, she did not always approve of modern young women. In 1897, Kate had been one of a group of female artists who signed a petition supporting women's suffrage, but when the suffragette Mary Richardson launched a protest by slashing a painting by Velázquez in the National Gallery she would have been appalled. Kate and her peers lived through decades of great—and terrible—inventions, seeing the world change almost beyond belief.

Kate's year of presidency of the Dickens Fellowship (beginning in 1912) saw a flurry of activity from her "camp." Georgina Hogarth was still an active force to be reckoned with, despite her advanced age, and Henry had started to give regular talks about his father and public recitals of his books. Kate's friends, such as Lady Lucy Mathews, were also encouraged to come to events and lend their support. Another of her and Anny's mutual friends was the American novelist Henry James, who was currently living in London, on fashionable Cheyne Walk (once home to the artists Whistler and Dante Rossetti). In 1913, Kate presided over a special dinner at the George and Vulture pub, in London, held specially for visiting Canadian and American Dickensians. She and Carlo continued to hold their At Homes almost every weekend, which although perhaps rather intrusive must also have resulted in several sales of pictures.

As the world moved inexorably closer to war, Kate's nieces and nephews were at the right age to fall in love. In April 1913, Henry and Marie's daughter, Olive, married Robert Shirley Shuckburgh, known as Bob, at the Brompton Oratory, London's most fashionable Catholic church; the reception was held at the Alexandra Hotel. Neither Kate nor Georgina approved of the wedding service because of its Catholicism. (Despite Carlo's Italian parentage, he seems to have been brought up a Protestant.) The following March, no doubt painfully aware of the specter of conflict starting to loom over Europe, Henry and Marie's son Philip was married to Sybil Cunliffe Owen, also at the Brompton Oratory.

In April 1914, a month after Philip and Sybil's wedding, Ellen Ternan—now known as the respectable Ellen Robinson, wife of a schoolmaster whom she'd married after Charles' death, and mother of two children—died. Ironically, she is buried in Highland Road cemetery, a short distance from the grave of Charles Dickens' first love, Maria Beadnell (Mrs. Winter).

22

LIVING THROUGH THE "GREAT WAR"

On Tuesday August 4, 1914, England went to war with Germany. The wounds of the Boer War had not yet healed and those of Kate and Carlo's generation still remembered the Crimean War. Yet at this time the vast majority of people still believed in "the old lie," *Dulce et decorum est pro patria mori* ("It is sweet and honorable to die for one's country"). Tens of thousands of young men were sent to the Front, most of them gung-ho about the prospect—only to be massacred in the thousands. To begin with, the majority of Britons genuinely believed the war would be over by Christmas. The conflict that was predicted to last just four months endured heartrendingly for over four years.

Just as Virginia Woolf was to suffer from the terrible depression that led to her suicide during the Second World War, Kate found her own depression returned with a vengeance as the war refused to be brought to a civilized end. At first, she became rejuvenated by the feeling that she could be useful—in common with many others, she believed the war would be over swiftly—but as tales of terrible massacres, military incompetence, and atrocities started to leak back to those waiting at home, Kate became acutely aware of the fact that, had he lived, her own son would have been sent to fight. The situation was even worse for Henry and Marie: They had sons of fighting age.

Those who waited at home needed to be entertained to take their thoughts away from what was happening overseas. Henry began a series of recitals from his father's works, with the money raised going to the Red Cross; Kate and Carlo supported him by attending and persuading friends to do the same. In 1915, a stage version of *David Copperfield* played nightly to a full-capacity audience at His Majesty's Theatre in London's West End to boost morale and give at least temporary relief from the miserable realities of everyday life. Everyone who could was attempting to help the war effort. By now Carlo and Kate were feeling elderly, but while Carlo's health was fragile, Kate seemed to find resources of energy to bolster her through the first couple of years of the war. She and Carlo continued to paint (in 1914 Carlo exhibited *Hero* at the Royal Academy), but they were also mindful of the need to help those directly affected by the war. It seems Carlo was not capable of any great exertion, as many of Kate's letters make reference to his not being able to leave the house and to events that she had attended on her own as he wasn't well enough to go, too. In one undated letter, Kate confides to Anny that "Carlo who looks all right but is not really well, is afraid of going away for a whole day—for various reasons which you may perhaps understand. If he gets quite better I will let you know but for the present, perhaps it is wiser for him to stay at home." As well as angina, it seems likely Carlo had some kind of bowel or bladder problem as there are several of Kate's letters that allude to his being unable to spend too long away from their home and to the embarrassing nature of his infirmity. He began spending more and more time at home. He was not, it appears, in much pain or in need of constant nursing as Charlie Collins had been and his and Kate's relationship seems to have become more tender the older they grew, patiently nursing each other through the indispositions caused by their advancing years.

In 1915 Kate and Anny decided to work together for the war effort. A large two-day fête was being organized at the White City, an enormous complex of exhibition halls built in Shepherd's Bush in London to house the 1908 Olympics. With their combined illustrious parentage, a charity book stall seemed the obvious way for the two women to take part. Despite both being in their late seventies, they worked with a fervor. The fête was a great success, raising money for St. Dunstan's Home, a brand-new hospital set up for servicemen who had been blinded. It seems the effort of organizing and running the stall was exhausting for Anny, as Hester was soon writing to Kate saying that her mother was unwell, but Kate herself appears to have been rejuvenated with energy for this new project.

In the same letter in which she had written about Anny being ill, Hester asked permission to call Kate "Aunt Kitty." The two women had grown into the habit of sending each other very loving letters, a few of which remain in existence. Kate's reply in August 1915 shows that she was in good spirits, despite the previous twelve months of the war. Hester had been to visit the Great Bed of Ware on display in London and had sent Kate a postcard:

Dearest Hester. Thank you for sending 'the great bed of Ware' in which I am much interested. It looks however not only a beautiful but rather a bogey and buggy bed and one which I should scarcely care to sleep in. It adorns the chimney-piece of this little 'morning room' and here it will remain as long as the smoke and dust of London allow.

I am so very sorry my dear Annie is not well. With her, I am sure it is 'only the weather', please tell her so with my fond love. With me I don't know what it is but believe that charcoal, far from adding fuel to the fire is the only remedy that keeps me going. However, why worry, when 'This way to the Skeleton' is the inevitable end of all things and some people get thinner & thinner! 'Small by degrees and beautifully less,' or is that beautifully less, 'a mere chimera?' By the way—is a thin old lady a less or a more agreeable object than a fat one? There is certainly less to look at, which may have charms for the observer, but I ha'e me doots or should have if I could spell that expression but this I do know: When I was a mite of a thing, my father used to sing us a song about an old lady 'who dwindled to a speck' a process in which we took the most absorbed and canny delight. I believe I am that same old lady though I've taken a long time about it, but even the speck is beginning to be invisible at last, and when I go out of this world like a stick of barley sugar, you too will remember the song I have never forgotten. Until then, and long long after, I hope, may the sun smile upon you and shine on all your undertakings wherever you may be—in other words may you be as happy as I would have you—you and all belonging to you.

Ever my dear your very affectionate
Aunt Kitty

The maid who buys my pens is off on holiday so I'm blotting about all over the place. Please forgive. Why should you feel grateful to be my niece? A lady (or is she a lady?) who can't spell 'ha ma doots' is not a lady to be grateful to, but despised. I asked Carlo just now if he could spell it, but with [word illegible] diplomacy he said, he should avoid the phrase, which I call real mean don't you?

The letter shows Kate in a cheerful frame of mind, not yet experiencing the depression the war would cause. For many of those in England, the horrors of the so-called Great War were unrealized. One of the most difficult experiences for returning soldiers was the jingoistic joviality with which their overseas experiences were perceived by those they came home to, their friends and families, who really believed that the war was noble and high-minded. This was probably Kate's own experience at least during the first couple of years of conflict, as the war and modern fighting machinery were things of which she had little—if any—understanding.

At the end of 1915, she and Henry launched an appeal via the newspapers, asking for Dickens books to be sent out to wounded soldiers in hospitals. In 1916, Kate and Anny organized another book stall, this time for a sale at Hyde Park House on November 22, which was patronized by Queen Alexandra. The profits went to "the French Wounded Emergency Fund."

Before the sale, Anny wrote an amusing letter to a friend in which she confided that she was hoping to dissuade Kate from carrying out her idea of decorating the stall with a picture of Charles Dickens wearing a laurel wreath. At great personal sacrifice, Kate included in the sale Luke Fildes' original drawing of his famous painting, *The Empty Chair*, depicting Charles Dickens' desk and chair shortly after he had died. She also sold the letter that Fildes had written to her to accompany it.

During the second winter of the war, Kate was extremely depressed. Until now, she had continued her regular "At Homes" for the Dickens Fellowship, but during the winter months these ceased, as did her correspondence. One of the Fellowship members, Mr. Osborne Walford, who with his daughters had become very close to Kate, thought that her silence was an indication that he had offended her in some way and wrote to apologize. Kate was quick to reply to him, on her last remaining piece of writing paper:

If I have not written to you lately or invited you to our house, it has simply been because I have been very much occupied and have not given any tea parties this winter; nor have I liked to ask friends to come and see me because of the intense darkness that has descended upon London. But now that the days are getting longer I should be so pleased if you and your daughters would come any fine Saturday afternoon and have a cup of tea with me.

As the spring advanced, Kate forced herself to start taking part in a social scene again. She had become very scathing of, but also empathetic toward those people who fled London during the war. Staunchly determined to stay in the city in which she had lived for most of her life, Kate was continually depressed and, perhaps, wished she had the strength to run away herself. By the end of 1916 she was almost overwhelmed by the misery of what was happening in the world. In August she wrote a letter to Hester Thackeray Ritchie, in which she tells of her "not too cheerful" "existence"; Carlo is not well nor is Georgina Hogarth, to whom Kate is now a constant visitor. Again she mentions the weather, such a prevalent factor in determining her moods:

All things seem dark just at present. But . . . it is only because of the war—because of the weather—because of people being away and because, perhaps, that I have just read 'The Aspern Papers' for the first time and devoured them at one gulp, that I feel depressed—that is all.

It is no wonder that Henry James's *Aspern Papers* had such resonance for Kate. The story centers on a scholar who, researching the life of a deceased poet, Jeffrey Aspern, is desperate to get his hands on private papers owned by the poet's former lover. The lover, Miss Bordereau, is now a very elderly lady with a middle-aged niece. Not only does the book reveal what deceitful lengths a researcher is prepared to go to in order to dig up scandal about a dead writer, but also his private thoughts show he is quite revolted by the middle-aged niece's infatuation with him. As an elderly lady who had spent so much of her life being adored by men, Kate possibly found the book upsetting on more than one level.

The following month the family was shocked by the terrible news that two of Henry and Marie's sons had been badly wounded on the same day, in the same battle. Major Cedric Dickens, aged just twenty-seven, had died on the battlefield at Ginchy, in the Somme; although injured, the newly married Philip survived. Henry and Marie were devastated by Ceddy's death. Several years later, Henry wrote about his son:

> *My wife could not bear the idea of having my son's body moved to the military cemetery; she wanted him to lie where he fell—in the midst of a wide and open field. Happily she obtained permission for this; we acquired the right to the piece of land on which he died, and my wife has turned it into a beautiful little garden which is carefully looked after by one of the representatives of the Imperial War Graves Commission.*

After the war, Marie was to devote much of her life to helping the poverty-stricken people of war-torn Ginchy, to whom she felt indebted for burying her much mourned son. On the eightieth anniversary of the battle, in 1996, a large party of Dickens family members returned to Ginchy to take part in a memorial service for those who had been killed so senselessly.

On September 26, 1916, Kate attended the memorial service for Ceddy, held—of course—at the Brompton Oratory. She broke down in tears and was embarrassed about her outpouring of emotion while all the others were being so stoic and "brave." She wrote in a letter to Anny, "The service at the Oratory was very beautiful in spite of certain little bobbings about and little bells and so on—The music, divinely lovely, but painfully so to one who is always upset by music to her own very great shame—for they were all so calm and bearing their grief so bravely."

Kate sank into an unspecified illness, probably depression, after the death of her nephew, which had brought the realities of the war so very firmly into their lives and also the remembrance of her own son's death. She was, however, roused back into an interest in public life after the resignation, in December 1916, of the Prime Minister, Herbert Asquith. As Kate wrote to Anny, the commotion had made her too interested to continue to be ill:

> *Lord Derby's was a noble speech and could not have been better and if all Englishmen had so gallant a spirit,—perhaps we should not be in this agony of suspense and anxiety. Oh how will it all end! This, surely, is the worst moment, or almost the worst, that we have had during these last two years. I am better; too interested to be ill, I am like the rest of the world only longing for news and never satisfied. I am in a way sorry for Asquith (one is always sorry for the man who is down) but I am thankful he's gone! So thankful.*
> *With best love from us both your K.E.*

Despite her dwindling artistic output, Kate remained famed and adored on account of her father. She once commented to Gladys Storey, "I always wanted to be loved for my own sake, but I am very happy to be loved for my father's sake." Having needed to worry about money ever since she left home to marry Charlie Collins, she was stunned when, at his death, Mr. Wagg, the father of two women with whom Kate was friendly, left her an annuity of £300. He made the bequest in gratitude because he was a "lifelong fan" of Charles Dickens. When one considers that, after Charley's death, Bessie Dickens and her daughters were living on an annual income of £100, Mr. Wagg's gift was extremely generous. It marked a welcome end to Kate's constant nagging anxiety about money. Her friend Lady Fanny Fildes remembered calling to visit Kate on the day she had received the letter telling her about the money; Kate told her that she had "come into a fortune!"

In 1917, Kate was honored to receive a letter from a member of the Scottish Dickens Fellowship. Mr. Herbert D. Down, a resident of Edinburgh, requested permission to name a hospital bed after her. The bed was in the Scottish Women's Hospital and Mr. Down also gave £50 to the hospital—enough to cover the expenses for that particular bed for a year. In the same year, she was proud when Henry was made Common Sergeant of London. This was a very great honor, making him one of the highest-ranking legal members of the City of London.

By the spring of 1917, Kate had been nursing two patients of her own for several months: Georgina, who was now in her nineties, still living on her own (with servants, of course) at 72 Church Street, Chelsea, and rapidly becoming senile; and Carlo, who was suffering from angina. After a cruel and lingering descent into dementia and physical dependency, Georgina Hogarth died on Thursday, April 19, 1917, at the age of ninety-one. Her death came as a relief. It had been extremely distressing for Kate and Henry to watch their always capable aunt deteriorate so humiliatingly. Her funeral was held the following Monday and she was buried in Mortlake Cemetery, not far from Charley and Bessie Dickens. Despite the problems most people unfairly assumed Georgina had caused in Charles and Catherine's marriage, the Dickens children had adored her. In his book, Henry was moved to defend her against the slurs that prevailed even after her death (and over half a century after his parents' separation) by describing her as "one of the dearest friends I ever had."

The Dickens family was out in force at the funeral, although Carlo is not mentioned as attending. This was probably because he was ill; certainly he and Kate chose to spend two months that summer out of London, recuperating. In that summer of 1917, Kate did not anticipate being greatly entertained by a wartime convalescent holiday and urged Anny and Hester to write to her as often as possible; no doubt she was also scared of leaving behind those she loved at such a dangerous time, in case she never saw them again.

Throughout the war years, Hester was a regular visitor to the Peruginis' home, taking them roses from the garden. Kate seems to have been much closer to Hester than she was to any of her real nieces and nephews. In an effort to help with the war effort, Hester was working in a charity kitchen, providing food for the needy. She was kept so busy that her visits to Victoria Road became, necessarily, less frequent, prompting Kate to write her a short poem during the last year of the war,

Public kitchens my Hester, are all very well,
But Friendship calls out at least for a spell;
Give me five minutes' grace, I ask for no more, –
Then back you shall go to your communal door.

I *know you are busy. Pay no attention to the above, which is only
sent—as a reminder that there is an old person somewhere who loves
you! KP*

In the summer of 1918, Kate and many of her peers were appalled
by the strikes that began to plague Britain while the country was still at
war. Kate wrote at least two poems about the strikes, one of which, dated
August 1918, was entitled "The Policeman's Strike is not a happy one"
(in homage to Gilbert and Sullivan). During these last few months of
conflict, Kate wrote a number of poems; a few survive, but it is highly
probable these are just a small percentage of her output.

With the benefit of hindsight, we know that in October 1918 the war
was drawing to a close, but to those living through it, who had spent so
many years seeing their prayers for an end to the bloodshed unanswered,
it must have felt that it would never be over. That month, seventy-nine-
year-old Kate sent Hester another poem. It was about the misery of getting old and about everyone she knew dying and leaving her. No doubt
she could see that both Anny and Carlo were becoming increasingly frail.
The poem includes the verse:

I tell you something sad my dear,
As sad as sad can be,
All those I knew and loved so well
Have gone away from me.

23

THE PASSING OF LOVE

The end of the so-called "Great War," in November 1918, was not to bring happiness to everyone. Those at home were painfully learning the horrors of what had really been happening overseas. Henry and Marie were able to welcome home three of their sons and their two sons-in-law, all of whom had been serving at the Front. As stories trickled through about families in which every male had been killed, they perhaps felt they had been—in a twisted way—quite fortunate to lose only one beloved son.

For Kate the relief at the war being over was to prove sadly short-lived. The Peruginis were now an elderly couple, fast approaching their eightieth birthdays. Carlo's health had been growing steadily worse over the previous few years, making his life difficult. While he and Kate were happily preparing for their first non-wartime Christmas in four years, Carlo became dangerously ill. One of the maids discovered him gasping for breath in his studio and summoned Kate at once. He died at their home, 32 Victoria Road, on December 22; his death certificate records that he succumbed to angina. For several days, his body was kept in the room in which he had died. Kate placed sprigs of holly around him, so that he would not miss out on Christmas, and kissed him every day, in death, just as she had done in life.

Carlo's funeral was held at St. Nicholas's Church in Sevenoaks. He was buried in the same grave as their baby son, Dickie. Henry, who had registered Carlo's death on Kate's behalf, now became one of the most important people in his sister's life. Many years later, after Kate's own death, Henry was to describe her as "universally beloved. She had wonderful charm and a very strong sense of humour. I was devoted to her and I think she had the same feeling for me." He remained, even as an old man himself, the adoring younger brother eager to please his clever, popular sister.

A couple of months after Carlo's death, Kate lost her oldest and dearest friend, Anny Thackeray Ritchie. Anny died at her home in Freshwater, on the Isle of Wight. Her body was brought back to the mainland, to be buried at Highgate, and Kate traveled to the funeral with their mutual friend and fellow artist Marie Spartali Stillman.[92] Marie was a beautiful Greek who, in her youth, had been taught to paint by Ford Madox Brown and had worked as a model for Dante Gabriel Rossetti, Edward Burne-Jones, and Julia Margaret Cameron. After her marriage to the American journalist William Stillman (against her family's wishes)—which had followed a scandalous love affair with Lord Ranelagh—Marie had spent much of her life living abroad. An extremely talented artist, she had often exhibited at fashionable London galleries. Just four years younger than Kate, by the time of Anny's funeral, Marie was also an old woman. The two artists comforted each other on their journey to and from the funeral and no doubt reminisced about happier times.

After being widowed, Kate made the decision to leave Victoria Road, unable to cope with living in such a large home by herself. She moved to 3 Argyll Mansions, a little flat in Chelsea, on the corner of King's Road and Beaufort Street. The move was distressing and it was some time before she stopped hating her new home. For the first months, she was miserable, complaining she couldn't sleep because of noisy traffic. The flat was cold and small and the miners' strike meant there was no coal for an open fire. Kate had continued to paint and draw and would keep doing so for several years to come, but the few remaining pictures from the late 1910s and 1920s are poorly executed and show nothing of the skill she had owned at the peak of her career. This was partly to do with general physical infirmity, but largely to do with an ever-failing eyesight. Throughout her life Kate, like her father, had been short-sighted (a defect both strove to prevent other people from knowing, choosing to wear glasses only in

---

92 Her devoted family friends the Tennysons lent Anny's family the same funeral pall—cream, with elaborately embroidered roses—that had been used to cover the coffin of Alfred, Lord Tennyson.

private).[93] In old age this infirmity grew much worse and her eyes became sore and troublesome. Several letters survive in which she says her eyes have "been bad" again. She began walking around her flat with her eyes closed, convinced she was going to go blind and determined to learn how to get around without being able to see.

My grandfather's cousin Cedric Dickens remembered being taken to see Kate at around this time. He was born in 1916 and he told me of his memory of meeting "Aunt Kitty" when he was still so young that he was small enough to be carried. At Kate's home (perhaps Victoria Road but more likely to be Argyll Mansions as it seems likely his memory dates back to after Kate was widowed) he was held by his nanny tantalizingly close to Kate's mantelpiece, on which stood a small carved wooden bear. He purloined it—he remembered that it fit neatly into his hand—and sneaked it home. On being discovered, he was taken sternly back to Kate's home to return the bear and apologize. He remembers Kate as being "a very elderly lady dressed in a lot of stiff black material" and that she was very small like "a fluffy ball"—no doubt this latter image was because she still wore Victorian-style dresses, so very different from those worn by most of the women he would have known. He also remembered she was nice to him, despite the fact he was expecting to be told off.

At around the time Kate moved into her new home, she wrote a letter to George Bernard Shaw, in very shaky handwriting. When viewed alongside her earlier letters it illustrates painfully that old age had finally caught up with her. It says, very simply:

Dear Mr. G.B.S

Would you be kind and spare me a few moments of your valuable time? I live in a tiny flat at above address, up one flight of rather steep stairs. When you arrive at the top, come straight along to end of passage and knock at my door on right hand side; inside, you will find an old friend and a warm welcome.

Yours very sincerely
Kate Perugini

---

93 Kate also inherited her father's "slow pulse" (perhaps low blood pressure).

Much as she disliked 3 Argyll Mansions when she moved in, it was to prove a sociable home. As the years progressed, Kate became reluctant to venture outside her flat, but she still enjoyed the company of a constant stream of visitors, including Hester, Lucy Mathews, J. M. Barrie, Luke and Fanny Fildes, Marie Stillman, and T. P. O'Connor. The weather continued to affect her, though, and she spent much of the last years of her life in a depression, missing Carlo and pondering on the indignities and infirmities of old age. One of her poems, simply entitled "Winter," was written at around this time. The first verse demonstrates how Kate viewed life as an elderly widow.

Winter
The flowers are dead, the branches bare
And Age beside the fire,
Stares silent into empty space
That held his heart's desire;
For gone is joy and hope of Spring
Its vague but longed for glory,
The past has fled beyond the stars
And finished is the story.

At about the time Kate moved to Argyll Mansions, she became increasingly friendly with Gladys Storey and her mother. She and Carlo had first been introduced to Gladys, the daughter of Royal Academician Graham Storey (by now deceased), in 1910, when Gladys was a young actress. Gladys later recalled that it had been at a party at the Mansion House (the grand home of the Lord Mayor of London) and was a "reception given *In Honour and in Friendship of Art*" (Gladys's italics). They had kept in touch and after Kate's move to Chelsea Mrs. and Miss Storey became Kate's most regular visitors. By 1919, Gladys seems to have forsaken the stage entirely and was concentrating on building a career as a writer. Their friendship is interesting and in some ways controversial. The bulk of information about it derives from Gladys's own notes and diaries, kept during her visits to Kate. For the last nine years of Kate's life, the Storeys would visit every Sunday, if possible, and occasionally on other days as well, to take tea with the elderly artist. Kate's family, in particular Henry and Marie, had mixed feelings about it. My great-uncle Eric used to complain that Gladys and her mother had monopolized Kate, turning her against her family, and that no one was ever able to see Kate on her own, as one or other of the ubiquitous Storeys was always visiting. It is hard to get to the truth. Gladys does seem to have adored Kate, but one also gets the impression that on occasion she was rather more interested in Kate's grand parentage and her useful contemporary connections than in her.

At some point during their friendship, Kate asked Gladys to write her biography. It was, she stipulated, not to be published until after her own and Henry's deaths. Having worked so hard on the manuscript about her parents' marriage, Kate had decided she could not bring herself to get it published—it was too truthful and too raw and would cause irreparable damage to her father's reputation. She burned the only copy, because "I only told the half-truth about my father, and a half-truth is worse than a lie, for this reason, I destroyed what I had written." The loss of Kate's manuscript is something I regret keenly.

Despite only having been able to bring herself to write a "half-truth" about her father, Kate wanted the whole truth to be told—but after her death. Her conflict between wanting to exonerate her mother and yet not being able to bear sullying her father's memory is perhaps what led her to deface Mamie's book so vehemently: Mamie had no qualms about recording only what the world wanted to hear and what she wanted to remember about her idealized father. Kate remained, however, eaten up with guilt about her father's treatment of her mother, about her own "selfish" behavior, which she now saw as amounting to collusion, and about the lies that still persisted about Catherine. She decided to dictate to Gladys the story of her life—and the truth about her parents' marriage— so that Gladys could publish it and let the world see what Catherine Dickens had really been like. The book, *Dickens and Daughter,* was published in 1939, one hundred years after Kate's birth. It remains a controversial book. The press at the time were incensed and many reviewers rubbished everything that Gladys had written, some of them declaring (erroneously) that Kate had been senile for the last decade of her life and that the book contained only the ravings of a madwoman. J. W. T. Ley of the Dickens Fellowship wrote a particularly vindictive review claiming

Kate's brain had been affected—an interesting irony when one considers that the Fellowship had been happy to listen to all Kate's memories and record them as the gospel truth even at the end of her life.

Several years before the publication of Gladys's book, the journalist and biographer Thomas Wright published an article about Charles Dickens and then a biography of him. He had been working on his research for several decades, advertising for letters and other private information not previously known to the public. (In the 1890s Georgina Hogarth had written to him, appealing to him not to publish.) He became acquainted with a clergyman, Canon Benham, who had known Ellen Ternan and to whom she had apparently confessed. Astonishingly, Wright later claimed that Canon Benham had told him Ellen's confidences. If this were true it was a terrible violation of her privacy and of ecclesiastic principles. In 1934, the *Daily Express* published his article, in which it was claimed Ellen was Charles' mistress. His biography followed in 1935. The public was appalled and his credibility was attacked on many fronts by furious Dickensians and academics, as well as public feeling.

Gladys' revelations were, therefore, not the bombshell she had intended, but she had the edge over Thomas Wright through her association with Kate. This did not mean that the book was well received. If anything, Kate's involvement made people even more irritated. It was claimed that Gladys had manipulated an elderly woman's words or that Kate and Gladys had both lied, in order to make themselves seem important. Public affection for Charles Dickens remained at such a height, even sixty-nine years after his death, that the firm of printers employed by Gladys' publishers actually refused to print the manuscript, claiming it was "a dangerous book." Although the book, which is essentially a collection of anecdotes rather than a biographical account, remains at times disjointed and occasionally incorrect, it is actually more correct and more carefully researched than most reviewers—and almost all family members alive in 1939—would give it credit for.

Gladys' papers are now at the Charles Dickens Museum in London. Having spent many hours painstakingly going through them, I was surprised how well documented her research was and how often Henry Dickens had backed up Kate's assertions. Of course, as Gladys was writing in an age before dictaphones and portable recording equipment, we have only her handwritten notes as "evidence" that either Kate or Henry made such comments to her. There is, however, a signed letter from Marie, written after the publication of the book, making reference to the comments and not refuting them, just expressing a wish that Gladys had not published.

The most thrilling revelation in the book is that Charles not only carried on an affair with Ellen Ternan, Kate tells Gladys, but also that they had had a baby, a son who had died in infancy. There are still people today who refuse to believe this assertion, but Gladys' papers show that not only did Kate tell her the story, but also that Henry reiterated it. It makes absolutely no sense that either Kate or Henry would make up the story. The fact that there was no official recognition of the baby, such as a birth certificate, is no surprise, considering that illegitimate children did not need to be registered at that time. Claire Tomalin suggests the baby was born in France and may not have been registered or the records may have been lost. Dickensians and scholars will continue to debate this issue furiously, with the majority refusing to accept that Charles fathered an illegitimate child (though never explaining how or why the man whose sex life with Catherine was obviously very passionate suddenly chose to live a life of monkish celibacy), but the very fact that it was his own children who told the story convinces me it is genuine.

Additionally, certain letters written by Charles came to light many years after his death. W. H. Wills' great-nephew C. E. S. Chambers wrote, in 1934:

> *Certain members of my family had great intimacy with C.D. and remember being told many years ago [by Nina Lehmann] that C.D. had actually lived for some 12 years with a well-known actress, I forget the name. . . . All of D's letters to Wills had been preserved and on the death of Mrs. Wills became the property of a cousin, from whom they were purchased by myself and my cousin the late Rudolph Lehmann for the sum of £300. We discovered that some of this correspondence was of an extremely private nature. It contained instructions to Wills*

written from America during D's second visit, regarding the welfare of a certain lady, then apparently sickening for her confinement. These instructions were of the most intimate nature and contained in letters which should have been destroyed at the time. Rudolph L. and myself finally decided to send these half dozen letters to Sir Henry Dickens and that we did, and what became of them only his executors can now tell![94]

By the time Gladys's book was published, both Kate and Henry had died—Henry was killed in 1933, after being run over by a motorcyclist. Marie Dickens was still alive when the book was published and protested greatly against many of the comments. Publicly and to her family Marie dismissed much of what Gladys had written as nonsense, yet Gladys retained letters that show Marie was aware of the truth, she just had not wanted Gladys to reveal it to the world. In July 1939, Marie wrote to Gladys:

As for the silly Beadnall love affair and the Ternan affair every one has heard these stories over and over again, 4 generations know about it, published in letters, in books and in papers, and now you give it to a 5th generation! Every one of these people are no more. Why not speak only of Charles Dickens for the good he did to the poor & to the sufferers. His books belong to all, but his private life to himself alone, and I wish, oh how I wish that these blemishes & shortcomings of this great writer, should be unmentioned once and for all. May my great grandchildren admire and revere their great ancestor for the good, a kindness he brought to all . . . forgive my criticisms. I cannot help it, neither Harry nor Kitty ever spoke of their father but with great admiration; his private life they preferred to be very little known about.

---

94 In *The Invisible Woman* Claire Tomalin records a note made by Dickens scholar Madeline House, who met and talked to Gladys Storey and believed her assertions. House recorded, "I'm convinced Mrs. T was with Ellen at the time of the baby's birth. This I have from Gladys Storey, who—with Kate Perugini—read the letters from Dickens to Wills making plans concerning the baby, before destroying them. –It was something of a triumph to get this out of Gladys, who is a jealous guarder of her secrets; but I'm convinced by the way it was said and the way it came up that it was the truth G was telling me." Claire Tomalin states that the letters were read by both Henry and Kate and then destroyed.

Dickens and Daughter was universally hated by the family. I was fascinated to discover a comment written by my great-uncle Eric Hawksley on the inside flap of another book in the library at the Charles Dickens Museum. It is Hebe Elsna's book *Unwanted Wife: A Defence of Mrs. Charles Dickens*. Eric wrote on it: "This is a thoroughly bad vindictive book *and* inaccurate.... It all comes from taking 'Dickens and Daughter' seriously."

Whatever the family feelings about Gladys—and my own feelings became distinctly less impressed as I delved deeper into their friendship—I owe her a large debt for the careful note-keeping. That is not to say, however, that her information is completely accurate and, obviously, it is biased. It is also apparent that there was a great deal of carefully suppressed enmity between Gladys and Marie Dickens; although it must be said that Hester, and Kate's cook and maid, also seem to have found Marie hard to bear. Perhaps these feelings emanated from Kate, despite her fond assertions of friendship and the very loving comments Kate was to write about Marie in her will. The friendship between Kate and her sister-in-law seems to have been complicated—they grew to love each other but also often found one another's presence too much to take. As their personalities were so very different, this is not altogether surprising. Quite naturally, if Marie had annoyed her, Kate probably let off steam to her servants and friends such as Hester and Gladys, but that does not mean that her attitude toward Marie was actively hostile.

Just as her feelings for Marie were changeable, so was Kate's general mood. Although after moving into her new home in 1919 she spent the first few months unhappy and depressed, as often seemed to happen Kate's natural vivacity and interest in life surfaced again. Instead of sinking into her widow's weeds and letting herself fade away of a broken heart, which was perhaps at first what she intended to do (she was, after all, a Victorian), she could not help taking an interest in what was happening in the world. She loved people and she loved charming them. Even as an elderly lady she could captivate men, including those many years her junior. She never grew out of being the flirtatious, "fast," pretty Miss Dickens.

Although in August 1919 Kate was writing to Gladys that "everything has been going wrong," by October Marie Stillman reported that

Kate was feeling better, that she had grown accustomed to the traffic on the King's Road and was able to sleep through the noise. She also had a niece getting married (yet again at the despised Brompton Oratory), Henry and Marie's younger daughter, Elaine, known as "Bobbie." Even I can remember Aunt Bobbie. An incredible woman who lived until the age of ninety-five, she was a regular visitor to our house in the 1970s, when I was very young and she very old. She used to play endless games of ludo and snakes and ladders with me—I am the youngest in my family, so everyone had grown out of board games before me. I have often wondered if Bobbie was similar to Kate in old age; everything I have read about Kate's personality seems to suggest it. Bobbie was formidable and amazing; to us children she was wonderful. She would never fail to bring us bars of Fry's Chocolate Cream, which she would hand over with an air of great secrecy as though they were forbidden, and she never talked down to me. She would speak to me as though I were an adult and I was expected to behave very well and reply in grown-up fashion. At the time we lived in a hilltop Regency house with a very large number of steps up to it. Cars had to be parked at the bottom and then everything, luggage and all, carried up to the door. My mother was always worried about elderly visitors not being able to manage the steps. Bobbie, even when she was well into her nineties, would make her way up them far more easily than I could; according to my mother, she was the first person to count exactly how many there were.

Bobbie married Major Alec Waley, just over a year after Armistice Day, on November 18, 1919. I am not certain whether Kate attended, though it would have been perfectly understandable, less than a year after being widowed, if she felt she could not cope with a wedding (also, this time there would be no empathetic Georgina or Anny to make rude comments to about the "little bobbings about and little bells"). At around the time of Bobbie's wedding, Kate was becoming increasingly frail, or at least she believed she was. In August 1920 she wrote that she had developed a terrible "dread" of leaving her flat. Gladys, with the fervor of youth, had apparently been trying to persuade her to go out and to visit theaters and cinemas and friends. She also wanted to introduce Kate to a family friend, Lord Leverhulme, who was longing to meet her. Kate replied with the bald truth:

My dear Gladys, It is all very well my talking about going to see cinemas and other things but when it comes to the point—I cannot. The fact is, I have grown into such solitary ways that I dread going anywhere!

But, I am more than pleased to see those who are good enough to come to me. Pray tell Lord Leverhulme with my kind regards, I should be charmed to receive him any day he could manage to come. A warm welcome and a cup of tea awaits him any afternoon from 4 to 6.30 and on Sundays I am always 'at home'.

Kate continued these Sunday afternoon "At Homes" just as she had at Victoria Road. Almost every week she had numerous visitors come to take tea with her at her tiny flat. She was beginning to take more pleasure in her new home and even wrote a poem about how—despite its small rooms, the dim entrance hall and steep stairs—on a sunny day the flat would be flooded with light.

Kate's distaste for going out intensified into what could amount to a phobia; she would arrange appointments, but then cancel them, usually owing to "ill health." The only place she could be tempted to visit was Henry and Marie's home at 8 Mulberry Walk, just a few minutes' walk from Argyll Mansions. She was an old woman who wanted nothing more than to be with those she loved in familiar surroundings. She had no desire to see all the rapid changes that were taking place in the London that had once been so familiar to her. So many of the places she knew had been transformed, either by the ravages of war or by the twentieth-century obsession with modernity. Buildings were being erected in strange new "futuristic" styles; the fashions were vastly different from anything she had ever worn; and popular music had changed beyond recognition. Henry, who had been so up with the latest fads during his and Mamie's weekly outings to the Pops, was no longer enthralled with popular music. My favorite part of his book, *Recollections of My Father*, is the sentence "I can only regard jazz as a passing phase in music, and not one that is likely to endure."

Despite no longer having the luxury of her studio, Kate continued attempting to draw and paint, but sadly her eyesight was increasingly poor and her hands were becoming unreliable. Her works from this time are less accomplished and she exhibited nothing new. Her walls at Argyll Mansions were hung with paintings by Carlo and some of her own. Her fire was kept well stoked with burning pictures she was unhappy with, both those she attempted to draw now and, sadly, pictures she had painted in the past and had become dissatisfied with. Unable to paint, she threw herself into writing: letters, poems, and even the occasional article (always written with a quill pen, in emulation of her father). In the autumn of 1920 Kate was supposed to make a speech to the London branch of the Dickens Fellowship; she cried off shortly beforehand, claiming she was too ill to leave home. In place of her speech, she wrote an article called "On Women Old and New," which was later published in the Fellowship's journal, *The Dickensian*. In it, she makes slight apology for her father's depiction of women, but mainly defends it, saying that he was a very young man when he began to write:

> . . . *with no doubt a sincere admiration for the young women of his generation which indisposed him from any dissection of their characters for the benefit of an inquisitive public. . . . I will also claim for my father . . . he had no fondness for silliness* per se, *but was rather impatient of it and kept his admiration for those members of the sex who were strong, bright and capable.*

Kate also remembers back to her youth:

> *I . . . can recall vividly mid-Victorian days when women and girls of the higher and middle classes lived a pleasant if uneventful life of peace and plenty: plenty of rather monotonous amusements such as garden parties, croquet, long walks, drives and rides and in the evening occasional rather dull dinner parties, dances and the always popular opera and theatre parties. . . . Their manners were gentle and unobtrusive, their voices held the low music that Shakespeare loved—now raised to shriller tones. . . . Not a few of the Victorian ladies were timid and took rather roundabout ways in getting their ends, whereas, the new women go direct to the point and are unafraid. But you can never*

tell—perhaps they may be trembling in their very decorative shoes all the time, in spite of their commanding looks and martial stride.

She writes of the admiration she felt for women such as Harriet Martineau and Florence Nightingale, who were "daring" and broke out of the conventions. She is scathing of the methods used by suffragettes but lauds "a new and splendid race of women" who appeared in 1914, stepping into the shoes of men who had been called to fight. She is pleased that women have taken their "rightful place by man's side," after having been finally awarded the vote, and asks men not to sigh wistfully for the meeker woman of old but to realize that the woman of 1920 "is a new and better edition."

The following year, 1921, Kate finally made the acquaintance of the art collector Lord Leverhulme, who had been asking Gladys to introduce them. Several years before, Leverhulme had purchased *The Black Brunswicker*. Rather than attend a Sunday afternoon "At Home" in Chelsea, Leverhulme asked Gladys if she would bring Kate to tea with him at his house, The Hill, in Hampstead, so she could see the painting again. He sent his car to fetch them and Kate was finally coaxed out of her flat. She was not entirely happy with the experience of traveling for some distance in a motor car, but she was thrilled to see *The Black Brunswicker*. Gladys recorded her own impressions of that visit:

> *As past and present stood facing each other, it was interesting, and not difficult, to trace in Mrs. Perugini the outline of the forehead and the still beautiful nose, little changed since the great artist painted the picture.*

Kate became instant friends with Leverhulme and his sister, who were to become regular visitors to Argyll Mansions. Even toward the end of her life, Kate had enough vitality and personality to want to forge new friendships. At the end of this first tea party, after seeing her safely home, Leverhulme visited Kate's flat, where he admired *Flossie*. Kate later presented it to him and it was as a part of his family's personal effects that the painting was to sell for such a record sum, over eighty years later.

After being offered the painting as a present, Leverhulme and his sister came to visit Kate, bringing with them an amusing array of presents in exchange for the painting. Their offerings included "a little old fashioned [eighteenth-century] cabinet . . . some cigarettes, and soap."

24

"YES, I HAVE AGED . . ."

Throughout the 1920s, the little sitting room at 3 Argyll Mansions, described by Kate as "a tower-shaped room with three windows," was a sociable, happy salon. Kate was looked after very capably by her long-serving cook-housekeeper, Emily Elmer, known to everyone only by her surname (and often misspelled as Elma), and by a couple of maids, Alice Glancy and Ellen Eakins. When either Alice or Ellen was away, one of Kate's former models, Mary Lloyd, came to help out. Kate had inherited her father's attitude toward servants and was a kind, interested employer, disinclined to pay attention to class differentiations, preferring instead to like or dislike people on their own merits or defects, regardless of whether they were servants or her social "equals." On one occasion, when Gladys had stayed to supper, they were served an inedible pudding; desperate not to hurt Elmer's feelings by sending it back uneaten, Kate devised a plan whereby they would wrap the pudding up in brown paper and Gladys would take it home with her, like a parcel, to dispose of it.

Toward the end of her life, her domestic staff, in particular Ellen and Elmer, took on the roles of companion and nurse; Kate gave several of her sketches and poems (as well as other presents) to Ellen in gratitude for her companionship. One of the poems begins:

> Yes, I have aged, I who often was told
> That long as I lived I should never be old!

It tells of how old people are dismissed as being beyond love, no longer able to feel with a passion, but that they are the same inside as they ever were, and they still "feel and we care—perhaps to our cost ..." In it Kate bemoans her own physical weakness in old age as well as the attitudes of other people toward her. It is not a great poem—as was often the case, Kate was more preoccupied with finding words that rhymed than those that made sense but it ends with the poignant lines:

'Tis only the crust that is worn – that is dead –
the sap is still there on which we were fed.

Kate also wrote an affectionate poem about her maid, a short little rhyme that was simply entitled "Our Ellen":

Our Ellen is thoughtful though she is gay
Her spirit is lively and clever
She makes her friends happy and through the day
No grumble is heard from her ever!

Ellen Eakins was a remarkable young woman and their relationship was one of mutual affection. After her time with Kate was over, Ellen—who had been given glowing references by Kate's friends and family—would be employed by the composer Vaughan Williams to look after his elderly mother. Mrs. Vaughan Williams lived in the country, which Ellen hated and longed to exchange for London. She described her employer as "a funny huge man, but very nice" and commented, "Everyone here seems to think his music wonderful, but I don't."

In 1917, while she was still working for Kate, Ellen's brother and his wife died of influenza. Ellen and her sister Margaret took charge of their orphaned nephews, giving them a home and becoming devoted guardians. While Ellen worked for Kate to earn money to keep them all, Margaret kept house with the children. Later Ellen returned to live with them. The two unmarried sisters brought up their nephews lovingly and for the rest of her life Ellen would relate to them stories about the time she worked for Charles Dickens' daughter.

Kate loved to have young people about her and often asked Hester and Gladys to introduce her to their friends. She particularly liked one of Gladys's close friends, Ishbel MacDonald, daughter of the then Prime

Ellen Eakins, Kate's loyal maid and companion during her years living in Chelsea. Ellen would later work for the composer Vaughan Williams and become a part of the Bloomsbury Set's outer circle.

Minister, Ramsay MacDonald. She asked Gladys to bring Ishbel to tea on several occasions and was introduced to Ishbel's fifteen-year-old sister, Shelah, too. Kate also retained a love of the theater and, upon discovering Gladys knew the actress Lottie Venne, asked for her to be brought to tea. The two women seem to have discovered an affinity for each other and Kate was deeply saddened when, four years after meeting her, she heard of the younger woman's death. Henry and Marie had always socialized with thespians, including many "names," such as Henry Irving. The whole family retained their parents' love of the theatrical, a love that was passed on to Charles Dickens' grandchildren and continues in the family today.

Fascinated by Gladys and her young friends, Kate wrote a poem about the young women of the 1920s, who were so very different in appearance from how she and her friends had been. It is strangely titled "The Constant Lover":

> In modern days a woman's form
> Has nearly been abolished;
> Straight lines and few, are now the rule,
> And pair of shoes well polished.
>
> In modern days a woman's hair,
> Is surely rather skimpy;
> O why are all her lovely locks,
> So quaintly 'bobbed' and crimpy!
>
> In olden days a woman's ways,
> Were often soft and pleasing;
> But now alas! she wears a stare,
> That frightens us to freezing.
>
> And yet methinks, our modern girl,
> Who seems so high and mighty:
> Is no less charming than of old –
> when girls were fair and flighty.

In personality, Kate was an intriguing mixture of conformity and modernity. Gladys recalls in her diary how she and Kate would relax in the Chelsea sitting room, smoking cigarettes and talking. Kate had developed a great fondness for cigarettes, perhaps because of the whiff of scandal that still attached to women smoking, especially in public. It was something that had been almost unheard of in her day. In May 1921, Leverhulme invited Kate, Henry, Marie, and the Storeys to dine with him and his sister at The Hill. After dinner, the parlormaid who was handing around cigarettes neglected to offer them to Kate, assuming a woman of her generation would disapprove of the habit, and probably scared of offending her. Kate later admitted that she had been "dying" for one but had had to sit there and endure watching the men smoking.

Another regular visitor to Argyll Mansions was T. P. O'Connor. A few days after Carlo's death, T. P. had sent Kate an affectionate note of condolences wrapped about a bottle of alcohol, which he described as "a drop of comfort." They were obviously close friends by that time as he apologized for not having called around to see her owing to illness, adding that he would visit her very soon. He was nine years Kate's junior, but, although it seems he first made Kate's acquaintance when she was almost eighty years old, Ellen and Elmer were convinced he was in love with her. He would send her chocolates, flowers, and presents on a regular basis. His flowers always cheered her up, seeming to bring sunlight into her flat, as she was to describe in a sentimental poem entitled "Flowers in Winter." Kate would also send T. P. flowers, and in 1925 he sent her a very fond telegram: "The flowers were beautiful in themselves but more beautiful as a token that you remembered me affectionately & constantly as I do you." On her eighty-eighth birthday, in October 1927, he sent her a very loving telegram that reads: "My best wishes and fond love my dearest sweetheart." Ellen related how, when she knew he was coming to visit, Kate would disappear into her room to change into her "best jacket," brush her hair, and put on jewelery and make-up. On one of his visits, she drew a ring from her finger and gave it to him; he put it on his watchchain and wore it every day.

T. P. suffered so dreadfully from rheumatism that he found it impossible to make the ascent to Kate's flat without assistance from his chauffeur. A large man, by the end he needed almost to be carried up the difficult stairs by two strong men, but he was determined this should not deter him from visiting. One of Kate's poems seems to have been written about her affection for T. P. It is a witty little rhyme, almost worthy of Dorothy Parker.

> Each night he came – for long they talked
> And parted with tender feelings; –
> 'Ah, would my dear that thou wert mine
> Yet where should I spend my evenings.'

By the time Kate and T. P. met, he had enjoyed a long and successful career as a Liberal MP. An immigrant from Ireland who had worked as an MP in the Irish Nationalist party, he began his career in London as a journalist on the *Daily Telegraph*. (He later founded *The Star* and *The Sun* newspapers.) A fervent believer in Irish Independence, T. P. ended up as an MP for an English constituency, at the same time using his many press contacts to put across his views on Ireland. In 1918 became Father of the House of Commons and was appointed a Privy Councillor in 1924. Concurrently, he was also president of the newly established British Board of Film Censors.

On one of his visits, T. P. became concerned about Kate's lack of entertainment; with her eyesight deteriorating there were times when she could not draw or read. He insisted on buying her a portable gramophone, which could be wound up by hand. Although Kate declared she didn't need it, she seems to have enjoyed and made use of his gift. She was entertained too by Hester, Ellen, Gladys, and Mrs. Storey reading aloud to her so she didn't have to strain her sore eyes. Also she was visited often by Henry, Marie, and their children and family friends from the old days, such as Luke and Fanny Fildes and the MP Augustus Birrell. Her nieces, daughters of her brother Charley, also visited her, as did a cousin on her mother's side, yet another Mary Hogarth.

It seems J. M. Barrie also called to see Kate when he was in London and that he introduced her to the young publisher Peter Llewellyn Davies, now grown up but one of the family of children for whom Barrie had originally created the story *Peter Pan*. Peter Llewellyn Davies took tea with Kate in Chelsea on at least one occasion. Lucy Mathews,

Marie Stillman, and another prominent artist, Annie Swynnerton, were regular visitors who would sit and talk with her for hours about the old days. Annie Swynnerton and Kate had known each other for many years and, when Kate moved to Chelsea, lived close to each other. Kate loved this reminiscing with friends, though there were times when it made her understandably sad. She wrote Hester a poignant letter in the 1920s (the enclosure she mentions in the letter is missing and unidentified):

> . . . *In looking over some old papers the other day I came upon enclosed.* *. . . To me the thing brings back so many memories. Those dread-* *ful times when we never went to bed without the thought that we* *might be unpleasantly disturbed—but it also brings memories of you* *and your mother and poor Dick and my own dear, kind Carlo. Years* *ago—centuries! And now everything changed and gone . . .*
> *Aunt Kitty*

Kate's final decade was also marred by debilitating patches of depression. She would comment with sad regularity that she should never have been born and how glad she was that her son had not lived, as she was certain he would have inherited all her "faults." These periods of depression seem usually—though not always—to have been alleviated by visitors—and she was very cheered in the early 1920s by the news that her brother Henry had been awarded a knighthood. As had always been the case, Kate grew particularly low in wintertime and became happier with the arrival of good weather. She was also always cheered by people showing affection and attention to her and in June 1922, when she had been feeling especially sad, it was her friendship with J. M. Barrie that caused her to smile again. Perhaps Barrie knew that his friend was feeling depressed, or maybe it was serendipity that he decided to contact her on a specific day, but one evening when she was feeling especially low the postman arrived with a late delivery. It was a small parcel sent from St. Andrew's containing Barrie's book *Courage*. Kate was thrilled and saw the title as portentous, telling her to take courage. He had inscribed the book "To Kate Perugini from her friend J. M. Barrie." (She later promised the book to Gladys Storey.)

As her health grew worse, Kate refused to leave her home. In her first years at Chelsea, she had become accustomed to going for walks in the morning, but when she grew scared of falling she stopped going out at all. It is perhaps not surprising that she became frightened of walking: First she would have to negotiate the twisting steep stairs to the block's front door; then outside, the streets were now so crowded and, with the advent of cars, much more dangerous. Annie Swynnerton, whose home and studio were nearby, was twice run over while crossing the road. On the first occasion, she had the good fortune to be only lightly bruised and to have been run over by a doctor who was able to examine her immediately. On the second occasion, she was less lucky and ended up in hospital for several weeks with broken bones.

Kate's own doctor was perpetually worried about his patient's health, particularly as the flat was cold and rooms that weren't used all the time were difficult to keep warm; after a time he advised her no longer to sit in the dining room, so she began taking all her meals at a little table in her sitting room. She was her own worst enemy where her health was concerned, entertaining the delusion, as do so many elderly people, that she must not spend any money—believing she must leave it all to her brothers' children—and often living in great discomfort because of it. When she moved to Chelsea she had not been able to keep her and Carlo's bed, as it was too big to fit into her little bedroom; but instead of buying a new one she brought with her a small, uncomfortable bed that had stood for many years in Carlo's dressing room. The Dickenses tried in vain to persuade her to buy a new bed, but it was Gladys and her mother who eventually talked her around and then went out to buy the bed for her. Although Henry and Marie might have been pleased with the result, the fact that it was the Storeys who had had the success must have rankled.

There seem to have been several small clashes between the family and the Storeys, although outwardly they remained on very friendly terms, with Henry and Marie often inviting Gladys and her mother to tea or to family occasions. There is an unintentionally amusing entry in Gladys's diary for 1927, when Henry's granddaughter Aileen, always known in the family as "Gypsy," came to visit. Aileen was alluring, vivacious, and several years younger than Gladys; she was also starting out on a stage career, just as Gladys had originally hoped to do. The entry is short and attempts not to be acerbic, but the latter fails and Gladys's jealousy is apparent. It states, "she is 19 has gone on the stage & is with Master Harvey calls herself Gipsy Raine, plenty of confidence. Seems quite a nice girl."

Poor Marie continually received short shrift from Gladys, Hester, and Ellen, especially in letters written after Kate's death when they seem to have banded together in disapproval of her. Marie also managed to get on the wrong side of T. P. O'Connor. Once again, it was because of her religion. T. P., who had been brought up Catholic but rejected it, did not know that Marie was Catholic. On one Sunday, while he, Marie, and the Storeys were all taking tea with Kate, he started talking about religion. T. P. began with the comment, "I have always envied the happy way the English Protestants were brought up. I was brought up in the Roman Catholic faith and was taught that if I did not believe certain things and go through certain practice[s], that the earth would open and flames would consume me (and I was terrified) and that I should go right down to hell." Whereupon Marie piped up frostily, "I am a Roman Catholic." Diplomatic Mrs. Storey attempted to resolve the situation by commenting blandly, "Oh well, it is very nice to feel we are going to meet everyone again," to which T. P. reportedly replied ("with a twinkle"), "Not everyone!" This fairly lukewarm exchange was the beginning of a mutual dislike.

It is understandable that the family resented Gladys and her mother for their apparent hold over Kate, yet it must also be taken into consideration how much time the Storeys devoted to her and how happy this constant companionship made the elderly Kate. Gladys's papers and diaries demonstrate genuine feelings for Kate, but there is also a particularly unpleasant element: Gladys's grasping eagerness to accept presents, especially family memorabilia, and the air of secrecy with which she did it. Gladys claimed that Kate always told her as she bestowed the presents, that it would be best for Gladys to take them now as otherwise the family would contest them in the will; this seems strangely at odds with Kate's reluctance to spend money on a bed because she wanted her savings to go to her "descendants." Gladys's own notes make for painful reading as they record how she would turn up with a present for Kate—some flowers or a cake—and how Kate would then begin searching her rooms for a gift, feeling obliged to give her a present in return. Gladys never seems to have said no.

Among the presents Kate gave her were books once owned by Charles Dickens; family letters, including some written by Kate's mother; a diamond and aquamarine pendant that had once been a tie-pin belonging to Charles Dickens, which he had had made into a pendant especially for Kate; and a chair with a seat worked by Catherine Dickens (something Henry would have loved as a memento of his mother). She gave Gladys and her mother various other pieces of jewelry, most of which were not family pieces, but she also gave Gladys the original plaster cast of *Athlete Wrestling with a Python* made by Leighton and given by him to Carlo. I can't help thinking that Carlo's nephew, the author Mark Perugini, should have received that particular gift.

Mark was another regular visitor of Kate's; his sisters, Florence and Stella, and his brother, Laurence, are not mentioned in Gladys's diary but may also have visited. Mark seems to have felt a compassionate sense of duty and often took Sunday afternoon tea with his aunt. Kate, however, seems to have found him something of a bore and, just as she had been so many years ago about Hans Christian Andersen, was quite unkind about him after he left. Gladys recorded in her diary that she couldn't understand why Kate didn't like him as he seemed very pleasant to her.

Kate also received the occasional visit from overseas Dickensians, in particular the American Jordan Mott and his wife, Kitty. His wife was a cousin of Winston Churchill's wife, Clementine (though Kitty estranged herself somewhat from the family by sending a telegram to the Kaiser of Germany during the First World War). Another Sunday tea visitor was Major Henry Lygon, who called Kate his "best girl" and was distraught when she died. After Kate's death his sister, Lady Maud Hoare, wrote to Gladys, saying that her brother had been "very much attached to Mrs. Perugini and often talked to me about her."

Kate delighted in remembering anecdotes to relate at her many tea and supper parties, reveling in her ability to make her guests laugh. She would recount stories to do with her childhood or the famous people she had associated with throughout her long life. When she and Henry were together they became a hilarious double act, making their guests roar with laughter as they described scenes from the past—just as their father once did at his parties. Kate also enjoyed carrying on the family traditions. Christmas was no longer a happy time, carrying the weight of the anniversary of Carlo's death, but she rejuvenated her childhood memories of Twelfth Night. In emulation of Angela Burdett-Coutts, Kate started giving an annual Twelfth Night cake to Mrs. Storey.

In Kate's new little world, the home she never left, her constant companions were the servants, and she grew very close to her employees. Ellen Eakins's few remaining letters demonstrate a friendship and respect that grew up between mistress and maid. In June 1928, Ellen wrote to Gladys, making changes to a proposed visit. It is a cheery, chatty letter suggestive of a warm personality. The maid relates with candor an incident that has just taken place.

> It's now eight o'clock lovely and bright, but [Mrs. Perugini] has made me light up and pull down the blinds, so when she went to the 'little place', I pulled up the blinds thinking she would have forgotten and would not notice, but—the moment she entered the room, she made a bee-line and drew down again each blind, and because I was helpless with laughing, she was so annoyed, and told me to leave the room at once, which I did. In a few minutes, the bell was set ringing and 'Ellen come back here at "ONCE" and dont [sic] ever dare to laugh at me, and when you have fully realised how rude you are, we will make it up, and be friends again.['] Dear old soul, how can one help loving her.

Another of Ellen's letters tells of the occasion Kate determined to pay her doctor back for his constant attempts to make her do things she didn't want to. At this time, Kate was refusing to see anyone and all the doctor had been trying to do was to encourage her to start seeing her friends again. However, Kate, who had always been opposed to anyone attempting to order her about, stubbornly refused. The following day, knowing the doctor was due to call, she explicitly instructed Ellen and Elmer in what to say: "Mrs. Perugini sends her dear love, and is sorry she is too ill to see him, but will he call next week, when she is better."

After Kate's death, Ellen would write regularly to Hester and Gladys so she could reminisce about what seems to have been one of the happiest times of her life. She loved Kate and also loved living in Chelsea. She called Kate her "little lady," and as her employer grew increasingly frail and unable to look after herself Ellen took on greater responsibility, both for running the home and taking care of her mistress, without patronizing. She bought Kate treats (presumably the money was provided by Kate's friends), such as her favorite lavender water, as an attempt to cheer her up, or a pair of knitted gaiters, when her mistress complained of always feeling cold. If she thought Kate was particularly low she would phone exactly the right person needed to cheer her and ask him or her to visit.

In 1928, Henry became very concerned that Kate would be upset by a newly published novel, *This Side Idolatry*, by Mr. Bechhofer Roberts. It was based on the life of Charles Dickens and ends with his marriage

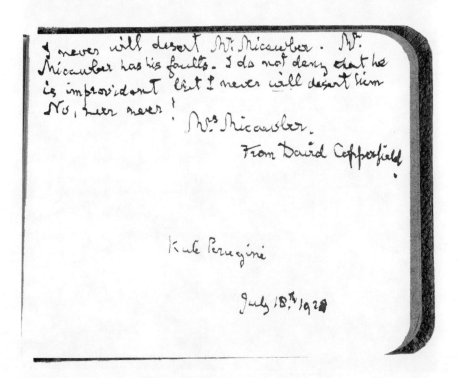

A dedication by Kate, written in Ellen Eakins' autograph book on July 18, 1928

breaking down because he has become infatuated with Ellen Ternan. The book stops short of claiming they had an affair, but readers are left to draw their own conclusions. Henry, Marie, and Ellen took great pains to ensure no one mentioned to Kate that such a book existed.

Kate Perugini in later life

As she grew more elderly, Kate developed a great fear of dying. She convinced herself that if she got into bed she would never leave it, so she refused to go to bed. Instead she slept every night on her favorite sitting-room chair, in which she also spent most of the day. This refusal to get into bed seems to have been an extension of the superstition that had led her to check underneath it every night and the nightly task of running her hands around the inside of the wardrobe three times before going to sleep. She began to talk increasingly about her childhood, her siblings, and her parents. She also began talking of her first marriage, how very "poor" they had been, of how she and Charlie had worried constantly about money. As happens to many elderly people, the distant past became more lucid than events that had happened just a few days previously. On occasion, she made sweeping and controversial comments, such as the time she told Gladys, "My father was really a wicked man—a very wicked man." These words caused widespread outrage when *Dickens and Daughter* was published. Looking at Gladys's notes, one can see that Kate had made the comment in regard to Dickens' treatment of Catherine and of his attitude toward women in general. The words were spoken less than a year before Kate died, at a time when she was depressed, angry, and terrified of dying. It was these words that led many of the book's critics to declare Kate had been insane by the end of her life. Gladys's decision to put that particular quotation in the book caused fury among the Dickens family. *The Times Literary Supplement* was particularly virulent in its claims about Kate's mental health, prompting Gladys to write to George Bernard Shaw, pleading with him to refute in writing the claims that Kate had lost her mind. He did so willingly.

Despite Gladys' and Shaw's outrage, Gladys' own notes show that there were several isolated episodes during Kate's last years when she became very confused and when her mind started wandering. This was obviously upsetting, and perhaps embarrassing to witness too, as in 1925 Marie was prompted to write a very short list of those people outside the family who were allowed to see her "in her present state." The only people on it were the Storeys and Lucy Mathews. Other friends, such as T. P., Hester, and Annie Swynnerton, colluded with the servants and contin-ued to visit just as frequently, avoiding the times Henry, Marie, or any of the family would be there. The indispensable Ellen Eakins must have spent a great deal of time on the phone, arranging Kate's visiting schedule. This period of confusion was overcome—perhaps it had been part of an illness—and Kate returned to being totally lucid, with only occasional moments of mental wandering, over the next few years. Until the end, she was almost always in control of her mental faculties.

From time to time, Kate would suddenly be against the idea of having visitors and Ellen or Elmer would be called upon to tell callers that Kate was "not at home," a lie that would have been ludicrously transparent as Kate had not left her flat for several years. In 1928, Lucy Mathews was terribly upset at being refused entry and had to contact Gladys and ask for her help as Kate would apparently see only the Storeys. It is incidents such as this that make one understand why the family felt so unhappy about Gladys and her mother. The Storeys do seem to have delighted in the power of being Kate's chosen friends and influenced her to avoid certain people.

Humiliatingly, Marie was often rebuffed and one cannot help wondering if Gladys and T. P. colluded in turning Kate against her because they did not like her. In her will, Kate left Marie a special bequest of £100 (in addition to the items that she and Henry would inherit jointly) "as a mark of my affection and gratitude for all she has done for me," suggesting the two women were not on such bad terms as history would have us believe. Kate was not the kind of woman who would have left Marie that fond legacy out of duty. Yet Gladys delighted in recording in her diary every instance when Kate spoke slightingly of her sister-in-law and the occasions on which Gladys and her mother would sit silently in Kate's sitting room, listening to Marie being told that Kate was not receiving visitors today. On one occasion Gladys gleefully recorded a conversation in which Kate commented, "I'm not a lady, you know, I'm too much of a socialist to be a lady. My father was not a gentleman—he was too mixed to be a gentleman. My mother was a lady born and by Education also my grandfather." Then Kate added of Marie, "She's not a lady but thinks she is."

As well as episodes of confusion and her great fear of death, Kate began experiencing what the doctor described as a "type of sleeping illness." She slept for hours at a time, all through the day as well as at night, a sleep from which it was almost impossible to rouse her. This continued for many years. There were several occasions on which Kate was presumed to be dying, but every time she rallied and returned to her normal, lucid, and witty self, astonishing her visitors by how quickly she could deteriorate and then recover. She seemed truly to believe that, as long as she avoided her bed, she really would be able to cheat death out of claiming her. With every report of the passing of another friend, such as the deaths of Luke and Fanny Fildes within a few months of each other in 1927 and the death of Ellen Terry in 1928, Kate would become increasingly depressed and even more frightened of her own mortality. It seems anomalous that someone with Kate's strong belief in the Christian faith (and with so many of those she loved having died already) should have such a fear of dying. Every new death recalled those from the past, and she often dwelt morbidly on the demise of her parents, Thackeray, and Millais. The anniversaries of deaths, especially those of her parents, Dickie, and Carlo, plunged her into misery. She also began to hate her birthday, celebrating it—and apparently enjoying it—every year but making herself ill for weeks beforehand by fretting over it.

On her eighty-ninth birthday, she held a tea party to which Henry and Marie, Gladys, Mrs. Storey, and Henry Lygon all came. T. P. had wanted to attend but was laid up with chronic rheumatism. In lieu of himself he sent her a handwritten birthday telegram. Several of the words are illegible, suggesting he was in great pain when he wrote it. "I cannot [*word illegible*] without sending you a line for your birthday. I am sure you realise how much I admire and love you. The crippling [*word illegible*] of rheumatism makes it impossible for me to pay a visit to my dear friends at the moment I am [*two words illegible*] and may be sure I will pay you a visit. Ever your affectionately T. P. O'Connor." In addition to his telegram, T. P. sent Kate a large box of deliciously rich chocolates, which she "devoured" with relish, despite Ellen's warnings of indigestion. J. M. Barrie, who regularly had red roses delivered to her on her birthday, also sent a birthday telegram, to which Kate dictated the following reply:

My dear Sir James, It was a great treat to get your telegram and your greetings on my birthday—I could have wished that my birthday was a little less weighty but alas! Perhaps we shall meet again in another and a better—when I shall be more worthy of my wonderfully gifted old friend—as it is I am a poor old thing! I bless you dear for the pleasure you have given me and remain your affectionate Kate Perugini.

This tea party, on October 29, 1928, was the last time Kate was to celebrate her birthday. Two days afterward she was feeling ill and listless. Ellen's nephew Stanley Eakins had sent Kate a letter or card (presumably for her birthday) and on October 31 she replied to the little boy, whom she had never met, with great affection: "My dear Stanley How kind of you to send me a word. I am not well or should write some more. I hope to send you some when I am better. Yours affectionately, Kate Perugini."

By now Kate was suffering regular bouts of an unspecified pain, which would rack her body and lead her to shout out to God for help. She began to have a terror of sleeping alone and often tried to persuade Gladys to stay the night. On the one occasion Gladys did so they both slept in the sitting room, with Gladys on the sofa and Kate in her usual chair. Gladys was terrified at about two o'clock in the morning by Kate suddenly beginning to groan; the older woman then got up and haltingly wandered around and around the room, staring out of the window and going through her routine of touching all the furniture, piece by piece.

The death of one of her oldest friends, Lucy Mathews, on Boxing Day 1928, seems to have affected Kate badly. She had entered her ninetieth year and became increasingly frail over the next few months, frequently dwelling on the memories of her mother, Georgina, Mamie, and Carlo, and becoming sad and contemplative over the fact that Catherine and Georgina had been estranged for so many years. She also began what amounted to a kind of mania about Marie and religion, convinced that her sister-in-law would connive to bury her with a Catholic service and often refusing to allow Marie into the room to see her, in case she tried to convert her. It seems to have escaped her mind that her adoring brother Henry was not a Catholic nor had Marie insisted he give up his faith. Henry would never have allowed Kate to be buried with anything but the type of service she wanted (nor would a Catholic priest have permitted it), but she seems to have convinced herself otherwise.

One cannot help wondering if, when Georgina Hogarth was no longer around to support Kate in deriding Marie's faith, that Gladys, her mother, and T. P. enjoyed spurring on this anti-Catholic fervor. If so, it backfired very sadly, making their friend confused and given to rambling—and upsetting Henry deeply.

On Wednesday May 8, 1929, Kate Perugini finally allowed Ellen and Elmer to carry her into her new brass bed. She died the following morning. Her death certificate, registered by Marie and certified by Kate's long-term physician, Dr. Maclaren, lists one of the causes of death as "exhaustion." Kate was alive until beyond the first quarter of the twentieth century, but her death certificate remains firmly a relic of the nineteenth century: Under the heading "Occupation" Kate's own work has been almost entirely dismissed with the words "Widow of Carlo Perugini Artist (Painter)."

As Kate lay in peace at 3 Argyll Mansions, she was visited by a stream of mourners who came to place roses around her open coffin and to sit with her for one last time. Marie earned their shocked disapproval as she and Bobbie stayed by it for hours, repeatedly saying the rosary. The servants were scandalized.

25

A BRIGHT FLAME

On May 10, 1929, *The Times* published a glowing obituary, which seems to have been written by someone who knew and loved Kate. It describes her as "a lady of rare charm and humour, who if she had not been a painter would assuredly have made a name as a writer" and states that "from her early childhood she won the hearts of all who knew her." Her union with Carlo is described thus: "If ever there was a happy marriage, this was one." It continues:

> *In their charming house where each had a studio, and each happy in their own work, Mr. and Mrs. Perugini gathered round them a remarkable circle of people eminent in literature, art, and music, and every one fell in love with 'Kitty' as most of them called her. Her charm and natural gift for genuine friendship, and the happy companionship in which she and her husband lived made a visit to their home a sheer delight. For Mrs. Perugini inherited her father's characteristics of wit, whimsicality, common sense in all things, and a broad outlook on life and humanity. She was a brilliant but at the same time thoughtful talker. Her conversation was full of fun, her eyes seemed to sparkle in the enjoyment of it, her radiant and honest smile lighting up her beautiful face. . . . Mrs. Perugini possessed the secret of growing old gracefully; indeed she seemed to grow more beautiful and charming with the years. All her faculties were bright and luminous to the end, and at her ripe age was as to the friends around her as in those early exciting, youthful days in her father's house.*

I did not see the obituary until some years into the researching of this book. Its final paragraph (below) struck me as echoing sentiments that I had begun to feel about Kate, through the distance of almost a century:

She was a lovable woman most fascinating in manner, with a sense of humour that she must have inherited from her father, an artist to the tips of her fingers, ever loyal to her friends and with a wonderful patience in the physical discomforts of her later years. It is given to few people to make as many loyal and loving friends as she did, and to leave such kindly memories behind her as she will to those who survive her.

After Kate's death, Hester wrote to Gladys, "It was a horrible shock to read of her death—for though one knew her age, one never thought of her as old—her bright flame always inspired and encouraged. I don't think there ever has been or ever will be anyone in the least like her again. Every time one saw her one carried something precious away with one."

On the first anniversary of Kate's death Ellen would write simply, "I never thought I could still be missing her after all these months, I loved her so." Six months later she wrote again, "I still miss and miss the little soul, I don't think there will ever be another like her." Ellen was also struck by the sadness and romance of T. P. O'Connor dying very shortly after Kate; she was convinced he had died of a broken heart.

Kate Elizabeth Macready Perugini's funeral took place on Monday, May 13, at 11:00 a.m. It was a cold day in Sevenoaks, and the temperature was even colder inside the church, making the attendees relieved that the service—which was most definitely not Catholic—was relatively short. Kate had left a written request that no one wear mourning clothes. Once again Marie had managed to incense Kate's friends by requesting in the newspaper that no flowers be sent, asking instead for money to be donated to the Radium Fund.

Hester (who was away in Paris and sadly unable to come back for the funeral), T. P., and Gladys were furious that Kate "who so loved flowers" was being denied them. Defiantly, they all sent huge wreaths of flowers, and Gladys and her mother dropped white roses onto the coffin once it had been lowered into the grave. Even the large respectful cross of lilies that poor Henry and Marie themselves provided was despised by Gladys (as Kate had "disliked arum lillies [*sic*]"). Gladys didn't consider that Kate's brother might have known the real Kate better than she, who had known her only for the last few of her eighty-nine years.

It is unlikely that Marie intended her request for no flowers to be adhered to by those closest to Kate; the notice was presumably to deter the many hundreds of Kate's acquaintances, including the ever-growing ranks of the Dickens Fellowship, from sending flowers that would merely pile up and rot on the grave. She was also probably correct in her assumption that Kate—who had been so fervent a fundraiser for good causes—would have appreciated money being sent to a charity instead.

Kate is buried in the graveyard of St. Nicholas's Church, Sevenoaks, Kent. She was laid to rest in the family grave with Carlo and Dickie. The grave is next to Mamie's, and there is a sense of perfect symmetry in the two sisters being once again by each other's side as well as Kate being reunited forever with her husband and son.

The poignant words on the card that accompanied Hester's wreath of red roses, sent from Paris for the funeral, celebrated not only Kate's long life, but also the great gift she had for enchanting and befriending people of all generations. It simply read: "For my grandfather's friend, for my mother's friend, for my own darling friend."

ACKNOWLEDGMENTS

There are a large number of people to thank for their help with this book, first and foremost my parents, Sue and Henry Hawksley, for their love, support, and encouragement. At Globe Pequot Press I'd like to thank Lara Asher who has been incredibly supportive despite the time difference and my crazy schedule. Also Janice Goldklang, Ellen Urban, and Lauren Brancato. I'd also like to thank my American agent, Jonathan Lyons, and my English agent, Broo Doherty, for their hard work.

Thanks also (in alphabetical order) to: John Aplin for his Thackeray wisdom; Joe Beard for timely information on Dickens and copyright law; Dr. James Bennett-Levy for answering medical queries about depression; Brigitte Berg for information about the Scwabe family; Simon Bowring for kindly contacting me and giving me information about Katey's association with the Hagborgs; Colin Bruce at the Imperial War Museum; Dr. Simon Butcher for invaluable advice about 19th-century illnesses and medicine; Erin Coffin at the Royal Canadian Mounted Police archives; Evelyn Cook for her information about Dorothy de Michele; Dr. Caroline Dakers for advising about Val Prinsep research; the inimitable Cedric Dickens (no more need be said) who is very much missed; Clare Double, for selflessly risking life, limb, and fingernails helping me clear away decades of brambles and ivy from Katey's grave; Isabel Eakins for her information and help about the last years of Katey's life; the Richard Green Gallery; Thelma Grove for a very interesting tour of Gad's Hill Place; Colin Harris at the Bodleian; Elizabeth Hawkins for allowing me to search through her family archives; the late Eleanor Hawksley for many family reminiscences; Sue Hawksley for help with research; Jo Hodder at the Society of Authors; Michele Hutchison, my editor at Doubleday; Crispin Jackson at Christie's; Dr. Maria Lazari for medical advice; Sue Meynell for Val Prinsep research help; Geoffroy Millais for help, advice, and a wonderful tea; Jo Micklem who worked so hard on the book at Doubleday; the late Belinda Norman-Butler for telling me so many stories both about the Thackeray family and about my own ancestors; Peter O'Toole at the Artists' Rifles and SAS archives; Sandra Penketh at the Lady Lever Art Gallery; Peter Selley at Sotheby's; Becky Sherrington for providing answers about midwifery and childbirth in the 19th century (and for all those encouraging phone calls); Christopher Sinclair-Stevenson, who first believed in *Katey*; Professor Michael Slater—not only for his excellent book *Dickens and Women*, but also for his interest, invaluable research advice about Charles Dickens, and for reading a long manuscript at very short notice; Reena Suleman at Leighton House Museum; Simon Toll at Sotheby's; Malcolm Warner for invaluable Millais advice; Christopher Wood for Carlo Perugini information; Richard Wragg at the Royal Holloway archives for his diligent research on Bedford College; and Andrew Xavier, former Director of the Charles Dickens Museum (and friend), for providing constant advice and help and for reading the manuscript. I wish you were still here to see this edition of *Katey*. Thanks also to those people who still work or have worked at the Charles Dickens Museum including Don H., Don S., Gayle, Sophie, and Robina. Thanks also to all the various Dickens family members who showed encouragement, interest, and support (very much appreciated).

Thanks to the Society of Authors and to staff at the British Library, Family Records Office in Islington, Hammersmith Library, Kensington Local Studies Library, National Art Library, National Portrait Library's Heinz archives and picture library, Royal Academy Library, Tate Britain archives, V&A archives (at Olympia), and the Witt Library (at the Courtauld Institute).

For help with the pictures I would like to thank: Chris and Gill Bottomley, Jennifer Camilleri at the Royal Academy, Chris Forrest, Robina Lamche-Brennan at the Charles Dickens Museum, and last, but certainly not least, my picture researcher Jo Walton.

A very special mention must go to the late Kitty Mellon, who was not only so generous in allowing me to use images of her Katey painting but who also became a friend. I miss receiving her emails and phone calls.

Thanks to my friends for putting up with me obsessing about people who died over a hundred years ago. Thanks to my ever-fabulous sisters, Jo and Ginny, for always being at the end of the phone or email connection when I needed to let off steam, and to my niece and nephews, Sarah, Archie, and John for being just perfect and for always managing to make me laugh.

BIBLIOGRAPHY

Ackroyd, Peter. *Dickens.* Sinclair-Stevenson Ltd: London, 1990.

_____. *Dickens: Public Life and Private Passion.* BBC: London, 2002.

Adrian, Arthur A. *Georgina Hogarth and the Dickens Circle.* Oxford University Press: London, 1957.

_____. *Mark Lemon: First Editor of Punch.* Oxford University Press: Oxford, 1966.

Ash, Russell. *Sir John Everett Millais.* Pavilion: London, 1996.

_____. *Victorian Masters and Their Art.* Pavilion: London, 1999.

Ashley, Robert. *Wilkie Collins.* Arthur Baker Ltd: London, 1952.

Baker, William, and Clarke, William M. (eds). *The Letters of Wilkie Collins,* Vol. I, 1838–1865. Macmillan: Hampshire, 1999.

Bennett, Mary. *Artists of the Pre-Raphaelite Circle: The First Generation* (Catalogue of Works in the Walker Art Gallery, Lady Lever Art Gallery and Sudley Art Gallery). National Museums and Galleries of Merseyside in association with Lund Humphries: London, 1988.

Beresford, Richard. *Pre-Raphaelites and Olympians.* Art Gallery of New South Wales: Sydney, 2001.

Black, Clementina. *Frederick Walker.* Duckworth & Co.: London, 1902.

Bonham Carter, Victor. *Authors by Profession,* Volume I. Society of Authors: London, 1978.

Bowen, W. H. *Charles Dickens and His Family: A Sympathetic Study,* privately printed by W. Heffer & Sons Ltd, Cambridge (no date given).

Cherry, Deborah. *Painting Women: Victorian Women Artists.* Routledge: London, 1993.

Chesterton, G. K., and Kitton, F. G. *Charles Dickens.* Hodder & Stoughton: London, 1903.

Collins, Charles Allston. *A Cruise Upon Wheels: The Chronicle of some Autumn Wanderings along the Deserted Post-Roads of France.* Peter Davies Ltd: London, 1926.

Collins, Philip (ed.). *Dickens: Interviews and Recollections.* Macmillan: London, 1981.

_____. *Thackeray: Interviews and Recollections,* vols i & ii. Macmillan: London, 1983.

Coombs, James H., Scott, Anne, Landow, George P., and Sanders, Arnold (eds). *A Pre-Raphaelite Friendship: The Correspondence of William Holman Hunt and John Lucas Tupper.* UMI Research Press: Ann Arbor, Michigan, 1986.

Dakers, Caroline. *The Holland Park Circle: Artists and Victorian Society.* Yale University Press: New Haven and London, 1999.

Dark, Sidney, and Grey, Roland. *W. S. Gilbert His Life and Letters.* Methuen & Co.: London, 1924.

Davis, Nuel Pharr. *The Life of Wilkie Collins.* University of Illinois Press: Urbana, 1956.

Dewy, Robert Cullen. *A Manual of the Law Relating to Divorce and Matrimonial Causes, with a Chapter on The Married Women's Property Act, 1870.* Longmans, Green & Co.: London, 1872.

Dickens, Charles. *The Life of Our Lord.* Collins: London, 1970.

_____. *Our Mutual Friend.* Penguin: Harmondsworth, 1988.

Dickens, Charles, and Dickens, Catherine. *Mr. & Ms. Charles Dickens: His Letters to Her* with a foreword by their daughter Kate Perugini. Constable & Co. Ltd: London, 1935.

Dickens, Charles, and Perugini, Kate. *The Comedy of Charles Dickens.* Chapman & Hall: London, 1906.

_____. *Character Sketches from Dickens.* Raphael Tuck & Sons Ltd: London, 1924.

Dickens, Henry Fielding. *The Recollections of Sir Henry Fielding Dickens, K.C.* Windmill Press: Surrey, 1934.

Dickens, Mamie. *My Father as I Recall Him.* Roxburghe Press: London, 1897.

Dickens, Mary. *Charles Dickens by His Eldest Daughter.* Cassell & Company: London, 1894.

Dickens, Mary, and Perugini, Kate. *The Charles Dickens Birthday Book.* Chapman & Hall: London, 1882.

Dickens-Hawksley, Enid. *Charles Dickens Birthday Book.* Faber & Faber: London (no date given).

Dickens-Hawksley, Lucinda. *Charles Dickens.* Andre Deutsch: London, 2011.

Dickens McHugh, Stuart. *Knock on the Nursery Door: Tales of the Dickens Children.* Michael Joseph Ltd: London, 1972.

Dickensian Magazine, The. The Dickens Fellowship: London, 1905–2005.

Dolby, George. *Charles Dickens as I Knew Him.* T. Fisher & Unwin: London, 1885.

Elsna, Hebe. *Unwanted Wife: A Defence of Mrs. Charles Dickens.* Jarrolds Publishers: London, 1963.

Elwin, Malcolm. *Thackeray.* Cape: London, 1932.

Flanders, Judith. *The Victorian House.* HarperCollins: London, 2003.

Fleming, G. H. *John Everett Millais: A Biography.* Constable: London, 1998.

Forster, John. *The Life of Charles Dickens,* in 2 volumes. Chapman & Hall: London, 1876.

Foulkes, Nick. *Scandalous Society.* Abacus: London, 2004.

Funnel, Peter, Warner, Malcolm, Flint, Kate, Matthew, H. C. G. and Ormond, Leonée. *Millais Portraits.* Princeton University Press: Princeton, 1999.

Garnett, Henrietta. *Anny.* Chatto & Windus: 2005.

Gaunt, William. *The Pre-Raphaelite Tragedy.* Jonathan Cape: London, 1975.

Gérin, Winifred. *Anne Thackeray Ritchie: A Biography.* Oxford University Press: Oxford, 1981.

Goldman, Paul. *John Everett Millais: Illustrator and Narrator.* Lund Humphries in association with Birmingham Museums & Art Gallery, Aldershot and Vermont: 2004.

Greaves, John. *Dickens at Doughty Street.* Elm Tree Books: London, 1975.

Hardwick, Michael, and Hardwick, Mollie. *As They Saw Him . . . Charles Dickens.* George G. Harrap & Co. Ltd: London, 1970.

_____. *The Charles Dickens Encyclopaedia.* Futura: London, 1990.

Hibbert, Christopher. *The Making of Charles Dickens.* HarperCollins: London, 1967.

Hibbert, Christopher, and Weinreb, Ben. *The London Encyclopaedia.* Macmillan: London, 1993.

Hilton, Timothy. *The Pre-Raphaelites.* Thames & Hudson: London, 1993.

Holman Hunt, Diana. *My Grandfather, His Wives and Loves.* Hamish Hamilton: London, 1969.

Holman Hunt, William. *Pre-Raphaelitism and the Pre-Raphaelite Brotherhood* (publisher not given): London, 1905.

Holman Hunt, William, and Stephens, F. G. *William Holman Hunt and His Works: A Memoir of the Artist's Life with Descriptions of His Pictures.* James Nisbet & Co.: London, 1860.

House, Madeline, and Storey, Graham (eds.). *The Letters of Charles Dickens.* Clarendon Press: Oxford, 1969.

Johnson, Edgar. *Charles Dickens: His Tragedy and Triumph,* Vols I & II. Hamish Hamilton: London, 1952.

_____. (ed.). *Letters from Charles Dickens to Angela Burdett-Coutts 1841–1865.* Cape: London, 1953.

Kaplan, Fred. *Dickens: A Biography.* Hodder & Stoughton: London, 1989.

Landow, George P. *William Holman Hunt's Letters to Thomas Seddon.* John Rylands University Library: Manchester, 1983.

Laurence, Dan H., and Quinn, Martin. *Shaw on Dickens.* Frederick Ungar Publishing Co.: New York, 1985.

Lazarus, Mary. *A Tale of Two Brothers.* Angus & Robertson: Sydney, 1973.

Lehmann, John. *Ancestors and Friends.* Eyre & Spottiswoode: London, 1962.

Lehmann, R. C. *Familiar Letters, N.L. to F.L., 1864–1867.* Ballantyne, Hanson & Co.: London, 1892.

_____. (ed.). *Memories of Half a Century: A Record of Friendships.* Smith, Elder & Co.: London, 1908.

_____. *Charles Dickens as Editor.* Smith, Elder & Co.: London, 1912.

Lemon, Mark. *The Enchanted Doll.* Alexander Moring: London, 1903.

Ley, J. W. T. *The Dickens Circle: A Narrative of the Novelist's Friendships.* Chapman & Hall: London, 1918.

Litzinger, Boyd (ed.). *The Letters of Robert Browning to Frederick and Nina Lehmann, 1863–1889.* Baylor University: Texas, 1875.

Marks, John George. *Life and Letters of Frederick Walker, A.R.A.* Macmillan & Co. Ltd: London, 1896.

Meynell, Viola (ed.). *Letters of J. M. Barrie.* Peter Davies: London, 1942.

Millais, John Guille. *The Life and Letters of Sir John Everett Millais.* Methuen & Co.: London, 1899 (repr. and abridged in 1905).

Pope-Hennessy, Una. *Charles Dickens.* Chatto & Windus: London, 1945.

Priestley, Lady. *The Story of a Lifetime.* Kegan Paul, Trench, Trübner & Co. Ltd: London, 1908.

Ritchie, Hester (ed.). *Letters of Anne Thackeray Ritchie.* John Murray: London, 1924.

Robinson, Kenneth. *Wilkie Collins: A Biography.* Davis-Poynter: London, 1974.

Rossi-Wilcox, Susan M. *Dinner for Dickens: The Culinary History of Mrs. Charles Dickens.* Prospect Books: London, 2005.

Sartoris, Adelaide. *A Week in a French Country House.* Smith, Elder & Co.: London, 1902.

Slater, Michael. *Dickens and Women.* J. M. Dent & Sons: London, 1983.
_____. *Charles Dickens.* Yale University Press: New Haven & London, 2009.
Stedman, Jane W. *W. S. Gilbert: A Classic Victorian and His Theatre.* Oxford University Press: Oxford, 1996.
Storey, Gladys. *All Sorts of People.* Methuen & Co. Ltd: London, 1929.
_____. *Dickens and Daughter.* Frederick Muller Ltd: London, 1939.
Taylor, George. *Players and Performers in the Victorian Theatre.* Manchester University Press: Manchester, 1989.
Thackeray Fuller, Hester, and Hammersley, Violet. *Thackeray's Daughter: Some Recollections of Anne Thackeray Ritchie.* Euphorion Books: Dublin, 1951.
Tomalin, Claire. *The Invisible Woman.* Penguin: Harmondsworth, 1991.
Toynbee, William (ed.). *The Diaries of William Charles Macready 1833–1851,* Vol II. Chapman & Hall Ltd: London, 1912.
Trewin, J. C. *Mr. Macready: 19th Century Tragedian.* George G. Harrap & Co. Ltd: London, 1955.
Warre Cornish, Blanche (ed.). *Some Family Letters of W. M. Thackeray.* Houghton Mifflin Company: Boston and New York, 1911.
Williamson, George C. *Frederic Lord Leighton* (Bell's Miniature Series of Painters). George Bell & Sons: London, 1902.
Wilson, Angus. *The World of Charles Dickens.* Viking Press: New York, 1970.
Wilson, A. N. *The Victorians.* Arrow Books: London, 2003.
Yates, Edmund Hodgson. *Mr. Thackeray, Mr. Yates and the Garrick Club. The Correspondence and Facts. Stated by Mr. Edmund Yates,* printed for private circulation. Taylor & Greening: London, 1859.
Yates, Edmund. *Fifty Years of London Life: Memoirs of a Man of the World.* Harper & Brothers: New York, 1885.
_____. (ed.). *Celebrities at Home,* reprinted from "The World." Second Series: London, 1878.

INDEX

Note: The name "Kate" refers to the same person with the name Catherine Elizabeth Macready Dickens as her maiden name, and her married names of Kate Collins and Kate Perugini. Name references to "Catherine" identify Catherine Thomson Hogarth; "Charles" refers to Charles John Huffman Dickens; "Charley" refers to Charles Culliford Boz Dickens; "Charlie" refers to Charles Allston Collins; and "Carlos" refers to Charles Edward Perugini. Use of "Mamie" refers to Mary Dickens. Page numbers followed by n indicate footnotes.

A

Albert (Prince Consort of England), 8, 63, 84, 188
Alexandra (Queen of England), 340
All for Her (Merivale), 190
All The Year Round (periodical), 131–132, 146, 154, 156, 174, 179, 217, 303n89
Alma-Tadema, Lawrence and Laura, 328, 334
America
   book tours, 15–21, 213–214
   death and burial of Alfred, 329–330
   death and burial of Frank, 279
   Dickens book sales and royalties, 268n81
Anderson, Hans Christian, 46, 65, 104–105, 116, 369
Anne (Dickens servant), 43, 46
Artists' Rifle Corps, 240–241
Aspern Papers (James), 341–342
Athlete Wrestling with a Python (sculpture, Leighton), 369
Austen, Jane, 3
Austin, Henry, 26, 65, 173

Austin, Laetitia Mary Dickens, 65, 91, 173, 302
Australia
   Alfred's relocation to, 207–208
   Alfred's return to England, 329–330
   Plorn's indebtedness, 269–271, 288, 315–316
   Plorn's marriage, 267
   Plorn's relocation to, 217–218, 227
   relocation of British prostitutes, 28n9
Ayrton (Miss, godmother to Kate), 14

B

Barnaby Rudge (Dickens, 1841), 15n6
Barrie, J. M., 314, 321, 325–326, 349, 365, 366, 375
Beadnell, Maria. *see* Winter, Maria Beadnell
Beard, Thomas, 84, 147–148, 177
Beardsley, Aubrey, 237
Beckett, Gilbert à, 90, 100–101
Beeton (Mrs.), 68, 202
Bell, Vanessa, 259
Benham, Canon, 351
Bentley's Miscellany (magazine), 3
Berengaria's Alarm at Seeing the Girdle of Richard Offered for Sale in Rome (Collins, 1850), 58
Berg, Brigitte, 266
Bianca Capella (Prinsep, 1862), 189
Birrell, Augustus, 365
Black, Charles, 36–37
The Black Brunswicker (Millais, 1860), xv, 139–144, 358–359
Blackwood, John, 135
Bleak House (Dickens, 1853), 12, 66, 78, 204
Bloomsbury Group, 185, 219, 362
Boer War, 315, 337
Bonolis, Guiseppe, 239
Book of Household Management (Beeton, 1861), 68, 202

ABOUT THE AUTHOR

Lucinda Hawksley is a prize-winning travel writer and a direct descendant of Charles Dickens. Having completed an MA in History of Art, Lucinda pursued her fascination with Dickens' artist daughter, Kate Perugini, organizing and curating an exhibition of her paintings in 2002 at the Dickens House Museum. She is the author of the critically acclaimed *Lizzie Siddal: The Tragedy of a Pre-Raphaelite Supermodel.* Lucinda lives in London. For more information visit the author's website at lucindahawksley.com